Lucasta Miller

THE BRONTË MYTH

Lucasta Miller was educated at Oxford. She was the deputy literary editor of *The Independent*. Her articles and criticism have appeared in *The Times*, *The Times Literary Supplement*, *The Independent*, and *The Sunday Telegraph*.

THE
BRONTË MYTH

Lucasta Miller

ANCHOR BOOKS

A DIVISION OF RANDOM HOUSE, INC.

NEW YORK

In memory of my father

The Library of Congress has cataloged the Knopf edition as follows:
Miller, Lucasta.
The Brontë myth / Lucasta Miller. — 1st American ed.
p. cm.
Includes bibliographical references and index.
1. Brontë family. 2. Novelists, English — 19th century — Biography.
3. Women novelists, English — Biography. 4. Haworth (England) — Biography.
5. Brontë, Charlotte, 1816–1855. 6. Brontë, Emily, 1818–1848.
7. Brontë, Anne, 1820–1849. I. Title.
PR4168.M49 2003
823'.809 — dc21 [B] 2002040620

Anchor ISBN: 978-1-4000-7835-6

Book design by M. Kristen Bearse
Author photograph © Neil Libbert

www.anchorbooks.com

Contents

Illustrations

Preface and Acknowledgments

Some years ago, when I was supposed to be working on a thesis about Milton, I used to find myself going home from the library and compulsively reading books to do with the Brontës. Their novels—which I had first read in my early teens—provided emotional nourishment, but the legendary tale of their lonely moorland lives, which had gripped my imagination even before I was old enough to read *Jane Eyre* or *Wuthering Heights,* seemed to offer the allure of a more escapist fantasy.

Around the same time, I read Terry Eagleton's *Myths of Power: A Marxist Study of the Brontës* (Basingstoke and London, 1975; 1988), and began to think more questioningly about the role the Brontës played not only in my own imagination but in culture at large. In his introduction, Eagleton remarked that "the Brontës, like Shakespeare, are a literary industry as well as a collection of literary texts, and it would have been worth asking why this should be so and how it came about" (p. xix). A decade on, this book is my personal attempt to answer that question.

As critics have often recognized, the two most famous Brontë novels have become established not just as literary classics but as what might be called modern myths. Both *Jane Eyre* and *Wuthering Heights* have burst their generic boundaries and found their way into mass culture through Hollywood, stage versions, television, and even pop music. Yet what, for me, makes the Brontës so extraordinary is that unlike the authors of comparable modern myths—Bram Stoker, say, who wrote *Dracula*—the sisters themselves, plus their entire family, have become mythic figures in their own right. Since 1857, when Elizabeth Gaskell published her famous *Life of Charlotte Brontë,* hardly a year has gone by without some form of biographical material on the Brontës appearing—from articles in newspapers to full-length lives, from images on tea towels to plays, films, and novelizations.

Like *Jane Eyre,* like *Wuthering Heights,* the tragic story of the Brontë family has been told and retold time and again in endless new configurations. Cliff Richard may have starred as Heathcliff, but Sinead O'Connor has played Emily Brontë; *Wuthering Heights,* and more recently *Jane Eyre,* may have been adapted as operas, but the lives of their original creators have inspired ballets and a musical. George Eliot has never rivaled Maggie Tulliver in the imagination of readers. Thomas Hardy does not compete with Tess. Yet the Brontës of Haworth have become popular characters on a level with Jane Eyre and Rochester, Cathy and Heathcliff.

Henry James had a particularly suspicious attitude toward this "romantic tradition" of the Brontë story, which he thought got in the way of serious critical appreciation of the sisters' works. He felt that their life history had "been made to hang before us as insistently as the vividest page of *Jane Eyre* or *Wuthering Heights,*" resulting in an unprecedented muddle in the public mind. My purpose is to trace the historical route by which the Brontës' lives came to take on this unusual prominence and to show how years of cultural accretion have shifted the sisters' position in the collective consciousness from the level of history onto that of myth.

This book, therefore, is not so much a biography of the Brontës as a book about biography, a metabiography. Occasionally, when focusing on the sentimental excesses of the Brontë cult, it may even read more like an antibiography. But while I share Henry James's anxiety about overemphasis on the Brontë story, that is not to say that I reject the biographical approach per se. The Brontës' lives *are* legitimately fascinating, but their value lies less in the simple rehearsal of the story—however melodramatic it has been made to seem—than in the ways in which, as writers, these women transformed experience into art.

What I do not claim to be able to do—as too many biographers have claimed in the past—is to sweep away all previous "false" versions of the story and resurrect the "true" Brontës in their place, as if the dead could be brought, definitively, back to life. Although recent scholars have made enormous progress in reclaiming the factual circumstances and historical background of the Brontës' experience, facts alone cannot provide the final word on a life, and there will always be a need for interpretation. I am only too aware that some people may trace my own reading of the Brontës—which emphasizes their role as conscious and ambitious literary artists—to my background as a literary critic. Had I been a romantic novelist or a social historian I might have formed a very different image of them in my mind. Nevertheless, I strongly believe that Emily Brontë in particular has too often been deintellectualized since her death, and I have become aware of how much work still needs to be done on reclaiming the literary and cultural background of her writings.

To acknowledge that all biographers have their own agendas and to reject the possibility of the definitive biography is not, however, to deny that there are rights and wrongs when it comes to life-writing. The history of the Brontës' posthumous lives is littered with examples of apocryphal stories and fantastical claims which can indeed be dismissed as mere "myths" in the commonplace sense that they have no basis in documentary fact. Yet this book is also concerned with the idea of myth in a more subtle sense of the word. Even a true story can become a myth by being endlessly repeated and woven into culture. To call an event in history mythic does not necessarily denigrate its reality or truth value. But it does acknowledge the penumbra of emotional, aesthetic, and ideological resonances which have clustered around it.

Facts, then, can become mythic through the way in which they are packaged and perceived. That there were three—and not four or five—Brontë sisters is, for example, a historical fact. But the motif of the three sisters has a cultural mystique stretching back into fairy tale, which unconsciously—or consciously, as when Ted Hughes calls them the "Three weird sisters" after the witches in *Macbeth*—contributes to the sense of mystery which surrounds them. The historical accident by which three of Patrick and Maria Brontë's five daughters lived beyond childhood, grew up to develop literary talent, and became famous as a trio melds at some level in the cultural consciousness with the atavistic magic associated with the idea of the three sisters.

As a group, Charlotte, Emily, and Anne Brontë are collectively known as "the Brontë sisters," and I therefore feel I ought to offer some explanation for why this book concentrates almost exclusively on the developing biographical image of the two elder sisters at the expense of the youngest. The reason is that Anne—who did not become the subject of a proper full-length life until a century after the first biography of Charlotte appeared—has never taken on the mythic stature of her sisters in her own right. Though she has by now been rediscovered, for most of her posthumous life she was regarded as very much the least interesting sister, mentioned, it seems, merely to make up the number three. Similarly, I have discussed the myths surrounding the sisters' father, Patrick, and brother, Branwell, only insofar as they impinge—which they often do to a large extent—on Charlotte and Emily. Although these men have been enshrined, as one critic put it, in the Madame Tussaud's of the collective psyche, they would never have become famous had it not been for the literary achievements of the women in their family.

This book has had a prolonged gestation, taking what seems like an age to develop from embryonic idea to finished text. Work on it was slowed down first by a full-time job as deputy literary editor for the *Independent*, and then by four years of debilitating illness. Since I first thought about the topic, Brontë studies seem to have flowered into something of a golden age, and I have been lucky enough to be able to take advantage of the superb new scholarship which has emerged during the writing and researching of this book. In particular, I would like to mention the work of Lyndall Gordon, whose *Charlotte Brontë: A Passionate Life* came out in 1994. Not only have I found her reading of Charlotte inspiring, but I also have to thank her for her friendship and generous support. Her unstinting encouragement, and her belief that I could finish this book even when I thought I would never manage to do so, did me so much good.

I am also indebted to Juliet Barker's *The Brontës*, another book published in 1994. The ambitious scope of Barker's research and her clear eye for historical detail make this a landmark biography which no subsequent writer on the Brontës will be able to ignore. Thought-provoking in a very different way was Stevie Davies's more literary *Emily Brontë: Heretic* (also 1994), whose approach to its subject's intellectual context chimed in with my own feelings about how we should read the woman dubbed the sphinx of English literature. I am also extremely grateful to Patsy Stoneman, who helpfully let me see some of her work in draft and whose book, *Brontë Transformations: The Cultural Dissemination of "Jane Eyre" and "Wuthering Heights"* (1996) analyzes an unparalleled array of rewritings of the two most famous Brontë novels. The critical zeitgeist does indeed seem to be moving in the direction of interest in the Brontës' reception and afterlife: in 2000, just as I was completing this book, the Brontë Parsonage Museum put on an excellent exhibition, "A Passionate Response," featuring information on Brontë biographies and on adaptations of *Jane Eyre* and *Wuthering Heights,* as well as the coat worn by Cliff Richard in his role as Heathcliff!

One of the most important Brontë projects to have begun to take shape in the 1990s is Margaret Smith's edition of *The Letters of Charlotte Brontë,* the first volume of which appeared in 1995 and the second in 2000 just in time for me to be able to take it into account. I feel very fortunate to have been able to rely on Smith's scholarship for letters up until 1851, not only because of her standards of textual accuracy but also for her fascinating footnotes. For letters after that period I have, as I explain in my bibliography, had to rely on the outdated Shakespeare Head Edition while acknowledging its inadequacies. Lastly, I want to thank the compilers of two book-length Brontë bibliographies which have proved invaluable in my search for source material: firstly, G. Anthony Yablon and John R. Turner, and secondly, Anne Passel. Two other books I want to mention, both brilliant, which came out after I started working on *The Brontë Myth* and have been indirectly influential, are Janet Malcolm's study of Sylvia Plath and her biographers, *The Silent Woman* (1994), and Jonathan Bate's *The Genius of Shakespeare* (1997).

The staff of the British, London, and Fawcett Libraries deserve my thanks, as do Rachel Terry and Ann Dinsdale of the Brontë Parsonage Museum in Haworth and Robert Parks of the Pierpont Morgan Library in New York. If I have ever felt tempted into adopting the cynical pose of the out-and-out demythologizer, I have made myself remember how extraordinarily moved I was when I first read and handled the manuscript of one of Charlotte Brontë's diary fragments written while she was a young teacher at Roe Head. No amount of rationalization can fully account for the magical sense of sharing in a private world, and of the past coming suddenly to life, which such experiences engender.

In England, where this book came out in 2001, I would like to thank my agent, Bill Hamilton, and my publishers at Jonathan Cape, especially Philippa Brewster, who first commissioned it in 1992, Dan Franklin, who continued in the most touching way to believe against the odds that it was ever going to materialize, and Jason Arthur. Owing to circumstances described below, I was unable to compile the bibliography or read the proofs myself; I thank Alexandra Butler at Cape and Myra Jones for doing this for me. Pamela Norris read through the entire manuscript with her eagle eye and made many valuable and interesting comments. In America, I would like to thank my agent, Kathy Anderson, and my editor at Knopf, Vicky Wilson, and her team, who gave me the opportunity to make a number of additions to the text that was originally published in the United Kingdom, particularly in the chapters on Emily Brontë. I was so pleased to be able to include an account of Emily's Latin translations, with their bizarre scribbled images, which I spent a fascinating day exploring at the King's School, Canterbury. Colleagues and friends have also helped, whether by reading bits of the manuscript or offering advice, information, or just encouragement, in particular, Juliet Carey, Donna Choo, Sarah Christie-Brown, Linda Kaye, Simone Ling, Michael Meredith, John Mullan, Rosie Parker, Fiammetta Rocco, Natasha Walter, and Robert Winder. My brother-in-law, Mark Bostridge, deserves a special mention for having shared his long-held love of the Brontës with me.

The completion of this book was overshadowed by two overwhelming events in my life. Just as the manuscript was about to be sent to the typesetters, my son, Oliver, was born; a couple of days after the proofs were returned my father was tragically killed, aged fifty-nine, in an accident. Both my parents were endlessly supportive during the writing of this book, but my father, who gave me a treasured first edition of Mrs. Gaskell's *Life of Charlotte Brontë*, always encouraged me with an enthusiasm which it is almost too painful to recall. I cannot express how sad I am that he will never read it. My greatest debt is to my husband, Ian Bostridge, whose constant love and care have helped me so much.

THE

BRONTË MYTH

CHAPTER ONE

To Be for Ever Known

I f the twenty-year-old Charlotte Brontë had been told that she would
one day be a household name, that her picture would hang in a future
National Portrait Gallery, and that pilgrims would travel to Haworth on
her account from as far away as Japan, she would have been delighted but
not altogether surprised. The image of the Brontës presented in Charlotte's own "Biographical Notice" of her sisters casts them as "unobtrusive
women" shunning fame.[1] Yet Charlotte's early ambition was not merely to
write but "to be for ever known."[2]

By the time she died, at the age of nearly thirty-nine, in 1855, she had
indeed become a celebrity. Two years later, with the publication of Elizabeth Gaskell's *The Life of Charlotte Brontë,* she became a legend. Yet her
journey from private individual to public persona was less straightforward
than her naive twenty-year-old self might have hoped. Instead of a triumphant progress out of obscurity into the "light & glory" of literary
renown, she would have to travel a tortuous route, characterized as much
by evasion and self-effacement as by self-exposure.[3]

She soon realized that, as a woman writing in an age in which
"authoresses" were "liable to be looked upon with prejudice," it was expe-
dient to disguise herself under a male-sounding pseudonym if she was to
make her work public.[4] In her novels, that pseudonym would give her the
freedom to use her own emotional life as the basis of her art, allowing her
to revolutionize the imaginative presentation of women's inner lives. She
was so uninhibited in her portrayal of the female psyche that her heroines
shocked many of her contemporaries and were accused of unwomanly
assertion, morbid passion, and anti-Christian individualism.

So when her pseudonym began to slip and her real identity became
known in literary circles, Charlotte had to seek out a new sort of protective
"veil" to distract attention from the unacceptable elements of her fiction
and deflect attacks on her personal morality.[5] She found this shield in her
social persona as the modest spinster daughter of a country parson, disin-

genuously insisting to those she met on the literary circuit that she bore no more than a fleeting external resemblance to the rebellious Jane Eyre. Unlike the French novelist George Sand (1804–76), who wore men's clothes and took a stream of high-profile lovers, Charlotte never sought a bohemian lifestyle. Sand's novels, with their frank portrayal of female desire, may have influenced her writing.[6] But Charlotte the clergyman's daughter was not prepared to sacrifice her respectability. She was well aware that she lived in a society where "publicity . . . for a woman . . . is degrading if it is not glorious" and where the line between celebrity and notoriety was perilously thin.[7]

If Charlotte Brontë was her own mythologizer, she invented two distinct and conflicting myths, the second designed to deflect attention from the first. One was the positive myth of female self-creation embodied by her autobiographical heroines, Jane Eyre and Lucy Snowe, who forge their own sense of selfhood in conflict with their social environment. The other, which eventually inspired the saintly heroine of Elizabeth Gaskell's *Life of Charlotte Brontë,* was a quiet and trembling creature, reared in total seclusion, a martyr to duty, and a model of Victorian femininity, whose sins against convention, if she had unwittingly committed any, could be explained away by her isolated upbringing and the sufferings she had endured. Both had their elements of truth in aspects of Charlotte Brontë's private character, but both were imaginative constructs, consciously developed.

Charlotte's perception of the writer's self as material for mythology derived from her Romantic inheritance, as did the lifelong belief in her own genius which enabled her to achieve what she did in literature against the odds. Her youthful faith in writing as a route to immortal fame had been established early on in childhood. Because of the way her public image was molded after her death, her family has, over the past century and a half, been primarily remembered for its tragedies. But what made her able to transform herself into one of the major novelists of the nineteenth century was the fact that she grew up steeped in literature, defining herself as a writer from a very young age. Charlotte was five when her mother died and eight when she was sent with her sisters to the Clergy Daughters' School at Cowan Bridge, where the eldest two, Maria and Elizabeth, contracted the tuberculosis that killed them. Yet within a year or so of these damaging experiences, Charlotte had recovered sufficiently to form an intense bond with her three surviving siblings, Branwell, Emily, and Anne, in boisterous imaginative games fueled by the literary tastes their father encouraged. Like Samuel Taylor Coleridge, who talked meta-physics with his infant son Hartley, the Reverend Patrick Brontë took a Romantic interest in his children's development and encouraged their precocity.

Charlotte and Branwell later recorded how their "plays" began in 1826 with the present of a box of toy soldiers. In real life, death had intruded as an arbitrary force. In play, they could take control when, as four gigantic Genii, they held the power of life and death over the diminutive wooden men. Soon, they began to make tiny magazines for the soldiers, writing out their own compositions in microscopic script. This scribblemania contin-ued long after they had outgrown the toys which had originally inspired it and eventually became a purely literary adventure. By the time they were into their teens, their understanding of the term "Genius" was more metaphorical than it had been, but no less potent. Eventually, the siblings split off into two separate camps, Charlotte and Branwell chronicling the history of the imaginary kingdom of Angria while Emily and Anne invented their own fantasy world, Gondal.[8]

At an early age, the young Brontës formed a habit of treating writers as heroes. In one game, played when they were aged between seven and eleven, each had to pick an island and its chief men.[9] Their chosen leaders included literary figures such as Sir Walter Scott, J. G. Lockhart, Leigh Hunt, and "Christopher North" (John Wilson) of *Blackwood's* magazine, all of whom were clearly believed to be as powerful as a man of action like the Duke of Wellington, who was also selected.[10] Though Emily's and Anne's early prose has not survived, Angria and its predecessor Glass Town are vividly documented in Charlotte's and Branwell's voluminous juvenilia, which reveal their fantasy world as a place where writers were important figures.

Charlotte's early-established belief in the writer as an exceptional indi-vidual derived from her sophisticated childhood and teenage reading and continued into adulthood. During the 1820s and 1830s, *Blackwood's Magazine,* and later *Fraser's,* formed the core of her cultural education.[11] Unlike today's magazines, these periodicals were not mere ephemera but would have been kept and reread like books. They offered an often highbrow mix of poetry, fiction, satire, criticism, philosophy, history, and political commentary, often sustained to booklike length. *Blackwood's,* in particular, turned its contributors into cult figures, such as James Hogg, "the Ettrick Shepherd." A serialized "Gallery of Literary Characters" in *Fraser's* during 1832 reinforced the celebrity status of the writer. Steeped in the fallout from the Romantic movement, these magazines fostered the belief that poets were not mere linguistic craftsmen, but privileged souls whose personalities were as important as their actual literary output. One *Blackwood's* article on Byron in 1828 casually refers to "Great Poets" as "the Chosen Few."[12] Another, two years later, also on Byron, describes famous poets as "fixed stars" forming their own "celestial clubs."[13]

In their imaginary city of Glass Town, Charlotte and Branwell could aspire to join this heavenly clique by writing poetry and prose under the pseudonyms of their favorite characters. These alter egos were all, without exception, men. As Christine Alexander points out, writing was regarded in the Brontë household as "very much a male domain."[14] At this stage, Charlotte had no conscious anxiety about unquestioningly identifying herself with the power and privilege of her narrators, who were male simply because she had few female models to emulate (there was no Jane Austen, for example, on the Parsonage shelves). The conflict between her gender and her desire to write would only become explicit later, particularly when she made contact with the real-life world of professional letters. Even so, it still provoked latent tensions in her juvenilia which would not be finally exploded until *Jane Eyre*, in which she used a woman's voice. Charlotte's best mature fiction is remarkable for the subjective intensity of its female first-person narrators, but in her juvenilia she tended to adopt the pose of a cynical and detached male narrator. Something held her back from total engagement, except as a voyeur.

When thirteen-year-old Branwell threw himself enthusiastically into the character of Young Soult, an inspired poet, fourteen-year-old Charlotte could only stand back and mock in a satirical drama, *The Poetaster*. Soult is turned into Henry Rhymer, a drunken coward who writes trite little verses about his own Orphic powers, stamps his foot, and treats his social superiors with absurd flattery one minute, insults the next. When Lord Charles Wellesley, Charlotte's cynical alter ego, reads Rhymer's effusions, he can hardly contain his giggles. Rhymer ends up being kicked out of the room by another of Charlotte's alter egos, the Angrian prose author Captain Tree. Rhymer responds by murdering the unfortunate Tree, but is reprieved on the gallows when Tree is magically brought back to life.[15]

There is no doubt that Branwell at this age could be infuriatingly bumptious and probably deserved everything he got. Yet the very mercilessness of Charlotte's attack suggests how threatened and excluded she felt by her brother's confident identification with the poet who knows that after his

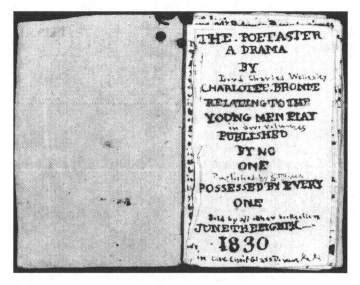

Part of the manuscript of Charlotte's 1830 satire, *The Poetaster,* in which she lambasts her brother for his high-flown literary ambitions

death he will become (quoting the *Blackwood's* article on Byron of a few months before) "a fixed star ascending to the heaven of literature and there establishing its glory, in the midst of poets which are its fellows, to all eternity."[16] This is Henry Rhymer speaking in Charlotte's satire, but his words sound remarkably similar to her own Romantic ideals. Indeed, his Keatsian belief that true poetry comes as naturally as the leaves to the tree—"The thoughts should come spontaneously as I write or they're not the inspiration of genius"[17]—is almost identical with the credo earnestly expressed by Charlotte thirteen years later. In an essay written while she was studying in Brussels in 1843, she argued that for the true poet "inspiration takes the place of reflection" and that "the man of genius produces, without work."[18] If the teenage Charlotte found her brother's posturing unbearable, it was because she would herself have liked to identify with the high Romantic conception of the man of genius, but felt prohibited from giving herself fully to the fantasy because she was a girl.

When Charlotte does write in a nonsatirical poetic voice, we find her bewailing the fate of the "neglected genius" who dies unrecognized:

None can tell the bitter anguish
Of those lofty souls that languish,
With grim penury still dwelling:
Quenched by frowns their sacred fire,
All their powers within them swelling,
Tortured by neglect to ire.[19]

It may be written in the voice of the Angrian Marquis of Douro, but this poem reflects Charlotte's angry sense of her own unacknowledged worth. In it, she goes on to address Genius as a "Spiritual essence, pure, divine" which purifies the vision of the favored mortals to whom it is given.[20] Though awkwardly expressed here, the faith she held at fourteen in the God-given origin of her own artistic creativity would change little as she matured.

Through her early reading, Charlotte absorbed the influence of two distinct types of Romanticism which both informed her view of what the creative writer ought to be. On the one hand there was the visionary Romanticism found in her poem on the neglected genius. This enshrined the imagination as the "divine faculty,"[21] which allowed the gifted individual to see beyond appearances into spiritual reality and was ultimately derived from Wordsworth, Coleridge, and lesser figures such as John Wilson of *Blackwood's*.[22] When Wilson exhorted "us visionaries" to apply their transcendent imaginations to a sublimely craggy landscape, Charlotte would have included herself in the invitation.[23]

Charlotte quotes Wordsworth and Coleridge in her juvenilia, but in her prose writing she was less interested in their visionary aesthetic than in chronicling the political and amorous intrigues of the Angrian scene. As a result, the two authors she most admired in her late teens, and whose impact on her writing is most apparent, were Scott—she believed all other novels after his were "worthless"—and Byron.[24] Scott's legacy can be seen in her stories of abducted damsels and civil war, Byron's in her cynical men-of-the-world narrators and her obsession with the amours of her aristocratic hero, Zamorna. Both writers were among the biggest celebrities of their age and would have informed Charlotte's idea of what it was to achieve literary success.

Sir Walter Scott (1771–1832) was, as Carlyle put it in a review of Lockhart's biography of 1837–38, "like some living mythological personage, and ranked among the chief wonders of the world."[25] Lord Byron (1788–1824) had not only been the most famous poet of his day, but had notoriously lived out his private life on the public stage. His glamour and fame were reinforced by Thomas Moore's biography of 1830, which was devoured by the Brontë children.[26] In a review, Macaulay commented on the interchangeability of the writer and the work, suggesting that Byron had consciously set out to become a legend: "He was himself the beginning, the middle, and the end of all his own poetry—the hero of every tale—the chief object of every landscape. Harold, Lara, Manfred, and a crowd of other characters, were universally considered merely as loose incognitos of Byron; and there is every reason to believe that he meant them to be so considered."[27]

After her death Charlotte Brontë would come to rival Byron in personal fame. But in her early prose fiction she was not so much trying to be Byron as to look through the keyhole onto Byronic scenes of aristocratic seducers and swooning ladies in glittering silks.[28] Her contact with Byron's life and works (including his racy *Don Juan,* which she had read herself by the time she was eighteen, but which she advised her ladylike friend Ellen Nussey to avoid)[29] exposed her to the frank literary portrayal of sexuality which would reemerge, in modified form, in her adult novels to upset many readers of the 1840s and 1850s.

Instead of plunging directly into this risqué world of Angrian amours, Charlotte habitually described it through the eyes of a noncommital narrator, "Charles Townshend." This was a safety valve designed to prevent her from getting too involved. For she was beginning to feel increasingly guilty about her reliance on this secret fantasy life, which jarred more and more with the social identity she was expected to develop as the demure daughter of the local parson, whose duties included organizing tea parties for Sunday-school teachers who would never have suspected what was going on in their young hostess's mind.

While a frustrated junior teacher at Roe Head (the kindly boarding school where she had been a pupil in her teens, not the notorious Cowan Bridge of her childhood), Charlotte's habit of escaping into vivid voyeuristic daydreams—often erotic, as when she conjured up the image of a heaving-chested African warrior sprawling lasciviously on the sumptuous couch of a beautiful queen—became all the more intense, as did her guilt about them. Sometimes her lurid visions dissolved into ambitious fantasies of her own literary talents. Scribbling in almost illegible script in the ad hoc journal she kept at the time, she described the intensity of the feeling:

"Then came on me rushing impetuously. [*sic*] all the mighty phantasm that this had conjured from nothing to a system strong as some religious creed. I felt as if I could have written gloriously—I longed to write."[30]

At Roe Head, Charlotte experienced an often frantically suppressed sense of conflict between her outward self—the dutiful young teacher—and her secret inner dreams. This conflict at work reflected a similar contradiction in her home upbringing. On the one hand, her father, the Reverend Patrick Brontë, expected his daughters to behave as model churchwomen, concerning themselves with parish duties and behaving with the appropriate decorum. Yet, on the other, his own career proved that it was possible to break away from the station into which one was born and make a life for oneself of one's own choosing. Himself a published poet, Patrick offered his children a tangible example of the potentialities of self-creation. As a young man, he had symbolically shed his humble Irish background when he arrived at Cambridge University: on arrival he was registered at St. John's College under the name of "Branty," but this was soon crossed out and replaced with the more flamboyant "Bronte," possibly in imitation of Nelson, who had recently been made Duke of Bronte by the King of Naples.[31] Through the transforming power of books, Charlotte's father had been able to adopt a completely new class identity as a Church of England cleric. This gave an edge to her own ambition.

Charlotte must have been very ambitious indeed, for while on holiday from Roe Head in December 1836, she found the courage to write to the Poet Laureate, Robert Southey (1774–1843), enclosing some of her own poems and confessing her desire "to be for ever known." In her private writings so far she had usually chosen to be the passive observer of her Byronic heroes rather than allowing herself to pose as the man of genius. Yet in her first attempt to make contact with the public, professional world of letters, she explicitly acknowledged her covert hope of being recognized in her own right for her talents.[32] Southey—himself a remnant of the Romantic vanguard Charlotte admired—was generous enough to write back a substantial letter. But though well meant, his response was dispiriting. While he conceded that she had "the faculty of Verse," the core of his message was unequivocal: "Literature cannot be the business of a woman's life: & it ought not to be."[33]

What seems to have troubled him most about Charlotte's letter was her frank ambition to be publicly acknowledged. His attempt to dampen her naive enthusiasm—he was embarrassed to find himself described as

The Brontë sisters (left to right, Anne, Emily, and Charlotte), painted in 1834 by their brother, Branwell.

Charlotte kept the painting all her life. Though she showed it to her future biographer Mrs. Gaskell in 1853, she clearly wanted to keep it private, as she told her publisher she had no portrait of either of her sisters. After she died, her widower, Arthur Nicholls, took it to Ireland, where it remained until 1914, folded up on top of a wardrobe, hence the creases in the canvas. Though neither Charlotte nor her husband would have welcomed the publicity, it has since become the most widely disseminated image of the Brontës, reproduced on countless book covers and souvenirs and even, in the 1980s, taken to Japan for an exhibit in a department store.

"stooping from a throne of light & glory"—is understandable.[34] Having mellowed into respectable middle age, he had long since abandoned the Romantic idealism of his own youth.[35] Even so, one gets the feeling that he might have considered a lust for fame more excusable in a young man than in a girl. Once she had buckled down to her "proper duties" as a woman, he advised, she would be "less eager for celebrity."[36]

Southey's response to her plea for recognition confirmed Charlotte's fear that her passion for writing was something socially unacceptable, to be concealed. As it was, she had kept Angria a secret outside her own family, though in moments of religious guilt, she would hint to Ellen Nussey—whom she had met at Roe Head and who was to remain a life-long friend—that she was eaten up by the unhealthy workings of her "fiery imagination."[37] So when none less than the Poet Laureate questioned the legitimacy of her ambitions and daydreams, she tried to make the effort to suppress them. In her reply to his letter she reassured him: "I carefully avoid any appearance of pre-occupation, and eccentricity, which might lead those I live amongst [i.e., at Roe Head] to suspect the nature of my pursuits."[38] She admitted that she would rather be writing than sewing or teaching, but, she added dutifully, "I try to deny myself."[39] The double meaning—does she simply mean "resist temptation" or is there an implication of "erase myself"?—speaks for itself.

Though Charlotte may have been chastened enough by the poet to write "Southey's Advice To be kept for ever" on the envelope to his next letter—a brief acknowledgment of her reply which urged her to "endeav-our to keep a quiet mind"—she did not accept his verdict for long.[40] Instead, she kept on writing in the hope of one day embarking on a literary career, which she saw as an escape route from the drudgery of teaching, either in a school or, far worse, as a governess in a private family—the only paid employment then open to most women of her class. The real differ-ence made by Southey's letter was that in future contacts with the literary world she would be careful to "deny" her real name, which the Poet Lau-reate, ironically, had suspected of being made up (which in a sense it had been, by her father). As an author, she would never attempt to publish as "Charlotte Brontë."

When, three years later, she sent some fiction to the well-known writer Hartley Coleridge (son of Samuel Taylor and nephew of Southey) for his comments, she signed herself "C.T."—after "Charles Townshend," one of her Angrian alter egos. The pseudonym gave her the freedom to let rip when he wrote back an unflattering reply. Her second letter to him is bursting with frenzied sarcasm and swaggering contempt for the man who had failed to give her the encouragement she craved. (Her fury at being snubbed may have been exacerbated by the fact that earlier that year Coleridge had responded to a similar letter from Branwell by praising his poetry and inviting him to spend a day with him.)[41] Coleridge had suspected his correspondent was a woman, but, C.T. reminded him with a swipe at male authors in general, "Several young gentlemen curl their hair and wear corsets — Richardson and Rousseau — often write exactly like old women — and Bulwer and Cooper and Dickens and Warren like boarding-school misses."[42]

The tale Charlotte sent to Hartley Coleridge derived from the Angrian saga. Though she disguised its origins by relocating the action in the more realistic West Riding of Yorkshire, it remained rooted in the artificial world of high-society intrigue, complete with Byronic antihero, which still dominated her imagination.[43] Coleridge's criticisms were probably valid. At this stage in her literary apprenticeship Charlotte had not yet learned to get inside her protagonists and create the sustained psychological portraits which characterize her mature work. She did not come into her own as a novelist until she developed the confidence to base her fiction on her own emotional experience and to enter her creations empathetically rather than hovering voyeuristically outside them.

The influences which would enable her to make this creative leap were not English. In 1840, Charlotte discovered George Sand, the French writer who had created her own female form of Romanticism in novels which put women's erotic passion at center stage. In the 1832 preface to *Indiana,* Sand had described her heroine as "desire at odds with necessity . . . love dashing her head blindly against all the obstacles of civilisation."[44] The story is unashamedly about forbidden sexual relationships, one consummated, one endlessly deferred. Though it includes no anatomically explicit descriptions of sex, it leaves the reader in no doubt as to when the act is taking place. Though her writing would never be as voluptuous as Sand's, such "wicked" reading (as she put it) would enable Charlotte to legitimize her focus on women's passion in her mature novels.[45] But the most important influence on her development was her decision to leave Haworth for the Continent in search of new intellectual experiences.

In 1842, Charlotte went, with her sister Emily, to study French and German at the Pensionnat Heger, a girls' school in Brussels whose headmistress was married to one of Belgium's finest teachers of literature, Constantin Heger, a professor at the Athénée Royal. Southey and Hartley

Coleridge had dismissed her ambitions. But here, for the first time, at the age of twenty-five, Charlotte met a high-powered literary man who actively encouraged her talent for writing while challenging her intellectually. Under Heger's instruction, she and Emily produced French compositions which were subjected to rigorous critique, not merely as language exercises, but for their style and content. He expected his pupils to develop their own prose by emulating that of famous authors, and he made Charlotte think hard about the technical side of writing.

Heger also gave Charlotte a forum in which to explore her own feelings about creativity. With him, she debated the subject of genius. In one essay, "Letter From a Poor Painter to a Great Lord," Charlotte dramatized her own quest for recognition in the defiant voice of an artist who wanders through Romantic forests, poor, but confident that he possesses "a few grains of that pure gold which is called Genius."[46] Rather than mocking the self-belief of the aspiring artist—as she had mocked Branwell's pretensions all those years before in the character of Henry Rhymer—she poured all her own hopes into the sincere ambition of the struggling young painter.

Where Charlotte wanted to believe that great art was the product of intuition alone, Heger insisted that study and experience were just as crucial. The fact that his tuition yielded such results suggests that his classical emphasis on craft and hard work was in reality as important to Charlotte's artistic development as her own more Romantic belief in spontaneous inspiration. She did not abandon that belief, but she modified it in the light of Heger's teaching, accepting that the craft of writing could be worked on and improved. As well as helping her technique, he made her more aware of the needs of writing for an audience rather than as a personal escape. Most significantly, he gave her the self-confidence which comes from recognition. She even seems to have trusted him enough to have shown him some of her Angrian fiction.[47]

Charlotte and Emily spent an initial nine months in Brussels, from February 1842 until they were called home by the death of their Aunt Branwell, who had come to live at the Parsonage to help bring up the children after their mother's death. In January 1843, Charlotte returned alone for a further year, during which she became more and more dependent on her "Master" and more and more alienated from his wife. When she came home again, she experienced agonizing feelings of emotional withdrawal. The result was a series of increasingly desperate and passionate letters to her professor. These probably had as much to do with a need for artistic recognition as they did with romance. In one she describes her ambition to write a book and dedicate it to him.[48] Despite her agony when Heger failed to reply, writing these intense letters had a cathartic effect. Once the one-sided correspondence came to an end, she became filled with a firmer resolve than she had previously been able to sustain. Two months after writing her last letter to Heger in November 1845,[49] she had begun to put her literary ambition into practice by approaching the publishing firm of Aylott and Jones.[50]

She later described how her chance discovery of Emily's notebook spurred her into action. "One day, in the autumn of 1845, I accidentally lighted on a MS. volume of verse in my sister Emily's handwriting. Of course, I was not surprised, knowing that she could and did write verse: I looked it over, and something more than surprise seized me,—a deep conviction that these were not common effusions, nor at all like the poetry women generally write." Fired by the discovery, Charlotte set about persuading Emily that "such poems merited publication." Anne too offered some of her verse, and the three sisters at length decided to put together a joint volume and bring it out under ambiguous pseudonyms which, while not "positively masculine," would effectively disguise the fact that the writers were women.[51]

Poems, by Currer, Ellis, and Acton Bell, was published at the authors' own expense by Aylott and Jones the following year, 1846. It may not have been the sisters' very first venture into print—it seems that the odd poetry translation by Charlotte and lyric by Anne had perhaps appeared anonymously in the press[52]—but it was their most significant step yet. Published in a period of particular sluggishness in the market for poetry, the volume was a commercial failure. But although it sold only two copies, it marked the moment at which the sisters began to construct a public identity as writers. The few critics who noticed the book were immediately intrigued by the Bells and suspected by instinct that the name was pseudonymous. One reviewer speculated that Currer, Ellis, and Acton were in fact three aspects of a single poet.[53] Though no critic suspected the truth—that they were women—another was perceptive enough to realize that the authors had disguised themselves because they "desired that the poems should be tried and judged upon their own merits alone, apart from all extraneous circumstances."[54]

The sisters had by now decided to follow up the *Poems* with three prose tales, which they intended to publish under their new *noms de plume.* In the summer of 1847, Emily's *Wuthering Heights* and Anne's *Agnes Grey* were accepted "on terms somewhat impoverishing to the two authors" by the London publisher Thomas Cautley Newby.[55] Charlotte's novel, *The Professor*, was yet to find a home. It was based loosely on her Brussels experience, but, written in the voice of an emotionally repressed male narrator, it lacked the intensity of her later treatment of the same material in *Villette*. In early August she received a rejection letter from the publishing house of Smith, Elder & Co. full of such kind encouragement and enthusiastic advice that it gave her more pleasure than a curt acceptance might have done. Smith, Elder, thought that *The Professor*, though well written, was too short and lacking in excitement, but they expressed an interest in any three-volume work Currer Bell might have to offer.

By August 24, Charlotte had sent off *Jane Eyre*, on which she had been working while her other manuscript did the rounds. According to his account, George Smith, the energetic young head of the firm, had planned to spend his Sunday out riding with a friend, but found himself so engrossed in Jane's story that he canceled his plans and locked himself away in his study, preferring to snack as he read rather than join his family for dinner. The following day he wrote to Currer Bell offering £100 for the copyright. Six weeks later the book was published.[56]

It caused an immediate sensation. Like anyone who reads it for the first time today, its original audience was overwhelmed by its passion and emotional honesty. It was a book "to make the pulses gallop and the heart beat,"[57] which had "little or nothing of the old conventional stamp upon it."[58] William Thackeray was so caught up in it that he missed a deadline and was found in tears by the astonished servant who had come in to see to the fire.[59]

Jane Eyre's tale of a poor governess who eventually marries her employer—but only after his mad first wife has perished in a climactic conflagration—offered a highly original mix of gothic melodrama on the one hand and detailed naturalism on the other. Yet the real secret of its extraordinary force was what G. H. Lewes, the critic and future partner of George Eliot, called its "strange power of subjective representation."[60] Jane must be the most irresistible first-person heroine in literature. The reader cannot help but think her thoughts and feel her feelings. As Lewes put it, "it is soul speaking to soul; it is an utterance from the depths of a struggling, suffering, much-enduring spirit: *suspiria de profundis!*"[61]

Jane Eyre was the first fiction Charlotte had written in the authentic voice of a female narrator. It offered access, unheard of in the novel at the time, into the depths of the individual psyche: the "I" of it was revolution-ary.[62] Charlotte had found a way of relocating the Romantic individualism that had shaped her literary ambitions in the outcast figure of the small, plain, shabby-genteel governess, the social persona into which she herself had often felt boxed. Instead of trying to emulate male writers in her quest for literary identity, she had found a path of her own, distinct from the exhibitionism of a Byron. Disbarred by her gender from the public postur-ing of the man of genius, she instead poured her egoism into a new and specifically female form of self-expression. In Jane, she let out the pent-up emotions of a woman who feels the world against her, and in doing so she indicted the society that had told her to suppress her passions and ambi-tions in the interests of womanly duty.

The full title of her novel was *Jane Eyre: An Autobiography*. Like Wordsworth, like Byron, like De Quincey (to whom Lewes alluded in his use of the phrase *"suspiria de profundis,"* sighs from the depths, the title of a prose piece which appeared in *Blackwood's* in 1845), she believed that personal experience was the most valid basis for art there could be. As G. H. Lewes intuitively recognized, the novel contained elements taken from the author's own life. Charlotte's childhood misery at the Clergy Daughters' School at Cowan Bridge was reworked in *Jane Eyre*'s Lowood; her elder sister Maria, who had died as a result of the school's poor hygiene, bad food, and inhumane regime, was transformed into the poignant char-acter of Helen Burns. Fifty years later, it would become fashionable among Brontë enthusiasts to obsess over the minutiae of the real-life originals of the people and places in the sisters' novels. But Lewes, in 1847, realized that the novel's psychological truth was more important than its documentary aspect: "It is an autobiography,—not, perhaps, in the naked facts and cir-cumstances, but in the actual suffering and experience."[63]

Lewes realized that the author of *Jane Eyre* had transformed personal experience, through art, into something universal with which every reader could identify. "It reads like a page out of one's own life,"[64] he wrote of the passage in which the child Jane hides in the window seat with a book to escape her vile cousins, the Reeds. Jane's resistance to the Reeds' attempts to subdue her personality is apparent as she symbolically creates a world for herself in the space between the curtain and the window. Later on, when Mr. Rochester, her employer, takes advantage of his male power and privilege to toy with her emotions, Jane will assert not only her passions and desires, but her individual worth as a human being:

Do you think I am an automaton?—a machine without feelings? and can bear to have my morsel of bread snatched from my lips, and my drop of living water dashed from my cup? Do you think, because I am poor, obscure, plain, and little, I am soulless and heartless?—You think wrong!—I have as much soul as you,—and full as much heart! . . . I am not talking to you now through the medium of custom, conventionalities, nor even of mortal flesh:—it is my spirit that addresses your spirit; just as if both had passed through the grave, and we stood at God's feet, equal—as we are![65]

Her final reunion with Rochester, and their subsequent marriage, can only happen on the basis of equality of souls.

Jane Eyre's status as a modern myth—its dissemination into mass culture—can be explained by its ability to be broken down into the basic building blocks of a simple Cinderella story, or Bluebeard narrative. But Charlotte's real achievement in the novel was to create a different kind of myth: a positive concept of the emerging female self in a society whose predominant models of middle-class femininity were self-denying, dutiful, and passion-free. By using her own life as the imaginative starting point for fiction—which she did in all her novels, especially *Jane Eyre* and *Villette*—she instigated a myth which was both personal and universal. The difference, however, between her and a myth-maker such as Byron was that while he, as Macaulay put it, expected the public to see straight through his incognitos, she wanted to remain concealed beneath the veil of "Currer Bell."

From the start, however, *Jane Eyre*'s readers wanted to get behind that veil. "It is a womans [*sic*] writing, but whose?" was Thackeray's first comment in a private letter to the publisher William Smith Williams.[66] Publicly, reviewers would soon begin to voice similar suspicions. In her contacts with the male-dominated literary world as "Currer Bell," Charlotte had so far made every effort to maintain her disguise by aping a tone of masculine confidence. Her letters to publishers had been businesslike. When she sent complimentary copies of the *Poems* to the leading male writers of the day (including Hartley Coleridge, who had snubbed her seven years before), her accompanying note could have come straight out of *Ranthorpe,* G. H. Lewes's novel, published that very year, about the trials on Grub Street of a young man with poetic ambitions.[67] Such ventriloquism may have disguised Charlotte's gender, but Jane Eyre had spoken in such an authentic female voice that many readers began to speculate that "Currer Bell" was not what he appeared.

Speculation only intensified after the appearance, in December 1847, of *Wuthering Heights* and *Agnes Grey* by Ellis and Acton Bell. Their publisher, Thomas Newby, who had been sitting on the manuscripts for months, had been stung into action by the best-selling success of *Jane Eyre*. Soon it seemed that the Brontës' decision to use pseudonyms had had almost the opposite effect to that intended: instead of securing an objective hearing for their work, they had unwittingly invited a hoard of amateur detectives to speculate on their identities. The authors, not the books, increasingly became the focus of interest. Was "Currer Bell" an anagram?[68] Were the brothers Bell a trio of Lancashire weavers? References in *Jane Eyre* to cookery and fashion would be scrutinized as clues to the author's sex. Some scurrilous gossips even started the rumor that *Jane Eyre* had been written by Thackeray's governess and mistress, capitalizing on the fact that the author of *Vanity Fair*, like Mr. Rochester, was unwillingly bound in marriage to an insane wife.[69]

The mystery had deepened when Newby intentionally began to confuse the Bells' identities in the public mind. He advertised *Wuthering Heights* as "Mr. Bell's new novel," implying that it was by the author of the recent best-seller *Jane Eyre*.[70] To begin with, the sisters were rather amused by the confusion. But Newby went on to offer Acton's second book, *The Tenant of Wildfell Hall*, to an American publishing house as another work by the author of *Jane Eyre*. George Smith was understandably concerned when he got wind of this proposed deal, wondering why his prized author was apparently offering a new novel to another publisher behind his back. A letter was promptly despatched to Currer Bell, demanding an explanation. It was this enquiry which prompted the celebrated journey Charlotte and Anne made to London in the summer of 1848 (Emily, reclusive as ever, stayed behind in Haworth).[71] Appearing out of the blue in the Cornhill offices of Smith, Elder, these two "odd-looking countrywomen"[72] finally revealed themselves as the real Currer and Acton Bell.

"[M]ystery is irksome, and I was glad to shake it off with you and Mr. Smith, and to shew myself to you for what I am," wrote Charlotte, on her return, to William Smith Williams, the Smith, Elder & Co. reader with whom she had, over the preceeding months, developed an increasingly relaxed epistolary relationship.[73] While her earliest letters to the firm could easily have been a man's, her neutral, businesslike tone had gradually grown more intimate. Encouraged by Williams's kindness and quiet intelligence, she had expressed herself more and more freely, particularly on the question of a woman's right to work. Yet while she implicitly helped

him to guess her sex, she had been firm on one point: " 'Currer Bell' only—
I am and will be to the Public; if accident or design should deprive me of
that name, I should deem it a misfortune—a very great one."[74] Her desire
to be "for ever known" had mutated into a fear of being found out.

In particular, Charlotte was determined that her writing should not
become known among her Yorkshire acquaintance. When her close friend
Ellen Nussey mentioned local gossip about the new novel *Jane Eyre*,
Charlotte fired back the following: "[T]he report—if report there be . . .
must have had its origin in some absurd misunderstanding. I have given *no
one* a right either to affirm, or hint, in the most distant manner, that I am
'publishing'—(humbug!). . . . Though twenty books were ascribed to me, I
should own none. I scout the idea utterly. . . . The most profound obscurity
is infinitely preferable to vulgar notoriety; and that notoriety I neither
seek nor will have."[75]

Charlotte may have been afraid of the scandal that might erupt if
she was recognized as the author partly because she had based her most
terrifying villain on a real-life local figure: William Carus Wilson, the
Evangelical patron of the Clergy Daughters' School, who inspired Mr.
Brocklehurst, the evil genius behind *Jane Eyre*'s Lowood. Indeed, in January 1848 she reported to William Smith Williams that an elderly clergyman
of her acquaintance had recognized the portrait, though she was relieved
to say that she was not suspected of its authorship.[76] Deeper, however,
than any fear of this nature was her habitual reluctance to reveal the passionate depths of her imagination to her everyday acquaintances. At this
stage, the only one of her old friends whom she told about *Jane Eyre* was
the strong-willed feminist Mary Taylor, whom she had met at Roe Head,
but who was now thousands of miles away in New Zealand.

Charlotte had always been secretive about her writing, but she now had
every reason to fear notoriety and to cling to "the advantage of being able
to walk invisible."[77] In London, while she and Anne revealed themselves
to their publishers, they were otherwise determined to keep a low profile.
They reluctantly refused invitations to meet with leading men of letters
and insisted on being introduced to George Smith's bemused mother and
sisters as the "Misses Brown." It was not until after Emily and Anne died
that Charlotte would finally consent to becoming generally known in literary circles as the author of *Jane Eyre*.[78] This desire for incognito is more
than understandable if one considers the sort of comments the Bells were
attracting in the press. Although *Jane Eyre* had been an instant success, the

near-universal approval of the earliest reviews had begun to show signs of cracking.[79]

The first hints of the Bells' notoriety had appeared soon after the publication of *Wuthering Heights*, which had impressed reviewers but also shocked them with its "coarse and loathesome" passions and scenes of violence.[80] *Jane Eyre* also began to attract the odd hostile comment, and, in December 1847, Charlotte had written a preface for the second edition in which, in the strident voice of Currer Bell, she had defended herself with the cry that "Conventionality is not morality." She thanked those among the press and public who had responded positively, but fingered "the timorous or carping few who doubt the tendency of such books as *Jane Eyre*: in whose eyes whatever is unusual is wrong; whose ears detect in each protest against bigotry—that parent of crime—an insult to piety, that regent of God on earth."[81]

Rather than converting the carping few, these comments may in fact have inflamed the public sense that *Jane Eyre* was a controversial book when the second edition appeared in January 1848. Certainly, Charlotte's fulsome praise of Thackeray, to whom she dedicated it, had the unintended effect of intensifying the scandal attached to *Jane Eyre* by starting the rumor that Currer Bell was Thackeray's lover. (Being outside the charmed circle of London literary gossip, she had been unaware that Thackeray had a mad wife, and was mortified when she discovered the embarrassment she had inadvertently caused him.)

The negative comments about *Jane Eyre* began to intensify as they became more closely bound up with the debate over the mystery author's gender. Once the novel was widely supposed to be the work of a woman, it seemed far less acceptable than had previously been the case. In April 1848, the *Christian Remembrancer* castigated the book's "masculine hardness, coarseness, and freedom of expression" as inappropriate in a female author.[82] The question of Currer Bell's gender was soon being used by critics as an occasion for pontificating on what was acceptable "feminine" writing and what was not.

Attacks intensified further with *The Tenant of Wildfell Hall*, Anne's brave account of a young wife who decides to leave her abusive, alcoholic husband. The first reviews coincided with the sisters' visit to their publishers in London. The very day they arrived, the new issue of the *Spectator* came out, containing a review of Anne's novel which accused its author of having "a morbid love for the coarse, not to say the brutal." The critic went on to vilify the sisters' entire oeuvre: "There is a coarseness of tone throughout the writing of all these Bells, that puts an offensive subject in its worst point of view."[83] It is hardly surprising if Charlotte and Anne were resistant to "being made a show of"[84] among the capital's literati during their visit, if this is how they were perceived. By September, the *Rambler* was decrying "that truly offensive and sensual spirit which is painfully prominent in *Jane Eyre* and the tale now before us." *Jane Eyre* was now judged "one of the coarsest books which we ever perused."[85] *Sharpe's London Magazine* made a special effort to warn lady readers off the "revolting" *Tenant of Wildfell Hall.*[86]

The "coarseness" to which so many critics objected was a catch-all moralistic term which encompassed a range of elements considered unfeminine and indecorous. Linguistically, it included the Brontës' use of slang and swear words as well as their supposedly inappropriate use of biblical quotation (in fact, Charlotte's frequent scriptural allusions pay testimony to the fact that she was so saturated in religion that no area of human experience, serious or humorous, intimate or public, was considered outside its range). More fundamentally, the word "coarse" was applied to the novels' depiction of passion and violence, which were held to challenge the modesty and refinement of normative femininity.

Quite how seriously all this was taken by the reading public is debatable. An article in the *North American Review* of October 1848 takes quite a humorous view of "*Jane Eyre* fever" in its survey of how the novel had so far been received in Britain: "The book which caused the distemper would probably have been inoffensive, had not some sly manufacturer of mischief hinted that it was a book which no respectable man should bring into his family circle. Of course, every family soon had a copy of it, and one edition after another found eager purchasers."[87] Yet this confirms that, whatever individual readers may have felt, the novel had developed an undoubted *reputation* for scandal. Two months later, that reputation would be confirmed by Elizabeth Rigby's notorious article in the *Quarterly Review* of December 1848.

Writing anonymously, Rigby not only attacked *Jane Eyre* for its "coarseness of language and laxity of tone"[88] but lambasted the heroine's character as an affront to conventional ideas of womanly humility. Jane's individualism, independence, and self-assertion were not merely unseemly but subversive. The novel was accused of being "anti-Christian," and its heroine was described as "the personification of an unregenerate and undisciplined spirit" who had "the strength of a mere heathen mind which is a law unto itself."[89] To the religious daughter of a clergyman—which is what Charlotte still was, despite her rebellious streak—such comments must have felt particularly cruel. Rigby's remarks on the authorship question were even more spiteful: if this book had been written by a woman, she concluded, it must be by one who "has, for some sufficient reason, long forfeited the society of her own sex."[90] The implication was that the author was a fallen woman who, through sexual indiscretion, had ostracized herself from the company of respectable ladies. (When Marian Evans, the future George Eliot, took up with G. H. Lewes a few years later, hostesses stopped inviting her to dinner parties. Male friends did not drop her, but as the mistress of a married man she was no longer acceptable in mixed company.)

Vilification such as this was not what the young Charlotte had had in mind when she told Southey of her ambition to be forever known. But by the time the *Quarterly* came out, its power to wound was minimal compared to the tragedy which had begun to unfold in the Brontë family. Branwell, the brother whose early promise had ended in misery and addiction, had died suddenly in September at the age of thirty-one. Emily began to decline soon after his funeral. She never recovered, dying of consumption after a terrible struggle, on December 19. Anne, who suffered from the same disease, would cling on to life for another few months. She died on May 28, 1849, in Scarborough, where Charlotte had taken her for a last look at the sea.

At the time of Branwell's death, Charlotte had been making good progress with a new novel, *Shirley,* but she was unable to concentrate on writing during the terrible months that followed. It was not until after Anne's death that she threw herself back into her work, certain that "Labour" was "the only radical cure for rooted Sorrow."[91] In some ways, *Shirley* was more ideologically explicit in its feminism than *Jane Eyre* had been. Through the character of Caroline Helstone, it argued that society should allow middle-class women more opportunity to express themselves and fulfill their talents. Yet *Shirley* lacked the emotional force of the earlier novel and consequently had less power to shock, although its resolutely "unfeminine" (Charlotte's own word) opening scene, a bitingly satirical portrait of an all-male gathering of curates, would raise eyebrows.[92]

Shirley was published in October 1849. Charlotte had originally intended to take this opportunity to attack her critics in a preface entitled "A Word to the *Quarterly.*" Taking on the voice of a man, an "old bachelor," she wrote in a sarcastic, satirical voice, very similar to that in which she had lambasted the ungenerous Hartley Coleridge.[93] Smith, Elder, were, however, anxious that her tone was both too flippant and too aggressive. They suggested instead that the time had come for her to drop her veil and reveal the identities of the Bell brothers to the world. Charlotte was initially forthright in her desire to let rip against the *Quarterly* while retaining her anonymity, writing to William Smith Williams on August 31, " 'C. Brontë' must not here appear; what she feels or has felt is not the question—it is 'Currer Bell' who was insulted—he must reply. Let Mr. Smith fearlessly print the preface I have sent."[94] In the event, however, she dropped the idea, having been persuaded that going on the offensive in such tones was ill-advised. Instead, she was gradually becoming reconciled to the idea of revealing herself to the literary world as Charlotte Brontë.

The identity of Currer Bell had in fact been seeping out for some time. It had even reached Haworth. Despite Charlotte's denials, Ellen Nussey had finally discovered the truth. Some time before Emily's death, Charlotte had also told her father about *Jane Eyre*. She must have been relieved that their pride in her overweighed any disapproval they might have had of the novel. Now that her secret was out among her Yorkshire acquaintance, and now that Emily—who had been more determined than either of her sisters to maintain their cover—was dead, there seemed little point in trying to maintain a charade of secrecy.

"Currer Bell" would of course remain the name on Charlotte's book covers. But her curiosity about seeing the "literary coteries" of London was beginning to get the better of her. Since the days when she had read *Blackwood's* as a girl, she had always been excited by the idea of contact, even if only as a passive observer, with the celestial club. "I long to see some of the truly great literary characters," she told William Smith Williams in September 1849, though she declined as yet to sacrifice her incognito.[95] As Currer Bell she had already corresponded with G. H. Lewes and sent a copy of *Jane Eyre* to the novelist Julia Kavanagh. She now sent *Shirley* to two other novelists, Harriet Martineau and Elizabeth Gaskell, though for the time being she maintained her "resolution of seclusion."[96]

In mid-November she was still recoiling from "the éclât and bustle which an open declaration of authorship would certainly entail" but was now open to the idea of accepting an invitation to stay privately with George Smith and his family.[97] By the end of the month she was preparing to make the first of what was to become a series of visits to London. The week before she left, she told Ellen Nussey: "What I *am,* it is useless to say—those whom it concerns feel and find it out. To all others I wish only to be an obscure, steady-going private character."[98] This was the character in which she had decided to appear before the "literary coteries," who would be disappointed to find her manner so different from that of the passionately outspoken Jane Eyre. She had turned down a previous invitation to London partly out of fear that her provincial manners would show her up. Now she began to realize that her outward persona as a "country spinster" could in fact be used as a protective shield in much the same way as her pseudonym.[99]

Charlotte's encounters with Thackeray are a case in point. While he was amused to point out the similarities between the passionate Jane Eyre and her equally passionate creator, Charlotte was determined to deny the link. She first met Thackeray at a dinner party given on December 4, 1849, by her publisher, George Smith. After the meal, the novelist approached her, smoking, and flirtatiously asking if Charlotte had "perceived the secret" of his and Smith's cigars—a clear reference to Mr. Rochester's customary cheroot. Charlotte, wanting to dissociate herself from Jane, pretended not to get the allusion.[100]

The following June, at a dinner given by Thackeray at his house in her honor, Charlotte took her revenge by embarrassing him so much that he slipped away to his club in the middle of his own party. Refusing to play up to her reputation as the author of a shockingly outspoken novel, she was quiet and self-effacing to the point of rudeness, preferring to converse in low tones with the governess than to hold forth for the entertainment of the guests. When Thackeray addressed her as "Currer Bell" on the way down to dinner, she replied curtly: "I believe there are books being published by a person named Currer Bell, but the person you address is Miss Brontë—and I see no connection between the two."[101] On a later occasion, when he audibly introduced her as "Jane Eyre" at a public lecture, she literally shook with rage, though her response was interpreted by ladies such as George Smith's mother (who was there) and Elizabeth Gaskell (who heard about it later) as the frightened trembling of a delicate woman overcome by shyness.[102] Afterward, she rounded on him in anger.

The split public persona of Charlotte's celebrity years went back to her time at Roe Head, and would play a key role in the creation of the posthumous Brontë myth. Aspects of her personality which she showed to intimates were not willingly exposed to public view. Her humor, her passion, her energy and determination, her occasional sharp-tongued tartness were dampened whenever she felt she was on show. Even to close friends, the fire of her creative self remained hidden. This self she had shared with her sisters, and Heger. She would continue to share it—soul speaking to soul, as Jane speaks to Rochester—with those readers who were prepared to look deeply into her novels. In a more equivocal way, she also let it flare up in the presence of literary men such as Thackeray and Lewes. But this aspect of her character, which had gone into Jane Eyre, was not something she was prepared to acknowledge openly, as it was what had inspired the press to lambast her as "a woman unsexed."[103]

The men of letters Charlotte met, such as Thackeray and G. H. Lewes, found something titillating in the idea that a single woman could have written a novel as passionate as Jane Eyre. Lewes had enraged Charlotte with a review of Shirley which revealed to readers that the novel was the work of a clergyman's daughter but said that the vigor she displayed in her writing amounted to coarseness and was "the very antipode to 'lady like.' "[104] He also teased her to her face by suggesting that he had something in common with her since they had both written "naughty" books.[105] (As Lewes's "naughty" book, his 1848 novel Rose, Blanche and Violet, featured a female poet who takes a lover, comes to London to pursue a literary career, fails, and ends up a fallen woman, it is hardly surprising Charlotte did not appreciate the comparison.)[106] Unlike many of Charlotte's female critics, who were often genuinely prudish, Lewes rather admired her for her naughtiness. But not being quite respectable himself—he lived a ramshackle, bohemian existence and would soon be living in sin with Marian Evans—he did not understand how much it meant to her to retain her social position.

Charlotte's disconcerted, humorless response to Lewes's teasing is only too understandable considering what a precarious hold she had on her respectability. She was, after all, an Irish peasant's granddaughter, who craved social acceptance as a lady, but whose novel had genuinely shocked the upper classes. As her publisher George Smith recalled in his memoirs, "Jane Eyre was really considered in those days by many people to be an immoral book. My mother told me one evening that Lady Herschel, having found the book in her drawing-room said: 'Do you leave such a book as this about, at the risk of your daughters reading it?' "[107]

The one subject on which Charlotte would fire up, breaking her general resolve to appear meek and "steady-going," was that of literature—and then, only when provoked by literary men. Thackeray used to annoy her by referring to his books with exaggerated unconcern "much as a clerk in a bank would discuss the ledgers he had to keep for a salary." He considered Charlotte's elevated and Romantic conception of the artist to be "high falutin'."[108] What he did not consider, though, was the urgency of Charlotte's need to believe in this exalted aesthetic. Without a belief in her own genius she would never have had the motivation or confidence to achieve what she did. Her conviction that "genius," "poetry," or "inspiration" were a gift to the artist from some transcendent force—which she often identified with the Christian God, hence her frequent use of biblical language in discussing artistic creativity—was essential if she was to gird herself against social disapproval.

Torn between the desire to rebel and the need to conform and be accepted, Charlotte had to some extent internalized that disapproval. At Roe Head, she had felt guilty about the strength of her imagination, afraid that it was idolatrous in its escapism. As a mature artist she still needed to find a way of internally purifying her own creative powers, which were potentially threatening to her status as a respectable woman. She did this by attributing them to an exalted, even divine, spirituality (just as Florence Nightingale, similarly, had the need to define her unfeminine-seeming ambition as a call from God). As she wrote, in a letter to Lewes, of another woman writer who had taken a male pseudonym, "It is *poetry*, as I comprehend the word which elevates that masculine George Sand, and makes out of something coarse, something godlike."[109] In Charlotte's Romantic vocabulary, "poetry" did not simply mean verse, but "the divine gift" of transcendent imagination.[110]

Accusations of "coarseness" were something with which Charlotte herself continued to have to contend. Although *Shirley* had on the whole been considered by the public and critics alike as less "disagreeable" than *Jane Eyre*, it did little to change the fixed popular perception of the Bells.[111] A year on, Charlotte made a decided attempt to clear her dead sisters—and, by association, herself—from any imputation of immorality. In December 1850, she republished *Wuthering Heights* and *Agnes Grey*, together with some of Emily's and Anne's poems, as a memorial to her sisters which, she hoped, would "wipe the dust" from their reputations and "leave their dear names free from soil."[112]

When the sisters first decided to publish, they had taken masculine names in an attempt to protect themselves from prejudice. Instead, this had produced a wave of speculation which turned to vilification as soon as the real gender of the writers was suspected. Now, in an attempt to change the public mind, Charlotte adopted a new tactic. In social situations, she had been accustomed to project a timid, ultrafeminine persona to hide her inner fire. The way she presented her sisters to the world would be an extension of this strategy. She decided to make their identities public, but to use the fact that they were female as a plea in mitigation rather than a stick to beat them with. If readers were to know that her sisters were in fact a pair of "unobtrusive women," they might forgive where they had once condemned, especially if they were told about the quiet and blameless lives these retiring virgins had led, and were given a harrowing account of their tragic early deaths. Charlotte would concede that her sisters' novels had dubious elements, but she would paint a picture of their lives which would, she hoped, exonerate them.

So, for the first time, Charlotte revealed the truth about the sisters' gender to the general public in the "Biographical Notice of Ellis and Acton Bell," which appeared in the reissue of their selected works together with a Preface to *Wuthering Heights* and a few remarks on the poetry. To clear her sisters of the charge of coarseness, she presented them as a couple of simple, uneducated country girls who did not really know what they were doing when they wrote *The Tenant of Wildfell Hall* and *Wuthering Heights.* Keen to dissociate herself from Anne's novel, which had shocked critics the most, Charlotte dismissed it as "an entire mistake"[113] and pointedly refused to reprint it; her remarks on Emily were clearly designed as exoneration more than celebration. She argued that her sisters were innocent girls, inhabitants of a "remote district where education had made little progress":[114] if they had committed errors, she pleaded, it was not through willfulness. Anne had been forced into writing on such an unspeakable subject by the dreadful events she had witnessed in real life (a veiled reference to Branwell's dissipation); Emily was merely the passive vessel through which "Fate or Inspiration" had poured.[115]

Charlotte presented her sisters as naive artists responding only to the dictates of nature, rather than as knowing and ambitious writers who had produced consciously constructed novels. This defense combined her Romantic ideal of the natural genius with the conventional ideal of feminine modesty and simplicity which, she hoped, would counterbalance public perceptions of the Bells as women unsexed. It also relied on an exaggeratedly romantic view of Haworth as a place of complete isolation inhabited only by mythic "unlettered moorland hinds and rugged moorland squires."[116] If *Wuthering Heights* was at all coarse, Charlotte blamed these people, whose rough manners and unbridled passions, she claimed, were the only example of humanity Emily had had to draw on.

As a public relations exercise, the "Biographical Notice" turned out to be less successful than Charlotte had hoped. In some ways it even had the opposite effect to what she wanted. Her eagerness to concede the "faults" of her sisters' novels meant that she failed in her efforts to rescue the Bells from critical opprobrium. Writing in the *Leader,* G. H. Lewes now seemed to find their works even naughtier than he had before, expressing amazement that a couple of reclusive girls could have written books which he now described as "coarse even for men, coarse in language and coarse in conception, the coarseness apparently of violence and uncultivated men."[117]

In publicly accepting that her sisters' novels had faults and describing their personal circumstances as a means of exculpating them, Charlotte appeared to have made a mistake. Long term, however, she set the agenda which would turn the Brontës into icons. When Elizabeth Gaskell set about writing her seminal *Life of Charlotte Brontë,* she would use the sisters' life story as a strategy for distracting attention from the shocking aspects of their books. Southey may have warned Charlotte that personal celebrity was unwomanly. Ironically, the story of the Brontës' private lives—though not the truth about their inner selves—would turn out in the long run to be their ultimate shield against accusations of impropriety.

CHAPTER TWO

Poor Miss Brontë

I confess that the book has made me ashamed of myself. . . .
I [had given] up the writer and her books with the notion that she
was a person who liked coarseness. How I misjudged her! . . .
Well have you done your work, and given us the picture of a valiant
woman made perfect by sufferings.[1]

This response to Elizabeth Gaskell's *Life of Charlotte Brontë* was written soon after it came out in 1857 by the Christian Socialist and future author of *The Water Babies,* Charles Kingsley. It shows how successful the biography was at revolutionizing readers' attitudes. A man who had previously reviled the dubious Currer Bell now revered Charlotte Brontë as a saintly icon of female suffering. The *Life* had done what Charlotte's "Biographical Notice of Ellis and Acton Bell" had failed to achieve: it had reinvented the Brontë image.

Where did this new vision spring from? How did Charlotte's biographer come to see her in this transformative light? Elizabeth Gaskell (1810–65) was one of the literati among whom Charlotte began to mix when she finally agreed to shed her anonymity. The biography sprang out of the friendship between the two women, which began when they met for the first time at a house party in the Lake District in August 1850.

Like Charlotte, Gaskell was one of the up-and-coming women novelists of the day, having had a success with *Mary Barton* the year after *Jane Eyre.* Unlike Charlotte, she was married (to a Unitarian minister), metropolitan (she lived in Manchester), and comparatively conventional in her attitude toward the female imagination. But she was a warm, if sometimes interfering, person, eager to like and be liked, who was keen from the start to minimize the unsettling aspects of *Jane Eyre* and search out what she thought of as the best in Charlotte. Charlotte, on her side, was anxious to display a social persona which would dispel any suspicions of coarseness from the minds of those she met. The *Life* evolved out of a subtle interplay between Gaskell's preconceived assumptions and Charlotte's own self-projection.

The "Miss Brontë" whom Mrs. Gaskell met in 1850 was not the fiery visionary who had created *Jane Eyre* but the figure of "gentle unassuming manners" Charlotte was accustomed to present socially, whether at home, when her father invited a bishop to the Parsonage, or at literary gatherings.[2] Quietly—or was it ostentatiously?—stitching away at her needlework, she would offer a picture of unimpeachable propriety. This passive and ladylike image was not quite a facade. As the dutiful daughter of a clergyman, Charlotte had been brought up to it and it was part of her being. But she was also conscious that she was playing a role. As her novels—particularly *Villette*—show, she believed that being a woman in her society often involved putting on a social mask to guard the deeper self.

Whatever she might write as Currer Bell, Charlotte still felt a real need for social acceptance as well as artistic recognition. This was particularly the case in her relations with the female literary community, whose support would be vital in her quest for respectability. In December 1849, on her first trip to London sans incognito, she called on the author and journalist Harriet Martineau, anxious to find a friend and ally in a well-established woman writer whose work she respected. When the subject turned to reviewers, however, she discovered that Martineau shared some of their strictures against Currer Bell's coarseness.

Instead of attempting to justify herself with a thundering counterattack, as she had done in the preface to the second edition of *Jane Eyre,* Miss Brontë meekly accepted the verdict and asked to be put right if she ever overstepped the mark again.[3] Anticipating her later defense of Emily, she also adopted what looks suspiciously like a naive pose, claiming that she did not understand what it was the critics objected to. (Charlotte's apologists would often claim that she was "unconscious" of the fact that there was anything subversive in her work, but it is hard to believe that such a sophisticated writer could have been so unknowing.) Before she left Martineau's company, Charlotte reportedly told her "in a simple, touching manner, of her sorrow and isolation."[4] Was she aware of the sympathetic effect such personal disclosures would make?

Certainly, she must have presented herself rather differently to her fellow women writers than she did to their male equivalents. In a letter to Mr. Hunt (probably Leigh Hunt's son Thornton, editor of the *Leader*), Harriet Martineau later expressed astonishment that he and Lewes found harshness and sarcasm in the Miss Brontë whose strength, as she saw it, consisted in a personality "gentle & composed,—meek & self-possessed." Indeed, Charlotte seems almost to have erased herself in the company of Martineau, who found her "so sympathizing that her consciousness seems to pass into others, leaving none for herself,—she is as opposite to the creature of passion & prejudice as to the marble-hearted self seeker."[5]

Charlotte must have been alive to the fact that women writers such as Martineau and Gaskell needed to believe in a version of Currer Bell who was beyond reproach. Men like Lewes and Thackeray could derive schoolboy amusement from the supposed naughtiness of her novels, arousing Charlotte's wrath. But *Jane Eyre* posed a stickier problem for literary women. On the one hand, they felt the need for solidarity in the face of prejudice, as some critics still held, with Coventry Patmore, that women were naturally debarred by their limited abilities from the "properly masculine power of writing books."[6] Yet on the other hand, a book such as *Jane Eyre,* which had been labeled coarse, might bring women's writing into disrepute. Charlotte's sister authors could not ignore the sensationally successful Currer Bell, whose literary talents were too obvious not to recognize. But they felt uncomfortable about her, perhaps fearing that her passionate aesthetic might inflame prejudice toward authoresses in general.

The solution to this discomfort was to pathologize Charlotte's literary imagination, while clutching at the mitigating evidence of her personal delicacy, miserable life, and isolated upbringing. While Martineau tended to be judgmental, Gaskell preferred to offer sympathy. But both coped with the disturbing passion and intensity of Charlotte's work by regarding it as morbid, the sad consequence of a mind made sick by a life of continual suffering and deprivation.[7] "Her faults," as Gaskell put it, "are the faults of the very peculiar circumstances in which she has been placed."[8] It was important for them to see Charlotte as a figure of pity, even if that meant exaggerating the isolation and misery of her life. In this way, they could dissociate themselves from the unpalatable aspects of her work without feeling that they were betraying the cause of women's writing.

This is not to say that Charlotte had not really suffered. In childhood, she had had to face the deaths of her mother and elder sisters, as well as the never-forgotten misery of school at Cowan Bridge. As an adult, she had borne the appalling bereavements of 1848–49, which left her in a state of chronic depression. Gaskell, however, invested such suffering with an intense moral meaning distinct from its actual emotional impact on Charlotte. Indeed, a focus on suffering seems to have been essential to her acceptance of the author of *Jane Eyre*. Sometimes she exonerated Charlotte by suggesting that her imagination had been coarsened by dreadful experiences; at other times, she seems, conversely, to have believed that sufferings had in fact purified Charlotte's soul. But whichever way she looked at it, she always came back to the same idea. In the *Life*, she would go on to propagate the misleading notion that Charlotte's whole existence was one of unremitting martyrdom.

One visitor to Haworth in the late 1850s, who was shown round the Parsonage by the servant, asked whether the Brontë sisters were "always of a melancholy disposition." "Oh no, sir!" came the retort. "They were as cheerful and full of spirits as possible . . . they used to be full of fun and merriment."[9] Yet Gaskell's air of tragedy would encourage future commentators to imagine the Brontës' house as a place of gothic horror in which "every movement, even to the flicker of their eyelids, was fatal and ominous."[10] The very title of one study from the 1970s, *Charlotte Brontë's World of Death*, suggests an overwhelming morbidity so out of keeping with the life-affirming energy of Jane Eyre, who is above all a survivor, that one wonders how such a partial view can have taken hold.

For all the anguish Charlotte undoubtedly experienced at periods in her life, she was also a woman of toughness, ambition, and creative boldness, able to break the mold of the conventional English novel. She had the self-belief not only to brave rejection after rejection before she found a publisher, but also to see her own inner life as the valid material of art. Her fiction reveals deep knowledge of human emotion; her correspondence with her closest friends shows her to have been funny, opinionated, sarcastic, and bitchy as well as depressive, dutiful, and damaged. Yet the woman who emerges from Gaskell's *Life* is sapped of all brightness by the age of nine.[11]

Elizabeth Gaskell never fully engaged with the powerful, intense, and uncompromising side of Charlotte's personality—the part which went into her novels under the name of Currer Bell. She responded ambivalently when she read *Jane Eyre* for the first time, in April 1848. Though she praised its originality—it was, she felt, an "uncommon book"—it made her feel distinctly unsure: "I don't know if I like or dislike it," she told a friend. "I take the opposite side to the person I am talking with always in order to hear some convincing arguments to clear up my opinions."[12]

She was never able to shed these initial reservations. Unlike the abrasive Harriet Martineau, who told Charlotte straight out that she disapproved of her too-passionate treatment of love, Gaskell never confronted her with her true feelings. To Charlotte's face she winningly confided that she would keep her works as a treasure for her daughters;[13] but behind her back she was actually so concerned about *Jane Eyre*'s moral tone that she seems to have forbidden her eldest girl to read it until she was twenty.[14] After Charlotte's death, she was quite explicit about her doubts, admitting in the—otherwise hagiographic—*Life:* "I do not deny for myself the existence of coarseness here and there in her works, otherwise so entirely noble."[15]

Gaskell's difficulty with Charlotte's books was intensified by their very different beliefs about the nature and purpose of the novel. Despite their eventual friendship, the two were ideologically poles apart. Mrs. Gaskell remarked after their first meeting that they had "quarrelled & differed about almost every thing,—she calls me a democrat and can not bear Tennyson."[16] Charlotte's politics were Tory and aristocratic, and her Romantic aesthetic was introspective and individualistic. Gaskell, on the other hand, was a dissenter who came out of the Nonconformist tradition, which still, at some vestigial level, had doubts about the morality of fiction per se, and certainly about fiction which did not have an improving purpose.

Unlike Charlotte, whose art drew on her deepest personal experience, Mrs. Gaskell began to write fiction in the hope that it would take her *out* of herself after the death of her baby son left her inconsolable. Her fiction took on social and political issues. Set in the Manchester factory community, *Mary Barton* (1848) tackled questions of labor and capital in emotive, humanitarian tones; *Ruth* (1853) would focus on the plight of the fallen woman. For her, the novel was ideally a practical agent of reform, in which the author should look out to the world, not into his or her interior life. Significantly, Gaskell's philanthropic approach could more easily be assimilated into conventional Victorian ideals of femininity than Charlotte's aesthetic, which she had inherited from the male Romantics and from George Sand. Unlike Charlotte, Gaskell was looking for ways in which she could define her literary work as an extension of women's traditionally moral and caring role.

That role, particularly in relation to domesticity, was of prime importance to Gaskell, who was nevertheless honest enough to acknowledge the difficulties of combining womanly duty with artistic work. She regarded art as a positive emotional outlet which could enhance women's lives, but she was also worried that it could seduce them away from ideal feminine self-sacrifice. A letter she wrote to her friend Eliza Fox in February 1850 shows her working through her confused feelings on the subject:

One thing is pretty clear, *Women*, [*sic*] must give up living an artist's life, if home duties are to be paramount. It is different with men, whose home duties are so small a part of their life. However we are talking of women. I am sure it is healthy for them to have the refuge of the hidden world of Art to shelter themselves in when too much pressed on by daily small Lilliputian arrows of peddling cares; it keeps them from being morbid . . . and soothes them with its peace. I have felt this in writing, I see others feel it in music, you in painting, so assuredly a blending of the two is desirable. (Home duties and the development of the Individual I mean.)[17]

After reading this over she went on to add, somewhat anxiously, "If Self is to be the end of exertions, those exertions are unholy, there is no doubt of *that*—and that is part of the danger in cultivating the Individual Life."[18] Though Gaskell did believe in the individual's duty to make the most of a God-given talent, she did not have Charlotte's fearsomely Romantic faith in her own genius. It may be that when she got to know Charlotte she would be particularly eager to uncover evidence of self-sacrifice and femininity precisely because she feared that Currer Bell was lacking in these qualities.

Like many Victorian critics, Gaskell probably found too much ego in the heroine of *Jane Eyre*. Nevertheless, when the book first came out, she could not help joining in the general excitement over its mysterious authorship. According to her biographer, Jenny Uglow, "[s]he was always hungry for stories, for involvement in other lives."[19] Unlike the Brontës, who were capable of extraordinary self-sufficiency in their private imaginative worlds, she found other people more interesting than she found herself, and was dying to find out the secret identity of the new author.

Gossip suggested that a certain Dr. Epps—in fact the physician whose advice Charlotte had sought during Emily's last illness—might be able to furnish her with the answer, but her enquiries drew a blank. She finally learned the truth in November 1849, when Charlotte decided to take the first steps toward making herself known in literary society by sending copies of her new novel to a few select authors. Mrs. Gaskell could hardly contain her excitement when she received Charlotte's note and immediately fired off a tantilizing letter to her friend Catherine Winkworth: "Currer Bell (aha! what will you give me for a secret?) She's a she—that I will tell you—who has sent me 'Shirley.' "[20]

Over the next few months, she eagerly snatched up whatever snippets of information she could. She leapt at an account of the meeting between

Currer Bell and Harriet Martineau, writing excitedly to her friend Anne Shaen about the "very little, bright haired sprite," who had appeared in the drawing room of the London house where Martineau was staying.[21] Rumor had already begun to exaggerate the isolation and unsophistication of Charlotte's life, and Gaskell happily spread the erroneous claims, confidently but incorrectly asserting that this was Charlotte's first visit to London, and that her father had "never slept out of his house for 26 years," again untrue.[22]

By May, Mrs. Gaskell was corresponding about Charlotte with Lady Kay-Shuttleworth, the woman who would eventually bring the two novelists together. The author of *Jane Eyre* and *Shirley* had by now become an attractive prize for ambitious hostesses, and Lady Kay-Shuttleworth and her husband, Sir James, had recently sought out the acquaintance of the famous Currer Bell. Sir James, who had originally trained as a physician, was a prominent public figure who had worked tirelessly for the good of society in the fields of health and education, but he was a rather blundering and insensitive character whose literary pretensions Charlotte found irritating. His pressing invitations were, however, difficult for her to resist, especially since they gratified her father's snobbery. Lady Kay-Shuttleworth, whom Charlotte described as "a little woman 32 years old with a pretty, smooth, lively face,"[23] was less of a trial. She did, however, share Mrs. Gaskell's penchant for gossip.

Mrs. Gaskell, of course, wanted to know all about Lady Kay-Shuttleworth's celebrated houseguest, eager to hear more of the woman behind *Jane Eyre:* "No! I never heard of Miss Brontë's visit; and I should like to hear a great deal more about her, as I have been so much interested in what she has written. I don't mean merely in the story and mode of narration, wonderful as that is, but in the glimpses one gets of *her*, and her modes of thought, and, all unconsciously to herself, of the way in wh [*sic*] she has suffered."[24]

From the start, Gaskell seems more interested in the character of Charlotte Brontë, whom she had already begun to package as a woman of suffering, than in the novels of Currer Bell. She turns abruptly from an acknowledgment of the author's writerly achievement ("wonderful as that is") into a vision of the woman's private pain. The distinction between what Gaskell later called the "two parallel currents" of Currer Bell the author and Charlotte Brontë the woman would become central to the *Life*.[25] In making this split, she may have hit on something very real about Charlotte's divided self, yet her underlying motive was to sanitize the woman by detaching her from the artist. In the biography she would push Currer Bell so decisively to the sidelines that, as one of its first reviewers put it, "we have no trace here of the higher workings of her genius. . . . We see the woman, not the authoress, in these annals of Haworth parsonage."[26]

At this early stage, however, Mrs. Gaskell's bias in favor of Charlotte Brontë the woman was partly the natural result of her gossipy temperament, her interest in people's lives. But it also reflects the discomfort she felt with Currer Bell's fiction and exemplifies her accustomed way of dealing with it: diffusing the threat by focusing on the author's suffering. Though the rest of her letter to Lady Kay-Shuttleworth makes little direct comment on Charlotte, it is indicative of the context in which she chose to view her. Swerving off into a long and pitying digression on the problems of single women and their place in society, Mrs. Gaskell, a happily married mother of four surviving children, implicitly defines the spinster Miss Brontë as a victim.

The unmarried woman was a topic of public debate in the 1850s, a period which saw a demographic surplus of females over males in the population. What, it was asked, should society do with these spare women? In her correspondence with William Smith Williams, Charlotte had answered that question by proposing the expansion of employment opportunities, wondering whether there might be room "for female lawyers, female doctors, female engravers, for more female artists, more authoresses."[27]

What is significant about Gaskell's account of the "trials" and "purposelessness" of single women's lives is that she does not entertain the possibility that they might find fulfillment in work (as many in fact did, such as the Brontës' feminist friend Mary Taylor, who emigrated to New Zealand and opened a shop). Nor does she propose Charlotte as an example of redemptive professional achievement in a single woman. Her train of thought does not lead on from "Miss Brontë" into a discussion of literature—Charlotte is not bracketed with Dickens and Thackeray—but into a long account of the inevitable misery of women who are "deprived of their natural duties as wives & mothers," which she contrasts with her own contentment: "I am always glad and thankful to Him that I am a wife and a mother and that I am so happy in the performance of those clear and defined duties."[28]

Gaskell's use of the phrase "natural duties" suggests she is referring not just to the socially anomalous position of spinsters but to a more basic, biological concept of womanhood. In some Victorian medical textbooks, spinsters were presented as not merely sad but also sick. Unable to fulfill the "great *physical* end of her existence"[29]—married sexuality defined by maternity—the old maid was regarded as what the historian of science Sally Shuttleworth has called "a form of physiological disaster."[30] Her natural energies were held to be unhealthily blocked, causing untold ills. According to an article in the *Journal of Psychological Medicine and Mental Pathology* of 1851, the spinster had two options, which the writer presents in moralizing terms. Either "the love that should have found its natural outpouring on a husband or children, may be directed by religious feelings to suffering humanity" and she will develop the admirable qualities of "self-denial and humility"; or she will suffer the untoward fate of becoming a "strong-minded" virago, "bold and unfeminine in her manners."[31]

In *The Life of Charlotte Brontë,* Gaskell would go out of her way to emphasize Charlotte's qualities of humility and self-denial; she would re-create her as a nunlike figure providing succor to the poor of the parish and a dutiful daughter who put her father's needs before her own. As such, she would present her as the good spinster rather than the virago. But she would always retain the sense that Charlotte's singleness, as much as the bereavements she had suffered, defined her as damaged, and suspected that the unacceptably coarse or unfeminine elements of her novels were morbid symptoms of her unhealthy single state.

In contrast, Gaskell presents herself as an essentially healthy maternal figure, in a position to care for the deprived Miss Brontë. She had already been encouraged by Lady Kay-Shuttleworth to think that she could "do her [Charlotte] good."[32] That impulse to protect Charlotte would underlie *The Life of Charlotte Brontë* to such an extent that one reviewer complained that "Mrs. Gaskell is, indeed, lavish of her sympathy; but it is of the patronising apologetic kind, feeling for rather than with the sufferer."[33]

Thus, before she had even met Charlotte, Gaskell had formed a vivid mental picture of her, derived from a mixture of gossip and prejudice. She had adopted an attitude of pity which would never essentially change. Even though she admired Charlotte's literary brilliance, she felt uncomfortable about her writing and believed that only a damaged woman could have produced it. She therefore channeled her fascination for the mysterious new novelist into pitying curiosity about her private suffering. Reassuring accounts from Harriet Martineau and Lady Kay-Shuttleworth revealed that in person Miss Brontë was the soul of ladylike modesty.

Gaskell was all prepared to meet Charlotte in a spirit of protective sympathy, and to draw her out on the subject of her sad life.

When the meeting between Charlotte and her future biographer finally took place, in August 1850, at Briery Close, the Kay-Shuttleworths' summer retreat in the Lake District, Gaskell was able to spend more time than she had hoped putting her preconceptions to the test. As their hostess had a bad cold, the guests were much dependent on each other's company during the few days of their stay. Afterward Charlotte, pleasantly impressed, was able to write that she found Mrs. Gaskell "a woman of the most genuine talent—of cheerful, pleasing and cordial manners and—I believe—of a kind and good heart."[34] Mrs. Gaskell's response was more excited. Despite her considerable expectations, Miss Brontë did not disappoint.

Where Charlotte summed up her impressions in a couple of sentences, Mrs. Gaskell immediately set down as much as she could about the author of *Jane Eyre* in long and vivid letters to her friends. After only a few days' acquaintance, she felt the impulse to communicate Charlotte's history, which would find its ultimate expression in the *Life*. These letters, in particular the one she wrote to Catherine Winkworth on August 25, have a breathless feel, as though she could hardly write fast enough to pack in all the details: "[N]ow is not this enough material for one letter. . . . I have so much to say I don't know where to begin."[35] Even at this early stage she regarded Charlotte's life as "material" to be molded into literary shape.

Mrs. Gaskell's letter to Catherine Winkworth begins with a description of her first glimpse of the "little lady in the black silk gown," whom she at first could not see clearly owing to the "dazzle in the room."[36] As Charlotte comes into focus and Gaskell has "time for a good look at her,"[37] she begins to anatomize her with a dehumanizing clarity which is uncomfortably close to a contemporary psychologist's description of the sick virago-spinster, whose appearance was said to be marked by, among other characteristics, "a lean figure" and "shattered teeth":[38] "She is, (as she calls herself) *undeveloped;* thin and more than ½ a head shorter than I, soft brown hair not so dark as mine; eyes (very good and expressive looking straight & open at you) of the same colour, a reddish face; large mouth & many teeth gone; altogether *plain;* the forehead square, broad, and *rather* overhanging."[39] Yet as soon as Gaskell moves from external description into Charlotte's life story, her tone becomes increasingly sympathetic and involved, and one soon realizes that, despite her chatty style, she is creating a highly controlled narrative that pre-echoes the *Life* in microcosm.

Much of the content of Gaskell's letter is inaccurate or exaggerated in such a way as to make Charlotte's life, painful though it had been, appear in a light of heightened deprivation. Although she had never been there, Gaskell opens her account with an emotionally charged and visually vivid depiction of Haworth—in reality an industrial township—as "a village of a few grey stone houses perched up on the north side of a bleak moor—looking over sweeps of bleak moors." She then focuses in on the Parsonage itself: "There is a court of turf & a stone wall,—(no flowers or shrubs will grow there) a straight walk, & you come to the parsonage door with a window on each side of it."[40] (There were in fact flowers growing in the beds under the windows, as Gaskell discovered, perhaps to her disappointment, when she finally visited Haworth for herself.) Having reached the door, she opens it to disclose the Brontës' mother, a "pretty young creature"[41] rejected by her parents on her marriage (Gaskell must have derived this false impression from Anne's novel *Agnes Grey*, in which the heroine's mother is indeed disowned by her family for marrying a poor clergyman)[42] and driven to death by frequent childbearing, the inhospitable Yorkshire climate, and "the strange half mad husband she had chosen"[43] (in fact she died of cancer).

It is amazing to realize that in these first few hastily scribbled sentences Gaskell has already laid the foundations of a legend which would eventually be propagated far and wide. The mythic status of Haworth as a pilgrimage site begins here, with Gaskell's decision to open Charlotte's story with a description of her home as a romantically isolated spot on top of a windswept moor. She would use the same almost filmlike technique in *The Life of Charlotte Brontë*, which starts with an account of the journey up the hill to Haworth from Keighley railway station and on up the narrow cobbled street to the Parsonage and church at the top of the village. Like a narrative formula from a folk tale, this would, over the years, become the standard opening for Brontë biographies.[44]

Of all the inaccuracies and half-truths which Gaskell had so far picked up about the Brontë family, none were to become more legendary than her apocryphal stories about Patrick, which would resurface unchanged seven years later in *The Life of Charlotte Brontë*. In Gaskell's letter to Catherine Winkworth, he becomes a mad misanthrope given to lurid acts of violence:

Mr. Brontë vented his anger against *things* not persons; for instance once in one of his wife's confinements something went wrong, so he got a saw, and went and sawed up all the chairs in her bedroom, never answering her remonstrances or minding her tears. Another time he was vexed and took the hearthrug & tied it in a tight bundle & set it on fire in the grate; & sat before it with a leg on each hob, heaping on more colds [*sic*] till it was burnt, no one else being able to endure in the room because of the stifling smoke.[45]

Full of circumstantial detail as this account is—particularly the way she has him "sitting with a leg on each hob"—it in fact had its origins in the tall tales, picked up by Lady Kay-Shuttleworth, of an ex-servant who had been dismissed from the Brontë household and whose testimony was thus extremely suspect.[46]

Mrs. Gaskell removed these stories from the third edition of the *Life* after Patrick, not unreasonably, complained. But the image of the saintly Brontë sisters patiently clinging to filial piety in the face of such colorful domestic violence was to prove hard to shift from the popular imagination and would reemerge time and again in later biographies. Even in the 1990s, Juliet Barker felt compelled to devote much of her vast biography, *The Brontës*, to rescuing Patrick from Gaskell's caricature, using the evidence of contemporary newspapers to reveal him as a respected figure of some standing, closely involved in local politics as well as with the church.

The rest of Mrs. Gaskell's letter follows the sweep of Charlotte's life, never failing to make it as miserable as possible. It continues with an account of the sisters' neglected education: "Their father never taught the girls anything—only the servant taught them to read & write."[47] (In fact, the girls were taught by their aunt and possibly by Patrick, who encouraged the intellectual development of all his precocious children and certainly gave formal lessons to Branwell.)[48] It then moves on to their disastrous time at the Clergy Daughters' School at Cowan Bridge, followed by the deaths of Maria and Elizabeth. Charlotte eventually goes out as a governess. Then she goes to study in Brussels. Here, she is presented as lonely and unsupported, saving up her meager governessing money (in fact her aunt provided the funds) and traveling all alone (on her first journey to Brussels she was accompanied by Emily and Patrick, who chaperoned his daughters all the way, as well as two Yorkshire friends, Mary and Joe Taylor, who traveled with them).

Back in Haworth, we have the writing of *Jane Eyre* and the deaths of Emily and Anne. Finally, Gaskell creates a sense of aesthetic closure by ending her tale with the imagined death of Charlotte herself, who is described as "already tainted with consumption."[49] (She was not in fact infected, and by starting this rumor Gaskell possibly did her a real disservice. Lyndall Gordon even suggests that the circulation of such negative accounts of Charlotte's health may have blighted her marriage prospects at a time when she could have expected a proposal from her publisher, George Smith, to whom she had become close.)[50]

On receiving this letter, Catherine Winkworth was so taken with it that she sent it straight on to her sister, whose reaction uncannily prefigures Charles Kingsley's response to the *Life*, quoted at the beginning of this chapter. Entranced by Mrs. Gaskell's lively powers of description, Emily Winkworth could not "get the look of the grey, square, cold, dead-coloured house out of [her] head."[51] She was immediately filled with so much sympathy for "poor Miss Brontë" that she was prepared (though rather grudgingly) to reassess her attitude toward her work: "One feels that her life at least *almost* makes one like her books, though one does not want there to be any more Miss Brontës."[52] Even at this early stage, Gaskell's tragic—if inaccurate—presentation was making Charlotte more acceptable in conventional eyes.

By the time she wrote *The Life of Charlotte Brontë,* Gaskell had corrected some of the mistaken impressions she had gathered during this first meeting with her subject. In her opening chapter, she would, for example, concede the existence of a "narrow flower border" beneath the Parsonage windows (though in case that sounded too cheerful, she quickly added that "only the most hardy plants could be made to grow there").[53] Yet her views were to change remarkably little over the remaining five years of Charlotte's life, despite subsequent meetings and correspondence. Lady Kay-Shuttleworth's gossip was the source of some of her errors, such as the false stories about Patrick. But Charlotte's own self-presentation contributed to Gaskell's perceptions too.

Mrs. Gaskell's excessive emphasis on suffering has often been explained by the fact that, at the time they first met, in August 1850, Charlotte was still in a low state following the loss of her brother and sisters in 1848–49. Bereavement had, it is true, hit her hard. Without Emily and Anne, her life had totally changed. Day to day she experienced loneliness and depression, and she would find it much harder to get down to her next novel, *Villette*, without her sisters, with whom she had always discussed her

The author of *Jane Eyre,* drawn by George Richmond in 1850, shortly before her first meeting with Elizabeth Gaskell. Ambivalent about publicity and self-exposure, Charlotte found it an ordeal to sit for the portrait, which had been commissioned by her publisher. Richmond had a reputation for flattering his sitters, but though he softens Charlotte's features, he also seems to capture a glint of her hidden fire about the eyes.

work. Yet it would be a mistake to suppose that she was no longer capable of taking pleasure in life. The month before her visit to the Lake District, she had enormously enjoyed a holiday in Scotland, squired around by charming young George Smith. If her manner seemed more subdued at the Kay-Shuttleworths', it was because she felt socially uncomfortable there.

Charlotte never warmed to Sir James. She could not relax in his presence. Like Thackeray and Lewes, he was one of those men who expected to be entertained by a firework display from the passionate author of *Jane Eyre*, something which Charlotte, as ever, was reluctant to provide. She was such an instinctual Romantic that she responded intensely to the Lakeland scenery, but with Sir James at her side she felt "obliged to control, or rather, suppress" her emotions "for fear of growing in any degree enthusiastic, and thus drawing attention ~~as~~ to the 'lioness' the authoress—the she-artist."[54] Mrs. Gaskell noticed Charlotte's quiet demeanor—"poor thing she can hardly smile"—and interpreted it as a sign that she had "led such a hard cruel . . . life."[55] In fact, such behavior may simply have been Charlotte's accustomed response to being put on show. She certainly felt that Sir James, with his "Utiltarian" instincts, had no hope of understanding the true artist within her, and her solution was to retreat into ladylike reserve.[56]

That reserve did occasionally slip enough for her to fire up in self-defense. During one conversation, some tactless person—Sir James?—brought up the subject of women novelists, who "outstepped the line which men felt to be proper in works of this kind." The remark was quite clearly directed at Currer Bell. Those present—shepherded presumably by the sensitive and protective Gaskell—quickly agreed that "such violations of propriety were altogether unconscious" on the part of these naive authoresses, who could not possibly know what they were doing.[57] Charlotte went on the defensive: "I trust God will take from me whatever power of invention or expression I may have, before He lets me become blind to the sense of what is fitting or unfitting to be said!"[58] Her honest moral vehemence must have pleased Gaskell, but the words were actually ambiguous. Although Charlotte was deadly serious in what she said, she did not mean quite what her listeners took her to mean. She must have been mentally adding that her sense—and God's sense—of what was fitting was very different from the standards set by "conventionality" and shared, most probably, by the other people in the room.

At the Kay-Shuttleworths', Charlotte found her conversations with Mrs. Gaskell a welcome relief from the attentions of Sir James. Here, instead, was someone who did not expect—indeed would have shrunk from—any displays of indelicate vehemence on the part of a fellow authoress, and who came ready prepared with a sympathetic ear. Gaskell did not want to talk about the disturbing passion of Charlotte's fiction. Instead, she wanted to hear about her life, asking questions in a caring tone, rather than trying (as Thackeray did) to provoke her into an explosive response. (Gaskell noticed how Charlotte would shy away from any-

thing that might lead to "too much conversation on one of her books.")[59]
We have to wonder to what extent Charlotte actively promoted the exaggeratedly tragic, and thus exonerating, view of her own life which Gaskell
later transmitted. It seems that she responded receptively to her fellow
guest's concern by choosing to dwell on those episodes, such as Cowan
Bridge, where she had suffered most or felt most lonely.

One story which could only have come from Charlotte herself was her
account of how she boarded the Ostend packet on her way to Brussels.
The image of a defenseless female forced to travel alone on her first trip
abroad made such an impact on Gaskell that she described the events in
some detail in her letter to Catherine Winkworth: "She had never been out
of Yorkshire before; & was so frightened when she got to London—she
took a cab, it was night and drove down to the Tower Stairs, & got a boat
& went to the Ostend packet, and they refused to take her in; but at last
they did."[60]

In reality it was only when Charlotte returned to Brussels for the second time that Patrick allowed her to travel without a chaperone. If she did
not tell Mrs. Gaskell about her first journey, made with her father, sister,
and two friends, it was because she sensed that her listener would rather
hear about the sad trials of the single woman. She must also have known
what a good story the episode made, as she later reused it in chapter 6
of *Villette,* where Lucy Snowe, deprived of family or other support, braves
the black night and the boatmen's oaths on her lonely journey into the
unknown. One telling difference is that where Charlotte described herself
to Gaskell as "frightened," this conventionally feminine reaction would be
absent from the bolder Lucy, who is "animated and alert, instead of being
depressed and apprehensive" in the face of danger.[61]

When Charlotte exposed some of her deepest emotions in *Jane Eyre,*
reviewers had vilified her. Talking with Mrs. Gaskell at Briery Close, she
found a way of telling her own story which elicited sympathy instead. Their
conversations may even have contributed to her decision, only a fortnight
later, to agree to William Smith Williams's suggestion that she publish
an account of her sisters. Charlotte had been thinking about doing this
for some time, but had previously not felt ready for it. Gaskell's warm
response may have convinced her that an account which stressed her sisters' life of isolation and the wildness of their moorland home would
secure a more understanding attitude from the critics. At any rate, the
romantic impression of Haworth Gaskell took away from Briery Close
was similar to that offered by Charlotte in her "Biographical Notice of

Ellis and Acton Bell," which she finished on September 19, and her preface to *Wuthering Heights,* written a couple of weeks later.[62]

The Brontës' home was not, in reality, as isolated as these accounts—the basis of subsequent legend—suggested. Even today, visitors to the Parsonage are often surprised to find that it is not a lonely unprotected structure surrounded on all sides by miles of windswept moor, but is seconds from the nearest pub and post office. As Juliet Barker's exhaustive research has shown, in Charlotte's time the place was "not some remote rural village of Brigadoon-style fantasy" but "a busy, industrial township" which already contained thirteen small textile mills when the Brontës arrived there in 1820, and it continued to expand.[63] In his book, *A Month in Yorkshire,* one visitor of the 1850s, Walter White, recalled the clattering clogs of the factory people and paired his account of Haworth with a description of the wonders of Saltaire, the extravagant industrial complex built by Tobias Salt at nearby Bradford.[64] "Isolated" and "lonely" are not, Barker suggests, really appropriate terms for a sizeable village that was equidistant between the three major towns of Bradford, Halifax, and Burnley, situated on one of the main routes between Yorkshire and Lancashire, and possessed of no fewer than six public houses.

Barker has also shown that Haworth had a very different social makeup from that described in Charlotte's preface to *Wuthering Heights,* which appears to consist solely of rude peasants and brutal, uncivilized landowners. The inhabitants included "a respectable number of professional people and tradesmen," including a surgeon, a wine merchant, a watchmaker, five butchers, two confectioners, eleven grocers, and three cabinetmakers.[65] If the Brontës held aloof from friendship with such people, it may have been, as Tom Winnifrith has suggested, out of class insecurity. Separated by only a generation from a very humble Irish background, they clung jealously to their newfound gentility and may not have wanted to compromise it by "visiting with" confectioners.

However, their acquaintance included educated men such as William Dearden, a poet and schoolmaster who got to know the family while teaching in nearby Keighley in 1829–30. Branwell later became part of the same literary and artistic circle as Dearden, publishing poems in Yorkshire newspapers, while Charlotte's correspondence with Ellen Nussey is full of the names of forgotten individuals and gossip about local clerical circles. In the course of researching her own family history, Margaret Connor recently unearthed a real-life woman by the name of Jane Eyre who turned out to be a cousin of one of the Brontës' fellow pupils at Roe Head.

While this unexpected find tells us nothing about Charlotte's novel, except a possible source for a name, it incidentally reveals much about the complex web of social ties in which the Brontë family could not help but be involved.[66]

Nor did the Brontës live in a cultural vacuum. Apart from their reading, which was haphazard, perhaps, but broad and deep, they were not ignorant of the wider world of culture. Juliet Barker shows, for example, that Europe's most celebrated pianist, Franz Lizst, performed at nearby Halifax in 1841; Branwell was probably in the audience.[67] Similarly, recent work by Christine Alexander and Jane Sellars on the art of the Brontës has shown them to have been more involved with the cultural goings-on of the area than had previously been thought. They reveal that the Brontës not only attended the summer exhibition of the Royal Northern Society for the Encouragement of the Fine Arts in Leeds in 1834, but that two drawings by Charlotte herself were accepted for exhibition alongside the work of established professional artists.[68]

Yet while this sort of research can give us an objective sociological picture, it does not tell us how the young Brontës experienced their home subjectively. Isolation is as much a state of mind as an external reality, and it is hard to imagine that Emily could ever have been anything but "isolated" even if she had lived in a bustling metropolis. From an early age their lively imaginations latched onto the moors above the Parsonage rather than the village below, and they tended to view their world through literary spectacles. Their Romantic inheritance informed their love of nature, but also inflamed their frustration with the dull workaday aspects of their surroundings. Charlotte's references in her early letters to "the solitude of our wild little hill village"[69] and "the little wild, moorland village where we reside"[70] suggest a desire to Romanticize her home, as does the letter Branwell wrote to William Wordsworth at around the time Charlotte wrote to Southey. Hoping to appeal to the older poet's sensibility, the teenager portrayed himself as a child of nature who had "lived among wild and secluded hills" from the day of his birth.[71]

Even before her biographers got around to it, the youthful Charlotte had already exploited the literary potential of her home in her private diary. The Brontë children may even have been encouraged to see romance in the graveyard in front of their house by a series of tales in Blackwood's, "Chapters on Churchyards."[72] In a daydream Charlotte recorded while homesick at Roe Head, she imagined herself back in the Parsonage in terms which one twentieth-century biographer would find disappointingly "like any and every commentator who has written on the Brontës" when it was published in the 1940s.[73] The fact that, toward the end of this passage, we can see her crossing out a word to choose a more poetic one shows that she is consciously transforming her memories into literature:

> [M]y eyes fixed on the window, through which appeared no other land-scape than a monotonous stretch of moorland, a grey church tower, rising from the centre of a church-yard so filled with graves, that the rank-weed & coarse grass scarce had room to shoot up between the monuments. Over these hangs in the eye of memory a sky of such grey clouds as often veil the chill close of an October day & low on the horizon ~~appear~~ glances at intervals through the rack the orb of a lurid and haloed moon.[74]

The focus on moor, church, graves, and stormy sky indeed prefigures the grisly imagery at the heart of the Brontë legend, iconized by Gaskell and endlessly reformulated, for example in this spectacularly purple version from an American biography of 1940:

> The house I am about to describe is a grey, two-storied dwelling standing bleak and weather-beaten between church and moor.
> I seem to see it from the churchyard—it fronts that way; rather paler than the sky behind it, which wears the leaden hue of a coming storm. Its pallor is livid; the colour of fear, or of feverish meditation. It would appear to be haunted. Its windows look out on graves; and the dead lie rib to rib in a triple layer awaiting the day of doom under those quarried stones.[75]

Like her later mythographers, the homesick young Charlotte does not conjure up visions of the mills and factories down toward Keighley or pic-ture Haworth's eleven grocers going about their business. It is hardly likely that she would have mentioned them to Mrs. Gaskell if asked to describe her home during their conversations at the Briery. The moors and Charlotte's sense of isolation were what Gaskell asked about;[76] the banal-ities of everyday life would not have seemed worth mentioning.

Three years later, when she invited Mrs. Gaskell to stay at the Parson-age in 1853, Charlotte would humorously exaggerate the wildness of Haworth: "When you take leave of the domestic circle ... to come to Haworth, you must do it in the spirit which might sustain you in case you were setting out on a brief trip to the backwoods of America. Leaving

behind your husband, children, and civilisation, you must come out to bar-
barism, loneliness, and liberty."[77] Gaskell may have missed the full extent
of the satire in these comments and taken Charlotte too literally at her
word. The myth of Haworth was already entrenched in her imagination.

The first meeting between Charlotte and Mrs. Gaskell had been a success.
Thrown together for much of the visit, each had been keen to please the
other, and both came away with the intention of keeping in touch. Charlotte had appealed to Gaskell's protective insincts by putting the subdued
and needy side of her personality to the fore; Gaskell had appealed to
Charlotte as a sympathetic ally in the literary world who accepted her as a
lady. Yet the friendship that developed, warm though it was, was never
truly intimate, as there were parts of herself Charlotte would always keep
veiled. On the surface it was a cordial relationship, but it was not without
its hidden ambiguities.

As soon as they returned to their respective homes, the two women
began to correspond. Charlotte's letters, though genuinely friendly, are
also revealing about the way she wanted to be read by her new friend.
Researching the *Life* after Charlotte's death, Gaskell was struck by "how
much the spirit in which she wrote varies according to the correspondent
whom she was addressing."[78] Socially, Charlotte was acutely sensitive
to others' expectations. In *Villette,* her autobiographical heroine, Lucy
Snowe, reflects on how her character changes depending on whom she is
with: to flighty Ginevra she is "old Crusty" or "Diogenes" the sour old
cynic,[79] to Dr. John she is "quiet Lucy . . . inoffensive as a shadow,"[80] to
Paul Emanuel she has the sexual energy of a "coquette."[81]

In her relations with the literary world, Charlotte could be equally
chameleonlike. To G. H. Lewes, she could write in the voice of Currer Bell
that *Jane Eyre* had been written in a calculated attempt to please the market.[82] Yet she told Mrs. Gaskell, on the contrary, that she would never be so
indelicate as to write novels for the money.[83] This contradiction reveals
much about the difficulty of self-definition for a professional woman
writer in the 1850s, but it also shows how keen Charlotte was to project a
ladylike image to Gaskell.

The first letter Charlotte wrote Gaskell after their meeting was sensi-
tively tailored to fit her correspondent's sensibility. Gaskell was fascinated
by the relationship between dutiful unmarried daughters and difficult widowed fathers—it became a recurrent motif of her novels—so she must

have leapt at the following tantalizing glimpse of Charlotte's domestic life, presented against a suitably Brontëan backdrop of graves and wuthering winds: "Papa and I have just had tea; he is sitting quietly in his room, and I in mine; 'storms of rain' are sweeping over the garden and churchyard; as to the moors—they are hidden in thick fog."[84]

When Charlotte goes on to discuss the less personal topic of the books she has read recently, her tone is different, say, from the more high-flown style she used in her literary letters to G. H. Lewes, written as Currer Bell. She recommends a mealymouthed article on Sarah Lewis's book *Woman's Mission* in the *Westminster Review,* which casts women as moral muses rather than creators in their own right. Though the author accords some respect to women who work, he still regards woman's primary role as being to inspire heroic creativity in men.[85] Charlotte goes on to express the view concerning the condition of women that there are "evils—deep rooted in the foundations of the Social system—which no efforts of ours can touch—of which we cannot complain—of which it is advisable not too often to think."[86] Yet though she recommends turning a blind eye to these unsolvable problems in life, in her art she was in fact prepared to think the unthinkable about such issues. Though Currer Bell may have described the female mind as a place of rebellion in *Jane Eyre,* as Miss Brontë she was keen to present a moderate, conciliating face when she discussed the woman question with Mrs. Gaskell.[87]

In December 1850, Mrs. Gaskell reported to Lady Kay-Shuttleworth on how her relationship with Charlotte was getting on: "I wrote her a long letter of almost impertinent advice, (at least it would have been impertinent if it had come simply from the head, and not warm from the heart which ached for her loneliness,) and she replied by return of post, so very nicely and warmly, thanking me for all I had said."[88]

Charlotte genuinely welcomed such sympathy in periods of poor health and depression, as Gaskell was happy to indulge her in as much moaning and misery as she felt like. Though Charlotte needed to be in a good mood to write to George Smith,[89] she would be more likely to write to Gaskell on bad days.[90] There were, however, times when she was privately not so grateful for her friend's concern. In April 1851, she complained to George Smith that two "ladies"—Mrs. Gaskell and Harriet Martineau—"seem determined between them that I shall be a sort of invalid." They had a habit of spreading "derogatory" rumors about her "physical condition" if she forgot to answer their letters by return of post. "Why may I not be well like other people?" she wailed.[91]

If those ladies would not allow Charlotte to be strong and healthy, it may have been because they preferred her that way. The passion of her writing was only explicable to them in terms of sickness and suffering on the part of the author. Though both were radicals in their own ways— Gaskell had written about a strike from the viewpoint of the workers, Martineau inclined to atheism—both remained conventional in their idea of what was fitting in female sensibility. In their attitude toward Charlotte's novels they inclined to the view that the expression of frustrated libido in an unmarried woman was a symptom of mental ill health. The enormous gulf between Gaskell's and Charlotte's attitudes toward art, femininity, and sexuality becomes blindingly clear when one compares the novels they were writing during the period in which they got to know one another. Gaskell was working on *Ruth,* Charlotte on *Villette.* Both were published in early 1853.

Gaskell's *Ruth* was written with a clear moral and social purpose. She had, through Charles Dickens, been in contact with a charity for saving "fallen" women—usually prostitutes—by helping them to emigrate and start new lives abroad. Her novel was designed to secure sympathy for the plight of these pariahs, by showing how innocent girls could be led astray. Ruth Hilton, her vulnerable, orphaned teenage heroine, works as a seamstress in sweatshop conditions, but runs away with a young man of good family who seduces and then abandons her, having made her pregnant.

She spends the rest of the novel atoning for her sin, seeking redemption first in motherhood and finally in an act of transfiguring self-sacrifice. Working in a fever hospital, she discovers her seducer among the patients, contracts typhus while nursing him, and dies a martyr. Despite her original fall, Ruth is in every other respect so excessively virtuous as to stretch credulity. As one unconvinced reviewer pointed out, Gaskell contrives to make her heroine lose her virginity while remaining in angelic ignorance of sexuality.[92] She approaches her corruption in a state of childlike passionlessness, devoid of sexual desire: "Ruth was innocent and snow-pure. She had heard of falling in love, but did not know the signs and symptoms thereof; nor, indeed, had she ever troubled her head much about them."[93]

Culturally, Charlotte's *Villette* belongs to a completely different world. As G. H. Lewes recognized in a review, its passion, power, and "[c]ontempt of conventions" aligned it with the works of George Sand and made it as unlike *Ruth* as sunlight from moonlight.[94] Its heroine, Lucy Snowe, is the opposite of Ruth Hilton: quiet and conformist in her external behavior, but inwardly seething with rebellious desires. Unlike Ruth, she does not fall. But Charlotte's vivid portrayal of her mental landscape would be more disturbing to some Victorians than the morality tale painted by Gaskell.

It is not surprising that Charlotte found writing *Villette* a struggle. No longer able to hide behind her pseudonym, she knew that next time she published she would be vulnerable to personal abuse. It says much for her courage that she resolutely followed her artistic instincts and returned to the intense autobiographical aesthetic that had animated *Jane Eyre*, digging into the painful depths of her own psyche for material. Socially, Miss Brontë may have conformed to decorously feminine standards of behavior and conversation. But artistically, Currer Bell was absolutely committed to her own original vision, regardless of whether or not it fulfilled what she called the critics' "notion of ladyhood."[95] Having to appear in drawing rooms as the acknowledged author of *Jane Eyre* had made her more aware than ever of the disjunction between her inward and outer selves. The conflict between outward conformity and inner passion was to become the central theme of *Villette*.

Inspired by Charlotte's time in Belgium, the novel tells the story of Lucy Snowe, an English orphan who finds herself teaching at a school much like the Pensionnat Heger in a fictitious version of Brussels. It tells of her relationships with two men: the charming but superficial doctor, John Graham Bretton, who does not return her love (based on George Smith); and the passionate, mercurial professor, Paul Emanuel, who does (based on Constantin Heger). The melodramatic plot, which looks back toward gothic and forward to the sensation novels of the 1860s, includes perfidious Jesuits and an evil headmistress (based on Heger's wife) bent on destroying Lucy's chances of happiness with Monsieur Paul. But the real subject of the book is the heroine's turbulent inner world.

The setting and some incidents are based on Charlotte's own experience. Like Lucy, Charlotte made a desperate visit to a Roman Catholic confessional during the lonely summer vacation of 1843, tormented by her unresolved relationship with her "master" and his wife's increasing chilliness. But it would be a mistake to regard the novel as a naive transcription of real life. As she said herself, she only allowed reality to suggest, not to dictate. In this, her most sophisticated fiction, Charlotte achieved a depth and complexity of analysis that went way beyond literal autobiography.[96]

Matthew Arnold would find *Villette* "hideous, undelightful, convulsed," and it is true to say that it is not a comfortable read.[97] *Jane Eyre* had opened her heart unreservedly. "Reader, I married him" is one of the most appealing sentences in literature because it speaks to us as to a friend.[98] Yet Jane had been rudely rebuffed by those who found her coarse and overassertive. In Lucy Snowe, Charlotte offered an equally intense but far less trusting narrator, who frequently conceals vital information from the reader and offers misleading interpretations of her own character and behavior. In a society in which unmarried women could not admit to sexual desire without compromising their claims to femininity, Lucy keeps denying the obvious: that she is in love. Her attempts to suppress her inner feelings eventually result in mental collapse. This is a novel about breakdown and recovery, about identity and the unconscious in which, as the recurrent images of burial suggest, much of the action takes place beneath the surface.

Lucy is a spinster in a society which does not know what to do with independent single women. This, of course, was a topic Mrs. Gaskell and Lady Kay-Shuttleworth had discussed in relation to Charlotte. But where they had envisaged such women bearing their "trials" in a state of uncomplaining renunciation and substituting self-denial for the fulfillment of marriage and motherhood, Lucy is not so docile. She would shock Victorian readers not because she suffers, but because she responds to that suffering with what Matthew Arnold disapprovingly called "hunger, rebellion, and rage."[99] When she visits an art gallery, Lucy finds that culture divides women into two stereotypes, neither of which is fully human. On one wall is a Rubensesque Cleopatra, obscenely sensual, a sluglike nude devoid of spirituality. But the alternative is the sickly piety of a sentimental genre series showing scenes from the life of a woman, focusing on marriage and motherhood.[100] Unable to conform to either of these bankrupt options, is it really surprising that Lucy breaks down?

Lucy's—and Charlotte's—great achievement is to find words for the inarticulate impulses of a powerful personality in a state of internal and external repression. Her breakdown—described with a phantasmagoric intensity that edges toward the surreal—stems from the effort of suppressing unruly desires. Some readers would find in *Villette* confirmation of the medical view that sexual frustration caused hysteria in morally weak spinsters. Yet Charlotte's position differs radically from that of the doctors who were so keen to label and objectify women. Not only does she allow the patient to map the subtleties of her emotions in her own subjective voice, suggesting that sexuality involves more than the reproductive instinct. She also avoids moral judgmentalism and does not pretend that Lucy would be cured by a course of self-abnegation and charity work.

Most significantly, she suggests that social, rather than purely biological, factors are at work: it is not the fact that she has unfulfilled desires, but the fact that conventionality will not allow her to acknowledge them, which drives Lucy to mental collapse.

The vision of *Villette* is not, however, without optimism about the human mind's capacity for resilience and renewal. Eventually, Lucy manages to pull the scattered fragments of her life together. Despite the famous open ending—we do not get the traditional closure, marriage, but are left with the suggestion that Lucy's lover will probably drown in a shipwreck rather than return to her—she finds a measure of fulfillment in work and independence, becoming the headmistress of her own flourishing school. The fact that she has had to acknowledge her own desire for love, even if it is never fully consummated, leaves her a more integrated person. Despite the unflinching moral realism of this novel of disillusion, Lucy Snowe is, in her own way, as much a survivor as Jane Eyre.

The writing of *Villette* was a stop-start process punctuated by frequent blocks, but Charlotte did not want to discuss it with her new novelist friend, realizing that Mrs. Gaskell might not altogether empathize with her heroine. Gaskell, on the other hand, was always asking for advice about *Ruth*.[101] This reflects their different attitudes toward their art. Where Charlotte's main concern was to express her inner vision without compromise, Gaskell was more worried about the effect she would have on her readers, since her ultimate aim was not personal expression but philanthropic reform.

In a perceptive letter, Charlotte once asked Mrs. Gaskell whether she found it easy when writing

> to be quite *your own woman,* uninfluenced unswayed by the consciousness of how your work may affect other minds; what blame, what sympathy it may call forth? . . . In a word, are you never tempted to make your characters more amiable than the Life, by the inclination to assimilate your thoughts to the thoughts of those who always *feel* kindly, but sometimes fail to *see* justly? Don't answer the question; it is not intended to be answered.[102]

Villette shows that, artistically at any rate, Charlotte was utterly committed to being her own woman. She certainly did not soften Lucy Snowe's personality to please readers. It is amazing that, despite the loss of her anonymity, she was still willing to use the darker recesses of her own interior life as the starting point for her creative vision. She was also quite ruthless about using people she knew as models—in particular George Smith and his mother, who appear as Dr. John and Mrs. Bretton—even when she must have known they would be able to recognize themselves in her none-too-flattering portraits.

In *Ruth,* on the other hand, Mrs. Gaskell knew that she had chosen a controversial subject and was afraid the public might not accept a fallen woman as a heroine. In fact, her urgent need to protect her own moral reputation may be what motivated her, in January 1853, to beg Charlotte to postpone the publication of *Villette,* so that the two novels, originally scheduled to appear at the same time, would not be reviewed together. The reason Gaskell gave Charlotte was that she did not want the critics, prejudiced as they were against women authors, to make invidious comparisons. But it is also possible that she did not want to be tarred with the same brush as the "naughty" Currer Bell.

In the event, *Ruth* received a mixed response. Soon after publication, Gaskell reported that a copy had actually been burned in Manchester. But this isolated incident does not reflect the reactions of literary reviewers, many of whom seemed more worried about its failure to convince as fiction than about the author's immorality in choosing such a central character. Gaskell's desire to make Ruth sympathetic had compromised her commitment to psychological realism, making the heroine seem, as one critic put it, to be "derived from cogitation rather than from life."[103] Like many readers, Charlotte found the ending unnaturally tragic, wondering why Ruth, who had suffered so much already, should be made to die.[104] Gaskell's strategy, of course, was to make Ruth so pitiable that it would be impossible for the most hard-hearted critic to withhold forgiveness, to punish her so thoroughly that no one could suggest she had not paid the price for her crime. In this respect *Ruth* anticipated *The Life of Charlotte Brontë,* in which the heroine's feminine virtues and tragic suffering would be used as a means of blotting out her supposed errors.

Though she did not want the critics to compare her novel to Charlotte's, Gaskell did exactly that when she read *Villette* for the first time. She told Lady Kay-Shuttleworth: "The difference between Miss Brontë and me is that she puts all her naughtiness into her books, and I put all my goodness. I am sure she works off a great deal that is morbid *into* her writing, and *out* of her life; and my books are so far better than I am that I often feel ashamed of having written them and as if I were a hypocrite."[105] She was not the only reader to find disturbing morbidity in the novel, which she felt detracted from the "transcendent grandeur" Charlotte could have achieved had she been "brought up in a happy & healthy atmosphere." In Mrs. Gaskell's eyes, Miss Brontë's sad life of "duties to her father, to the poor around her, to the old servants" was irreproachable, but her artistic vision, though "wonderfully clever," remained contaminated.[106]

Charlotte must have anticipated that her uncompromising presentation of the female psyche would cause consternation in some quarters. She even asked George Smith if he would be prepared to publish *Villette* anonymously, so that she might hide behind the "sheltering shadow of an incognito" once more.[107] Not surprisingly, he refused to drop the famous "Currer Bell" name.

Elizabeth Gaskell, drawn by Samuel Lawrence in 1854, the year of Charlotte's marriage

When the first reviews came out, Charlotte found that her fears were justified. As the morally upright Miss Brontë she had cultivated a friendship with the bristly Harriet Martineau, and therefore assumed she could rely on her support. But Martineau attacked the book in an unsigned but easily identified review in the *Daily News* which reiterated what had, since *Jane Eyre,* been the set critical response to Currer Bell: acknowledging her "stamp of originality" and artistic powers but bridling at her passion. Moreover, the review publicly labeled the book morbid. Martineau found Lucy Snowe's mentality too complex to be healthy and declared that her inner conflicts and sexual desires were far from the experience of normal women and should never have been written about: "[T]here is an absence of introspection, an unconsciousness, a repose in women's lives," she went on, "of which we find no admission in this book."[108]

Less conciliating than Mrs. Gaskell, Miss Martineau let Charlotte know her objections directly, telling her in a letter: "I do not like the love, either the kind or the degree of it."[109] Her hypersensitivity to what she saw as morbid passion led her to blame Charlotte where Gaskell merely pitied. Unmarried herself, her extreme reaction may have stemmed from a fear that the works of Currer Bell would play into the hands of those men who dismissed single women writers as sex-starved spinsters seeking compensatory thrills.

Charlotte responded angrily to Martineau's letter, which suggests she had not really meant it when she asked her back in 1850 to be unsparing in her criticism. She felt she had been trying to get to the heart of an emotional truth: that there was nothing wrong with single women having natural passions, whatever society may think. "I know what *love* is as I understand it," she wrote; "and if man or woman should be ashamed of feeling such love, then there is nothing right, noble, faithful, truthful, unselfish in this earth."[110] She was so hurt that she put an end to the friendship.

If Elizabeth Gaskell and Harriet Martineau found *Villette* hard to stomach, it is not difficult to see why. Gaskell in particular was trying to forge a definition of female writing founded on moral purity and philanthropy. In a world where some medical men defined both intellectual work and active sexuality as masculine, she was keen to show that literary labor could be perfectly pure and feminine. Charlotte, on the other hand, put passion at the heart of her vision in a way that was particularly worrying for women writers. Not only did she acknowledge erotic feelings in her heroines, but she made an implicit connection between sexuality and artistic creativity.

When Jane Eyre confesses to having passions of her own, this acknowledgment of desire merges into an assertion of women's need for professional fulfillment, both of which are conventionally considered the preserve of men: "Nobody knows how many rebellions beside political rebellions ferment in the masses of life which people earth. Women are supposed to be very calm generally: but women feel just as men feel; they need exercise for their faculties, and a field for their efforts as much as their brothers do."[111] In *Shirley,* Charlotte had expressed her view of the female imagination through a mythic metaphor of sexual union between divine genius and the woman artist. And in *Villette,* the tragic actress Vashti combined artistic and sexual power to a terrifying, amoral extent. If Gaskell (who compared herself to the holy martyr St. Sebastian)[112] was keen to promote authorship as a spiritually pure vocation for women, it is not surprising if she could not accept Charlotte's passion.

In literary terms, *Villette* was such a stunning achievement that most critics praised its power and sophistication, even though they continued to niggle at its "coarseness," "masculinity," or "morbidity." However, when the *Christian Remembrancer* came out in April, Charlotte was to find herself subjected to an onslaught as virulent as anything the *Quarterly* had thrown at her. Once more, the anonymous writer was a woman, again suggesting how particularly threatened female authors felt by Currer Bell.

The reviewer, Anne Mozley, summed up her view of gender relations in the words "We want a woman at our hearth."[113] Not surprisingly, Lucy Snowe did not appeal. She reminded readers of "the outrages on decorum, the moral perversity, the toleration of, nay, indifference to vice which . . . make *Jane Eyre* a dangerous book, and which must leave a permanent mistrust of the author on all thoughtful and scrupulous minds."[114] Then she attacked Currer Bell's heroines for being "without the feminine element, infringers of modest restraints, despisers of bashful fears, self-reliant, contemptuous of prescriptive decorum." Her critique was also personal. She described Lucy Snowe as embodying "the authoress's own feelings and experience."[115] Charlotte—who had done so much to convince literary society of Miss Brontë's respectability—found this *ad feminam* approach particularly threatening.

When *Jane Eyre*'s morality was first questioned, she had added a strident preface in the voice of Currer Bell. But now that she was generally known to be a woman, it would be impossible to print a public counterattack without, as Anne Mozley would have put it, infringing modest restraints. Instead, she wrote privately to the *Christian Remembrancer* in a more defensive tone. Echoing her "Biographical Notice of Ellis and Acton Bell," she tried, rather awkwardly, to use her upbringing as a shield. "I was born and have been reared in the seclusion of a country parsonage," she told the editor, hoping that her status as a clergyman's daughter would confer respectability, while her isolated upbringing would explain away anything in her works which offended polite society.[116] Yet a private letter to an editor could have little effect. She could still rely on the sympathy of the caring Mrs. Gaskell, but this did little to dispel the fact that her public reputation for coarseness was now confirmed.

That September of 1853, Mrs. Gaskell finally got to visit Currer Bell's country parsonage for herself. It turned out to be more cheerful and commodious than she had imagined. Charlotte had recently redecorated, and the sitting room was cozy and warm with its new crimson curtains. Mrs. Gaskell noted with approval how "exquisitely clean" the house was.[117] Signs that Charlotte took domestic duties seriously were particularly gratifying, and reinforced Gaskell's belief that though Currer Bell might be morbid, Miss Brontë was the soul of feminine delicacy. Patrick's formal, old-fashioned courtesy made Mrs. Gaskell feel uncomfortable, but most of the time she was alone with Charlotte, who became talkative in the presence of such a sympathetic listener. As she reported to her friend John Forster: "There are some people whose stock of facts and anecdotes are soon exhausted; but Miss B. is none of these. She has the wild, strange facts of her own and her sisters' lives."[118]

Charlotte was actually quite discriminating about which aspects of her life she wanted to reveal to her ever-sympathetic guest. They discussed *Villette*, but she did not reveal anything about her intense relationship with her mentor Constantin Heger, which had inspired the love affair between Lucy Snowe and Paul Emanuel. Gaskell had already guessed that the book related to Charlotte's Brussels experience, recognizing incidents, such as the ship-boarding scene on the Thames, which Charlotte had already mentioned. She had told Lady Kay-Shuttleworth that she believed it to be "a very correct account of one part of her life; which is very vivid & distinct in her remembrance, with all the feelings that were called out at that period."[119] So it was oddly tactless of her to announce, bluntly, that she did not like Lucy Snowe. This cannot have encouraged Charlotte to open up, and the book would remain an enigma to Gaskell until well into her research for the *Life*.

In other ways, Charlotte more than fulfilled her guest's appetite for stories. As a pupil at Roe Head, she had terrified the other girls with spooky tales after lights-out.[120] Now, she riveted Mrs. Gaskell with some of the more melodramatic local legends and scandals. Keen to confirm her preconceived view of Haworth as uncivilized, Mrs. Gaskell swallowed these "wild tales of . . . ungovernable families" as typical of everyday life in the area.[121] They would later resurface in the biography, in which Haworth is presented as populated by Heathcliff-like misanthropes threatening to shoot hapless visitors, uncouth addicts of cock-fighting and bear-baiting, and underage girls seduced by their brothers-in-law under their sisters' noses. Given that she would also quote an Elizabethan account of Haworth's lack of civility, it is not surprising that she made it seem excessively backward and untamed, but her views were initially encouraged by her hostess.

During Mrs. Gaskell's visit Charlotte may not have wanted to bare all about her Brussels experience, but she did confide one significant personal fact: that her father's curate, Arthur Bell Nicholls, had proposed to her. An intelligent, emotional man of great integrity but few intellectual interests, Nicholls had been in love with Charlotte for years. Initially, she had refused his offer out of hand, but over time she had been more and more moved by his obviously intense, Brontëan passion (he had responded to rejection with redoubled constancy and uninhibited fits of weeping). Her father, however, objected to the match ostensibly on the grounds of Nicholls's "utter want of money."[122]

Mrs. Gaskell must have thought that marriage and motherhood—those "clear and defined duties" for which she herself had thanked God—might prove Miss Brontë's salvation and perhaps cure her of her morbid streak. With her characteristic mix of generosity and interference she soon set about trying to remedy Nicholls's pennilessness, asking her friend Richard Monckton Milnes if he might be able to use his influence to sort out some sort of pension for the impoverished curate. Milnes did in fact manage to recommend him to two good curacies—neither near Haworth—both of which he turned down.

Charlotte's warmth toward Nicholls was increasing all the time, particularly after she heard in November that George Smith, whom she had once hoped to marry, was engaged. By January she had accepted Nicholls's proposal, and by April the couple had finally succeeded in gaining Patrick's blessing. Before the wedding, which took place in June, Charlotte paid one last visit to Mrs. Gaskell in Manchester, which proved the most enjoyable and relaxed time they had yet spent together. Catherine Winkworth was also there, a vivacious, easygoing person who made Charlotte feel at home. The mood was one of fun and laughing, and Charlotte felt able to confide the anxieties she felt about her impending marriage. Unlike her intense feelings for Constantin Heger, this was a subject which she could discuss freely, sure of an understanding and supportive response. To Mrs. Gaskell, the marriage must have seemed like the happy ending to Charlotte's story of loneliness and struggle.

This was the last time the two writers saw each other. Over the next year they fell rather out of touch. Charlotte found herself both busier and happier in her married life than she had anticipated; Mrs. Gaskell was anxious that Arthur Nicholls's Church of England dogmatism would prejudice him against his wife's dissenting friends and so held off. It came as a shock when, in the spring of 1855, she received news of Charlotte's premature death in a letter from John Greenwood, the stationer who had supplied the paper on which the Brontës had written their novels and whom Gaskell had met briefly on her visit to Haworth. (That she learned the news from a local busybody like Greenwood says much about her lack of rapport with Charlotte's family.)

Charlotte had died, probably in the early months of pregnancy, on March 31, 1855, less than a year after her wedding.[123] Mrs. Gaskell's immediate—and characteristic—response was to beg John Greenwood for "every detail" of what had happened: "I can not tell you how VERY sad your note has made me," she told him. "My dear dear friend that I shall never see again on earth! I did not even know she was ill. I had heard nothing of her since the beginning of December when she wrote to a mutual friend saying that she was well, and happy. . . . I want to know EVERY particular."[124] In a flush of unrestrained emotion, she even wondered aloud whether she could have prevented her friend's death, perhaps by persuading her to induce the pregnancy prematurely: "[I]t is no use regretting what has passed; but I do fancy that if I had come, I could have induced her,—even though they had all felt angry with me at first,—to do what was so absolutely necessary, for her very life."[125]

At the beginning of June, Mrs. Gaskell was still regretting the fact that she had not been at Charlotte's bedside. "I think I could have . . . perhaps saved her life," she wrote to George Smith on June 4.[126] Instead, she had begun to formulate a plan to save her dead friend's reputation, hoping one day to resurrect Charlotte on paper: "Sometime, it may be years hence— but if I live long enough, and no one is living whom such a publication would hurt, I will publish what I know of her, and make the world (if I am strong enough in expression,) honour the woman as much as they have admired the writer."[127]

If the public only knew of Miss Brontë's private sufferings and feminine virtues, they would forgive any touches of coarseness in the works of Currer Bell.

CHAPTER THREE

Life into Literature

The memoir Mrs. Gaskell began to contemplate in the weeks after Charlotte's death would turn out to be arguably the most famous English biography of the nineteenth century. Not only would it catapult the Brontës into the realm of myth, but it would, unusually for its genre, become a classic in its own right, still read today as one of the great works of Victorian literature. For one leading female novelist to publish a full-length life of another was a landmark event in the history of women's writing. Yet it would, ironically, have a deeply ambivalent impact on the Brontës' literary reputation.

Rather than offering a critical analysis of the novels which had made the Brontës famous, Gaskell's *Life of Charlotte Brontë* would redirect attention toward the moving, dramatic, and uplifting aspects of their lives. It was not designed to celebrate the work but to exonerate and iconize the authors. The legend it laid down—three lonely sisters playing out their tragic destiny on top of a windswept moor with a mad misanthrope father and doomed brother—was the result of the very particular mind-set Gaskell brought to it. Her philanthropic aim was to provide an apologia which would relaunch Currer Bell on the public stage as an irreproachable martyr-heroine and, in the process, sanctify the image of the woman writer more generally. But it is also important to remember that she was a novelist who had trouble disciplining her imagination. "[Y]ou see," she confessed while working on the biography, "you have to be accurate and keep to facts; a most difficult thing for a writer of fiction."[1]

Gaskell's tragic vision would feed imperceptibly into the collective mind. Half a century on, Henry James would complain that the Brontë story had become such a "beguiled infatuation" that it got in the way of critical appreciation of the Brontë novels, supplanting their rightful place in the cultural consciousness:

The romantic tradition of the Brontés [sic], with posterity, has been still more essentially helped, I think, by a force independent of . . . their applied faculties—by the attendant image of their dreary, their tragic history, their loneliness and poverty of life. That picture has been made to hang before us as insistently as the vividest page of *Jane Eyre* or of *Wuthering Heights*. If these things were "stories," as we say, and stories of a lively interest, the medium from which they sprang was above all in itself a story, such a story as has fairly elbowed out the rights of appreciation. . . . It covers and supplants their matter, their spirit, their style, their talent, their taste; it embodies, really, the most complete intellectual muddle, if the term be not extravagant, ever achieved, on a literary question, by our wonderful public.[2]

If the history of the Brontës had been transformed into "story," it was due to the long-term effects of Gaskell's biography. Reading over the *Life,* with its heightened emotions, vivid scene-painting, and use of melodrama, it does almost seem as though Gaskell the novelist was unconsciously trying to create a rival, morally redemptive, story so compelling that it could compete with the impure Brontë novels for popular attention and win.

Gaskell was so driven in her commitment to the project of rehabilitating Charlotte that she would complete the biography in a mere two years. The basic outline had been in her mind since the summer of 1850, when she had first met Charlotte at the Kay-Shuttleworths' and formed a view of her dominated by pity for her sufferings and an overexaggerated conception of the wildness and bleakness of her life in Haworth. But in the immediate aftermath of Charlotte's death, Gaskell had assumed that it would not be possible to publish the story she so desperately wanted to tell. She could not believe that Patrick Brontë would ever agree to having what she saw as his crazy eccentricities revealed to the world, but she knew that his cooperation would be vital if she was going to collect enough material for a publishable life.

However, in mid-June 1855, three months after the death, Gaskell received an unexpected letter from the bereaved father, who had no idea that she regarded him as a strange and violent character. To her surprise and delight, he actually invited her to do what she had been aching to do for weeks—to take on the role of official biographer. In his ponderous, antiquated style, he explained his reasons thus:

Finding that a great many scribblers, as well as some clever and truthful writers, have published articles in newspapers and tracts respecting my dear daughter Charlotte since her death, and seeing that many things that have been stated are untrue, but more false; and having reason to think that some may venture to write her life who will be ill-qualified for the undertaking, I can see no better plan under the circumstances than to apply to some established author to write a brief account of her life and to make some remarks on her works. You seem to me the best qualified for doing what I wish should be done.[3]

Ironically, the book which would create the Brontë myth was initially commissioned as a work of demythology—as the authorized life whose purpose was to silence the false prophets who had already begun clamoring to tell the dead woman's story.

The "scribblers" to whom Patrick referred included Harriet Martineau, who had published an obituary in the *Daily News* in which she repeated all her prejudices. She reiterated her views on the coarseness and morbid passion of the Brontë novels, presenting Charlotte's personal tragedy as both explanation and expiation, begging readers to remember her "terrible . . . experience of life" in a "forlorn house" in those "dreary wilds." Martineau—like Gaskell after her—could only explain Charlotte's failure to conform by assuming that she had been completely cut off from cultural norms. In reality, Charlotte had, from childhood, been an avid follower of contemporary politics and current affairs in the press. But Martineau described her as "living among the wild Yorkshire hills . . . in a place where newspapers were never seen (or where she never saw any)."[4] She erroneously claimed that Charlotte was too feeble to walk on the moors and that she looked out of her window directly onto her sisters' graves (in fact Anne was buried in Scarborough and the other Brontës inside the church). Matthew Arnold, another scribbler, published an obituary poem which made a similar mistake, assuming the sisters were buried outside in the grassy graveyard.[5] (The same error occurs in Emily Dickinson's tribute poem, possibly written to commemorate the fifth anniversary of Charlotte's death, in which Currer Bell's tomb is "All overgrown by cunning moss.")[6]

But the specific catalyst which inspired Patrick's request to Gaskell was an anonymous piece in *Sharpe's London Magazine* which had upset Charlotte's friend Ellen Nussey. Pained by its "misrepresentations" and "malignant spirit," Nussey had felt it should not go unanswered. Writing immediately to the Parsonage to express her outrage, she had suggested that the well-known author Mrs. Gaskell might be just the person to "undertake a reply, and . . . give a sound castigation to the writer."[7] Charlotte's widower had felt that Ellen had overreacted, but Patrick had taken up her suggestion with alacrity.

In a bizarre twist, the article which Ellen found so "malignant" was in fact adapted, often almost word for word, from the long letter which Mrs. Gaskell had written to Catherine Winkworth immediately after her first meeting with Charlotte in the Lake District five years before. Mrs. Gaskell and her circle were in the habit of circulating correspondence with enormous freedom, often without the writer's knowledge. Somehow, the letter—which Winkworth had sent on to her sister—had strayed into the hands of a journalist.[8] The strange result was that Mrs. Gaskell was now being asked to publish a corrective to a story for which she herself was ultimately responsible.

Gaskell agreed straightaway to the proposal, though she was still anxious that the hovering presence of Charlotte's father and widower might inhibit her from writing the truth about her subject as she saw it. "Relatives," as Janet Malcolm put it in her gripping account of Sylvia Plath's afterlife, "are the biographer's natural enemies."[9] Even in Charlotte's lifetime Mrs. Gaskell had never warmed to Patrick, the eccentric chopper-up of furniture, or Arthur Nicholls, whose religious scruples had gotten in the way of her friendship with Charlotte. In the immediate aftermath of the death she had felt too uncomfortable to communicate with them directly. Instead, she had deputed the creepily obliging stationer John Greenwood to find out what she wanted to know, getting him to make discreet inquiries about whether Thackeray had written a condolence letter to Patrick.

On July 23, taking Catherine Winkworth with her for moral support, she arrived in Haworth, where she found that the father and the widower had very different attitudes toward the project. Arthur Nicholls's "feeling was against it's [sic] being written; but he yielded to Mr Brontë's impetuous wish."[10] Strangely enough, considering the unflattering portrait she would paint of him, Patrick would remain one of her staunchest supporters, perhaps because it gratified his ambition to see the Brontë name rise from its obscure origins into the pantheon of fame. Nicholls, on the other hand, was not susceptible to the magic of celebrity and instinctively regarded the biography as an intrusive act of desecration. He submitted to Patrick, reluctantly conceding that an authorized life might stem the tide of gossip, because he felt duty-bound to keep on good terms with the father-in-law who had initially opposed his marriage, but with whom he would now live until the old man died, in 1861.

Mrs. Gaskell left the Parsonage with her first cache of material—a dozen or so letters written by Charlotte in her early twenties to members of her family.[11] She then proceeded to make contact with Ellen Nussey, who would give her the richest crop of letters, over three hundred,[12] assuring her that "the more fully she—Charlotte Brontë—the *friend,* the *daughter,* the *sister,* the *wife,* is known, and known where need be in her own words, the more highly will she be appreciated."[13]

This could have been the leitmotif of the *Life.* It perfectly expresses Gaskell's aim of painting a picture of the private Charlotte which would counteract the impression given by the public figure of Currer Bell. If Gaskell was particularly keen to get hold of letters to the respectable, unintellectual, ladylike Ellen, with whom Charlotte did not choose to discuss her literary ambitions, it was because they were bound to reflect the feminine, domestic image she was hoping to create in the biography. Charlotte would have been more open in her letters to the independent feminist Mary Taylor, her other close friend from Roe Head days, but unfortunately for posterity Mary destroyed them in a bid to save them from prying eyes.

The letters to Ellen may not have reflected Charlotte's whole self, but Gaskell was right to suppose that they would be extremely valuable in her quest to create a sense of intimacy. If she could quote Charlotte's own words to one of her oldest friends, she would be able to give readers the sense that they were sharing in the closeness of the relationship. Where the substance of the letters was superficially banal—discussions, say, about a new shower bath that Ellen had bought for Charlotte[14]—the sense of sharing in a private world would be all the more poignant. As a result, future enthusiasts would experience the illusion of a highly personal affection for their idol. In 1899, one sentimental author boasted that "Charlotte Brontë had come closer to my heart than many of my living friends."[15]

The intimate atmosphere Gaskell hoped to achieve was actually revolutionary for biography. The fact that Arthur Nicholls was so shocked when he discovered how extensively Gaskell intended to quote from Charlotte's personal correspondence goes to show how unimaginably intimate the *Life* was. The widower initially assumed that the biographer wanted access to her subject's letters for information purposes only, and he would have to be forcibly coerced—a joint effort by Gaskell and George Smith—into signing over the copyright.[16]

Contemporary biographies of men by men—such as Samuel Smiles's best-selling life of the engineer George Stephenson, which also came out in 1857—paid scant attention to their subjects' childhood, home environment, and emotional life, preferring instead to chart their public achievements.[17] Gaskell, on the other hand, was determined to foreground these private areas in her drive to domesticate Currer Bell's image.

Details which would never have made their way into the biography of a famous man are given unusual prominence. A whole page is given over to a letter to Ellen of 1851 in which Charlotte discusses the clothes she has bought recently: how she has changed a black lace cloak for a white one as it goes better with her black satin dress, how she has bought a bonnet with a pink lining, how she has resisted splashing out on expensive colored silks and gone for black instead. The quotation lets us share an everyday private moment between two female friends, but is also used by Gaskell as proof of Miss Brontë's "feminine taste" and "love for modest, dainty, neat attire," moral indicators of her irreproachable womanliness. When Gaskell goes so far as to quote Charlotte's comments on her underwear—". . . some chemisettes of small size, (the full woman's size don't fit me) both of simple style for every day and good quality for best"—it is not difficult to understand why the biography might have made Arthur Nicholls feel violated and embarrassed on behalf of his dead wife.[18]

In offering this private, domestic angle, Gaskell opened up a space to the public view which was specifically female but which was also the stuff of the Victorian novel. Her careful deployment of apparently trivial homely details—about clothing or housework or a servant's pleasure on being given a present by her mistress—simultaneously created a womanly atmosphere while providing the sort of texture typically used by classic realist novelists to create an illusion of real life. Her novelist's instinct had been activated almost as soon as she had begun to think about the biography. A couple of weeks before she first got in touch with Ellen, she had tellingly told another correspondent that her aim was "to form a picture of her [Charlotte's] character, & a drama of her life in my own mind," suggesting that she was already conscious of actively sculpting her material into an aesthetic shape.[19]

In the event, Gaskell's telling of the Brontë story would be such that, as one reviewer noted, "This biography opens precisely like a novel, and the skilful arrangements of lights and shades and colours—the prominence of some objects and the evident suppression of others—leave upon the mind the excitement of a highly wrought drama, rather than the simplicity of daylight and nature."[20] As we have seen, the basic idea for the opening—a sweeping view of Haworth narrowing to a close-up of the Parsonage—had in fact been in Gaskell's mind since her first meeting with Charlotte. The reviewer could have added that the novels it resembled were Gaskell's own: *Mary Barton* opens in the fields around Manchester, scanning the groups of early-evening walkers and eventually homing in on the Barton family, while *Ruth*'s first paragraphs describe the history and architecture of "an assize-town in one of the eastern counties," eventually closing in on one house to find the heroine on the stairs.[21]

In the *Life*, however, the journey up the hill to the Parsonage does not end there, but in the church, and discloses not the heroine herself but the Brontë funeral tablet, crowded with so many names, so many successive deaths (Gaskell got the ever-obliging John Greenwood to copy it out for her). From the very start, she brings us face to face with tragedy, thus overcasting the rest of the book with a shadow of sorrow to come, which the protagonists could never have anticipated as they went unknowingly about the business of day-to-day living.

This rhetorical technique—known as narrative prolepsis—is a prime example of the sort of literary trickery Gaskell liked to use in her efforts to seize the reader's sympathy. The fatalism which would become such an integral part of the Brontë myth derives from Gaskell's habit of constantly looking forward to the story's tragic end, her reminders that "the dark cloud was hanging over that doomed household, and gathering blackness every hour."[22] She can only ever bring herself to admit that the youthful Brontës might have had fun—for example, quoting a letter to Ellen in which Charlotte describes a visit from their friends Mary and Martha Taylor—by immediately adding that such merriment "is now utterly swept away."[23]

It was this dramatic fatalism that gave future generations—as one enthusiast put it in 1914—"the impression that, at the Haworth Parsonage, when the Brontës lived there, life and poetry went hand in hand, life was poetry; not seldom, indeed, tragedy and poetry were life."[24] This is exactly the sort of confused attitude Henry James had in mind when he complained that the Brontë story had become a beguiled infatuation. As he put it, "Literature is an objective, a projected result; it is life that is the unconscious, the agitated, the struggling, floundering cause. But the fashion has been, in looking at the Brontés [sic] so to confound the cause with the result that we cease to know, in the presence of such ecstasies, what we have hold of or what we are talking about."[25]

If Gaskell's legacy was to make the public mistake life for literature, it is not, however, surprising. All life-writing (as Virginia Woolf called it) is a paradoxical process whereby the fragmentary business of lived experience is molded into a formal literary structure and given an artificial sense of direction. Etymologically, even the word "biography"—"life-writing"—is an oxymoron. At some level, all biographers borrow some of their narrative techniques from fictional storytelling, but Gaskell had more literary skill than most, and in her hands the Brontés' history did indeed become poetic.

As Gaskell shaped the evidence—personal impressions, letters, anecdotes, local history—into her own drama of Charlotte's life, she adopted many tactics she had learned as a novelist. She had a particular talent for colorful scene-painting, which she exploited, say, in her depiction of Patrick's violent tempers, but she also knew how to wait for the right moment to pull out the rhetorical stops. Her account of the journey up to Haworth, for example, does not deny the factual realities of the place, tersely documenting the factories and other evidence of commerce and manufacturing on the hills. Yet she acknowledges the existence of these unromantic landmarks in such flat, unemphatic tones that they slip entirely from the reader's memory. What sticks is the highly colored poetic description of the "sinuous wave-like hills . . . crowned with wild, bleak moors—grand, from the ideas of solitude and loneliness which they suggest, or oppressive from the feeling which they give of being pent-up by some monotonous and illimitable barrier."[26] Here, as so often in the *Life,* the imagery of tragic isolation Gaskell creates overwhelms the facts she documents.

There was, however, one area in which Gaskell was determined to remain as unromantic as possible: Charlotte's relationships with men. *Jane Eyre* and *Villette* had been criticized for their too passionate treatment of love. As a result, Gaskell felt driven by the need to portray her heroine as irreproachably sexless. While she was keen to foreground Charlotte's friendship with Ellen, there were other relationships from which she averted her gaze. One of these was Charlotte's friendship with George Smith, who had published Currer Bell's novels and would now publish Gaskell's *Life.*

Though Gaskell would quote from some of Charlotte's letters to Smith in the biography, she would offer no real analysis of their relationship, which had in fact been far warmer than a simple business connection, though he eventually cooled toward her and she came to the conclusion that he was too superficial to deserve her complete respect.[27] Perhaps Smith succeeded in keeping Gaskell in the dark about the intimacy—he only let her see a very limited number of Charlotte's letters to him[28]—but since she was now dependent on his editorial support she would not have made any attempt to scrutinize it, even if she had suspected something. Gaskell's personal contact with her subject and those she knew gave her an enormous advantage over later biographers, but it also, in this case as in others, compromised her vision. She would never have risked embarrassing Smith by suggesting he had flirted with his prized authoress.

Gaskell's gossipy temperament meant, however, that other men were not safe from her embarrassing revelations. Those whose advances had been repulsed by Charlotte could be dangled in front of the reader to show that, whatever her books might have implied, Miss Brontë herself was not "easily susceptible" to "the passion of love."[29] Gaskell was happy to reveal that Charlotte had received—and turned down—a surprise proposal of marriage from another Smith, Elder employee, a choleric Scotsman called James Taylor (though unnamed in the *Life,* he would have had no difficulty recognizing himself). Since Charlotte found Taylor physically repulsive—his presence made her veins run ice—it was not hard to make her rejection of him seem like a rejection of passion per se. With amazing disregard for the widower's feelings, Gaskell would also describe Charlotte's refusal of Arthur Nicholls's first proposal to show how "quietly and modestly" the author of *Jane Eyre*—"she, on whom such hard judgments had been passed by ignorant reviewers"—had received a "vehement, passionate declaration of love."[30]

Gaskell's urge to prove that Charlotte was passion-free in her dealings with men was exacerbated by her desire to cover up what she discovered when she made a fact-finding trip to Brussels in May 1856. She had planned to interview both of the Hegers about Charlotte's time as a student at their school. But when she arrived, Madame, understanding that she was a friend of Charlotte Brontë's, refused to see her. She was received instead by Monsieur, whose wife's strange behavior was immediately explained when he showed or read her the passionate letters Charlotte had written him after her return to England.

Gaskell had always had her suspicions about Charlotte's time in Brussels. When she first read *Villette,* she told Lady Kay-Shuttleworth that "it

Patrick Brontë in old age. Gaskell's *Life* made
the Brontës so famous that photographs of
Charlotte's father were soon on sale in
Haworth as tourist souvenirs.

reveals depths in her mind, aye, and in her *heart* too which I doubt if ever
any one has fathomed."[31] Yet when faced with what looked undeniably
like unrequited love for a married man, she decided that as far as the *Life*
was concerned Charlotte's intense emotions for her teacher must remain
unfathomable. Such evidence could not possibly be used, as it went completely against the grain of the morally pure character she was trying to
create. In the finished book, she would quote a few innocuous passages
from the letters, which Heger had copied out for her. Yet she knew that as
long as the full texts existed they represented a ticking time bomb, capable
of exploding the image of propriety she was carefully constructing: "I can
not tell you how I should deprecate anything leading to the publication of
those letters," she told George Smith on August 1, 1856.[32] (The bomb
would not go off until 1913, but when it did it would indeed rip Charlotte's
public image apart.)

Back home after the Brussels trip, Gaskell was feeling more and more
tense about Charlotte's relatives and their relation to her project. She
urgently wanted to see Monsieur Heger's letters to Charlotte—perhaps

she suspected that he had encouraged his pupil in her feelings for him—but was afraid that Arthur Nicholls had destroyed them.[33] The letters have never turned up, but there was no particular reason to point the finger at Nicholls: Charlotte could easily have burned them herself, or buried them, as Lucy Snowe does with Dr. John's letters in *Villette*. But Gaskell had increasingly come to believe that the widower was blocking her access to material.

Nicholls, a cautious and very private man, had always been paranoid about Charlotte's correspondence getting into the public eye, so Gaskell was right to sense his reluctance to cooperate. In the early days of his marriage, he had been shocked at the gossipy freedom with which his wife wrote to Ellen Nussey about the personal affairs of mutual friends. As a result, Ellen had been told to burn Charlotte's letters, though—happily for posterity—she disobeyed his request. Not surprisingly, this had created tension between Ellen and the man she secretly felt had come between her and her oldest friend. When Gaskell started researching the *Life,* it was inevitable that she would find it easier to form a bond with Ellen—who had lovingly kept Charlotte's letters and was eager to share them—than with the husband.

In the summer of 1856, a year into the project, Gaskell realized that despite her fear of Nicholls she would have to pay another visit to Haworth. Even if the letters from Heger had disappeared, there was other material she wanted to see, especially the manuscript of Charlotte's first, unpublished novel, *The Professor.* She told Ellen that she was interested in it for purely literary reasons,[34] but she was also afraid that it might relate to Monsieur Heger "even more distinctly & exclusively than Villette does."[35] If it did, and was published, Gaskell was afraid that Heger might retaliate by making Charlotte's letters public in an attempt to protect himself from possible accusations that he had made advances to his pupil.

Too nervous to brave the Parsonage on her own, this time Gaskell chose as her chaperone the overbearing Sir James Kay-Shuttleworth. His remarkable insensitivity to others' feelings meant that he was able to make quite shameless demands without embarrassment. Janet Malcolm has memorably used the metaphor of the biographer as burglar. In this case, the epithet seems capable of being applied almost literally. As Gaskell excitedly told George Smith afterward: "I have had a very successful visit to Haworth ... accompanied by Sir J P. K Shuttleworth, to whom it is evident that both Mr Brontë & Mr Nicholls look up.—& who is not prevented by the fear of giving pain from asking in a peremptory manner for whatever he thinks desirable. He was extremely kind in forwarding all my objects; and coolly took actual possession of many things while Mr Nicholls was saying he could not possibly part with them."[36]

The material in question included the manuscript of *The Professor*. Once she read it, Gaskell was relieved to discover that its uptight British hero was nothing like Constantin Heger, but her hypersensitivity concerning Charlotte's image led her to find the novel "disfigured by more coarseness, —& profanity in quoting texts of Scripture disagreeably than in any of her other works."[37] Just as alarmingly, the irrepressible Sir James soon announced that he personally intended to edit the manuscript for publication, blind to the fact that he must have been the last person on earth to whom Charlotte would have entrusted her prose.

Eventually, Arthur Nicholls stepped in and took on the job himself. Though he toned down some of Charlotte's original language—"God damn your insolence!" for example, became "Confound . . ."—Nicholls was far less anxious about it than Gaskell, even though, as a conscientious clergyman, he would have had high standards of propriety.[38] Gaskell's determination to detach Charlotte from all that was "coarse"—even if that meant dissociating her from her own writings—was absolute. After she saw the revisions, she wrote to George Smith, "But oh! I wish Mr Nicholls wd have altered more! . . . For I would not, if I could help it, have another syllable that could be called coarse to be associated with her name."[39]

Also among the papers Mrs. Gaskell took away with the help of Sir James were some of the juvenile manuscripts which have subsequently become so celebrated. Gaskell was amazed by the tiny booklets filled with microscopic writing which she interpreted as examples of "creative power carried to the verge of insanity."[40] In this, she was slotting the new discovery into a preconceived idea of the morbidity of Charlotte's literary imagination. She did not view the early writings as the space where the apprentice author first began to hone her craft, but then Gaskell was less interested in Charlotte the ambitious emerging writer than in the suffering woman whose upbringing in an isolated village had fostered unhealthy fancies.

Yet after seeing the juvenilia even Gaskell had to admit that some of the jollier fragments gave a more positive impression of the Brontës' childhood than she had expected. As she wrote in a letter to Emily Shaen, the documents also gave her a "pleasanter" view of Patrick, who was now revealed—to her surprise—to have been the sort of father who brought home presents of toy soldiers and made the effort to share his enthusiasm for politics with his children in terms they could understand.[41] Yet despite this new evidence that Patrick was an involved and caring parent, Gaskell would remain wedded to the caricature she had carried around with her since her very first meeting with Charlotte, branding him in the biography as a man of "misanthropy," opinions "wild and erroneous," and "principles of action eccentric and strange."[42]

Gaskell was well aware that her proposed treatment of Charlotte's father would compromise readers' respect for him. George Smith bluntly told her so in the summer of 1856 after reading the portion of the *Life* she had already begun to draft.[43] Yet she steadfastly refused to tone down her account of the "domestic peculiarities" of Charlotte's childhood.[44] It was of prime importance to her project to establish that her heroine's early life had been one of uniform sorrow and deprivation, as that would secure readers' sympathy while offering both explanation and excuse for the disagreeable aspects of her adult fiction.

Charlotte had lost her mother and sisters, and had experienced the horrors of poor food, harsh discipline, sickness, and death at the Clergy Daughters' School at Cowan Bridge. Gaskell's treatment of this episode was actually comparatively dispassionate and documentary. Charlotte had already dramatized the experience in *Jane Eyre,* and Gaskell saw her duty as being to establish as best she could the facts behind the fiction, suggesting that the novel's "vivid picture" may have made an "over-strong impression" on the public, and distinguishing between the subjective effects of the experience on the child Charlotte and the objective facts of the case.[45] Even so, her researches led her to conclude that the management of the school—particularly the kitchens—really had been very bad, a conclusion accepted by modern scholarly biographers. Where her vision became distorted was in her treatment of the Brontë children's home life.

Gaskell clearly felt that Charlotte's sufferings at Cowan Bridge were not enough and added an unsubstantiated picture of Patrick as a withered eccentric withholding not merely affection but basic foodstuffs from his children. She propagated the completely false idea that he had purposely kept his children on a spartan vegetarian diet, thus contributing to their ill health and eventual early deaths. (The adolescent Charlotte, it is true, disliked meat and tended to avoid it, as was noticed by her fellow pupils at Roe Head,[46] but this personal aversion was not encouraged by her family. Emily and Anne's diary paper of November 24, 1834, refers to the boiled beef they are going to have for dinner.[47])

Gaskell would never quite resolve the disjunction between her preconceived idea of the Brontës' childhood as a time of monotonous misery and the joyful vitality which shone out of Charlotte's early writings. Perhaps her exaggerated emphasis on the harshness and cruelty of Charlotte's childhood can be partly explained by the fact that it tapped into novelistic expectation. *Jane Eyre* itself had been at the forefront of the mid-nineteenth-century interest in the fictional portrayal of children, though Gaskell's picture of a solemn little girl bravely playing guardian to her motherless siblings has a more Dickensian than Brontëan ring to it. Yet her prime need, as ever, was to present Charlotte's life as sanctified by unremitting suffering. This she did, even when the evidence opposed it.

For instance, she repeatedly tells her readers that the Brontë children were "grave and silent beyond their years,"[48] that they knew "nothing of the gaiety and sportiveness of childhood,"[49] or that "[t]o small infantine gaieties they were unaccustomed."[50] Yet she goes on to quote at length Charlotte's "History of the Year," in which the thirteen-year-old recalls with relish the "plays" she and her siblings invented two to three years before, remembering how she and Emily had jumped boisterously out of bed to snatch up Branwell's new soldiers as soon as he appeared with them at their door. The extract quoted reveals a warm and informal household, with Anne kneeling on a kitchen chair to look longingly at some cakes; another quoted passage is equally lively, with the children refusing to go to bed and cheekily asking the servant why she is looking so glum.[51]

Gaskell must have privately justified her treatment of Patrick—exploiting his support for a biography in which she planned to pillory him—by believing she was doing it for the greater good of saving Charlotte's reputation. As the *Life* began to take literary shape, she became as ruthless as Charlotte had been in her novels when it came to using real-life characters as raw material. But because she was writing nonfiction, Gaskell was treading on far more dangerous ground.

She must have been aware of this, since she asked Smith in October 1856, "Do you mind the law of libel[?]"[52] There were three people she thought she was in danger of libeling, including Emily and Anne's unscrupulous publisher Thomas Newby, and Elizabeth Rigby (now Lady Eastlake), the reviewer who had lambasted *Jane Eyre* in the *Quarterly Review* by arguing that if the author was female she must be a woman who had "long forfeited the society of her own sex."[53] In the event, neither of these two caused any fuss. But the third person she mentioned, Lady Scott, would indeed threaten legal action when she saw herself in the published *Life*.

During her previous marriage to a Mr. Robinson, Lady Scott had had an affair with Branwell Brontë, who was employed as tutor to her son. Anne Brontë, who had been working as a governess in the same household, had been in the excruciating position of having to witness the adulterers' relationship as it developed. As soon as Mr. Robinson got wind of the affair, Branwell was dismissed and returned to Haworth. By the end of that year, 1845, Charlotte, Emily, and Anne had begun to put together the volume of *Poems* which would start their literary careers. Branwell, however, had become increasingly distressed, particularly after the newly widowed Mrs. Robinson rejected him. By the time of his death, in September 1848, he was in a state of mental and physical collapse exacerbated by alcohol and drug abuse.

Though she knew that the former Mrs. Robinson might invoke the libel laws, Gaskell recklessly determined to use this story as one of the key episodes in the *Life*. It is not known whether she had documentary proof of the affair beyond what she had gathered from Patrick and Charlotte and from general gossip (Juliet Barker suggests, intriguingly, that she may have seen letters written by Branwell to his friend the Haworth sexton John Brown describing the process of the affair).[54] She did know, however, that what she was doing was risky. Yet she could not resist writing about it in such a way that the "wicked woman"[55] in question, though unnamed, was easily recognizable to those who knew her.

Why, when she knew the dangers, was she so ready to make such a passionate personal attack? The rhetoric with which she presented Branwell's affair was highly emotional and morally charged: Gaskell even used the *Life* as a public forum in which to exhort the fallen Lady Scott to repent. In reality, she was less concerned with the state of Lady Scott's soul than with her own need to find extenuating circumstances to show how Charlotte, Emily, and Anne could have produced such unwomanly novels. As she explained in a letter to George Smith: "[I]t is a horrid story, & I should not have told it but to show the life of prolonged suffering those Brontë girls had to endure; & what doubtless familiarised them to a certain degree with coarse expressions, such as have been complained of in *W. H* & the Tenant of Wildfell Hall . . . you see *why* I wanted to contrast the two lives, don't you?"[56]

The Robinson affair provided contrast both moral and aesthetic. On the one hand, Branwell and his lover could be represented as both the cause and the source of the unacceptable side of the Brontës' writing. Echoing Charlotte's defense of her sisters in the "Biographical Notice,"

Haworth Parsonage and church, photographed c. 1860

A romanticized drawing made by Mrs. Gaskell
to illustrate her *Life of Charlotte Brontë*

Gaskell could insist that the novels' passion, violence, and bad language were not the product of their creators' imaginations, but were naive copies from reality, derived from "the hard cruel facts, pressed down, by external life, upon their very senses, for long months and years together."[57]

On the other hand, from a narrative point of view, the story was irresistibly appealing to the novelist's imagination. Adultery was a key motif of nineteenth-century fiction (Flaubert's *Madame Bovary,* perhaps the greatest example of the adultery novel, came out the same year as the *Life,* 1857), and Mrs. Robinson also gave Gaskell the opportunity to create a Madonna/whore dichotomy familiar to readers of the Victorian novel. Cast as the unregenerate fallen woman, she could be used as a foil to Charlotte, who was presented as the embodiment of feminine purity. Even the matter of dress offered a study in contrast. Where Charlotte is frequently praised for "her love for modest, dainty, neat attire,"[58] Mrs. Robinson is castigated as "a showy woman for her age," desporting herself in the gay ballrooms of Mayfair.[59]

At the moment of crisis, when Branwell returns home in disgrace, Gaskell whips up her style to a pitch of alliterative melodrama in which the protagonists are reduced to histrionic silhouettes: "[T]he blind father [Patrick was suffering from cataracts, later cured by a successful operation] sat stunned, sorely tempted to curse the profligate woman, who had tempted his boy—his only son—into the deep disgrace of deadly crime."[60] As the emotional temperature increases, the accusations get wilder, until the "depraved" woman[61] is eventually accused not merely of having had an affair but of killing off the Brontë sisters, those "innocent victims, whose premature deaths may, in part, be laid at her door."[62]

As well as realizing the theatrical potential of Branwell's disgrace, Gaskell found that she could put it to a more specific narrative use. She had to suppress her knowledge of Charlotte's infatuation for Monsieur Heger, but she also had to find a plausible explanation, consistent with psychological realism, for why Charlotte left Brussels when she did and why she fell into such a deep depression on her return home. By massaging the chronology to give the impression that Branwell's downfall had occurred earlier than it really had, Gaskell could lay the blame for Charlotte's torment on anxiety about her brother.[63] Branwell's adulterous affair was thus neatly made to stand in for the unrequited feelings Charlotte herself had had for a married man, leaving the heroine of the *Life* unsullied by any hint of sexual passion.

In plot terms, Branwell's fall came just as his sisters began to write the books which would shock society and make them famous. From Gaskell's point of view, the order in which these events were narrated was important, not so much because she wanted to establish a correct chronology for the historical record, but because she wanted to have worked her audience into a suitable mood before mentioning the unmentionable novels. Her strategy depended on securing pity and forgiveness for Charlotte, Emily, and Anne by building up a picture of the domestic tragedies they heroically endured *before* acknowledging that they had been working away at their writing all the while. In a similar way, she gives us over three pages on the sisters' caring anxiety about Patrick's eye trouble before alerting us to the fact that *Wuthering Heights, Agnes Grey,* and *The Professor* had already been completed by this stage.

Jane Eyre itself is introduced only after a direct, emotional appeal to the reader. Gaskell piles on clause after clause of excuse before she can bring herself to refer to the novel itself at the end of the sentence: "Think of her home, and the black shadow of remorse lying over one in it, till his very brain was mazed, and his gifts and his life were lost;—think of her father's sight hanging on a thread;—of her sisters' delicate health, and dependence on her care;—and then admire as it deserves to be admired, the steady courage which could work away at 'Jane Eyre.' "[64]

This was the novel Gaskell worried about most, as its heroine had been so closely associated with its author. Where critics had called Jane bold, brazen, and improper, she was determined that the Charlotte of the *Life* would be modest, quiet, and a model of "patient docility."[65] Gaskell would prove that, while Charlotte's literary imagination may have taken the impress of her cruel environment, her behavior as a woman was beyond criticism. Rather than "murmuring against God's appointment,"[66] as the critics said the rebellious Jane had done, Gaskell's Charlotte was made to embrace woman's traditional role within the home, willingly accepting "the supremacy of that duty which God, in placing us in families, has laid out for us."[67]

Gaskell was keen to show that Charlotte's writing in no way interfered with her housekeeping. So she described how, during the excitement of composing *Jane Eyre,* she would never allow herself to become carried away and forget her duties. The old servant Tabby was losing her sight, but was too proud to admit that she could not see clearly enough to cut the bad bits out of the potatoes. Charlotte, therefore, would "steal into the kitchen, and quietly carry off the bowl of vegetables, without Tabby's being aware, and breaking off in the full flow of interest and inspiration in her writing, carefully cut out the specks in the potatoes, and noiselessly carry them back to their place." Just in case the reader had missed the point, Gaskell pointed out the moral: "This little proceeding may show how orderly and fully she accomplished her duties, even at those times when the 'possession' was upon her." The adverbs are signposts of Charlotte's womanliness: "quietly . . . carefully . . . noiselessly . . . orderly."[68]

While Gaskell believed that it was as much a sacred duty for a woman as for a man to make use of a God-given talent, she was also keen to show that Miss Brontë had not been unduly ambitious or pushy in her quest to become an author. The courage with which she and her sisters had doggedly sent their manuscripts from one publishing house to the next might have been read as a sign of unfeminine self-assertion. So Gaskell told her readers of "a little circumstance" which would convince them of "Miss Brontë's inexperience of the ways of the world, and willing deference to the opinion of others": "She had written to a publisher about one of her manuscripts, which she had sent him, and, not receiving any reply, she consulted her brother as to what could be the reason for the prolonged silence. He at once set it down to her not having enclosed a postage-stamp in her letter."[69] The point was to show the creator of the fiery *Jane Eyre* defering to superior male judgment. (Branwell's advice was less valuable than Gaskell implies. At the time, George Smith had thought it extremely odd when he received an unsolicited postage stamp from Currer Bell, who had clearly picked up some strange ideas about publishers' parsimony.)[70]

At other moments, Gaskell looked for evidence which would reveal her heroine's ladylike modesty. Writing to George Smith in December 1856, she enthused over a passage in one of Charlotte's letters in which she wrote approvingly of how Smith's mother used to watch over her in social situations: "I liked the surveillance; it seemed to keep guard over me." Gaskell thought this perfect for the biography, as it showed "a nice feminine sense of confidence & pleasure in protection—chaperonage—whatever you like to call it; which is a piece of womanliness (as opposed to the common ideas of her being a 'strong-minded emancipated' woman) which I should like to bring out."[71]

When Patrick had originally approached Gaskell, he had specifically asked for the account of his daughter's life to be "brief" and for a critical appreciation of her works. The biographer, who had always found Miss Brontë more sympathetic than Currer Bell, inverted this hierarchy, calculatedly refusing to offer an in-depth discussion of *Jane Eyre*. She made no attempt to defend the novel on a literary basis, lamely announcing, "I am

Arthur Bell Nicholls.
Unlike her father, Charlotte's husband
regarded Gaskell's
biography as a painful intrusion.

not going to write an analysis of a book with which every one who reads this biography is sure to be acquainted."[72]

Instead, she turned the full force of her wrath on the critics who had attacked the novel, working up her style to a climax of religious rhetoric in which she sounded more like a preacher than a biographer: Charlotte had led a wild and struggling and isolated life; her only social contacts had been "plain and outspoken Northerns, unskilled in the euphuisms [*sic*] which assist the polite world to skim over the mention of vice" (having put so much emphasis on Charlotte's friendship with the ladylike Ellen, it is hard to see how Gaskell could have justified these remarks); her poor lapsed brother had led her into further familiarity with vice; bereavement had left the hearthstone of her home bare of life and love. How, then, could the reviewer presume to judge? He should rather pray with the Publican than judge with the Pharisee.[73]

Emphasis on her heroine's patient submission to her sufferings, combined with a parallel emphasis on her "womanliness," formed the core of the iconic image Gaskell was trying to get across to her readers. She knew that strongly chiseled lines, rather than blurred edges, were needed if she was going to succeed in reversing public opinion on the subject of Currer Bell. However, despite a superficial consistency in Gaskell's characterization of Charlotte, the *Life* contains a far more complex undertow, and this is perhaps what makes it such a fascinating work of art. It is in the gaps and the contradictions beneath the surface that deeper truths come through about the inevitable struggles of the woman writer in Victorian England.

At the moment Charlotte becomes a published author, Gaskell writes: "Henceforward Charlotte Brontë's existence becomes divided into two parallel currents—her life as Currer Bell, the author; her life as Charlotte Brontë the woman. There were separate duties belonging to each character—not opposing each other; not impossible, but difficult to be reconciled."[74] This reflects the genuine inner tension between the two sides of Charlotte's personality, the respectable clergyman's daughter and the unconventional author. But it is also an acknowledgment of how difficult Gaskell herself was finding the process of transforming Currer Bell into an exemplar of modest, self-sacrificing femininity.

Although Gaskell was tempted to effect the reconciliation by suppressing or downplaying the unpalatable aspects of Currer Bell, she could not quite bring herself to silence the real Charlotte, who often seems to be trying to break out of her saintly straitjacket. In fact, some of Charlotte's own remarks, quoted in the biography, stand as a rebuke to Gaskell's feminizing strategy. It is particularly ironic when Gaskell quotes Charlotte telling G. H. Lewes, "I wished critics would judge me as an *author,* not as a woman," as the *Life*'s whole strategy is to get readers to judge Charlotte as a woman, not an author.[75]

In fact, the extensive quotations from Charlotte's correspondence often conflict with the womanly image Gaskell is trying so hard to construct. It is extraordinary how much of the ambitious, assertive Charlotte gets through. Gaskell even includes a section from the bitingly satirical letter the young Charlotte wrote to Hartley Coleridge after he had failed to praise the story she sent him.[76] She cuts the most unladylike passage—in which Charlotte ridicules Dickens and his fellow male writers as "boarding-school misses"—and apologizes for the flippant tone, which she explains away by supposing it to be derived from Branwell's unwholesome influence. But she includes enough of Charlotte's text to suggest a young woman of angry self-confidence.

Elsewhere, however, Gaskell turns a blind eye to Charlotte's ambition. She quotes a section of one of the letters to Monsieur Heger, in which

Charlotte expresses a terror of losing her sight (an understandable fear in the context of her father's blindness) and goes on to reveal her desire to write a book and dedicate it to her *maître de littérature*. These literary hopes are passed over without comment. Instead, Gaskell dwells on the eye problems. Shortsightedness, she tells us, meant that Charlotte the good housewife had to forgo sewing and take up knitting instead, and that she tried to avoid writing wherever possible at this period.[77] (Her bad eyesight may not have mattered too much. As the girls at Roe Head noticed to their astonishment, Charlotte had taught herself to write with her eyes shut, a telling metaphor for shutting out the external world and entering the inner life.)[78]

Despite such interpretations, the assertive Charlotte does emerge, particularly in the second half of the book, which covers the period of her success as a writer. Here, Gaskell's narrative is almost swamped by the number of letters which are quoted at great length. The novelistic feel of the earlier chapters gives way to a different style of presentation, which belongs more to the "life and letters" tradition of Victorian literary biography. Some of these letters contain accounts of the deaths in Charlotte's family, more moving in their unself-conscious emotions than Gaskell's melodramatic references to "doom" or apostrophes to the reader demanding sympathy. But if these letters chime in with the image of the woman made perfect by sufferings, others, addressed to literary men on literary subjects, show Charlotte to have been confident and even abrasive in her own opinions, not a modest creature meekly defering to her brother's views on publishers and postage stamps.

These lengthy, undigested passages of quotation, paying testimony to Charlotte the writer, would always be there for anyone who wanted to read them. But they could not compete for attention with Gaskell's direct emotional appeals, which grabbed the public by the throat. As a girl in the 1870s, for example, the novelist May Sinclair devoured the *Life* with a passion, but "skipped all the London part, and Charlotte's literary letters."[79] In this way, many readers would simply accept the biography's surface reading of its heroine as a domestic martyr, and fail to notice the more complex reality between the lines.

In fact, *The Life of Charlotte Brontë* is riven with conflicts and contradictions all the way through. Constantly treading an uneasy line between factual research and novelistic presentation, it seems unsure as to what sort of book it is trying to be. On the one hand, Gaskell lets out hints that she is knowingly in the business of myth-making, scattering her narrative with odd references to fairy tale, Classical mythology, and Norse legend. As her novels show, she believed that storytelling—from Greek tragedy to gossip—was part of the web that held society together.[80] In the *Life,* she is tempted to follow this instinct for archetypal narrative and often reduces her subjects to simplified stock characters—the scarlet woman, the dutiful daughter, the wastrel son. But this contrasts with, say, her more documentary handling of the Cowan Bridge episode, or with her subtler use of Charlotte's letters, which are often allowed to speak for themselves in all their complex humanity. Her interpretations are presented with a simplified moral or dramatic force which frequently belies the multitextured evidence she presents. There are many different, sometimes conflicting, strands to the narrative she tells.

Over time, this multiplicity would enable the *Life* to be read in different ways by different readers. Many would embrace the idea of Charlotte as a saint capable of superhuman suffering, while others would respond instead to the very ordinariness of the story as charted in the everyday intimacy of her very middle-class friendship with Ellen Nussey. In contrast, others still would only be able to see Gaskell's larger-than-life fatalism, concentrating on doom and melodrama and isolation; while yet others would see the biography as a testimony to the problems of self-definition for Victorian women writers. Its ability to be read in so many different ways is one of the reasons the *Life* continues to survive. Despite the fact that its accuracy has been questioned again and again by subsequent biographers, no new account has ever overtaken this ur-biography, whose literary power has never been matched by any other life of the Brontës.

Though she had been so desperate to write it, it is not surprising that "this unlucky book," as she later called it, caused Gaskell profound unease.[81] Apart from the artistic difficulties of working in an unfamiliar genre, the *Life* was also the repository of her tense relationship with Arthur Nicholls and Patrick Brontë, and her suppressed guilt about the way she had disregarded their feelings. As soon as she finished it she decided to run away, leaving the country for an extended Continental holiday on February 13, 1857.[82] She wanted to be completely incommunicado at the time of publication. At the back of her mind, fears of libel lawyers as well as critics were nagging.

The Life of Charlotte Brontë was published on March 25, 1857.[83] It was so successful that a reprint was needed within a matter of weeks.[84] Soon, however, Gaskell's anxieties materialized, in the form of a letter from solicitors representing Lady Scott. Acting in something of a panic on behalf of his absent wife, William Gaskell and his lawyers capitulated immediately. By the end of May, all unsold copies of the *Life* had been recalled and a retraction of the allegations against Lady Scott had been printed in the *Times*. The *Athenaeum* subsequently addressed its readers, apologizing for having given the *Life* a good review and for mistakenly placing its trust in a biographer as an "accurate collector of facts."[85]

The former Mrs. Robinson was not the only person to complain. When Gaskell finally got home she found herself "in the Hornet's nest with a vengeance" and was forced to revise whole sections of the book.[86] The chapter which dealt with Branwell's downfall was rewritten, omitting all accusations against Lady Scott. Yet the legal gag imposed by the "wicked woman" could not stop the story, once out, from propagating itself through culture in a number of melodramatic guises. Branwell's tale of fatal attraction would eventually take its place in the Brontë legend. In *Empurpled Moors*, for example, a play of 1932 by Oscar W. Firkins, an unlikely assignation takes place in Haworth between Mrs. Robinson and Branwell, who becomes a sub-Byronic hero in a cloak uttering such lines as "I am the flue by which passions that are not mine reach their surface . . . blackening the track by which they go."[87]

Nevertheless, Lady Scott's vigorous use of the law managed to inject enough doubt into the case to turn the Robinson affair into a tantalizing mystery, prompting speculation from future biographers as to what had really gone on. Branwell's acquaintance Francis Leyland published a biography in 1886 which claimed that the whole affair had been the delusion of a madman's brain, a theory designed to defend Branwell's morals but not so flattering to his mental health. (Unfortunately for his argument, he took as an analogy the allegation that Byron had had an affair with his half-sister Augusta. Leyland claimed this was an invention by Byron's spurned and maddened wife, but in fact the incestuous relationship had been only too real.)

In 1960, Daphne du Maurier would suggest that the story had been invented to cover up a far darker crime, hinting that Branwell had been dismissed instead for sexually abusing or otherwise corrupting the Robinsons' son.[88] Ironically, for the previous hundred years, proof of the affair had in fact been sitting in the commonplace book of Gaskell's friend the poet and politician Richard Monckton Milnes (Lord Houghton), who had visited Haworth in October 1859, seen Branwell's letters to John Brown detailing the affair, and made a note of some of their contents. Yet it took until the 1990s for this evidence to come, serendipitously, to the notice of

Juliet Barker, when Lord Houghton's notes were brought to her attention by Miss Diana Chardin of Trinity College Library, who had discovered them.[89]

The other major revisions Gaskell was forced to make for the third edition of the *Life* concerned the Clergy Daughters' School and its founder, William Carus Wilson, whose supporters started a campaign to justify him in the press.[90] By this time, Gaskell had little energy for a fight and soon climbed down, rewriting the chapter in such a way as to remove the blame for the Brontës' sufferings from Wilson personally, though she kept up her attack on the school's poor food, spoiled by a careless cook, and its unhealthy location.

Further complaints were made by numerous individuals who had been connected with Charlotte. "Every one who has been harmed in this unlucky book complains of some thing," Gaskell moaned.[91] Even minor characters were upset. Harriet Martineau was cross that her breach with Charlotte over *Villette* should have been publicized, and insisted on her version of the events being included in the third edition.[92] Two of the Brontës' former servants requested a reference from Patrick stating that they had not, as the *Life* had implied, been wasteful with food. A local girl could not bear to see herself described as having been "seduced"; the word was changed to "betrayed."[93] Unsurprisingly, Patrick asked Gaskell to remove the untrue anecdotes about his cruelties and eccentricities. She made the requested changes, but to little avail, since the overcolored portrait of the first edition would feed irreversibly into popular legend.

Certainly, Gaskell had allowed her literary instincts to obscure the fact that she was dealing with real people. But she had produced an image of the Brontë family which would imprint itself indelibly on the collective mind, often supplanting interest in the Brontës' novels. If Gaskell had never written the *Life,* one would not find later biographers, like this one from the 1920s, confidently declaring of Charlotte that "for every single individual who reads her books today, it is probably true to say that there are a hundred who find an absorbing interest in the story of her life."[94] Gaskell's intention may have been to promote an ideal of female authorship by showing that women writers need not compromise their femininity or moral virtue. Yet her underlying anxieties about the Brontë novels prevented her from straightforwardly championing the authors for their intellectual or literary talents and ambitions.

Her legacy can be seen in the entry under "Brontë" in the 1911 *Encyclopaedia Britannica,* still regarded as one of the monuments of reference literature. It provides fewer than twenty lines of comment on the works, compared to 236 lines on the lives. Heathcliff is not mentioned, but biographical trivia such as the fact that Charlotte visited the Great Exhibition in 1851 are considered crucial enough for inclusion. The author, Clement Shorter, admits that the "bare recital of the Brontë story can give no idea of its undying interest, its exceeding pathos" and goes on to opine, revealingly, "Their life as told by their biographer Mrs. Gaskell is as interesting as any novel."

A comparison with the *Encyclopaedia*'s entry for George Eliot shows how differently a canonical female novelist could be presented even at that date. Written, perhaps significantly, by a woman,[95] it offers a detailed critical appraisal of Eliot's fiction and nonfiction and compares her work with that of other leading novelists, such as Thackeray, Tolstoy, and Balzac. The implications are obvious. Eliot is as valued for her mind as are these men, while the Brontës, celebrated instead for the tragedy of their home lives, are still effectively barred from entering the male bastion of literary achievement.

CHAPTER FOUR

The Angel in the House

Elizabeth Gaskell's *Life of Charlotte Brontë* was intended as a memorial to the dead, but it also marked the birth of the Brontës as cultural icons. Within a few years of its publication in 1857, pilgrims began making their way to Haworth, shorter, derivative biographies began to appear, and Charlotte took on the status of a secular saint, redefined in the popular mind as a moral as much as a literary figure. By the 1880s, she had become so famous that a book offering a supposedly comprehensive list of the Worthies of the World included her as one of only four women on the roll call, the others being Joan of Arc, Elizabeth I, and Queen Victoria.[1] Gaskell had reinvented her in such a way that the appeal of "Charlotte Brontë" rested as much on her symbolic value as on her identity as a real, historical person.

The Life of Charlotte Brontë may have been dogged by controversy when it first came out, but in image terms it scored a brilliant public relations success, transforming the coarse Currer Bell into the valiant heroine perfected by sufferings. Under its influence, even the prickly Harriet Martineau seemed to forget that Miss Brontë had been merely human. In a review of the *Life,* she now assessed the woman she had criticized for excessive passion in idealized, explicitly saintly, terms: "[L]ittle as Charlotte Brontë [*sic*] knew it, she was earning for herself a better title than many a St. Catherine, or St. Bridget, for a place among the noble ones whose virtues are carved out of rock and will endure to the end."[2]

Such emphasis on Charlotte's moral and spiritual qualities, rather than on her achievements as a writer, was shared by most critics. The *Spectator* thought Charlotte "remarkable" for the "sense of duty to which everything in her life was subordinated": hers was a story of "the martyr's pang and the saint's victory."[3] The *Economist* found its "utmost admiration" excited by her "daily self denials" and "hourly proofs of moral rectitude," impressed by the way in which she "ever performed her woman's part with a persistency of gentle willingness."[4] And the *Manchester Examiner and Times* praised her "Christian fortitude . . . solemn resignation . . . and . . .

exemplary patience."[5] Considering how keen she was to feminize Charlotte's image, Gaskell would have been particularly gratified by the assessment in *Fraser's* magazine: "[I]t is a life always womanly."[6]

The decision to concentrate on Charlotte Brontë the woman rather than Currer Bell the author had paid off. Many readers must have shared Charles Kingsley's shame at having previously dismissed this saintly paragon as coarse. There were still a few dissenters who refused to forget that Charlotte had been charged with having written immoral fiction. *The Christian Observer* continued to find it necessary to fulminate against *Jane Eyre* as a tale whose moral "is obviously as bad as can well be conceived" and which "encourages the conviction that ungovernable passion is an apology for every other vice."[7] Yet this was the exception that proved the rule. In general, Charlotte's rehabilitation was accomplished at a stroke.

The immediate effect of the *Life* on the public imagination was to make Charlotte an icon of exemplary womanhood. In its emphasis on spiritual heroism, it appealed directly to the sensibility of its age. Belief in biography as a moral force capable of changing the lives of its readers was becoming increasingly influential in the 1850s. The Victorian habit of hagiography was not merely a question of sycophantic respect for the dead, since biography was a didactic tool, and as such, it needed to provide aspirational ideals rather than warts-and-all reality. In her review of Gaskell's *Life,* Harriet Martineau had echoed the views of many when she compared contemporary biography to the saints' lives of the Middle Ages, and to Plutarch's biographies, "the instructors of the pagan world." These works, she observed, were intended as a spur to action: "In the heroes, and the confessors, and martyrs, men saw before them examples of what they, too, might become."[8]

The classic exponent of biography designed to have an impact on the real lives of its readers was Samuel Smiles, whose full-length life of George Stephenson had come out in the same year as Gaskell's *Life.* Famous for the optimistic individualism of his classic tract, *Self-Help* (1859), he became one of the most influential Victorian popular biographers with his best-selling *Lives of the Engineers* (1861–62). In *Self-Help,* Smiles preached the benefits of independence, energy, industry, and thrift, promising readers that it was in their own power to improve their lot. Exemplary lives were an important part of his philosophy: "Good rules may do much," he wrote, "but good models far more, for in the latter we have instruction in action—wisdom at work."[9] Preferring "life rather than literature, action rather than study," he valued biography as a moral inspiration and a practical tool: "Biographies of great . . . men are . . . most instructive and useful as helps, guides, and incentives to others."[10]

Anthologies such as *Lives of the Engineers* looked back to Plutarch's pithy, moralizing Roman portraits and represented one of the most successful genres of the nineteenth century. Mostly, they taught by good example, though one pathetic title, *Wrecked Lives; or, Men Who Have Failed*, suggests there could also be a cautionary element.[11] An indication of the marketability of this type of book is shown in Trollope's novel, *The Way We Live Now* (1875), which opens with Lady Carbury, a hack author, writing to the editor of the *Morning Breakfast Table* in the hope of securing a good review for her latest offering. We are left in no doubt about her mercenary motives, and this is underlined by the fact that she has chosen a saleable genre, the biographical anthology. Her title, however, falls parodically short of the plain-living, high-thinking standards of Samuel Smiles. Rather than inspiring her readers with tales of moral fortitude, she offers them a mixed bag of *Criminal Queens*.[12]

Smiles's engineers were, of course, all men. A similar women's genre had, however, been growing up alongside the anthologies of male achievement, and it is here that Charlotte Brontë began to make her appearance in the first few years after Gaskell's *Life* came out.[13] With titles such as *Women of Worth*, or *Stories of the Lives of Noble Women*, or *Lives of Good and Great Women*, these were aimed at young, middle-class female readers. Like the male compendiums, they expressed an implicit faith in the power of reading to affect action by influencing the attitudes, behavior, and self-perception of their audience.

It is hard to know to what extent readers in fact responded by attempting to model their own lives on the exemplary women placed before them. But personalized inscriptions in two copies now in the Fawcett Library of *Heroines of Our Time* (1860) by Joseph Johnson (the Smilesian author of *Living in Earnest* and *Living to Purpose*) suggest that teachers and parents shared the author's belief in the book's didactic value. One is a Christmas present "from dear Mama and Papa" given in the hope that it might make their daughter dutiful; the other is a "Good Conduct Prize" presented to a schoolgirl "by the Misses Price and Richards with the fond hope and wish that she may endeavour to imitate those of whom it speaks."

The Misses Price and Richards and their prize-winning pupil would have been scandalized (or perhaps amused) to discover the discrepancy between the public face of Charlotte Brontë, as presented in *Heroines of Our Time*, and the private Charlotte who, as a young schoolmistress, had secretly despised her students as "fat headed oafs" or dolts who made her want to vomit.[14] Posthumously, Charlotte was being pressed into educational service once again, in texts which taught that "[a] good life is the best of sermons."[15] In her progress through the sanitizing pages of Gaskell's *Life* and into the anthologies, Charlotte's role in the public imagination became increasingly circumscribed. Gaskell may have heroized her subject, emphasizing feminine virtue in the face of suffering at the expense of writerly achievement. But the *Life* was still a complex and sophisticated work of art. The anthologies codified the Charlotte Brontë persona until she became the one-dimensional embodiment of the cultural values they were designed to promote.

Though written for girls, these books were often written by men, and their underlying ethos reflects Samuel Smiles's own attitude toward women: "We do not often hear of great women, as we do of great men. It is of good women that we mostly hear."[16] Such a division of the "great" and the "good" along gender lines echoes the divided personality—author versus woman—of Gaskell's Charlotte Brontë. In the mid-nineteenth century, "authorship," with its connotations of masculine authority, sat uneasily with "womanliness," a term whose moral implications went beyond the mere fact of gender. In her influential book, *Woman's Mission,* Sarah Lewis had exhorted her female readers to "[l]eave to men the grimy life of intellect and action," asserting that "the moral world is ours."[17] The anthologies inherited this tendency to place exaggerated importance on women's moral role, which reflected the separation of men and women into "the two spheres, public and private . . . which Victorian culture tried with extraordinary intensity to keep apart."[18]

This worldview placed a famous novelist like Charlotte Brontë in a contradictory position. Women were supposed to remain modestly within the private sphere, but publishing a book was, necessarily, a public act. How did the anthologists cope with the paradox of promoting the doctrine of separate spheres by pointing to exemplary women who were celebrated precisely because they had ventured beyond the domestic hearth? Male biographical collections, like those by Smiles, offered a catalog of energetic heroes striding out into the world to do great deeds. Heroines were expected to remain angels in the house, and yet the basic criterion for inclusion in the female anthologies, as in their male counterparts, was fame, which by its very nature had to be won in the public arena—an arena which the separate-spheres ideologues were keen to cordon off for the use of men only.

The author of *Stories of the Lives of Noble Women* (1867) attempted to resolve the problem by deciding to "fix upon women who have not been less distinguished by their domestic than by their public virtues," prefacing his work with the warning that girls must not forget "that their true happiness will always lie in the home circle."[19] This sounds uncannily similar to the advice Charlotte Brontë herself had received thirty years earlier from the Poet Laureate, Robert Southey, when he had tried to dampen her eagerness for celebrity by reminding her that literature was not the business of a woman's life. Twenty years after the publication of *Jane Eyre,* the Brontës' literary achievements seem to have had disappointingly little impact on the attitudes being fed to girls.

On the other hand, the very fact that the authors of these exemplary lives felt such a strong need to convince readers that a woman's place was in the home suggests that feminist ideas were already seen as a real threat. *Fifty Famous Women* (1864) poses the question, "What really is *woman's work*?" and propounds a scientific-sounding survival-of-the-fittest explanation for their exclusion from professions: "[F]rom a great many kinds of work, women are necessarily debarred by their own constitution and that of society, and equally by the universal law which, in a crowded labour-market thrusts out the weaker, until the strong are fully supplied."[20] The reader is comforted with the revelation that heroics are not confined to the masculine sphere. Passive female heroines are as worthy as active male heroes: "There is such a thing as fireside heroism,—the daily endurance of trial, the exercise of self-denial, all the more difficult, because the objects to be gained by them are small, and their surroundings humble."[21] Another anthologist admits that the lives of famous women might appear provocatively exciting, but encourages his readers to suppress their frustration at the limitations of their lot: "It is no doubt often a difficult matter for an enthusiastic young woman to settle into the harness of every-day life."[22]

In this context, Charlotte Brontë too was harnessed to an image of moral virtue within the home to such an extent that the fact that she had written books was almost forgotten. Ironically, she became the spokeswoman for the ideology which she herself had questioned in *Shirley.* In the novel, Caroline Helstone leads a life of enforced mental idleness within the confines of her uncle's home and eventually becomes dangerously ill. According to her aunt, who "would give a day to the mending of two holes in a stocking at any time, and think her 'mission' nobly fulfilled when she had accomplished it," Caroline should be devoting herself to the "duties of woman."[23] But Caroline cannot find fulfillment in sacrificing herself to household tasks. "Is it to live?" she asks. "Is there not a terrible hollowness, mockery, want, craving, in that existence which is given away to others, for want of something of your own to bestow it on? I suspect there is. Does virtue lie in abnegation of self? I do not believe it."[24]

Ironically, though Currer Bell had questioned the moral value of "abnegation of self," reviewers of Gaskell's *Life* had singled out Charlotte Brontë's "self-denial" for praise. In the anthologies, even more emphasis was placed on her "noble self-sacrificing nature,"[25] her "high sense of duty,"[26] and her domestic virtues. The values expounded in a book such as *Women of Worth*, published in 1859, give credence to J. S. Mill's 1861 account of "the exaggerated self-abnegation which is the present artificial ideal of feminine character."[27] Caroline Helstone may have raged in desperation against the confines of a limited domestic existence, but the Brontë girls as they appear in this anthology find their keenest pleasure in home duties.

Translated into a female context, the Smilesian work ethic became a housework ethic:

> Every menial office in the establishment was exacted of the children, not more as matter of necessity than of duty, and Charlotte continued to discharge them all until the year before her death, with the force of habit and the *penchant* of liking. Grates were scoured, furniture scrubbed, beds tossed, floors washed and swept, bread baked, and all sorts of plain cooking done by these little, quiet, heartbroken-looking children, who did every one of the same things daily after they became celebrated women.[28]

The fact that Patrick Brontë employed paid domestic help is ignored in this passage, as is the fact that neither Emily nor Anne actually lived to experience what it was to be "celebrated women." Historical accuracy is clearly less important than teaching the lesson of exemplary humility.

Gaskell had told her readers how the selfless Charlotte used to break off from the excitement of writing *Jane Eyre* to see to the potatoes which the elderly servant was too shortsighted to peel properly. The author of *Women of Worth* was keen to include the potatoes, but forgot to mention that Charlotte was writing *Jane Eyre* at the time. Gaskell's original chronology is confused in this derivative account. The potatoes incident is placed before the composition of *Jane Eyre*, and the author also forgets that Tabby in fact outlived Emily and Anne:

> With a delicate sense of kindness, which Charlotte ever displayed after Tabby's eyes failed her, and she did most imperfectly what she fancied she

had accomplished in her best manner, her young mistress used to steal away the dish from beneath her purblind vision, complete the process, and replace them on the dresser, as though no amendment had been made of the old attendant's botch-work. Had Tabby been the grandmother of the family, she could not have received more touching attentions from these admirable women; and when she died from their midst, at eighty years of age, and was buried by their care, they mourned as a loss what their affectionate kindness had made a voluntary burden of nursing and maintaining for years.

It was not *Jane Eyre* or *Wuthering Heights* or *The Tenant of Wildfell Hall* but "the regard maintained for the worn-out domestic" which "endears the names of Charlotte, Emily, and Anne Brontë to posterity."[29]

Women of Worth dates from the period (1859) when the Victorian cult of domesticity was at its peak, but it was still being reissued in 1904. Similar anthologies continued to be churned out into the twentieth century. In 1903, Joseph Johnson, who had been among the first popular biographers to make use of Charlotte in his *Heroines of Our Time: Being Sketches of the Lives of Eminent Women, with Examples of Their Benevolent Works, Truthful Lives, and Noble Deeds* (1860), was still going strong, regurgitating the same old story in a reissue of *Clever Girls of Our Time Who Became Famous Women.*

The dutiful daughter: Charlotte serves a cup of tea to her blind old father. (From *Women of Worth: A Book for Girls,* 1859)

Though some of the earlier versions tended to emphasize the tragedy of Charlotte's martyrdom with a particular grimness that became anesthetized in the more sentimental accounts of the later years of the century, her saintly, domestic image remained remarkably static. Invariably, she was represented as "a perfect household image."[30] Even in those accounts which acknowledged how much she had "shed a glory upon the annals of Literature," she remained, primarily, a symbol "for purity, goodness, and virtue."[31] One picture shows her as "the worthy daughter" wearing a neat little apron and serving a cup of tea to her blind old father;[32] in another, based on George Richmond's famous portrait, the illustrator has added a frilly bonnet in an attempt to emphasize her feminine respectability.[33]

As in the *Life*, Charlotte's sanctity is often contrasted with her male relatives' pecularities. In many of the accounts, Patrick Brontë, simplified to the level of caricature, remains the violent misanthrope originally created by Gaskell, which sits oddly with the emphasis on the girls' dutiful respect for the household patriarch. Branwell is mentioned only for the sake of moral contrast with his pure-minded sisters. In the interests of gentility, one author attempts to skate over the brother's role in the story, with a vague but intriguing reference to his "practices to which we cannot further allude."[34] Readers' imaginations must have run wild.

An indication of how inextricably Charlotte had become identified with the sanctified persona codified in the didactic anthologies can be found in the short, anecdotal memoir published by Ellen Nussey in 1871. Ellen offered some vivid new detail about the Brontë household, but she also described her friend in terms indistinguishable from those used by moralists such as the author of *Women of Worth*, who had praised Charlotte for the "high sense of duty which made [her] exertions through life a daily martyrdom."[35] In her urgent desire to defend Charlotte from the old "charge of irreligion" which had been made against *Jane Eyre*, Ellen regurgitated the prevailing rhetoric: "[D]aily she was a Christian heroine, who bore her cross with the firmness of a martyr saint!"[36] Even to one of her closest friends, Charlotte had come to embody an ideal stereotype.

It is hard to say how long the charges against *Jane Eyre* continued to stick. The evidence is ambiguous. On the one hand Thomas Wemyss Reid, who in 1877 published the first full-length reassessment of Charlotte's life since Gaskell's, suggested that her novels no longer possessed the shock value they had once had: "We hear nothing now," he wrote, "of the 'immorality' of her writings. Younger people, if they turn from . . . the most popular recent stories to 'Jane Eyre' or '*Villette*,' in the hope of finding there some stimulant which may have power to tickle their jaded palates, will search in vain for anything that even boarders upon impropriety."[37] Certainly, many of the so-called novels of sensation by writers such as Mary E. Braddon, which had been gaining popularity during the 1860s, were more knowingly outrageous than *Jane Eyre*, with their murderesses and unashamed amoralism. Yet other evidence suggests that *Jane Eyre* had not completely lost its air of danger by the time Wemyss Reid was writing.

Although the exemplary biographical anthologies tended to marginal-ize the Brontë novels almost to the point of extinction, *Jane Eyre* did not completely disappear in the decades after Charlotte's death. It was, how-ever, reimagined, repackaged, and redefined. In her fascinating account of the novel's afterlife, Patsy Stoneman has shown how Jane's character was increasingly tamed and domesticated in the surprisingly large number of stage adaptations which hit the theaters during the second half of the nineteenth century.[38] While the melodramas of the late 1840s and 1850s tended to remain close to Charlotte's original conception of her heroine, emphasizing Jane's spirited independence, those of the 1860s and 1870s attempted to transform Jane into a saintly exemplar of conventional femi-nine virtue. In other words, it was only in the pre-Gaskell period that Jane retained her fire. Mimicking the biographers who sanitized and domesti-cated Charlotte Brontë, playwrights writing after Gaskell clearly felt that Jane was just too threatening to be allowed onstage in her original form.

Theatrical adaptors, then, felt the need to re-create the subversive Jane in a submissive mold. But in the novels of the period, *Jane Eyre* went underground, emerging as a hidden literary influence on the very genre which Thomas Wemyss Reid found so different from it—sensation fiction. As early as 1855, the critic Margaret Oliphant was identifying Jane as the prototype sensation heroine: "She stole upon the scene—pale, small, by no means beautiful—something of a genius, something of a vixen—a dangerous little person, inimical to the peace of society."[39] Yet Wemyss Reid was right in supposing that there was a real and genuine difference between Jane and the calculating, egoistical, even perverse heroines who came later, such as Braddon's Lady Audley, whom Stoneman describes as "a positively active schemer, liar, bigamist and murderer," or the self-indulgent, manipulative Nell in Rhoda Broughton's *Cometh Up As a Flower* (1867), in whom Jane Eyre's famous self-respect seems to have evolved into a repellent form of narcissism.

"With hindsight," writes Stoneman with more than some justice, "it is distressing to find *Jane Eyre* identified as the fount of this kind of writ-ing."[40] It seems as though popular Victorian literary culture could only assimilate Jane Eyre at the expense of splitting her in two, as if a heroine who was both morally upright and socially subversive was an impossible contradiction. Either Jane was virtuous but stripped of her rebelliousness and passion, as in the stage adaptations, or her strength and independence were transformed into monstrous egotism and depravity, as in the sensation novels.

If *Jane Eyre* did become associated with the sensation school, this cannot have done its moral reputation much good. In any case, despite the sanctification of its author, it seems from anecdotal evidence that in some circles the novel retained an aura of impropriety until the end of the century and beyond, even after it had become an established fixture of the literary canon. Ironically, it is likely that many of the girls who were given Charlotte's life story as an improving example were also forbidden to read her fiction. *Jane Eyre* was a book that invited censorship. As recalled by her daughter, sometime in the 1880s Elizabeth Malleson, a woman of progressive views and a friend of George Eliot, read the novel aloud to her children "entirely omitting Rochester's mad wife, and so skilfully that we noticed nothing amiss with the plot!"[41] In 1889, some young teachers at a girls' boarding school wanted to read *Jane Eyre* but were forbidden to do so by the headmistress until they reached the age of twenty-five.[42] My own grandmother was not allowed to read *Jane Eyre* as a child in the 1920s, not so much because of its "irreligion," but because it was considered overexciting, frightening, a horror story.

It was possible, however, with careful selection, to read Charlotte's works in such a way that they reflected, rather than contradicted, her image as a moral paragon and spiritual guide: a book published in 1912, *Thoughts from Charlotte Brontë*, picked out sentences from her works and presented them as maxims which might help the reader with the ethical dilemmas of day-to-day living.[43] Though it was not the only way to make sense of her, Charlotte's image as a domestic saint retained its general currency until about the time of the First World War. As late as 1909, for example, *Bibliophile* magazine declared that "a good woman is an understudy for an angel. . . . Such a woman was Charlotte Brontë . . . she was content . . . in doing the common everyday tasks incident to the household."[44]

Charlotte's "spiritual" nature was capable of taking on the odd bizarre twist, as in a clairvoyant publication of 1894, *Twenty Photographs of the Risen Dead* by Thomas Wilmot. Wilmot offered reproductions of supposed photographic plates—"retouched negatives," he called them—which, he claimed, captured the visions of a lady medium. On one occasion, we are told, this lady received a visitation from "a glorified angel from earth, with messenger Spirits in her train" who gave her name as

Charlotte's ghost as supposedly captured on camera by a medium, 1890s. Do the disembodied heads represent the other Brontës?

Charlotte Brontë.[45] The resulting "photograph" shows a female figure stretching out her hand toward the viewer, surrounded by four disembodied heads (one has to ask if these are supposed to represent Emily, Anne, Branwell, and Patrick).

This was not the first time Charlotte Brontë had appeared from beyond the grave. In 1872, Harriet Beecher Stowe told George Eliot how she had had a chatty conversation with Charlotte's ghost during a séance.[46] This experience can be interpreted as an unconscious expression of the deep-seated emotional need shared by many women writers of the period to identify themselves with a female literary tradition. And it is not surprising that the martyr-heroine of *The Life of Charlotte Brontë* should have particularly appealed to the author of *Uncle Tom's Cabin,* a philanthropic work in the Gaskell tradition in which noble characters are sanctified by death, suffering, and self-sacrifice. Wilmot's photograph, however, suggests something rather different. With her head draped in a veil, his spectral Charlotte Brontë resembles no one so much as the Virgin Mary. Unlike Beecher Stowe's garrulous ghost, she remains silent. Spiritualizing Charlotte and turning her into a saint had the effect of depriving her of her voice.

Many of the popular authors who appropriated Charlotte as a symbol of ideal feminine behavior were men, but it would be a mistake to suppose that her image did not also genuinely appeal to women who were looking for something deeper than a wooden stereotype of housewifely virtue. During the 1850s, as Elaine Showalter has shown, many women were actively looking for figureheads with whom they could identify emotionally: "They wanted inspiring professional role-models; but they also wanted romantic heroines, a sisterhood of shared passion and suffering, women who sobbed and struggled and rebelled."[47] In this context, Gaskell's *Life of Charlotte Brontë* hit a nerve.

When the biography first appeared, the critic E. S. Dallas, who disliked what he saw as its souped-up, sentimental tone, had questioned why Gaskell had made such a meal of Charlotte's "struggles." Her experience, he said, was exactly the same as that of thousands of middle-class young women without occupation who had to make do with knitting stockings and inventing puddings.[48] In fact, Dallas unwittingly identified the very aspect of Gaskell's biography which made it so appealing. It was exactly the combination of romantic tragedy with ordinariness which made Charlotte so accessible a heroine, as her experiences really did mirror those of thousands of readers, even if her literary talents were unique. Because Gaskell had marginalized Charlotte's writing, which made her extraordinary, in favor of her domestic life, which was comparatively unremarkable, it was possible to see her as an Everywoman.

From the start, Gaskell's telling of Charlotte's story had read like a call for mutual support among lonely women fulfilling their duties within the home. The long, vivid letter she wrote Catherine Winkworth immediately after her first meeting with Charlotte had prompted Winkworth's sister Emily not merely to forgive poor Miss Brontë for having written *Jane Eyre,* but to consider how women might improve their lives through solidarity: "Oh dear," she wrote, "if the single sisters in this world were but banded together a little, so that they could help each other out."[49] At the time, Gaskell and Lady Kay-Shuttleworth had even been discussing the pros and cons of establishing lay sisterhoods for spinsters, though Lady Kay-Shuttleworth disapproved of these attempts to provide single women with an alternative to the family.

One of the paradoxes of the *Life* was that while presenting its heroine as a tragically isolated figure, it also strove to create a sense of female community. Not only did it show Charlotte sustaining her younger sisters in their trials. It was also punctuated by anecdotal stories of abused or suffering women, often with Charlotte in the role of comforter. Describing the mourners at Charlotte's funeral, Gaskell picks out the sorrowing women from among the crowd of Haworth locals. As the parson's daughter, and later the curate's wife, the real Charlotte would have inevitably been involved in informal social work in the parish. Gaskell sacralizes her into a nunlike "holy sister" who had given help and counsel to the unfortunate, including a girl who had lost her sight and another who had lost her virtue (this was the young woman who was so upset to see her sexual humiliation paraded in public that her family made Gaskell change the word "seduced" to "betrayed" in the third edition of the *Life*). Images like these created such a feeling of female philanthropy that Charlotte could enter readers' imaginations as a symbolic figure offering emotional support. Looking back fifty years on, the veteran novelist Margaret Oliphant described how Gaskell's biography had seemed like a plea "for every woman dropped out of sight."

The focus on Charlotte's personal sufferings rather than her professional achievements may indeed have played into the hands of those who believed that a woman's place was in the home. But it could also, paradoxically, be read as subversive. By putting the private world of a woman on public show, Gaskell was felt by some to have struck a blow for female emancipation by violating the conventional code of feminine modesty to reveal the hidden anguish behind its facade. As Oliphant put it, the emotionalism of the *Life* had "shattered indeed altogether the 'delicacy' which was supposed to be the most exquisite characteristic of womankind. The softening veil is blown away when such exhibitions of feeling are given to the world."[50]

Gaskell's biography was so complex and contradictory that it was possible to view it from a variety of angles. While some read it as a simple paean in favor of housework, others felt that Gaskell's continual emphasis on home duties made Charlotte's achievements as a writer seem all the more impressive in the circumstances. It is interesting that, whether they see it as cause for celebration or commiseration, most Victorian commentators regard Charlotte's performance of domestic duties in the light of self-sacrifice, even if it is a willingly embraced martyrdom. In reality, it may be that the life of the single daughter at home was precisely what the Brontë sisters needed to give them the mental space to develop their talents. Their brother, after all, who was not barred by his sex from making writing the business of his life, did not fulfill his potential. When the twenty-something Charlotte told Ellen Nussey that she would rather be a housemaid than a governess, it may not have been out of self-abnegation but because she realized that the physical labor of ironing and scrubbing would leave her mind free to roam.

As an icon of suffering, Charlotte became as appealing to women writers looking for martyr-heroines as she had been to moralists like Charles

Kingsley. The intellectually ambitious young May Sinclair (born 1863), who was to become one of England's leading female novelists of the early twentieth century, read Gaskell's *Life* "a score of times" after finding it in her father's library as a child.[51] The experience of this first encounter stayed with her as a defining moment. Opening the shabby volume, she had been seized with the "abiding gloom"[52] of its two illustrations, one of the Parsonage—"a grim, plain house standing obliquely to a churchyard packed with tombstones"—and the other of a memorial tablet.[53] Once she began to read, she could not put it down: "For the first time I was in the grip of a reality more poignant than any that I had yet known, of a tragedy that I could hardly bear.... There are pages in it that I shrink from approaching even now, because of the agony of realisation they revive."[54]

Sinclair was overwhelmed by the fatalism of Gaskell's account: "The passing bell tolled continually in the prelude; it sounded at intervals throughout; it tolled again at the close. The refrain of 'Here lie the Remains' haunted me like a dolorous song."[55] The biography's emphasis on personal tragedy meant that she gathered "a very vague idea of Charlotte apart from Haworth and the moors, the Parsonage and the tombstones." Yet this ambitious girl, who taught herself at home until, at eighteen, she finally spent a year at Cheltenham Ladies' College, was nevertheless aware that "something mysterious"—genius—had touched the Brontës' lives. As a result, Sinclair derived a view from the *Life* of the female artist as sanctified by martyrdom, viewing the Brontës' pain as integral to their literary talent. Their genius was "something that atoned, that not only consoled for suffering and solitude and bereavement, but that drew its strength from these things."[56]

Perhaps what the *Life* also did for Sinclair was to validate her own sense of suffering. Her father, who died bankrupt in 1881, was, like Branwell, an alcoholic. The experience left its mark on Sinclair, and would find its way into her fiction. Interestingly, reactions to her novel *The Divine Fire* in 1904 would show that, over half a century after the publication of the Brontë novels, male critics still had trouble with the idea of a woman writing about drunkenness: as the literary critic Frank Swinnerton recalled, "the most intelligent and sophisticated man known to me then shook his head over May Sinclair's knowledge of what a man felt like when he was drunk. My friend said, gravely: 'She knows too much.' "[57]

In addition, Sinclair's family life was dominated by bereavements on a Brontëan scale. Her childhood was haunted by a dead sister, just as Charlotte had been by Maria and Elizabeth, and her young adulthood would see the successive deaths of all her five brothers from the same congenital heart defect. As Sinclair grew older, the Brontës remained important figures, and she would eventually publish a biographical study of them in 1912. In many ways, her life was more somber, isolated, and deprived than theirs, which she perceived as being so tragic. Where they had each other, she was alone; where they had been hot-housed into intellectual precocity by an ambitious father, she had to fight for her education in the face of maternal opposition.

As the only daughter of a middle-class family down on its luck, the young Sinclair soon realized that her given role in life would be to act as companion and support to her mother, a woman whose gift for subtle emotional tyranny was matched by her desire to keep her daughter in a state of unintellectual docility.[58] In one of her early poems, written at sixteen, Sinclair describes a woman's fear that she may never fulfill her gifts because she is sacrificing her life — "Oh, death in life!" — to the needs of an aging parent.[59] Although she rebelled intellectually against her mother, rejecting conventional Christianity, Sinclair would continue to struggle to fulfill her duties as a conventional Victorian daughter. It may be that as she read and reread the *Life* she found, in Gaskell's Charlotte, a role model who had pursued a life of domestic self-denial without losing hold of her literary talent. Certainly, although her lonely determination to educate herself shows a dogged desire for personal fulfillment, morally and philosophically Sinclair idealized the notion of "self-abnegation" as the route to a higher plane of spirituality.[60]

Sinclair's early novels reveal a writer unsure as to what womanhood should be, particularly concerning what role sexuality should play in a woman's life. As Suzanne Raitt has shown, Sinclair was herself a woman of contradictions who stood on the cusp between the Victorian and the modern. Contemporaries tutted at her prim, ultra-formal, old-fashioned manners, yet she was keen to grasp hold of new ideas — from psychoanalysis to imagism — as soon as they appeared. She sympathized with the women's suffrage movement, yet she had a very Victorian fear of displaying herself in public by taking part in demonstrations.[61] Perhaps Sinclair identified so strongly with the Brontës because she found in them icons who held these oppositions in balance. In terms of her external behavior, especially as portrayed by Gaskell, Charlotte adhered to the Victorian values which Sinclair had inherited from her mother. Yet she combined this outer conventionality with a rich and untrammeled inner life which seemed, from

the perspective of the early twentieth century, to have been anachronistically modern in its intellectual daring.

Another writer who felt a lifelong kinship with the Brontës was the
American poet Emily Dickinson (1830–86).[62] During the early 1860s,
echoes of *Jane Eyre* and *Villette* run through Dickinson's letters and love
poems to her "master," a mysterious figure believed by some critics to have
been the newspaper editor Samuel Bowles and by others to have been a
purely imaginary construct. Uncannily, the correspondence echoes Charlotte's letters to Heger, which would not be published in full until 1913.[63]

In 1860, Dickinson, who had read Gaskell's *Life,* wrote a memorial
poem to Charlotte offering a suggestive reading of the relationship between Currer Bell the author and Charlotte Brontë the woman. The poem
begins with the image of Currer Bell as a dead nightingale who, forever
lost, will never return:

> *All overgrown by cunning moss,*
> *All interspersed with weed,*
> *The little cage of "Currer Bell"*
> *In quiet "Haworth" laid.*

> *The Bird—observing others*
> *When frosts too sharp became*
> *Retire to other latitudes—*
> *Quietly did the same—*

> *But differed in returning—*
> *Since Yorkshire hills are green—*
> *Yet not in all the nests I meet—*
> *Can Nightingale be seen—*

In the above version, Currer Bell is gone for good. But Dickinson also provided alternative second and third stanzas for the poem, which instead
assert eternal life after death, with a vision of "Brontë" transported to
heaven:

> *Or—*
> *Gathered from many wanderings—*
> *Gethsemane can tell*

Thro' what transporting anguish
She reached the Asphodel!

Soft fall the sounds of Eden
Opon [sic] her puzzled ear—
Oh what an afternoon for Heaven,
When "Bronte" entered there![64]

On one level the distinction between "Currer Bell" and "Brontë" suggests a Christian differentiation between the author, who achieved ephemeral worldly fame in the here and now but will write no more, and the eternal soul of the woman, which belongs to God. But the poem also casts an ambiguous light—though perhaps not intentionally—on Charlotte's after-life in the imagination of the Victorian public. While Charlotte the woman lived on in the collective consciousness surrounded by a heavenly penumbra of sainthood, Currer Bell's literary achievements often got lost.

However, popular emphasis on Charlotte's personal tragedy did not mean that no one was able to appreciate the Brontës for their books. Indeed, there were always some readers—if in the minority—who were ready to argue on behalf of their literary achievements. An early example can be found in the *English-Woman's Journal,* a progressive publication founded by women for women in 1858 which used rational argument rather than emotion to make the case for opening up career opportunities. In 1860, it published a long review of recent reprints of Gaskell's biography and Anne's novel *The Tenant of Wildfell Hall,* and of cheaper editions new to the market of *Jane Eyre, Wuthering Heights,* and *Shirley.*

Instead of using the Brontës' tragic lives as a means of excusing the supposedly improper elements of their novels, the reviewer took a notably nonjudgmental line, defending *Wildfell Hall,* and offering a thoughtful assessment of *Wuthering Heights:* "to those who think every book bad, which has not been written with one solemn, definite, and didactic purpose, we have nothing to say. To those who look deeper, many morals will present themselves, many human paradoxes and enigmas and theorems put forth for human consideration, which are much better than morals."[65] This was the sort of critique the Brontës had hoped for when they first brought out their novels, but which Gaskell's *Life* had purposefully avoided: it assessed the books dispassionately as works of literature.

Nevertheless, in the popular literature of the Victorian age, it was still the Brontë story rather than the Brontë novels which continued to attract

Four crude images of Charlotte derived from George Richmond's far more subtle portrait of 1850, by now an icon. The added details of costume (top right) make her seem smothered by the trappings of Victorian femininity.

didactic writers. As the nineteenth century progressed, however, and attitudes toward the education of girls began to change, the sort of moral messages Charlotte was used to convey began to change. No longer the angel
in the house, she now became an emblem of a new sort of womanhood. In
1889, a biographical anthology, *Some Eminent Women of Our Times,* was
published by Millicent Fawcett, sister of the medical pioneer Elizabeth
Garrett Anderson, friend of John Stuart Mill, and a well-known campaigner for women's education and the female suffrage movement. Charlotte and Emily Brontë were included along with women of achievement
such as Florence Nightingale, Elizabeth Fry, and Mary Carpenter. The sisters were still presented, as they were in the conventional anthologies, as
moral exemplars. But the morality was different—far more like that of
Rose Yorke, the young girl in *Shirley* who refuses to give herself over to
the "dark and dreary duties"[66] of the housewife and argues that, if God has
given her a talent, it would be wrong for her to shut it up in a china closet
or "hide it in a tureen of cold potatoes."[67]

Fawcett explicitly intended her book "chiefly for working women and
young people" as "an encouragement to them to be reminded how much
good work ha[s] been done in various ways by women." Her definition of
"womanly work" did not entirely reject the doctrine of separate spheres.
She was keen to demonstrate that "greater freedom and better education"
had enabled women to professionalize their traditional caring role—in
nursing, for example—rather than encouraging them to neglect it.[68] Her
portrait of Charlotte and Emily as pioneering working women treated
their writing as their real work, and not (as in the works of Joseph Johnson, for example) as a mere "accomplishment" or adjunct to the feminine
duties of the household. Fawcett takes a very different line from the earlier authors of exemplary anthologies. She retains the unsympathetic caricature of Patrick Brontë, derived ultimately from Gaskell, but shifts the
focus. No longer the moody patriarch pampered by dutiful daughters, he is
now criticized for not taking an active enough role in childcare and for
failing to support his wife.[69]

The book also reminds readers of the "prejudice against literary
women" with which the Brontës had to contend when they made their first
publishing venture, and points to the sisters' mutual cooperation, describing how they would discuss their work in progress.[70] Other popular books
of the period sentimentalized the idea of sisterly support, such as the sac-
charine *Golden Friendships,* where the Brontë sisters appeared side by
side with the Ladies of Llangollen, whose now famous lesbian relationship

was presented in a naive, desexualized light. But for Millicent Fawcett, an active campaigner for women's rights, the idea of female solidarity was an ideal with a practical and potentially political meaning.

Her reading of Charlotte's marriage to Arthur Bell Nicholls is strikingly unsentimental. *Golden Friendships,* for example, had treated the marriage as a conventional happy ending to a story which was then tragically cut short by the heroine's death: "[A]fter a glimpse of fuller life and love, [God] had taken her home to Himself."[71] Millicent Fawcett did not agree that marriage offered Charlotte the chance of a "fuller life." In fact, her husband—very unfairly—becomes the villain of the piece. He is not only accused of preventing her from writing but also of hastening her death by "remorselessly" sentencing her to "the routine drudgery of parish work."[72] Such self-sacrifice is no longer to be admired but instead represents a woman dragged away from her true vocation by a male-oriented conception of what constitutes women's work. "[P]earls have before now been cast before swine," concludes Fawcett, "and one cannot but regret that Charlotte was married to a man who did not value her place in literature as he ought."[73]

The redefinition of Charlotte and Emily as "working women" suggests that the message of the pioneers who had argued for women's careers in the *English-Woman's Journal* in 1860 was now getting through to a popular audience. Charlotte, like many living women, was beginning her emancipation from the cult of domesticity. By 1910, her appearance in an American critical study, *Women's Works in English Fiction* by Clara H. Whitmore, offered testimony to the progress being made in women's education: the book had started life as a master's thesis. The author was motivated "to fill a want which a schoolgirl recently expressed to me: 'Our club wanted to study about women, but we have searched the libraries and found nothing.'" Whitmore's modern-sounding aim was to rescue women's writing from the "oblivion" into which it had fallen as a result of "the fact that nearly all books on literature have been written from a man's standpoint."[74] These comments bear testimony to the fact that Charlotte's works had begun to be put to use in the service of girls' education, anticipating their later reclamation by the feminist critics of the 1970s.

In the early twentieth century, however, Charlotte often remained a simplified figurehead for feminists as much as for the earlier Victorian moralists. Her complexity as an individual and as a writer was sacrificed in favor of ideology in the fight for women's rights. As revealed in her novels and letters, the real Charlotte did not have a fully formulated theory of gender politics. She was less a political feminist than an artistic one. Sixty years on, however, she was claimed as a forerunner by radical activists. A curious report in the local *Evening Post* of 1913 links her name with an arson attack committed by Suffragettes at Shirley Manor in Yorkshire, said to be connected with her novel, though why they should want to set fire to the place remains a mystery.[75]

During the First World War, Charlotte was exploited as a symbol to activate the female workforce. Triumphalist rhetoric echoed through the pages of the *Lady's Pictorial:* "[A]t this tense moment, when disciplined, patriotic activity occupies hand and heart," the paper urged, "the daughters of to-day in their triumphant freedom" should look to Charlotte Brontë as the "pioneer" who "toiled to win them this liberty to work."[76] On a similar note, Maude Goldring's biography of 1915, *Charlotte Brontë: The Woman,* compared her, "in this hour of her nation's stress," to Joan of Arc, while championing her as a role model who managed to make the most of her abilities by fighting the obstacles put in her path.[77] The woman who had once embodied ideal feminine passivity was now allied to a fighting heroine in male dress. In both cases, however, Charlotte remained more icon than individual and was defined as a primarily moral inspiration.

One reason why Charlotte Brontë became such an appealing popular saint in the first six decades after her death was the fact that in Haworth she had an easily identifiable shrine. The almost religious awe in which she was held soon came to be focused on the place where she had spent nearly all her life, and a fully fledged cult developed, complete with pilgrims and relics. Although literary cults were not confined to the Brontës in the latter half of the nineteenth century, Charlotte inspired a uniquely intense devotion. As one newspaper put it, "Miss Austen and Thackeray have admirers; Charlotte Brontë has worshippers."[78]

Even before her death, a few determined fans had made the journey there to catch a glimpse of Currer Bell. One even called at the Parsonage during Gaskell's visit in 1853, only to have his homage dismissed by both ladies as impertinence.[79] Yet it was not until after *The Life of Charlotte Brontë* appeared in 1857 that pilgrims became a regular feature of the Haworth landscape. Gaskell had devoted an unusual amount of space to describing the environment in which Charlotte had been brought up. Her romantic account made it inevitable that readers would want to see the village, even though some who came were inevitably disappointed that the reality did not live up to expectation, as in this report from the *Bradford Observer* of 1857:

> We had supposed Haworth to be a scattered and straggling hamlet, with a desolate vicarage and dilapidated church, surrounded and shut out from the world by a wilderness of barren heath, the monotony of the prospect only broken by the tombstones in the adjacent graveyard. Our struggling hamlet we found transformed into a large and flourishing village—not a very enlightened or poetical place certainly, but quaint, compact, and progressive, wherein, by the bye, we observed three large dissenting chapels and two or three well-sized schools.[80]

Other early visitors were less disappointed by the experience. The Reverend Thomas Ackroyd of Liverpool, for example, was so excited by Gaskell's fascinating portrait of the Parsonage that he made the journey to the shrine at the first opportunity. Ackroyd was shown around the church by the sexton, a gossipy individual who features elsewhere in visitors' accounts as someone who relished his self-appointed role as chief purveyor of Brontë anecdote. His tales were often less than credible, such as his claim that Charlotte had once been joined in the Brontë family pew by Thackeray, Harriet Martineau, and Ralph Waldo Emerson.[81] After dinner, Ackroyd worked up the courage to call on Mr. Brontë, who received him courteously. When the visitor mentioned that he had just finished *The Life of Charlotte Brontë,* but that he supposed one should not take everything in it for gospel, Patrick responded with wry good humor: "Mrs Gaskell is a novelist, you know, and we must allow her a little romance, eh? It is quite in her line."[82]

Ackroyd was lucky to have been allowed an audience with the last surviving Brontë. As the old man told him: "Of course I cannot see all that come, you know. We have a great number of visitors now."[83] The number was indeed increasing. By 1858, pilgrims (as they openly called themselves) began to notice how the village seemed to have got used to the influx of strangers, and even to capitalize on it. Walter White was one of those who was surprised to find that some of the shop windows "denote[d] an expectation of visitors; the apothecary exhibits photographs of the church, the parsonage and Mr Brontë; and no one seems surprised at your arrival." In the Black Bull, where Branwell used to drink, the landlady told him "she had had a good many visitors but expected 'a vast' before the summer was over."[84]

Another visitor, the Irish economist John Elliot Cairns, who had been lecturing in Leeds and decided to make an excursion to Haworth, noticed that a grocer's shop on the hill up to the Parsonage was displaying copies of *Villette, Shirley,* and *Jane Eyre* "in great abundance."[85] By 1861, the range of souvenirs on offer had increased. Charles Hale—an acquaintance of the Gaskells and one of the many American pilgrims to be drawn by the Brontës during the nineteenth century—wrote to his mother from Haworth on specially produced stationery printed with the legend "the home of Charlotte Brontë" and a picture of the Parsonage.[86]

Hale, however, was not the sort of pilgrim to be content with souvenirs. He wanted the real stuff—relics. After the excitement of eating his supper in the Black Bull from a tray that had once belonged to Charlotte, his appetite for memorabilia was whetted. He was disappointed to discover that he had missed the sale of the Brontës' household effects held three weeks previously, in the wake of Patrick's recent death. But he managed to despoil the Parsonage itself of various bits and pieces, including segments of molding and woodwork, "the wire and crank of Mr Brontë's bell-pull, which he used daily for forty-one years" and, most impressively, "the whole lower sash of the window of the bedroom of Charlotte Brontë." Hale had woodwork from the house made into photograph frames which he glazed with Charlotte's windowpanes, so he could look at his pictures "through the same medium through which Charlotte Brontë saw the dreary landscape before her window."[87]

Such fetishization of physical objects, in themselves banal, was common among Brontë enthusiasts. In the aftermath of the *Life,* Charlotte's father had found himself cutting up her letters into small squares to cope with the demand for samples of her handwriting. Patrick's reply to one of these requests—from a certain T. Franklin Bacheller of Lynn, Massachusetts, in 1858—is preserved in the Pierpont Morgan Library in New York. Attached is a fragment in Charlotte's hand so small that it contains only the words "Dear Papa, I left S . . ." and then, on the line below, "having settled all."[88] Nothing could illustrate more graphically how Charlotte's celebrity had the effect of sucking the meaning out of her. Prized as physical relics rather than for their meaning, her words were essentially devalued. Amazingly, Margaret Smith, the modern editor of Charlotte's correspondence, has managed to reassemble much of the text of this letter—written while Charlotte was recuperating by the sea at Filey after Anne's death in Scarborough in 1849—from fragments which had been scattered far and wide.[89] In her quest to establish an accurate text of Charlotte's letters, Smith has also had to cope, among other obstacles, with weeding out forgeries, which began to enter the market in response to the demand for Brontë memorabilia.

The Victorians, who had a penchant for turning their dead relatives' hair into fashionable jewelry, took relics very seriously. In his book of 1841, *Extraordinary Popular Delusions and the Madness of Crowds*, the journalist and pioneering sociologist Charles Mackay treated this topic far more sympathetically than some of the other manias—haunted houses, witchcraft belief—he explored. Even the veneration of bogus saints' bones by superstitious Papists is treated with less scorn than one might have expected. The love of relics, he writes, "is a love which is most easily excited in the best and kindliest natures, and which few are callous enough to scoff at."[90]

Mackay's sympathy stemmed from the fact that he regarded all relics as being on a continuum with "home-relics," mementos of departed loved ones held as "sacred" by bereaved friends and relatives. This domestic and emotional context sits so easily with the aura of homely intimacy with which Gaskell had surrounded Charlotte that it is not surprising that Brontë relics took on a particular magic. In 1894, one young lady thought she would be "the happiest girl in America" if only she could have "but a small piece of an old dress, or the finger of an old glove once worn by Charlotte."[91] The veneration of Brontë relics would become integral to the cult. In the 1970s, a modern descendent of these earlier pilgrims described how she had been permitted by the curator of the Brontë Parsonage Museum to try on a shawl that had once belonged to Emily and claimed to have felt ghostly hands, heavy in death, pressing down on her through the fabric.[92] It was as if the relic had literally brought its onetime owner back from the grave.

It was not until the "Brontë epidemic" of the 1890s that tourists began to arrive in Haworth en masse. In the 1860s, visitors tended to be dedicated enthusiasts, people who had read the novels and Gaskell's *Life* and were prepared to go to quite some trouble to make their pilgrimage. In 1866, Miss Emma Cullum Huidekoper of Meadville, Pennsylvania, even made a special detour from her trip to Italy to fulfill her long-held ambition of seeing the Brontë homeland.[93] The actual number of visitors during the 1860s was still relatively small. In 1874, a French pilgrim counted "more than 3,000" names in the church visitors' book going back over the past fifteen years, an annual average of something over two hundred.[94] In the summer of 1895, however, Haworth attracted ten thousand visitors.[95]

The immediate cause of this boom was the new museum of Brontë relics which was opened in May that year, with a flourish of bunting and brass bands, in a couple of rooms above the Yorkshire Penny Bank.[96] The museum was the brainchild of the recently formed Brontë Society, which had been founded in 1894 at the suggestion of a Yorkshire journalist, W. W. Yates, with the intention of collecting and preserving manuscripts and other relics of the county's most famous literary family.[97] (An earlier, less well-organized museum, attached to a tea shop whose owners ran it as a sideline, had failed during the 1880s.) The opening ceremony included an address by Charlotte's biographer Sir Thomas Wemyss Reid, which, while acknowledging the Brontë genius, still stressed moral character over literary value: "Fame, even the highest literary fame, like riches, may take wings and disappear, but virtue will endure. We believe that the fame of the Brontës, as stars in the firmament of our literature, will long abide; but . . . we know that the heroic example of their lives will remain as an inspiration and encouragement for ever."[98]

The museum would foster Charlotte's already established personality cult, evoking an ambivalent response from the young Virginia Woolf, who visited in 1904. She found the case full of personal relics infinitely touching, but noted that, while they brought Charlotte Brontë the woman to life, they also made one forget "the chiefly memorable fact that she was a great writer."[99] The article she wrote about her Haworth trip—her first piece of published journalism—opens in an uncertain tone: "I do not know whether pilgrimages to the shrines of famous men ought not to be condemned as sentimental journeys."[100] Like Henry James, she seems to have been worried that unrestrained admiration would detract from true appreciation.

The keen public interest provoked by the museum when it opened in 1895 reflected a wider explosion of Brontë enthusiasm which took place during the 1890s. This "epidemic," as it was often called, was also fueled by the fact that the sisters' novels had come out of copyright in 1889, precipitating a wealth of new editions. In 1896, Clement Shorter, a journalist-turned-Brontë-expert who, together with the unscrupulous T. J. Wise, had managed to wheedle Charlotte's correspondence out of Ellen Nussey, finally put together a volume of letters, *Charlotte Brontë and Her Circle*, which also sparked new interest.[101]

At the top end of the market, the Haworth Edition of 1899–1900, *The Life and Works of Charlotte Brontë and Her Sisters*, offered introductions to the novels by the eminent novelist and critic Mrs. Humphry Ward. Providing literary criticism of a high intellectual caliber, Ward expressed concern over the public's sentimental overemphasis on the Brontë life story. Yet by including Gaskell's biography in the seven volume edition, the publishers Smith, Elder & Co. struck an ambiguous note, since they implicitly placed it on a level with the Brontë novels; this, as much as anything, must have fed Henry James's anxiety about the confusion of life and literature.

The main impact of the lapse of copyright, however, was the number of cheap editions of the novels, many produced by small local printers, which now flooded the market. (The particular popularity of the Brontës in America through the second half of the nineteenth century can be explained by the fact that English copyright did not apply there at the date.) At the time of *Jane Eyre*'s first publication, in 1847, a three-volume novel would have cost as much as a guinea,[102] when the annual salary for a governess in a private family, in addition to her board and lodging, might be as little as £16.[103] By 1900 you could buy *Jane Eyre* in a single volume for as little as sixpence.[104] Working-class consumers could now afford to buy books, and, newly literate since the Education Act of 1870, they were keen to read.

This was the period in which English literature began to take root as an academic subject. English was considered a suitable topic of study for women and the working classes, partly because they lacked training in Latin and Greek, and partly because of the subject's perceived moral value.[105] The workers education movement encouraged self-help through reading, and publications such as *Some Favourite Books and Their Authors*, in which Charlotte appeared in 1901, attempted to provide biographical sketches, synopses, and canonical lists of suitable titles. Interestingly, the extract from *Jane Eyre* chosen for this compilation suggests that the heroine's relationship with the hero, which we would today regard as the central relationship of the novel, was still considered morally dubious. The passage quoted does not feature Rochester; one of the St. John Rivers scenes is chosen instead.[106] Did readers go away with the same mistaken impression as the narrator in Jeanette Winterson's *Oranges Are Not the Only Fruit*, whose Evangelical mother leads her to believe that Jane, the perfect Christian heroine, ends up marrying the missionary?[107]

It is easy to see how Charlotte Brontë, celebrated—however inaccurately—as a self-taught writer, could have appealed to a mass audience seeking self-improvement through education. Hers could be seen as an exemplary tale of the individual triumphing over the disadvantages of material poverty, provincial obscurity, and undistinguished birth. For the members of the five detachments of the Yorkshire branches of the Workers Educational Association who made their way to Haworth in May 1913 for a Brontë pilgrimage ending in "a tea and symposium," Charlotte was a literary heroine with whom to identify.[108]

During the latter part of the nineteenth century, the rise in working-class education coincided with a new concept of leisure on a mass scale, with improvements in transport and the rise of the cheap holiday. According to John Urry in *The Tourist Gaze*, it was in the north of England that working-class holidays were first pioneered.[109] From the 1890s onward, Haworth begins to appear in an ever-increasing number of user-friendly travel guides, "compendiously written for popular use"[110] (as one put it) and offering (according to another) "an account of various short, happy, roaming, go-as-you-please holidays."[111] These books, with their pull-out maps and suggested walks, fed the Brontë epidemic by encouraging pilgrimages to the shrine.

With names like *Days Off, Where to Spend a Half-Holiday, Holiday Walks in the North-Countree, A Spring-Time Saunter Round and About Brontë Land, Best Ways to Visit Brontë-Land from Halifax,* and *Brontë Moors and Villages,* the guides were often aimed at residents of northern towns, offering them "cheap and pleasant recreation near home," suggesting walks and educational trips, and celebrating "the instinct which prompts man to seek recuperation."[112] In the imagination of tired city-dwellers, the place Gaskell had considered so dreary and untamed had turned into a comforting rural idyll, though one guidebook of 1911, *Nooks and Corners of Yorkshire,* warned that visitors might be disappointed in the unromantic "steep street, the stone houses, the general air of industry, the smell of oil and wood proceeding from the mills."[113]

Visitors to Haworth in the early part of the twentieth century were still barred, however, from entering the Parsonage itself without special permission from the resident clergyman, although, as one guide book peevishly put it, "some people, especially Americans, have thought they had a right to enter."[114] This was to change, however, in 1928, when the house was purchased by a wealthy local benefactor and given to the Brontë Society as a museum and library in which to house its—now substantial—collection of papers and other relics. In 1933 Rachel Ferguson opened her biographical play, *Charlotte Brontë,* with a present-day scene in the new Parsonage Museum in which a pair of overenthusiastic American

Crowds gather for the opening of Haworth Parsonage to the public, 1928.

tourists—"Why, the Brontës have *touched* that desk!"[115]—announce their intention to "check up on rock-bottom souvenirs,"[116] while an English girl denounces Patrick as "an awful old beast"[117] but admits, "I can't even begin most of the Brontë novels. I tried to get through *Shirley,* but I got stodged."[118] Brontëmania had reached a stage where the mania had become as worthy of remark as the Brontës.

Just as relic-hunters wanted contact with their idols through objects they had actually touched, visitors to Haworth were—and still are—after an authentic experience. Pilgrims wanted the village and the Parsonage to remain exactly as they had been in the Brontës' time, even though their idea of what that meant was often unrealistic. In 1994, complaints were raised about the proposal to erect windmills on the surrounding moors as an environmentally friendly source of energy. A group of leading cultural figures signed a letter to the *Times Literary Supplement,* deploring "the wholesale despoliation of a landscape with uniquely literary associations," which became the subject of a *Times* leader.[119] The visitor would, it was implied, no longer be able to admire the view that the Brontës had gazed at. Those complaining—who included Melvyn Bragg, Tom Stoppard, and Lady Antonia Fraser—did not, however, seem to mourn the disappear-

ance of the mills, with their attendant smoke and dirt, which had dominated Haworth in the Brontës' lifetime, or the piles of sewage that
had littered the streets.[120] (In a letter to William Smith Williams of 1848,
Charlotte gives a rare, unromantic glimpse of Yorkshire villages as "our
northern congregations of smoke-dark houses clustered round their soot-
vomiting Mills.")[121] Nor were they aware that similar complaints had been
being made by conservationists since the 1860s.

In 1861, Charles Hale had been able to snap up the sash of Charlotte's
bedroom window because the new occupant of the Parsonage, Patrick's
successor, the Reverend John Wade, had decided to replace the old-
fashioned small panes with modern plate glass. Visitors complained vocif-
erously about the loss. In 1867, W. H. Cooke expressed his affront in *St.
James's Magazine* that Wade, a man of "execrably bad taste," had even forbidden him from looking into the sitting room where the celebrated sisters
had written those works "which have conferred immortal lustre upon this
incumbent's present residence, and which will live long after he himself
has mouldered down to dust, and his bran-new [*sic*] window-frames have
rotted to decay."[122]

It is not surprising that Wade was less than keen to allow all and sundry
into his new home. He had little time for the Brontë cult. During the 1870s,
he changed the character of Haworth by adding a new wing to the Parsonage and presiding over the demolition and rebuilding of the church—only
the tower remains of the old church. This was done in the face of opposition from Brontë admirers keen to preserve the authenticity of the place
and was felt to have caused a fall in visitor numbers during the 1880s: a
guide to the Bradford area of 1890 explained that "of late" the number of
visitors to Haworth had diminished, probably because of the demolition of
the old church with its "quaint high-backed pews."[123]

Such destruction would never be allowed to take place today. Preservation is the core of the modern heritage movement, and the interior of the
Brontë Parsonage Museum has now been restored to look as authentic as
possible. Before the Second World War, some visitors thought that the
place, including the front room where the sisters used to write, felt more
like a shop than a lived-in space, with its glass display cases. But by 1956,
when the poet Sylvia Plath visited with her new husband, Ted Hughes,
the presentation was atmospheric enough to inspire an enthusiastic diary
entry, in which she scribbled a sketch of Emily's reputed death couch and
listed relics from samplers to sealing wax.[124] The first attempt to redeco-
rate the Parsonage so as to make it look as it did in the Brontës' time was

completed in 1959, along with the building of a sizeable extension to house the Brontë Society's unrivaled collection of books and manuscripts.[125]

Improvements have continued to be made; today the interior is presented with great attention to detail and a sensitive eye to historical accuracy. When the original furniture is not available, care is taken to provide authentic alternatives, such as an ornate carved bed which was recently commissioned, identical to one in a sketch by Branwell. The house is arranged as exquisitely as a theatrical set, and in the 1990s visitors could even eavesdrop on the conversations of Charlotte, Emily, and Anne, portrayed by actresses from a local theater company. A welcome emphasis has been put on education by the curatorial team. As well as being a center for scholarship, the Parsonage Museum now offers temporary exhibitions on particular themes and all sorts of programs for school parties.

Such innovations are appreciated by visitors, who expressed high praise in a recent survey for everything except the inadequate lavatory facilities[126]—though whatever Haworth offers today in that respect would have seemed bliss to the inhabitants of the Brontë era: a report into the sanitary conditions in Haworth of 1850 bemoaned the woeful inadequacy of the privies, noting that two, used by a dozen families each, were in the public street exposed to the eyes of passers-by.[127] In recent years, the museum has been regularly attracting more than 100,000 pilgrims annually, though the largest-ever number was 221,497, in 1974, in the wake of Christopher Fry's atmospheric television dramatization, *The Brontës of Haworth*.[128] The village has, however, become so famous for being famous that this represents only a fraction of the total number of annual visitors—more than a million[129]—many of whom want a day out unconnected with literature. In 1996, the Keighley and Worth Valley Railway, just down the hill from Haworth, which was the setting for the sentimental 1970 film *The Railway Children*, managed to pull nearly thirty thousand more visitors than the Parsonage.[130]

Perceptions of the Parsonage itself have changed over time. The box-shaped house seemed "grey, square, cold, dead-coloured" to Gaskell and her contemporaries; later writers gave it a gothic twist. By the 1970s, however, architectural tastes had changed, and the building now seemed to have an aura of nostalgic, Laura Ashley–ish charm: the fact that views of the Parsonage, looking very pretty, were used in *The Railway Children* shows how different the reality could be made to look from the "grim, life-prisoning shell"[131] of legend. The black-and-white photography of the late 1850s could make the house seem very grim and bleak, especially when taken from above from an uncompromisingly straight-on perspective. But a more flatteringly angled color picture in a 1990s tour brochure shows a very different aspect of the building, bathed in golden summer light and bordered by soft green flowerbeds.[132]

In the last century and a half, Haworth has thus become firmly established on the tourist trail. As the working mills and factories disappeared from the surrounding area, tourism became more and more important to the local economy and is now the biggest employer in Haworth.[133] The travel sections of today's newpapers continue in the tradition of the turn-of-the-century guidebooks, encouraging readers to wear their wellies to Wuthering Heights on trips to Brontëland.[134] In the 1990s, one finds a tourist board official quoted as comparing "Brontë" as a brand to "Coca-Cola," and local businesses use the name unsparingly, often for its recognition value alone.[135] A taxi company or a hairdresser's named after the Brontës has little to do with Haworth's most famous family, though one wonders about the cabinetmaker-cum-undertaker who, among other items, advertised coffins under the banner "Brontë Products" in the 1950s.[136]

Much of the imagery popularly associated with the Brontës today postdates the Victorian cult of Charlotte. In the twentieth century, Emily toppled her elder sister from her preeminent position and became enshrined as the free spirit of the moors. It was through the cult of Emily that the myth of the Brontës as forces of nature rising ineluctably out of the wuthering landscape gained currency. Images of storm-tossed passion associated with her—or with the Hollywoodization of *Wuthering Heights*—are now part and parcel of the Brontë brand. Yet if you visit the souvenir shops (with names like "Brontësaurus") which crowd up Haworth's steep Main Street, you can still detect the lingering presence of the domestic saint originally created by Elizabeth Gaskell.

Tea towels printed with the Brontës' faces or miniature brass warming pans send debased messages of homely nostalgia connected at some vestigial level to Gaskell's image of Charlotte the housewife rolling up her sleeves to peel Tabby's potatoes. Brontë Original Unique Liqueur (surely not a reference to Branwell's drinking problem?) comes in an olde worlde stoneware flagon straight from the kitchens of yesteryear. The former apothecary's shop, which supplied Branwell with laudanum, is now a sort of novelty chemist's, selling colored bath salts in Victorian-style packaging (the Emily Brontë soap has "the elusive fragrance of the wild moors"). During a visit in 1994, it was depressing to discover from the proprietor that the premises had previously been a bookshop which had closed down due to lack of demand.

Often, "Brontë" has come to stand for an all-purpose cozy nostalgia with no connection at all to literature. A souvenir teapot emblazoned with the word "Haworth" and purchased in the village transforms the Parsonage into a thatched cottage with roses round the door in a crude attempt to conjure ideas of traditional Englishness. In the case of "Brontë old fashioned recipe biscuits," a nationally marketed brand rather than a Haworth souvenir, the name is used as a watchword for what the packaging calls "traditional wholesome baking." It is meant to confer homemade status on a mass-produced product, reaching back through history to Victorian clichés of Charlotte the housewife. The deceptive illustration of the Parsonage on the packet—a prettified watercolor—sets the house in a rural oasis of lush green space, cutting out the buildings to its right and the graveyard in front.

Brontë products often embody a disjunction between reality and fantasy, such as Brontë Natural Spring Water ("Refreshingly sparkling, Serve chilled"). The bottlers allude to "the moorlands which were the playground of the Brontë children," but cannot have been aware of Haworth's notoriety in the Brontë period for its unhealthy water supply.[137] (In 1857, discomfited by guilt about her intrusive biographical methods, Elizabeth Gaskell tried to soften Arthur Nicholls by presenting him with the substantial gift of £100 to pay for a much-needed village pump, as Haworth was so "terribly off for water.")[138] The branding was, however, a canny piece of PR: the story was picked up on in the national press on account of the Brontë name.[139]

When Charlotte told Southey of her secret desire to be forever known, she imagined her name appearing on books, not biscuit packets. Such branding may increase the Brontës' fame, but there is an uncomfortable sense in which it has a belittling effect, obscuring the real truth about them: that it is their *writings,* in all their literary and emotional complexity, which are their most important gift to posterity.

CHAPTER FIVE

Secrets and Psychobiography

I

During the first years of the twentieth century, Charlotte Brontë's popular image remained that of the moral heroine originally created by Gaskell and codified by so many lesser writers. But if a single event could be said to have exploded her sainthood, it occurred on July 29, 1913, when the *Times* printed four letters she had written in 1844–45 to her Belgian teacher, Constantin Heger. The publication caused a storm of controversy. Issues of biographical ethics—of the propriety of exposing the private lives of public figures—were hotly debated. The guardians of Charlotte's moral reputation did not know how to cope with the evidence that their idol had fallen, all too humanly, in love with a married man.

In some ways, the sudden appearance of the Heger letters looks like a biographer's wish fulfillment, a real-life epiphany as exciting as the fictional account in A. S. Byatt's 1990 novel *Possession* of a researcher's discovery of a Victorian poet's hidden writings.[1] What the letters revealed soon came to be known as "the secret of Charlotte Brontë." But looking at the proliferation of subsequent interpretations, it becomes clear that their content is more fugitive than that suggests. The letters have been read as the expression of a conscientious pupil's gratitude toward a teacher;[2] as the culmination of a hysterical schoolgirl infatuation;[3] as evidence of a tragic unrequited *grande passion;*[4] as symptoms of a neurotic father fixation;[5] as an imaginative act of self-dramatization;[6] and as a comment on Charlotte's literary ambition.[7]

This diversity of interpretation demonstrates how malleable the raw material of biography can be, how dependent it is on the eye of the beholder. But even if we had a God's-eye view into Charlotte's mind, her feelings for Heger would probably still appear confused and contradictory.

Biographers trying to create a self-consistent interpretation may have been tempted to believe that there must be a single true reading, but it may be more realistic to allow the letters to remain inconclusive and multiform, and to take as an analogy Virginia Woolf's insight that "a biography is considered complete if it merely accounts for six or seven selves, whereas a person may well have as many thousand."[8]

What is most striking about the Heger letters is that they do *not* speak in a unitary voice. Written in French, though one has a postscript in English, their tone is shifting, changeable, unstable, which may explain why they have provoked such different responses. At times, Charlotte indeed writes in the courteous tone of a grateful pupil; at others, she seems to be dramatizing her feelings in the manner of a novel; elsewhere, her style reaches an unbearable pitch of desperate, needy emotion; yet the closest she gets to confessing to being in love is to tell Heger that she loves the French language for his sake.

If the letters are ambiguous, so was Charlotte's relationship with Constantin Heger. When they met, she was an ambitious twenty-five-year-old hungry for intellectual development. At thirty-two, he was still young, though married with a growing family. As teacher, and as husband of the school's headmistress, he was inevitably in a position of authority, but he could hardly have been a father figure in any literal sense.

She began as his pupil, but was a very unusual student, and she must have been a fascinating change from the recalcitrant teenagers he was used to dealing with. She went on to become his colleague, teaching classes in the school, and also his teacher, giving him and his brother-in-law English lessons (she found their accents highly amusing).[9] Perhaps it is not surprising that Heger's wife, the headmistress, began to cool toward this intriguing new inhabitant of their household. By July 1843, Charlotte believed that Madame Heger had become suspicious and told Ellen, "I fancy I begin to perceive the reason of this mighty distance & reserve; it sometimes makes me laugh & at other times nearly cry."[10]

At some level, Madame clearly felt threatened by the English teacher. Years later, while commenting on Charlotte's letters to her husband, she compared her to the hysterical schoolgirls she was accustomed to dealing with (one wonders whether she witnessed her pupils developing crushes on her husband with irritating frequency), though she went on to add that this independent, intense, older Englishwoman was far more dangerous because less easy to understand.[11] It seems, from the account of another pupil, that Heger was the sort of man who enjoyed being in a position of emotional power over his students: he liked to reduce girls to tears (as he did with Charlotte),[12] at which point he would melt and become gentle.[13]

This sort of manipulative flirtation may have been easy for Heger to get away with, as pupils and teachers at the Pensionnat seem to have habitually communicated in more emotionally charged language than one might expect. After leaving, Charlotte wrote to one of her pupils as "My dear little Victoire," telling her how she "loved" her students.[14] She reassured another pupil, Mathilde, of her "affection"; Mathilde responded by pouring out her soul, telling her teacher, "it seems to me that when I write to you the door of my heart opens."[15] Nothing could be further from the British formality of Roe Head, where Charlotte did not even call her pupils by their first names.[16] As a reserved if inwardly passionate Yorkshirewoman, she may have invested such freedom of expression, when it came from Constantin Heger, with a deeper significance than was intended.

And yet it seems hard to deny that there was a mutually intense element to the relationship, even though Charlotte felt more romantic about Heger than he did about her. He must have been gratified by her response to his teaching, and the high standards he set her reveal his high estimate of her abilities. His corrections to her essays suggest an element of mutual intellectual challenge; there is nothing flippant or noncommital about his attitude toward her work, which is, rather, highly focused and engaged.

Charlotte had returned alone to the Pensionnat in January 1843 after the death of her aunt had called her home from her first stint in Brussels with Emily. She went back alone, but as her emotional dependence on Heger increased, and his wife grew ever chillier, she became more and more isolated and subject to depression. By October—after the nightmarishly lonely summer vacation which would feature so powerfully in *Villette* and which drove her to the desperate measure of making a "real confession" to a priest in the Catholic cathedral of Ste-Gudule[17]—she felt so alienated and distrusting of Madame that she gave her notice, only to have Monsieur persuade her to stay.[18] By the end of the year, she had made up her mind. On January 1, 1844, she left Brussels for good.

The four "Heger letters" which survive from what must have been a larger correspondence were written between July 1844 and November 1845. The first, written on July 24, 1844, begins in a friendly but not intimate style. Charlotte is "well aware" that it is not her turn to write—Heger has not yet answered her previous communication—but feels she must take advantage of the fact that an English friend traveling to the Continent will be able to forward a letter (postage costs were not negligible at that date).

Suddenly, however, she bursts into a passionate cry which suggests that her previous letter had overstepped the mark: "Ah Monsieur! I once wrote you a letter which was hardly rational, because sadness was wringing my heart, but I shall do so no more."[19] She is afraid, she goes on, of forgetting French: afraid, in other words, of anything that might block communication with Heger.

Yet the real passion of the letter, its climax, has less to do with Heger himself than with the intense, long-standing literary ambition which his committed teaching had validated: she confesses that her dream is to write a book and dedicate it to her master, but she knows that the career of letters is closed to her. After such anguished honesty, she pulls back. The tone changes abruptly, as if she feels she has gone too far. *"Please assure Madame of my esteem,"* she writes in the voice of the respectful former pupil.[20]

The second letter, written on October 24, is much shorter, and was delivered by another English friend traveling to Brussels. Heger had still not replied, and Charlotte now begs him to write, carefully remembering nevertheless to ask after his wife and children. Her next letter, written on January 8, 1845, reveals that he has again failed to respond.

It opens in medias res without the customary "Monsieur," as if it is not a letter at all but a fragment of a novel:

> Mr Taylor returned, I asked him if he had a letter for me—"No, nothing." "Patience"—I say—"His sister will be coming soon"—Miss Taylor returned "I have nothing for you from M. Heger" she says "neither letter nor message."
>
> When I had taken in the full meaning of these words . . . I did my utmost not to cry not to complain—
>
> But when one does not complain, and when one wants to master oneself with a tyrant's grip—one's faculties rise in revolt—and one pays for outward calm by an almost unbearable inner struggle
>
> Day and night I find neither rest nor peace—if I sleep I have tormenting dreams.[21]

The agony of the post hour would become a repeated motif in Charlotte's mature fiction, inspired, it seems, by her experience of Heger's failure to reply to her letters. Yet Fannie Ratchford, the first editor of the Brontë juvenilia, noticed a similarity between the above passage and an episode in the Angrian saga Charlotte had written six years before in which the Duchess of Zamorna is neglected by her faithless absent husband.

Repeatedly asking if the mail has arrived, the duchess tells her attendant how she has been suffering "long, weary, sleepless nights" and that she could rest if only she had a letter. They are interrupted by a messenger returning from Zamorna empty-handed: " '[H]ave you no letter for me, Mr Warner? Do you bring no message, no word of his welfare, no enquiry after mine?' 'My lady, I have not so much as a syllable for you.' "[22]

Was the Heger correspondence inspired by Charlotte's literary imagination as much as it in turn inspired aspects of *Villette*? That novel would transform Charlotte's unrequited feelings for Heger into the mutual love of Lucy Snowe and Paul Emanuel, but perhaps she was already fictionalizing her relationship with her "Master" in her letters of 1844 and 1845. Some aspects of Heger which she appears to have fed into Emanuel are at second glance revealed to have a longer heritage in her imagination, going back to a time before Brussels—his ever-present cigar, for example. Heger may, like Emanuel and Rochester, have smoked,[23] but cigars had already been used by Charlotte to symbolize a hero's masculinity in her Angrian prose.[24]

Charlotte composed her last surviving letter to Heger on November 18.[25] Concluding with a final-sounding "Farewell" in English, was she signing off from what was really "an *invented* correspondence, close to an imaginative act"?[26] Writing into the void (his letters to her, none of which survive, were painfully infrequent),[27] was she using the correspondence as a way of consciously exploring modes of passionate subjective expression which would eventually be fully developed in *Jane Eyre* and *Villette*?

The final extant letter dwells on her attempts to forget Heger, the imbalance between her feelings for him and his for her, her feverish misery at the daily disappointment of not receiving a letter from him. Yet we know that, by the time she wrote it, other hopes had begun to take hold in Charlotte's mind. That autumn, she had made her momentous discovery of Emily's verse and set about galvanizing her sisters into preparing their *Poems* for publication. With biographer's hindsight we can see that she was no longer such a slave to the idea of Heger as she presents herself, that some sort of catharsis had begun to take place. This last letter is the most extreme expression of desperation and the most stylistic and emotionally consistent text of the correspondence. But its obsessional tone belies the fact that she had actually begun to move on.

In the end, the complex trains of thought and feeling aroused in Charlotte by her "Master" defy labeling. They slip through our fingers, not least because the correspondence is incomplete. From the available evidence we can try to reassemble her state of mind, but, as Bernard in Virginia Woolf's novel *The Waves* puts it, biography can do no more than "tack together torn bits of stuff, stuff with raw edges."[28] Gaps will always remain.

Uncannily, our fragmented vision is echoed by the fact that three of the four documents, now preserved in the British Library, are literally in fragments which have been carefully stuck and stitched together. After receiving Charlotte's letters, Heger had ripped all but one of them up and thrown the pieces away, but his wife had retrieved them, painstakingly reassembled them, and put them in her jewel box for safekeeping. She must have let her husband know what she had done, for as we have seen he showed—or perhaps read—the letters to Elizabeth Gaskell in 1856.

Twenty-one years after Charlotte left Brussels, the Hegers' daughter Louise, whose truthful little face had as a child inspired a particular affection in Charlotte,[29] went to a literary lecture about the author of *Jane Eyre.* The speaker mentioned, in passing, that Charlotte Brontë had been cruelly treated by the callous Heger family in Brussels. Hurt, Louise mentioned the matter to her mother, who showed her the letters.

When Madame Heger died in 1890, Louise went through her mother's papers, retrieved Charlotte's letters, and gave them to her father. Again, he tried throwing them away, but Louise rescued them from the wastepaper basket, as she knew they were important literary documents. Some years after Constantin Heger's death, in 1896, Louise finally discussed the matter with her brother Paul, a prominent scientist, who, on the advice of the critic M. H. Spielmann, decided to donate the letters to the British Library.

The main reason prompting the release of the letters was Paul Heger's desire that the record be set straight, as suspicion about Charlotte's relationship with his father had in fact been brewing for a long time. Though Charlotte's iconic image in the popular anthologies remained relatively static through the second half of the nineteenth century, other writers had begun to question whether Elizabeth Gaskell had told the full story.

The year 1877 had seen the first full-length life of Charlotte since Gaskell's. Its author, Thomas Wemyss Reid, the editor of the *Leeds Mercury,* had been given access by Ellen Nussey to correspondence of Charlotte's which Mrs. Gaskell had not seen.[30] The main thrust of his biography was to show that "the life of the author of '*Jane Eyre*' was by no means so joyless as the world now believes it to have been."[31] Though he still clung to the old moral rhetoric—Charlotte's was a life "made sacred and noble" by "self-repression"[32]—he was not above speculating on her relationship

Charlotte Brontë to Constantin Heger, January 8, 1845, in which she expresses her despair at his unresponsiveness. After he tore up the letter and threw it away, his wife retrieved it and carefully stitched the pieces back together.

with her teacher. Quoting a letter in which Charlotte told Ellen that she had returned to Brussels against her conscience,[33] he hinted darkly that Charlotte had "tasted strange joys"[34] at the Pensionnat Heger, evidence of which was to be found "not in her 'Life' and letters, but in 'Villette' . . . the revelation of the most vivid passages in her own heart's history."[35]

Augustine Birrell's biography, which followed ten years later, expressed similar suspicions. While apparently throwing up his hands in horror at the prospect of intruding upon "the secrets of a woman's heart,"[36] he left his readers in no doubt about how to interpret the two bald sentences with which he summarized the relationship: "Madame Heger became estranged. Miss Brontë got on better with the husband."[37] Birrell's slippery handling of the episode gives an indication of what it was and was not possible to say in a respectable biography of the 1880s: he counsels his readers to "read *Villette* between the lines" if they want to know Charlotte's secret, but he warns them "if they are wise, nay, if they are delicate, [to] hold their tongues about their discoveries."[38] Ironically, these roundabout attempts at euphemism allowed readers to infer something far more damaging than what was in fact suggested—the idea that Charlotte and Heger had had an actual affair.

This sort of speculation aroused bold attacks from writers who saw them as an insult to Charlotte's memory. Ever since Gaskell, biographers have tended to feel unusually possessive and protective of the Brontës, and Marion Harland, whose sentimental *Charlotte Brontë at Home* came out in 1899, was no exception. The rumors regarding Heger had reached such a pitch that it had become necessary, she thought, to quash "the romantic and unsavoury conclusion of a hopeless passion" which was being peddled on both sides of the Atlantic by "sensational penny-a-liners."[39] Harland's conviction that Charlotte could not have been emotionally attached to Heger derived not from a careful examination of the evidence, but from her devotion to an idealized image of her heroine.

The "sensational penny-a-liners" to which Harland refers with such scorn represented a type of short, downmarket biography which had begun to displace the didactic anthology in popularity. These offered leisure reading designed to entertain as much as educate, and a typical example is the American paperback of 1883, *An Hour with Charlotte Brontë, or, Flowers from a Yorkshire Moor* by Laura Carter Holloway. This book is riddled with inaccuracies and purple passages, from errors such as the claim that Charlotte's mother was a Yorkshirewoman[40] to the bold assertion that Charlotte never grew an inch after going to Cowan Bridge at the age of eight[41] to the idea that she only ever "exhibited herself" to her London publishers on one occasion.[42] Letting her imagination run riot over the evidence, Holloway not only repeats Gaskell's unsubstantiated claim that Patrick had viciously cut up his wife's best dress, but embellishes the story with an imagined reference to its "pretty figured" fabric.[43]

It would have been hard for such a sensation merchant to resist including the spicy rumor that Charlotte had been the victim of "a great tempest" of unrequited love.[44] But there were other writers who went further and explicitly stated that there had been not merely love but mutual passion. One of these was an obsessive enthusiast named John Malham-Dembleby, in whom the "Brontëmania" of the turn of the century reached proportions that can only be described as pathological.

Malham-Dembleby's book, *The Key to the Brontë Works* (1911), offers an extreme example of the intellectual muddle Henry James found so disturbing. For a conspiracy theorist, the fact that Charlotte had based some of her fiction on real-life experience proved frighteningly fertile.

Gaskell had tried to defend the Brontë sisters from charges of willful coarseness by claiming that they had merely written down what they saw before them in the shape of Haworth's rude inhabitants and their brother's debaucheries. Malham-Dembleby takes this claim to its hyperbolical conclusion, asserting that there was nothing in Charlotte's novels that was not a direct copy from life (if a detail does not fit, it is always "for obfuscation's sake").[45]

He often begins with a sane or semi-sane hunch—such as the idea that Mrs. Gaskell had not told the full story of Charlotte's Brussels life and that Charlotte had felt passionately about Heger—but shoots off into completely other territories in which he is wholly incapable of distinguishing fact from fiction. To identify Heger as the love of Charlotte's life is one thing; but to claim equally insistently that Charlotte was the author of *Wuthering Heights* is quite another. Later on, he declares that the French popular novelist Eugene Sue, author of the best-seller *The Wandering Jew*, had presented the true history of Monsieur Heger's reciprocal passion for Charlotte in a serialized novel of 1850–51, *Miss Mary, ou l'Institutrice*[46]— though where Sue was supposed to have picked up this secret information about their "dangerous friendship"[47] we are not told.[48]

If Malham-Dembleby's mad views received more of a hearing than they deserved, it was because he offered a mutant version of the sort of agenda pursued by saner Brontë enthusiasts who were keen to identify the real-life persons and places of the novels.[49] In 1911, his *Key to the Brontë Works* was published with the imprimatur of W. W. Yates of the Brontë Society, who was one of the subscribers to the volume. And in 1906, he had acted as adviser to the director of the National Portrait Gallery, who, as a result, purchased what ought to have been recognized as an obvious forgery, a picture supposedly of Charlotte by Heger (the forger spelled Heger's name wrong and hadn't even bothered to rub out sufficiently an earlier inscription, which read "Miss Mary Vickers"). Questions were eventually asked in the House of Commons about the portrait's genuineness, and in 1913 it was finally unmasked as bogus.[50]

Malham-Dembleby may have propagated the unwelcome theory that there had been reciprocal but unconsummated passion between Charlotte and Heger, but even more damaging reports had also begun to circulate. A book was published in France alleging they had had a sexual relationship.[51] This was this sort of unfounded allegation that Heger's son was determined to silence and explains why he was so keen to make the letters public. Once published, he felt, they would "lay open the true significance of what has hitherto been spoken of as the 'secret of Charlotte Brontë' and show how groundless is the suspicion which has resulted from the natural speculations of biographers."[52] It seemed to him better "to lay bare the very innocent mystery, than to let it be supposed there is anything to hide."[53]

Despite this attempt to downplay Charlotte's "innocent" secret, the press responded with uninhibited excitement when the letters appeared in the *Times* in 1913. Since the 1890s, newspapers had been prepared to run stories on almost any Brontë subject, however trivial. The high-Victorian emphasis on martyrdom, sickness, and death had given way to a public appetite for romantic sentiment. But if the Brontë story was lacking in anything, it was love interest. Popular writers and journalists had been attempting to supply this want in books like *Stories of Authors' Loves* (1904) and *Twelve Great Passions* (1912), and in newspaper articles such as "Charlotte Brontë's Love Story," serialized in the *Weekly Sun* in 1896. These had attempted to find romance in Charlotte's relationship with her husband, but the marriage was lacking in the sort of sensation value readers were beginning to demand.

The search for Brontë love stories would eventually find its most ludicrous expression in the Hollywood film of the 1940s, *Devotion,* in which Emily, bizarrely, dies of unrequited love for Nicholls, and Heger is played as a lecherous French *roué* who takes Charlotte to the local funfair to teach her a thing or two in the tunnel of love. Before the release of the Heger letters, the press had had little opportunity to find romance in the Brontë story. Afterward they could not get enough of it: under the headline "More Brontë Love Letters," one paper even attempted to compete with the excitement of Charlotte's secret passion with an unpromising story about a Miss Burder, to whom Patrick Brontë had once made an unsuccessful proposal of marriage.[54]

Those who saw themselves as the guardians of Charlotte's reputation responded less enthusiastically to the Heger letters. The emotional quality of their knee-jerk defenses of their heroine suggests how threatened they felt. Clement Shorter was placed in a position of some embarrassment. As the editor of Charlotte's correspondence, he had carved out a niche for himself as a Brontë expert, and, in that role, he had previously thrown cold water on the "silly and offensive imputation"[55] that Charlotte could have been infatuated with a married man. It was as if anyone who suggested that her feelings for Heger had been warmer than the ordinary gratitude felt by a pupil for a teacher would be accusing her of discreditable conduct which would pull the pedestal from underneath her.

Yet the letters were unquestionably passionate. Unfortunately for Shorter, their appearance out of the blue also seemed to suggest to the public that he knew less about Charlotte than he had previously claimed. Called upon to comment on them, he blustered his way through, repeating what he had always said: that there was nothing there "that any enthusiastic woman might not write to a man double her age, who was a married man with a family, and who had been her teacher."[56] In his earnestness to remove the offensive imputation, Shorter's expert knowledge of Charlotte Brontë and her circle deserted him. Charlotte was born in 1816; Heger in 1809. Only an enormous stretch of the imagination could describe an age gap of seven years as constituting "double her age."

The problem was that the letters' intensity of emotion, however platonic, did not sit comfortably with the sanctified ideal Charlotte had come to represent. In response to their publication, Shorter's friend W. Robertson Nicholl printed a "Vindication of Charlotte Brontë" in the *Times* in a desperate attempt to keep alive the vision of the angel in the house. "The truest of daughters and a pattern of domesticity, life was for her not a home but a school, and her heart was ever going out to that world of teachers and pupils," he wrote in an awkward attempt at justification.[57]

Defensive responses were not confined to those who clung to the image of Charlotte as domestic saint. Her feminist supporters were equally disquietened. A letter in the *Yorkshire Post* decried the "recent aspersions that have been cast on the personality and character of Charlotte Brontë" while hailing her as a "leader in the movement for the intellectual uplifting of womanhood." The correspondent not only defended Charlotte's sexual "purity," but also pigeonholed her as a political figure who had "set forth the iniquity of the system that denies the womanhood their just rights in the making and administering of the laws of this country."[58]

One of the most strident critics of the decision to make the letters public was the novelist May Sinclair, who had been gripped by the tragedy of Gaskell's *Life* as a child. The Heger letters appeared between the first and second editions of her critical biography, *The Three Brontës*. Before their publication she had, like Shorter, dismissed claims that Charlotte could have been in love with her teacher. In a letter to the *Times,* and then in the revised edition of her book, she was at pains to underplay the discovery.

With an intellectual's disdain for newspapers, she denounced the vulgarity of dragging "Charlotte Brontë's poor little secret . . . into the day-light for all Fleet Street to gloat over."[59] The letters, she asserted, "add nothing of any value to our knowledge of Charlotte Brontë, even suppos-ing that we had the right to know."[60] On the face of it, this statement seems extraordinary. No subsequent biographer has agreed with Sinclair in deny-ing that the letters are literary and personal documents of the utmost significance.

Sinclair's refusal to accept the Heger letters as important evidence of Charlotte's personality was motivated by more than a strict regard for the ethics of revealing intimate details of people's lives. It was also related to her conception of the ideal woman artist. One of the leading authors of her day, Sinclair was in the vanguard of a generation of female writers who, in the words of one contemporary critic, were seeking "a new spiritu-ality."[61] Attracted from her youth onward to philosophy—particularly to idealist metaphysics, as well as to mysticism and even spiritualism—Sinclair had a highly nonmaterialist sensibility.

Unlike the New Women of the Nineties, who had used literature as a forum in which to articulate demands for political rights, Sinclair was more interested in the internal, spiritual, and subjective aspects of femininity, to the extent that, in her novel *The Creators* (1910), she advocated what almost amounted to a wholesale rejection of the external world. "Experi-ence? . . ." she wrote. "It spoils you. It ties you hand and foot. It perverts you, twists you, blinds you. . . . I know women—artists—who have never got over their experience, women who'll never do anything because of it."[62] The novel's central character, a woman writer, protects herself from such contamination: "To make sure her splendid isolation, she had cut her-self off by a boarded, a barricaded staircase, closed with a door at the foot."[63]

In this context, Charlotte became a heroine of otherworldiness for whom subjectivity was more important than relationships with others. Earlier biographers from Gaskell onward had interpreted Charlotte's sub-dued social manner as proof of vulnerable shyness or ladylike modesty. For Sinclair, this apparent rejection of worldly values became a sign of spiritual superiority. In Sinclair's view, the female imagination should be pure and self-sufficient. It was unthinkable that Charlotte could have derived inspiration from the outside world, and least of all from a man. "It is supposed, even by the charitable," she writes scornfully, "that whatever M. Héger [*sic*] did or did not do for Charlotte, he did everything for her genius."[64] She goes on to add a sarcastic swipe at what she takes to be the antifeminist assumptions behind the supposition: "So when a woman's talent baffles you, your course is plain, *cherchez l'homme.*"[65]

Sinclair rages particularly against the married critic Mrs. Oliphant, who, she feels, could never understand Charlotte's "unsanctioned knowledge of the mysteries, her intrusion into the veiled places, her unbaring of the virgin heart."[66] Single herself, she had personal reasons for her emphasis on the "virgin heart." At this period in her life she was becoming more and more convinced that there was a close kinship between celibacy and creativity in the female artist, perhaps as a way of justifying or coping with her own singleness. As her most recent biographer puts it, throughout her life she "continued to feel that she had traded sexual intimacy for intellectual independence,"[67] and she came to believe "that sexual intimacy could actually hinder women in their pursuit of artistic excellence."[68]

As a result, although her public response to the Heger letters was grudgingly to admit that they contained "some passionate element, innocent and unconscious," Sinclair was privately devastated by what they revealed about Charlotte's emotional and erotic needs. According to her protégée Rebecca West, "The publication of the Heger letters was a tragic and terrible blow to May—like a personal bereavement. She had wanted so much to think of the Brontës as virgin priestesses of art."[69]

Yet Sinclair's attack on Mrs. Oliphant, and on other critics who presented Charlotte's infatuation with Heger as the trigger which prompted her to write, had more than a personal significance. It was also an understandable reaction against the crude caricature, which went back to the days of Thackeray, of Charlotte as a frustrated spinster whose art was nothing more than a naive confession that she was desperate for sex. If Sinclair was particularly keen to discredit the idea of the single woman artist as a sort of warped, sex-starved hysteric, it was because similar views persisted among opponents of female suffrage, such as Sir Almroth Wright, professor of experimental pathology at the University of London, who argued that militant women were suffering from a mental disorder brought about by blocked sexual energies.[70]

Sinclair's own attitude toward sexuality was complex, evolving, and often contradictory. In 1913 she discovered psychoanalysis, and would go on to incorporate some of its insights into her existing idealist philosophy, developing her own concept of sublimation. Her 1914 novel, *The Three Sisters,* suggests that she came to believe that although sexual repression could cause hysteria in ordinary women, who needed the outlet of marriage, the spiritually gifted could purify or sublimate their desires by redirecting them into a spiritual channel. As she wrote in her 1917 treatise, *A Defence of Idealism*, "All sublimation is a turning and a passing of desire from a less worthy or fitting object to fix it on one more worthy or fitting."[71]

The germs of these ideas can be seen in her earlier work, which was marked by conflicting feelings about the place of sexuality in women's lives. On the one hand, her novel *The Helpmate* (1907) had opened, scandalously, in a marital bed and attacked the Victorian ideal of the sexless woman in the character of a frigid wife who eventually learns that physical love can be a form of spiritual experience.[72] Yet on the other, her need to spiritualize the sexual was as strong as her interest in sexuality itself. In the 1850s, Harriet Martineau had regarded the erotic feelings expressed by Charlotte's heroines as morbid and demeaning. Sixty years on, they still seem to pose something of a problem for Sinclair. In her introduction to the 1908 Everyman edition of *Jane Eyre*, she felt the need to interpret the heroine's passion in an exaggeratedly pure light as "a thing of strange innocences . . . rejoicing in service and the sacrifice of self. A thing superbly unaware of animal instinct."[73]

In *The Three Brontës*, similarly, Sinclair would praise Charlotte for having purified passion. Before she came along, "passion between man and woman had meant animal passion" and was a "thing . . . defiled, dragged in the mud." Charlotte "washed it clean; she bathed it in the dew of the morning; she baptised it in tears; she clothed it in light and flame."[74] Where Charlotte's novels undoubtedly do display an idealized attitude toward passion, which she indeed associates with the purifying energy of genius, Sinclair insists more strongly on its unsullied incorporeality. Thus, she assimilates Charlotte into a spiritual ideal of the female artist which reflects not just her personal preoccupations, but a common tendency among feminists of her generation to regard women as superior to men in their essential sexual purity and to promote a chaste, etherealized view of ideal human relations.[75] Ironically, the cultural origins of this ideology can be traced, in literature, less to Charlotte's novels than to a text like Gaskell's *Ruth*.

Old-fashioned believers in Saint Charlotte and feminist intellectuals like May Sinclair may have been as reluctant as each other to accept the evidence of the Heger letters, but their attempts to downplay their significance had little effect. In 1914, Frederika Macdonald, who had herself been a pupil at the Pensionnat twenty years after Charlotte, published a book with the seductive title *The Secret of Charlotte Brontë*. Though she provided valuable firsthand evidence about the Hegers' teaching style, her treatment of Charlotte's emotional life was gushing. She concluded that after Brussels her existence "was not only coloured, but governed by a tragical romantic love" that "broke her heart." It was not Heger's intellectual influence but the love "vibrations" he set in motion that "called her genius forth to life."[76]

Charlotte's passion, suppressed by Gaskell, had been recovered, but at a cost. Her relationship with Heger subsequently became established in many accounts of the Brontë story as a tragic romance with a Mills and Boon flavor, its significance to her literary development swamped in a bath of sentiment. Even Winifred Gérin, the otherwise clear-sighted and scholarly Brontë biographer, treated the episode with emotional indulgence. A play she wrote on the subject early on in her career, *My Dear Master,* was described in a review in 1955 as rising "no higher than a women's magazine serial."[77]

By 1963, the Heger-Charlotte relationship had been so frequently and inappropriately romanticized that it was ripe for ridicule. A parodic "opera," *Le Sorelle Brontë,* appeared in New York, in which the Belgian professor features as a Latin lover crying, *"Dammi uno baccio. . . . Sulla bocca, Carlotta."* Included in the libretto is an illustration, based on Branwell's famous portrait of his sisters, showing Charlotte in a provocatively low-cut dress and a come-hither expression.[78] The Victorian guardians of her moral reputation must have turned in their graves.

II

When Paul Heger decided to release Charlotte's letters he was largely motivated by the fact that those involved were dead; it was no longer necessary to spare their feelings. But the publication also took place at a moment in history when attitudes to biography were beginning to change. Thackeray's daughter Lady Ritchie (who remembered Miss Brontë freezing her father out of his own dinner party over sixty years before) may have complained that printing a lady's private correspondence in the *Times* showed a lamentable lack of chivalry. But at seventy-six she belonged to an earlier generation.[79] Biography had already begun to lose its didactic and hagiographic function, and biographers' freedom was increasing to explore the darker undersides of their subjects' personalities. In the 1890s, one writer on the Brontës had criticized "the illogical demand . . . that portraits of public men should have all the shadows left out."[80] By "shadows" he meant anything that might compromise a reputation, but he could also have been referring to the shadowy area of the inner life.

By the 1920s, biographers were actively seeking those shadows. Aspects of experience which had previously been passed over in silence began to take center stage, most notably sexuality. The period saw such a shift that Virginia Woolf came to the conclusion that the facts of biography "are not like the facts of science—once they are discovered, always the same. They are subject to changes of opinion; opinions change as times change."[81] Life-writing was becoming a revisionist art, and as Charlotte moved into the twentieth century her personality underwent some radical redrawing.

Historically, the Heger letters appeared between two landmarks of biography: Sigmund Freud's *Leonardo da Vinci and a Memory of His Childhood* (1910) and Lytton Strachey's *Eminent Victorians* (1918). Rather than pursuing new factual research, both these writers took subjects whose lives had already been documented, and subjected the old data to new ways of seeing. They had in common a desire to break with the idealizing tendencies of nineteenth-century hagiography, whether (in Freud's case) by uncovering the hidden workings of the unconscious mind, or (in Strachey's) by revealing unedifying motives behind revered facades. The influence of both Freud and Strachey would feed indirectly into perceptions of Charlotte, and would prepare the ground for a new sort of approach which began to appear in the 1920s: psychobiography.

This is not to say that Charlotte had never previously been viewed as psychologically problematic. Mrs. Gaskell and Harriet Martineau had always suspected that the passion of her novels stemmed from something pathological in her makeup. Though Gaskell had avoided discussing these anxieties openly in the *Life,* at least one reviewer had picked up on her suppressed suspicions. "We have to read between the lines," wrote the *Examiner*'s critic, who thought that the biography was "likely to be regarded by the inconsiderate as an unhealthy book" because "it discusses sick minds almost without admitting that they are unsound."[82]

Looking at the *Life,* one can see how it might have prompted alert readers to wonder whether Gaskell was dropping hints about Charlotte's mental health. Its continual emphasis on suffering means that the whole narrative becomes flooded with nonspecific negative emotion, often with no apparent object. As a result, it sometimes gives the impression that

Charlotte existed in a permanent state of irrational emotional distress disconnected from the external tragedies of her life.

This is particularly so in the Brussels period, where Gaskell is gagged and cannot mention that the true cause of Charlotte's inner torment is her intense feeling for Heger. In a climactic scene, she tells us how the ever-dutiful Charlotte longed to return to Haworth, but felt bound to remain at the Pensionnat to complete her studies. Charlotte had been thinking of starting a small school with her sisters at the Parsonage, which would, as Gaskell saw it, enable her to combine the impoverished woman's duty of contributing to the family finances with the unmarried woman's duty of keeping her father's house:

> A knowledge of German now became her object; and she resolved to compel herself to remain in Brussels till that was gained. The strong yearning to go home came upon her; the stronger self-denying will forbade. There was a great internal struggle; every fibre of her heart quivered in the strain to master her will; and, when she conquered herself, she remained, not like a victor calm and supreme on the throne, but like a panting, torn, and suffering victim. Her nerves and her spirits gave way.[83]

Gaskell wants us to believe that it was for the selfless end of fitting herself for future work as a teacher that Charlotte sought education, and that she was willing to suffer for its sake. Yet unknown to its original audience, the writing is colored by the biographer's private fear that Charlotte had in fact been suffering from the moral sickness of a morbid passion. As a result, the emotions indeed seem pathologically out of proportion to the situation.

Most of Gaskell's contemporaries, however, missed the ambiguities of such depictions of self-suppression, simply reading them as proof of moral heroism. In the 1920s, it would indeed become fashionable to redefine the Victorian virtue of self-denial as a sick symptom of masochism. But in the immediate wake of the *Life*, the idea that Charlotte was mentally "unsound" was a minority view. More typical of public opinion was the *Manchester Examiner and Times*, which had been quick to quash the aspersions, declaring that "if Christian fortitude ... solemn resignation ... and ... exemplary patience be considered proofs of mental sickness, we must confess our belief that the world would be none the worse for a general plague of such a malady."[84]

Gaskell's *Life* ensured that in its immediate wake Charlotte would be revered as a woman of such nobility that it would have seemed insulting to her memory to dig too deeply into the secrets of her psyche. Even those who saw her as something more than a one-dimensional moral paragon would have shrunk from questioning her mental probity. An unusual psychological reading of Charlotte's life, which appeared as early as 1858 in the *Journal of Psychological Medicine and Mental Pathology,* makes surprisingly little attempt to medicalize her. One might have expected a treatise on female morbidity, but rather than diagnosing mental ills, the anonymous article offers, in restrained, respectful, and generous tones, what might better be described as an "appreciation" of Charlotte's character.

The main purpose of the argument is to discuss the etiology of "intellectual capacity" in heredity and environment. Departing from the standard post-Gaskell agenda, it concentrates on Charlotte's remarkable "mental development" rather than on her moral or feminine virtues, praises Jane Eyre's character as a "psychical transcript" of her creator's self, and stresses the positive influence of Patrick's talent and energy on his daughter's abilities and achievements.[85] The author appreciates the *Life* for its graphic details, but feels that it exaggerates the wildness of Yorkshire society and that its portrayal of Charlotte's character lacks coherence. After examining Charlotte's correspondence and writings, he (or—which is less likely—she) sums up her personality as dominated by

> unmistakeable marks of an ardent, fiery temperament, constantly repressed—of an imagination vivid, scintillating, wild and eerie ... of a disposition warm and affectionate ... of a piety deep, sincere and practical ... of a habit of mind reserved, timid and observant—of an entire noble nature, enthusiastic and aspiring, quelled and worn down with unremitting care and suffering.[86]

Thus, Charlotte is given a more complex personality than in the populist Victorian readings of her life.

Although it appeared in a specialist scientific journal, the categories employed in this sympathetic 1858 article are no different from those a layman might have used. Nor does the author feel that his self-styled status as a psychologist allows him to break the normal bounds of decorum to probe the subject's love life: he half-raises the question of whether or not Charlotte's marriage satisfied "that perfect, expansive, all-comprehensive love of which her original nature was capable" only to withdraw with the abrupt acknowledgment that "we have no right to enquire."[87] But by the time the first Freudian reading of Charlotte's life came out in 1920, psychological biography had become both more technical and more fearless. Lucile Dooley's lengthy essay, "Psychoanalysis of Charlotte Brontë, As a Type of the Woman of Genius," which appeared in the *American Journal of Psychology*, was the first to apply the vocabulary of Freud's new science of the mind to Charlotte's case. As such it was revolutionary.

In his work on Leonardo da Vinci, Freud had attacked the "prudishness" of traditional biographers who failed to explore their subjects' sexuality, which he saw as the key to understanding the mental life.[88] If the release of the Heger letters had brought ideas of romantic love onto the scene of Charlotte's posthumous reputation, psychoanalysis brought with it the first unvarnished assertion that "she really had strong sexual feeling . . . we see the part that the sex theme plays in her novels."[89] In describing Charlotte's literary treatment of passion as "morbid," Harriet Martineau and Elizabeth Gaskell had employed a pejorative term which in 1853 had connotations of moral as well as mental weakness. Psychoanalysis attempted to remove the moralizing tone from the discussion of sexuality. As Virginia Woolf put it, "What was thought a sin is now known, by the light of facts won for us by the psychologists, to be perhaps a misfortune."[90]

But if this new perspective made it possible for Charlotte to be resexualized, it also repathologized her, not merely suggesting that she had a morbid streak but centering her entire life and art on her "abnormally developed personality."[91] Lucile Dooley's psychoanalytic reading redefined Charlotte as "essentially a neurotic."[92] Unlike Gaskell or Martineau, who felt that Charlotte's pathology spoiled her art, Dooley equated neurosis directly with genius. She acknowledged the brilliance and uniqueness of Charlotte's works, "those soul-searching tales in which the inner life of woman is set forth as never before or since by any English writer."[93] But she simultaneously removed any sense of conscious artistry or adult responsibility on the part of the novelist. The novels, she believed, had risen "whole and unalterable" from "the Unconscious."[94] Thus, Charlotte's true value as a writer was held to lie not in her powers of intellect or expression but in the repressed emotional conflicts which flowed "uncensored" into her work from "the lower strata of the subconsciousness," apparently without her knowledge, awareness, or control.[95]

Dooley diagnosed the central unconscious conflict in question as a "Father-fixation" or "Electra complex."[96] Gaskell had ensured that Patrick would forever after be seen as a dominating presence; Dooley reinterpreted Charlotte's celebrated filial piety (which had been singled out for praise by Victorian hagiographers) as symptomatic of a repressed childhood incest fantasy she was never able to grow out of. Thus, the adult remained "fixed in her infantile mould" and could never reach "full emotional maturity."[97] It was because the forbidden feelings for her father were repressed that the sexual energy associated with them was sublimated into artistic creativity.

More a mental safety valve than an intellectual achievement, novel-writing may have provided a therapeutic channel and prevented Charlotte from meeting the total "mental shipwreck seen in *dementia praecox* cases."[98] But her repressed desires were nevertheless held by Dooley to have caused symptoms of hysteria and neurasthenia (the two conditions most often diagnosed in women by early psychoanalysts). She interpreted the physical illnesses from which Charlotte suffered during the course of her life as psychosomatic responses to unconscious conflict. Though it would be hard to deny that the headaches, often accompanied by depression, which visited Charlotte, particularly after the terrible bereavements of 1848–49, were inextricably bound up with the mental anguish of mourning, Dooley's reading of her death and final illness was much more contentious.

Oddly perhaps, Charlotte's marriage is not held to symbolize the final throwing off of the oedipal bond but is instead described as a "regression" to a childhood need for security. Ignoring the evidence of Charlotte's letters that she had been happy with her "dear Arthur," Dooley describes the relationship in purely negative terms. Charlotte, she argues, could not cope with the adult reality of having, firstly, a husband but, more terrifyingly still, children. Her pregnancy activated "all the resistances of her most powerful complexes." Dooley is the first commentator to suggest that Charlotte's death—a perennial source of speculation among biographers—was caused by "psychogenic reactions" linked to her father fixation: "Death seemed the fitting solution of the struggle. . . . She, whose life was so strongly bound to him who gave her life, could not become a mother without a destroying conflict."[99]

To be fair to Dooley, she admits that there is no medical evidence to support this claim, and hedges it with qualifications. She is quite right when she says, "It would be but mysticism unsupported by any scientific facts to trace her death to the mental conflict involved in trying to bring forth life . . . in our present lack of knowledge as to the connection between the neurological and the psychological."[100] Her admission that there is simply not enough recorded data for an accurate diagnosis is also true. The symptoms included vomiting, fever, emaciation, and exhaustion, which could apply to a range of wasting diseases. The death certificate states "phthisis" (tuberculosis and a general wasting away), but this is too vague to have much clinical meaning. Posthumous diagnoses have ranged from consumption[101] to *hyperemesis gravidarum* (severe morning sickness in pregnancy, causing death in some extreme cases)[102] to Addison's disease[103] to typhoid.[104] We will probably never know for sure what killed her. But the need to define Charlotte's last illness as the working through of a death wish would become so strong among the psychobiographers who followed Dooley's lead that they would dogmatically assert where she had merely suggested.

Written in the early, exploratory years of psychoanalysis, Dooley's essay is in fact far subtler than many later accounts. This is mainly because of the gaps and tensions in her argument, which add welcome texture and save it from the dogmatism of trying to make Charlotte fit a theoretical blueprint at all costs. In the case, for example, of Charlotte's supposed Electra complex, we can see Dooley trying to pursue a simplified Freudian generalization, only to find herself caught out by her own close reading of Charlotte's writings.

Dooley is tempted to use Charlotte's "lifelong bondage" to her father as the universal key which will unlock all aspects of her character and behavior, an exaggerated emphasis which actually owes as much to the tradition of filial piety established by the Victorian hagiographies as to the writer's Freudian training.[105] So when it comes to the question of Charlotte's feelings for Heger, Dooley begins by confidently defining these emotions as displaced symptoms of the immature "father-fixation" which supposedly lay at the root of her subject's being. Yet a few pages later she is honest enough to admit that reading the Heger letters has changed her mind: Charlotte's love for her teacher was not, as she had previously argued, a regression to infantile incest fantasies, but instead had the validity of "a truly adult passion."[106]

Dooley's response to the Heger letters may reveal her to be torn between the psychoanalytical paradigm she is trying to construct and her own direct response to Charlotte's words. But perhaps the most significant crux in her argument comes toward the end of her essay when she moves away from pure biography and devotes a final section to analyzing *Villette*. Up until now, she has proposed that the artistic value of Charlotte's works comes from unconscious sources: that it was because she was unaware of her repressed father fixation that it was able to energize her art. Here, however, she suggests, on the contrary, that *Villette* in fact shows a *conscious* awareness of the Electra complex.

Having initially presented Charlotte as unknowing, Dooley now credits her with making "a great contribution to psychology" by exploring the process by which childhood relations with a parent are often relived in the sexual relationships of adulthood in her portrayal of the character Paulina. After we have been led to believe in Charlotte as the archetypal unconscious artist, she is now praised for producing a "masterly, detailed and consistent" depiction of neurosis, which suggests conscious authorial control and detached, analytical thinking rather than naive emotional outpouring.[107] Subtly, Dooley even seems to hint that Charlotte was herself something of a theoretical psychologist, responding and contributing to the very currents in nineteenth-century thought which would eventually produce Freud himself. Reading *Villette* seems to have convinced Dooley that, for all its autobiographical content, its author was doing more than naively spewing forth her own unacknowledged conflicts and complexes.

If Dooley seems unsatisfied by her own theory of the pathology of the artist, it is unsurprising. Even Freud came to doubt the ability of psychoanalysis to explain creativity, admitting in 1928 that "[b]efore the problem of the creative artist analysis must, alas, lay down its arms."[108] The trouble with the argument that Charlotte's novels were outpourings of the unconscious was that it infantilized her relationship to her work, crediting it with no more craft or conscious artistry than dreams, and implicitly denying or at least devaluing its relationship to culture at large. *Jane Eyre,* and particularly *Villette,* had indeed explored hidden areas of the psyche with unusual depth and frankness. They had made artistic use of dreamlike symbols and had acknowledged, albeit in metaphorical language, sexual desire and its suppression. Rather than reading her as a mature artist who had gained insight from self-analysis, or championing her as a pioneering precursor of psychoanalytical thinking, the psychobiographers tended to treat her as the victim of her own mental chaos, as if her writings were mere symptoms rather than sophisticated works of art. Instead of being appreciated as an active thinker, Charlotte was reduced to lying passively on the couch, without the benefit that a living patient would have of being able to answer back.

Despite these objections, psychobiographers continued to concentrate on Charlotte's pathology well into the 1970s. By the time Robert Keefe's gloomily titled *Charlotte Brontë's World of Death* came out in 1979, psychobiography had lost the vitality found in Lucile Dooley's work and become excessively reductive and schematizing. Less exploratory and more dogmatic than it had been, the genre had atrophied.

Boasting that he has "cut away" such "random details" as Charlotte's intellectual background or adult relationships with family and friends, Keefe believed he had gotten to the "central core of significance."[109] He traced the meaning of her entire life to the single trauma of losing her mother at the age of five (which he compared, with astonishing insensitivity, to the Nazi death camps). Keefe gave the impression that this left her in a permanent state of what amounts to a sort of infantile psychosis, unable in any way to face up to adult reality. Her death at thirty-eight—the very age her mother had been when *she* died!—must have been caused purely by an act of unconscious will: "Charlotte was repaying her final, mortal debt to the dead, punishing herself and rejecting her child as she herself had been rejected."[110] In a tone of fatalistic symbolism, he concluded: "A black core of depression had existed within her for thirty-three years. That dark mass began to spread like a cancer now, consuming the frame in which it resided. . . . The need to die had come from deep inside her."[111]

In his study *Charlotte Brontë and Sexuality* (1984), John Maynard offered a devastating critique of the oversimplifications indulged in by many psychobiographers, whose accounts, he felt, had so often failed to acknowledge the complexity of Charlotte's art and mind. Yes, Charlotte had an interest in depression, even in near breakdown, which derived from personal experience. But it was only one strand of emotional experience in a life which also contained much "happiness, much joy of friendship and creation, much deeper, less perplexing grief of loss."[112] It was, importantly, also a strand of experience of which she was able to make creative use, precisely because she was able to contain and interrogate it within her own mind. Books like *Charlotte Brontë's World of Death* overstated the psychic damage she had suffered through early loss to the extent that the Charlotte who emerged seemed on the very borderline of sanity, and it was hard to see how she could have achieved anything in literature or even to have functioned at all in ordinary, everyday life. Instead, one has to remember that in the five years following the agonizing bereavements of 1848–49, Charlotte was still able, while mourning her brother and sisters, to write a large portion of *Shirley* and her entire masterpiece *Villette*, as well as get married. Queen Victoria, in contrast, was unable to cope with public life for years after the death of Prince Albert.

Maynard overturned the frequent twentieth-century presumption that as an unmarried Victorian woman Charlotte would have had so little inkling of sexuality that any apparent awareness of it in her works would have been wholly unconscious. Charlotte's literary exploration of sexual desire was rooted firstly in her reading and secondly in intuition and intro-spection. As an adolescent she had ranged uncensored through a range of pre-Victorian literature—including Byron's *Don Juan* and the bawdy sections from Shakespeare's comedies—which she knew would shock respectable girls like her friend Ellen.[113] In addition, more recent research has revealed that Victorian culture was not as silenced on the subject of sex as the modern cliché suggests and that Charlotte would have been exposed to the public discourse of sexuality as found in medical literature and the contemporary press.[114] There is also the question of how much the young Charlotte may have been exposed to informal information on sex through gossip, jokes, or whispered innuendo. Harriet Martineau and Elizabeth Gaskell may have found the passion of Charlotte's novels morbid or denied that it existed at all. But that is not to say that Charlotte herself was in denial.

To explain why Charlotte had attracted such an unusual prevalence of psychoanalytic interpretation, Maynard pointed to the rich symbolic content of her novels, which attracted psychobiographers "as a well-designed playground attracts children."[115] But he could have added that the legacy of Gaskell's *Life* had played an equally crucial role. For a start, it had given unusual space and emphasis to the importance of Charlotte's childhood experiences, but there were other aspects of it which fed the psychobiographers' imagination too. Their assertion that Charlotte must have died of psychosomatic causes could be seen as a reflection of the fact that Gaskell had turned her into a character in the novelistic mode. In novels, nobody dies without a purpose or a meaning. Infection does not choose its victims arbitrarily. From the opening chapter, with its description of the Brontë funeral tablet, Gaskell's narrative had established a fatalistic pattern which looked forward inexorably to death.

Gaskell's insistence on the Brontës' total isolation also fostered a way of seeing which divorced them from the outside world. As a result, it was easy for psychobiographers to see them exclusively in the context of primitive family relationships rather than embedded in a whole web of social and cultural and intellectual contacts. Gaskell had blamed Branwell for the coarseness in *Jane Eyre*. Ironically, a psychobiographer who identified him as the original for Mr. Rochester—claiming that Charlotte had not developed psychologically beyond infantile sibling-incest fantasies—was to some extent participating in the Victorian tradition which had naively ascribed literalistic autobiographical content to the novels in order to exonerate the Brontë sisters from having imagined such horrors of their own free will.[116]

Psychobiography opened new doors but in the end imposed new limits on the way in which Charlotte was understood. Significantly, it shifted the focus from the external aspects of the Brontë tragedy to the subjectivity of Charlotte's emotional responses, acknowledging that mental suffering could have internal as well as outside causes and that the inner life could be as valid a subject for biography as the outer events. But in its path-ologization of artistic creativity, it remained—despite its sophisticated vocabulary—uncomfortably close to the patronizing assumption that only unbalanced women turned to authorship as a means of compensation. As a result, it often unwittingly rose no higher than the hackneyed view found, for example, in a facile study of 1892, *Women Writers: Their Works and Ways,* which argues that "happy women do not write. . . . Happy women whose hearts are satisfied have little need of utterance. Their lives are rounded and complete, they require nothing but the calm recurrence of those peaceful home duties in which domestic women rightly feel their true vocation lies."[117]

In addition, the psychobiographers' evident need for the totalizing explanation or single key to personality (whether they found it in, say, the dominant father, the dead mother, or the rivalrous brother) meant that subtlety and complexity were often sacrificed for the sake of fitting the evidence into a consistent, preordained pattern. But the most impoverished aspect of psychobiography was the fact that it tended to detach the subject from the social, cultural, and literary influences which must, in reality, have contributed to her life and work as much as her infantile unconscious needs.

From Lucile Dooley in 1920 to Robert Keefe in 1979, psychobiographers tended to aim their work at specialist academic audiences. Even though the idea of the Brontës as sexually frustrated Victorian spinsters became something of a twentieth-century cliché, it was usually the learned journals, not the popular press, which carried clinical analyses of, say, Charlotte's "masochistic character."[118] Yet during the 1920s, psychobiography was also repackaged for a general readership. Rosamond Langbridge's *Charlotte Brontë: A Psychological Study* (1929) was indirectly influenced by a bastardized, watered-down version of psychoanalytical thinking—psychosomatic illness and sexual repression feature in her account—but, despite its title, its biographical posture owed more to Lytton Strachey than it did to Freud.

Strachey's *Eminent Victorians* of 1918 had sought to bring about a revolution in biography. The book offered iconoclastic portraits of four massive nineteenth-century public figures—Cardinal Manning, Florence Nightingale, Thomas Arnold, and General Gordon—which were partly intended as an indictment of the establishment values for which the First World War had been waged. Its abrasive, even satiric, tone was designed to undermine the idols of a bankrupt age and reveal their feet of clay. Biography was no longer, as it had been in the nineteenth century, about celebrating the achievements of the great with a view to inspiring the reader to go and do likewise. Its purpose was instead to uncover the dubious underside of the subject's personality.

In her post-Gaskell public persona, the dutiful, suffering Charlotte Brontë was as much of an eminent Victorian as the figures chosen by Strachey. His undressing of Florence Nightingale—he replaced the angelic lady with the lamp with a ruthlessly ambitious, twisted, acerbic woman—set a precedent for later treatments of the saint of Haworth. Where Gaskell had seen her role as that of protector, Strachey regarded the biographer as the subject's enemy: "He will attack his subject in unexpected places; he will fall upon the flank, or the rear; he will shoot a sudden, revealing searchlight into obscure recesses, hitherto undivined."[119]

Strachey was as keen to change the aesthetics of biography as its ideology. In the preface to *Eminent Victorians,* he could have been thinking of a caricature of Gaskell's *Life* when he attacked the typical Victorian biography as "two fat volumes" of "tedious panegyric."[120] He emphasized the need for brevity, art, and formal structure in life-writing, and his own biographical essays are masterpieces of wit and polish. Unfortunately, in Rosamond Langbridge, Charlotte attracted a biographer who had Strachey's debunking approach without his literary virtuosity.

What Langbridge shared with both the psychoanalysts and the Stracheyans was the conviction that the truth, which had been veiled by the hypocrisy of those "easily-gulled Victorian times," had finally become accessible in the clear light of the modern age.[121] She made it plain that her biography was intended to explode what she called "the foolish fashion of canonising Charlotte."[122] Scorning "the invariable sentiment of the Victorian Biographer that the Dead are always Good," she would subject Charlotte's "martyrdom" to scrutiny and reveal it to have been anything but admirable.[123]

If only, imagines Langbridge, Charlotte had been alive today. Bloomsbury would have welcomed her with open arms. Augustus John and Epstein would have begged her to sit for them. Everything would have worked out right in this new, liberated world. But as it was, Charlotte was condemned to become the embodiment of repression, "the Woman in the Iron Mask,"[124] who "never once rebelled"[125] against the strict Victorian values to which she was brought up.

Despite her claims to truth, Langbridge was not really interested in uncovering the facts behind the myth. Her inclusion of some of the *Life*'s most glaring errors reveals that her portrait was more dependent on the fictions of the nineteenth century than on solid research. One of Gaskell's unsubstantiated stories about Patrick's temper (whose authenticity had long since been questioned) had him flinging his children's colored boots into the fire in a fit of puritanism. Langbridge not merely repeated the anecdote with gusto but enlivened it by attributing a precise color to each pair, Charlotte's green, Emily's purple, and so on.[126] She needed all the help she could get to turn Patrick into a memorable villain, the oppressive Victorian patriarch, the starver of his children's bodies and souls, the "revered Papa"[127] to whom Charlotte martyred herself.

Without realizing it, Langbridge was aiming her disapproval less against what she called the "real woman who was Charlotte" than against the simplistic image created by nineteenth-century hagiographers.[128] She saw only the dutiful and self-sacrificing side of the Charlotte persona, but reinterpreted these qualities as willful self-punishment. Langbridge's moral universe was a place in which suffering was no longer good for the soul, as it had been for the Victorians. Instead, she mused, "Life is, or should be, for people what it is for birds and flowers, one extended act of happiness."[129] (It seems quite shocking to find the author of a book as morally and psychologically complex as *Villette* in such crass hands.) Charlotte had been a slave to the "Duty that can kill," and if her life was sad it was her "own fault."[130] The movement away from the external tragedies of the Brontë story toward emphasizing internal suffering had resulted in a rhetoric of blame.

As conceived by Langbridge, Charlotte's personality was devoid of vitality and characterized only by grim conscientiousness. Even the juvenilia are denied their exuberance, used only to prove what "alarming little prigs" the young Brontës were.[131] In a spurious attempt at psychological diagnosis, Langbridge identifies Charlotte's problem as *"suppressed Personality."* This is, supposedly, the single key which will explain "the whole secret of [her] miseries, her sicknesses of mind, her sicknesses of body, the sickness of her Fate."[132] Yet the main reason why this biographer is blind to the more vigorous aspects of her subject's character is her astonishing lack of interest in the literary evidence of her writings. Charlotte, she claims, "had practised repression for so long in her life that she had forgotten the practise of self-expression, excepting through the medium of her art. But that, after all, is not Life. It is Personal Inclination sterilised and made harmless for the public sake."[133] Thus some of the greatest novels of the English canon are reduced to insignificance in the life of their creator.

Unsurprisingly, the figure who emerged from Langbridge's "psychological study" was not one with whom readers wanted to identify. During the 1930s, Charlotte reached the low point of her popular esteem. As the *Radio Times* remarked, "There is now a tendency . . . to belittle Charlotte; to sneer at her as the anxious Victorian governess."[134] The fact that Charlotte's novels had challenged convention was often forgotten. The year 1936 finds her described, with extraordinary inaccuracy, as a writer "whose conventional tastes and preference for writing about pretty-pretty heroines (who never spoke or acted 'coarsely') resulted in *Jane Eyre.*"[135] (In truth, when it was first published *Jane Eyre* was considered as remarkable for having a plain heroine as it was for its supposed coarseness.) Such opinions were clearly based not on the real Charlotte but on the icon she had become. For many, as for Langbridge, she had come to epitomize the current negative stereotype of the Victorian age: prim, priggish, and a prude.

This was the era of Emily's ascendency. Her wildness and apparent disregard for social norms, which had been vilified or ignored in the decades after her death, made her a more appealing figure to the biographers of the 1920s and '30s, who often attributed to her a timeless spirituality they denied to the too-Victorian Charlotte. It was Emily's turn for canonization, and her sister needed cutting down to size. Whatever sibling rivalry may have existed between the real-life sisters, it was as nothing compared to the conflict which had now arisen between the so-called Emily-ites of the 1920s and '30s and the Charlotte-ites of an earlier generation.[136]

Like many of his contemporaries, the novelist E. F. Benson, whose biography of Charlotte came out in 1932, hero-worshipped Emily in the religiose language of mysticism. But at the same time, he was keen to uncover every possible human failing in her elder sister. His determination to seek out the less pleasant aspects of her character was a reaction against what he saw as Victorian sentimentality. But, though he does not advertise the fact, his antipathy may also have been exacerbated by a family connection: in her twenties, Charlotte had spent a miserable few months as governess in the household of one of Benson's forebears, and had made cutting comments about her employers in letters to Ellen.[137]

Benson set out his manifesto in no uncertain terms, asserting that the biographer had "no right to suppress or soften harsh features . . . in his hero."[138] Gaskell's image of Charlotte, he felt, had robbed her of her individuality by presenting her "as entirely tender and loving and patient under cruel trials."[139] He saw his job as being to "clear away" such idealizing "embellishments,"[140] and to put in their place a true picture, which included his subject's moral failings and limitations. "We know from Charlotte's own letters," he added sternly, "that there was a vast deal of hardness and intolerance in her nature."[141]

Unlike Langbridge's, Benson's Charlotte was not a masochistic martyr to duty. Indeed, he described her as being "too much of a fighter to rank herself with the non-combatants who suffer long and are kind."[142] Charlotte had hated governessing; she had been shocked to find herself treated more like a nursery maid than a teacher, and found the anomolous social position of the governess, halfway between upstairs and downstairs, hard to negotiate and frequently humiliating. She also found her employers unsympathetic. Benson quoted her negative remarks, calling her ruthless and bitter and pointing mercilessly to her "ungraciousness" and "bleak censoriousness of others."[143] Grumbling about one's boss behind her back might seem petty on the general scale of human inadequacy. But for Benson it became a sign of an overweening tendency to judge others which prevented Charlotte from enjoying life like "a normal human being," resulting in "that absence of charity which . . . was the root of much of her unhappiness,"[144] As in Langbridge, she is blamed for her own misfortunes.

Benson's main assault on Charlotte, however, concerned her relationships with Branwell and Emily, both of whom, he felt, she had failed. During the last couple of years of Branwell's life, after his rejection by Mrs. Robinson, he had become more and more alienated from his elder sister. Sleeping all day, drinking at night, he was hell to live with, and Charlotte found his self-destructiveness so painful to witness that she had difficulty speaking to him at times. Although his book is conceived and presented as a biography of Charlotte, Benson makes no attempt to enter his subject's subjectivity. Instead of trying to understand the situation from her perspective, he passes judgment from above on her "pitilessness" and "ruthlessness," claiming that "she had more compassion for the profligate and the insane wife of Mr. Rochester in *Jane Eyre* than she had for Branwell in his lifetime."[145]

Benson contrasts Charlotte's "hardness" with what he saw as Emily's superior generous nature. He expresses this belief by inventing wholly imagined scenarios in which Charlotte ignores Branwell on his return from the Black Bull, while her warmer-hearted sister invites him into her room for a cozy chat. By the 1930s, the idea that Emily and Branwell (now biographical subjects in their own right) had enjoyed an unusual intimacy had become popular, though it was in fact unproved, deriving mainly from a speculative reading of her poetry combined with the wayward Victorian theory that Branwell must have collaborated with his sister on *Wuthering Heights* because it was too coarse to be the work of a woman alone.

According to Benson, Charlotte's hard-heartedness was also responsible for Emily's refusals of help and sympathy during her last illness, as she would not accept for herself the compassion that had been denied their brother. Charlotte, he felt, had forfeited Emily's love. Gaskell had described how Charlotte tried to cheer her dying sister by bringing her a sprig of heather from the moor, only to find that Emily could no longer recognize the flower she loved.[146] One of the most genuinely moving images from the Brontë story, Benson dismissed the act as "a cheap attempt to undo the irrevocable."[147]

In castigating Charlotte for her excessively fault-finding nature, Benson was of course being supremely judgmental himself. His style of biographical reevaluation, derived ultimately from the Stracheyan tradition, was, in its own negative way, as moralistic as the Victorian eulogies. Charlotte remained detached from her works in that the biographer's purpose was not to gain a deeper understanding of her literary imagination but to sit in judgment over her private life, as if higher personal standards were expected of a great novelist than of mere mortals. In his need to condemn and to take sides, Benson seems unable to appreciate the full subtlety and emotional complexity of Charlotte's relationships with her family. His desire to escape from the gushing praises of Victorian sentimentalists may have been admirable, but instead of replacing it with a spirit of neutral enquiry, he seems driven by the need to search out petty failings and personal limitations rather than by the desire to understand.

He did, however, put Charlotte-as-bitch on the map. It was a formulation of her character which would reemerge at intervals over the years, the inevitable—if sometimes pinched and ungenerous—reaction against idealization and sentimentality. Because Gaskell's *Life* has survived as a classic to be read by each successive generation, even today some writers feel the need to counterbalance its eulogistic perspective, often turning their irritation on the subject as much as her biographer.

In 1993, for example, Charlotte was vilified in the "Heroes and Villains" column of the *Independent* by the novelist Charlotte Cory, who worked herself up into a state of outrage against what she saw as the cruel use of real-life models in *Villette,* particularly the transformation of Madame Heger into the evil headmistress Madame Beck. Charlotte's character was summed up as "bigoted, vengeful, and morally perverse" and Cory ridiculed her as the sort of woman "who throws herself at every man who comes into her orbit with a desperation and obviousness embarrassing to behold"[148] (the fact that Charlotte refused offers of marriage from three other men before accepting Arthur Nicholls is not mentioned). This view derives, perhaps, from Thackeray's gossipy speculation that all the author of *Jane Eyre* really wanted was a man, only she was too plain and past it to get one.[149] Cory's character assassination goes on to conclude that Charlotte was so embittered by her lack of physical attractions that her novels became a mere channel for pent-up bile and viciousness.

Looking at Thackeray's comical and faintly misogynistic belittling of Charlotte, one has to wonder whether he felt threatened by her obvious ability and high seriousness about her art. Cory's motives, however, are harder to fathom. Though a novelist, she is clearly untouched by any feminist reverence for Charlotte as a literary foremother: does she instead feel the need to rebel against one of the massive icons in whose shadow she has to work? She certainly appears to have mixed feelings about the Brontës, an ambivalence which is perhaps an inevitable correlative of the adoration they still inspire. For while being keen to excoriate Charlotte in print, Cory has also encouraged the hero-worshipping urge to identify with the Brontës, even taking it to a ludicrous—perhaps consciously self-parodying—extreme. An active member of the Brontë Society, she was to be found organizing a canine-look-alike contest at the society's annual get-together in Haworth in 1993, in which fans brought along their dogs to see which most resembled the Brontës' pets Keeper and Grasper.

It is easier to understand why anyone should bother to make vituperative *ad feminam* attacks on a writer long since dead when one realizes the strange extremes of enthusiasm which still exist at the lunatic fringes of the Brontë Society. The 1994 annual general meeting of the society was interrupted—to the great embarrassment of its officers—by a vociferous monologue from a man who claimed to receive regular messages from Charlotte's ghost. An ex–Hell's Angel who said he had been converted to Christianity by Gaskell's *Life,* he believed he had been saved by the protective figure of the saintly Charlotte, and he wanted to register his disgust at a newspaper article (presumably Cory's) which had attacked his idol and called her ugly.[150]

A fly on the wall would have gained the impression that a shot of much-needed iconoclasm was required if Charlotte was to be saved from the clutches of her eccentric admirers. Yet, as we have seen, iconoclasm had in fact been a common biographical pose for a substantial part of the twentieth century. The release of the Heger letters, followed by the double revolution sparked by psychoanalysis and Stracheyism, had given biographers the freedom to explore areas of Charlotte's personality and experience which had previously been off-limits. Potentially, this gave them the opportunity to gain a deeper understanding of her life and art. In practice, however, it was often compromised by the very iconoclastic instincts which were in some ways such a positive force. Psychobiographers became determined to reduce the moral heroine of the Victorian age to a quivering wreck naively spewing forth her complexes into her books, while Strachey's heirs carped and criticized in a way which often prevented them from fully achieving the imaginative leap into a past life, which requires at least some attempt at empathy. Yet if Charlotte attracted such negative approaches, it was testimony to her enormous staying power as an icon. The Brontës had become such a permanent feature of the cultural landscape that they could by now withstand any assault.

CHAPTER SIX

Fiction and Feminism

I

I once had a conversation with a charming but unliterary accountant who was trying to take a polite interest in my book. "The Brontë sisters—weren't they fictional characters?" was his response when I told him what I was working on. The Brontës only existed on the vaguest fringes of his consciousness, but the space they occupied there—hovering between reality and fantasy—said a lot about their role in the cultural imagination.

By the time Henry James complained about popular romanticization of the Brontës in 1904, they had already begun to take their place in this no-man's-land between fact and fiction. In the half century which followed Gaskell's *Life,* the Brontë story had been retold so many times and in so many forms that through sheer force of repetition it had shifted from the level of history to that of myth. Writers had always been attracted to the story as much for its symbolic as its documentary value. But by the 1920s, the Brontës had begun to break loose of their moorings in factual biography and start new lives as characters in plays, films, and novels.

The development of fictional Brontë biography was perhaps inevitable. Gaskell's novelistic treatment had set a precedent, and many of the biographers who came after her, such as E. F. Benson, were novelists by trade. But if the distinction between history and fiction was not always clearly marked, this also reflected the fact that Charlotte herself had used personal experience as the raw material for creative writing. Once this became widely recognized, the consequent attempts of enthusiasts to trace real-life models for every character and place in the Brontë oeuvre were frequently naively literal, and could have some odd results: Clement Shorter even met an old man in America who claimed to be the younger brother of Mr. Rochester.[1] Nevertheless, it remains true that Charlotte, like Wordsworth, is at her greatest when inspired by her own experience, though (as G. H. Lewes recognized) it is the subjective power, rather than factual accuracy, of those re-creations that gives them their particular intensity.

Charlotte, in fact, fictionalized aspects of her own life so successfully that the efforts of the fictional biographers who came after her look embarrassingly puny by comparison. Few had much literary merit. The fictional format may have legitimized and even invited a more fluid attitude toward the idea of telling a life story. Ideally, by freeing writers from the need to document every fact, it could have enabled them to project themselves with greater imaginative empathy into the subjective life of the biographee. But sadly, few of the playwrights, novelists, poets, or filmmakers who approached the Brontës were stimulated by this freedom into true creative innovation. Though many propagated spurious legends about the events of the Brontë lives, few were myth-making in any positive sense.

The middlebrow writers of the interwar period were not aesthetic theoreticians and remained stuck in cliché and convention. They were out of sync with the more sophisticated thinking of their contemporary Virginia Woolf, who was hyperaware of the intellectual problems of biography, that "bastard, . . . impure art." Unable to see how the biographer could chronicle the external facts of a life while simultaneously doing justice to the subjective truth of it, she even wondered whether "the best method would be to separate the two kinds of truth. Let the biographer print fully, completely, accurately, the known facts without comment; Then let him write the life as fiction."[2] In the 1980s and '90s, postmodernism again raised the issue of the relationship between biography and fiction, which was explored by writers ranging from Julian Barnes (in *Flaubert's Parrot*) to Peter Ackroyd (whose biography of Dickens included fictionalized passages and whose novels characteristically mix fact and invention), A. S. Byatt (in *Possession*), and more recently Andrew Motion (in *Wainewright the Poisoner*). But for the writers of the 1930s and '40s the fictional format was more often a tool for popularization than philosophical exploration.

Although Gaskell's book, the ur-text of the story, had been the life of *Charlotte* Brontë, the narrative had always been seen as a family affair. After the publication of lives of Emily and Branwell in the 1880s, the eldest sister had gradually begun to lose her centrality. By the time fictional biographies began to appear in the 1920s, the structure of the story had changed. No longer centered around the struggles of a single heroine, it had become more of a family saga, often dominated by Patrick in the role of a rigid Victorian patriarch and Branwell as a drunken madman.

The relationship between Emily and Branwell was often put center stage. Far less well documented than any part of Charlotte's life, this aspect of the Brontë story invited speculation, and writers used fiction as a way of filling in the gaps. A long verse narrative of 1927, "Storm-Wrack: A Night with the Brontës" by a minor poet, J. A. Mackereth, took its inspiration from the tradition that Emily used to go to the Black Bull to bring Branwell home after a night of drinking. The return from the pub is embedded in twenty-eight pages of storm-stress, the action taking place on a "boding night" when the moon is "wild," the clouds "angry," the rain "thrashing," the thunder "eerie," the "gusts" screaming "like wild-haired maenads," the moor "barren," and the Parsonage a "grim life-prisoning shell" inhabited by the five "shuddering" and "tortured" Brontës, "mortals tossed betwixt heaven and hell."[3]

Inspired by the storm-tossed passion associated with *Wuthering Heights,* though not by the novel's terse laconic language, the poem transforms Emily into a Cathy-like figure—a "tameless soul and proud . . . with tortured hair"[4] who "wails like a soul on the edge of hell"[5]—calling to her Heathcliff-brother through the pub window. Then she becomes a Christ-like personification of Love, the only member of the family to show true Christian compassion to their Shame, the "carnal Branwell."[6]

As a poet, Mackereth is not bound by the constraints of fact and evidence, and he incorporates elements of established Brontë mythography in his vision. Attracted to melodrama—Emily's white face "vivid in livid pain" appears in a flash of lightning like something from an early horror film—he is particularly drawn to the fatalism of the family story. He foretells in incantatory tones the deaths of Branwell, Emily, Anne, and later Charlotte:

> *For the rune of fate is writ, is writ*
> *And the first to read shall be he:*
> *A rune in the dark is writ, is writ,*
> *And the second to read is she*
> *Four names hath the rune in it,*
> *But the nearer names are three.*[7]

Mackereth could hardly fail to respond to the tradition (of uncertain origin) that Branwell ended his life standing, and the poem ends with an ecstatic upright death.

Gaskell had of course paid tribute to the Brontës' love of the moors, but it was only after Emily began to be rehabilitated in the later nineteenth century that the wild, wuthering landscape started to be treated as the icon it is today (in the Northern Ballet Theatre's recent dance piece *The*

Brontës, the moors even appear as a sort of character, portrayed by the corps de ballet in "tie-dyed sarongs").[8] Through its implicit allusions to Cathy and Heathcliff, Mackereth's poem directly connects to the imagery of Emily's own writing. But many subsequent treatments had less sense of what literary critics call intertextuality. Interest remained focused on the lives rather than the works, as if the Brontës—whose day-to-day existence had once been described by the Victorian writer Mrs. Oliphant as "respectable, humdrum and uninteresting"—would have been just as extraordinary without their creativity.[9] Typical of this outlook is the following remark from a character in a 1931 novel: "[W]hat a family! Even if they'd never written a line, what a story!"[10] It was a story whose popularity was such that one melodramatic play, Alfred Sangster's *The Brontës of Haworth,* was staged twenty times between 1933 and 1988.[11]

Many of the stage versions which appeared in the 1930s and '40s had storm-tossed or melodramatic titles such as *The Tragic Race* or *Wild Decembers* or *Divide the Desolation* or *Empurpled Moors.* In *Moor Born,* Emily tells her brother, "Strange things can happen to you, for you are moor born, Branwell. Yes . . . moor born . . . and what the moors took from you they may return."[12] *Stone Walls* has Branwell rolling around the stage in a fit of violent insanity armed with a pistol. Once he has passed out, Emily gives him (as the stage direction puts it), "a look of sadness, then one of happy inspiration," before dreamily announcing "I'll go my own gait, over the moors, over the moors. I'll call it *Wuthering Heights.*"[13]

Few plays managed to treat the question of artistic inspiration with more subtlety than this, though some managed to make some insightful points. The novelist Clemence Dane's stage version of the Brontë story opens with Branwell painting Charlotte's portrait. His first words offer a comment on the disjunction between her Victorian image and her inner self, suggesting that she was herself responsible for her own public persona: "I shall never get Charlotte. She isn't a prig. She isn't a staring miss. And yet look what I've made of her. It's her fault. She sits there and defies me, damn her!"[14]

Dane goes on to contrast Charlotte's worldly ambition with the superior, spiritual values of Emily, who wants to keep her poetry a secret despite being the only true genius among the sisters. The same judgment is made in *The Brontës* by Alfred Sangster (1933) and in *Stone Walls,* where a sensible bespectacled Charlotte aspires to a successful career in teaching and dismisses the sensitive Emily as a "wet blanket" because she does not want to go to Brussels to improve her mind.[15] During this period,

Charlotte is rarely the most sympathetic Brontë. *Moor Born* makes her bossy and mumsy, ticking Emily off for not changing her wet shoes, while *These Were the Brontës,* a novel, criticizes her desire for fame, though it simultaneously praises her urge to become an author for its implicit feminism.[16]

In the 1940s, the vogue for plays and novels based on the Brontës' lives reached Hollywood, resulting in the sentimental movie *Devotion,* released in 1946. The American film industry had already gotten its hands on *Wuthering Heights* (1939) and *Jane Eyre* (1943), conventionalizing their love stories to fit the expectations of cinema audiences. According to the Warner publicity machine, *Devotion* would tell "ALL about those Brontë sisters! . . . They didn't dare call it love, they tried to call it devotion!"[17] Theirs was "a story as rare and remarkable as any they dreamed."[18]

The Brontë story had in fact been given the Hollywood treatment once before, in a twenty-minute short by Twentieth Century–Fox, *Three Sisters of the Moors,* made to promote *Jane Eyre.* Although it took the odd liberty with the facts—on their trip to London, Charlotte and Anne are shown dancing at a ball with George Smith and Charles Dickens—this treatment had something definite in its favor, since it focused on the sisters as *writers.* Covering the period of the publication of the first Brontë novels, it avoided melodrama or tragic fatalism, finding humor in the disapproval of critics. It may, inaccurately, have made the *Quarterly Review*'s onslaught pre-date Emily's final illness, and transformed the female writer responsible into the stuffy, be-monocled "Archibald Winton." But it was celebratory of the Brontës' talents, giving their literary achievement a central place.[19]

The same could not be said of *Devotion,* which, in contrast, submerged the sisters in a bath of romantic and wildly inaccurate slush. Here, the filmmakers provided a love interest in the form of an invented rivalry between Ida Lupino's Emily and Olivia de Havilland's Charlotte for the attentions of Arthur Nicholls, played with a disconcerting Austrian accent by Paul Henreid. In real life, Nicholls hardly knew Emily. (He told Clement Shorter that whenever he took tea with Patrick at the Parsonage, Charlotte and Anne would be present but Emily preferred to have hers alone in another room.)[20] But Warner Bros. felt the need to inject romance into the story of three young women who had in truth spent their most intense hours bent over their desks with pens in their hands, not much of a recipe for dramatic action.

The publicity material promised a melodramatic love triangle:

Emily: she ruled in that strange quiet house! None could resist the force of her will!

The Man in Black [Nicholls]: he fled from her demands into her sister's arms!

Charlotte: the sweetness of love and the meaning of torment—she learned them both together![21]

Audiences must have been disappointed by a film far more placid than this suggests. The darker elements of the film, associated with Emily, were swamped in a wash of sentiment. Emily may confess to seeing ghosts (shades of the 1939 *Wuthering Heights*, which ends with the see-through figures of Cathy and Heathcliff superimposed on a moorland backdrop); she may have an exquisite sympathy for her doomed brother (the idea is derived from Mary Robinson's 1883 life, but Branwell is played as a comic turn indulging in drunken slapstick rather than a demon); and she may eventually die of unrequited love. But the director seems less interested in these tragic motifs than in creating a cozy imagery of innocent, nostalgic Englishness.

The film has more in common with other Hollywood costume dramas than with the historical Brontë family. The initially bickering relationship between Charlotte and Nicholls bears some relation to Elizabeth and Darcy in *Pride and Prejudice* (1940), though when he kisses her in the conservatory he seems to have turned into Rhett Butler from *Gone with the Wind:* "There are two ways of dealing with young women of your perverse temperament. It is fortunate for you that I am not a woman-beater." (Such lines come oddly from the wimpish Henreid, whose previous role had been that of Bette Davis's sexless lover in *Now Voyager*.) Yet the representation of the Brontës' world draws as much from a film like *Mrs. Miniver* (1942) as from *Wuthering Heights* (1939) (both of which were directed by William Wyler).

Set in the present day, *Mrs. Miniver* was designed to make Americans feel good about entering the Second World War by showing a prettified England of rose-strewn cottages and traditional class structures worth saving from Hitler's bombs. In *Devotion,* also made in wartime, the industrial township of Haworth becomes a rural idyll of half-timbered houses, inhabited by caricature yokels with odd accents and a formidable elderly lady of the manor who invites the Brontës to the Thornton House Ball, an event which provides an opportunity to show the girls in their corsets preparing to squeeze into evening gowns. The studio-bound moors feature a backdrop of mountains, a dimpling stream, and a haunted house with a huge pointy gable (Wuthering Heights). Emily's fearsome bulldog Keeper metamorphoses into a fluffy Old English sheepdog.

Brussels provides the opportunity to show Charlotte as a shameless flirt, swinging her skirts and simpering whenever Monsieur Heger, a confirmed ladies' man, hoves into view. She reads some of her love stories to her teacher, who feigns astonishment that such a young lady should know about such things. Having witnessed the kiss in the conservatory, we know however that Charlotte has already been initiated by "that insupportable Mr Nicholls," whom she finds attractive despite her protestations. Her feminine wiles—she knows how to play hard to get—are contrasted with the self-denial of her spiritually superior sister. In the end it is the womanly manipulator who gets the man, not the dreamy Emily, who instead dies of unrequited love.

Although our sympathies are supposed to be with the tragic Emily, her elder sister provides most of the entertainment. It is Charlotte who gets to go to London, where she lords it over the fashionable dinner tables in glamorous décolletage. Literary society is evoked in the famous scene where two men greet each other on the stairs with the immortal lines: "Good morning, Thackeray." "Good morning, Dickens." Thackeray's comment on *Wuthering Heights* is to ask Charlotte how her sister "came to experience so great and tragic a love." The tragedy is supposed to be that the worldly Charlotte does not know the secrets of her own doomed sister's heart.

Devotion—which did disappointingly at the box office—twisted the facts without aspiring to any form of higher truth. But among the often pedestrian retellings of the Brontë story which appeared in the period between the wars, one fiction stands out for its humor and originality: Rachel Ferguson's novel of 1931, *The Brontës Went to Woolworth's*. Ferguson, a journalist, was also the author of a straight biographical play about the Brontës, but her novel shows how the imaginatively oblique approach could result in more insight than the conventional retelling. Though the novel is in some senses typical of the whimsy of its age, it also offers an idiosyncratic commentary on the role in the public imagination which the Brontës had come to play.

Set in the 1920s, the plot concerns three sisters with "artistic" leanings. Unlike the Brontës, they are upper-middle-class, wealthy, and London-based, with a Mitfordish sense of their own specialness and the complacent arrogance of youth and privilege. Deirdre, the eldest, is a rather

Twentieth Century–Fox's *Three Sisters of the Moors* was made to publicize the film of *Jane Eyre*. Despite its inaccuracies, it did the Brontës the favor of stressing their literary talent.

Warner Bros.' *Devotion* (1946) was a travesty of the Brontë story. Here, Branwell's famous painting of his sisters is sentimentalized.

amateurish journalist who writes trashy articles about "the modern girl"; Katrine is a drama student; while the youngest, Sheil, is still under the tutelage of the much maligned family governess, Miss Martin.

Like the Brontës, who created Angria and Gondal, the Carne sisters invent their own parallel universe, which they call "the Saga," peopled by an array of fantasy figures, ranging from Ironface, a doll with aristocratic pretensions, to Sir Herbert Toddington, a real-life high court judge they have read about in newspapers. Deirdre, who narrates the novel, claims to have rejected a marriage proposal because she was in love with Sherlock Holmes. Beneath its superficial glitter, there are hints that her fashionable infantilism (think Sebastian Flyte and his teddy) hides the fact that the trauma of her father's death has prevented her from growing up. Her frivolity seems forced.

Despite its surface wit and jollity, there are deeper, more disturbing strands to the novel, and the Brontës belong to this ambivalent subtext. To begin with, the Carnes have control over their fantasy life. Even when the flesh-and-blood Judge Toddington and his wife appear, the reader still has a grasp on where fantasy ends and actuality begins in the world of the novel. But when the Brontës appear after a table-turning experiment while the Carnes are on holiday in Yorkshire, we are left in the unsettling position of not knowing whether we are supposed to take them as real, ghosts, or figments of the imagination. What troubles Miss Martin about her pupil Sheil is the fact that "one sometimes can't make out when she knows she is 'making up' and when she believes she is telling the truth."[22] Thus, Ferguson registers both the seductive appeal and the dangers of escapist fantasy, but she may also be casting an oblique comment on the ambiguous space between reality and fiction which the Brontës had come to inhabit.

The Carnes indulge in all manner of make-believe, but what they lack is the capacity for imaginative empathy. As a result, the reader cannot identify with Deirdre's first-person narrative voice without wincing at her callousness. The Brontës are unsettling characters partly because the sisters feel no compassion for them. Instead, they are associated with the crushed and harried figure of the governess, Miss Martin, whom the girls treat with snobbery and contempt, despite the fact that she (secretly) shares their need for private romantic fantasy (a caricatured spinster, she invents her own imaginary lover). Along with Miss Martin, the Brontës become the target for mockery and satire: Deirdre presents Charlotte as a comically dowdy figure who is spotted buying a hideous mauve hair net in a cheap chain store, hence the novel's title.

The Carnes may adore Victoriana—as long as they can ironize it as kitsch. But in their self-consciously carefree modernity they feel themselves superior to nineteenth-century women. It is because the Brontës are perceived as having led impoverished lives that they become sinister, frightening, even aggressive figures who want to get their own back on the bright young things of the twentieth century. Charlotte is felt as a genuinely destructive force when she scribbles damning remarks on the manuscript of a novel Deirdre has been trying to write, leading the insecure first-time author to give up on it. Deirdre's scorn has thus turned the Brontës into envious avenging figures. When Judge Toddington asks her whether it has ever occurred to her that the Brontës have been drawn to her family by the appeal of "a happiness they never had themselves," Deirdre bursts into tears of genuine emotion.[23] Lady Toddington then suggests placating the frightening ghosts by showing them warmth and inviting them to a Christmas party. Thus, as the novel moves toward its end, compassion of a sort begins to show through its brittle surface.

Much of the appeal of *The Brontës Went to Woolworth's* comes from its oddness and idiosyncrasy, but it nevertheless betrays (and questions) the common prejudices of its time. For all the popularity of the Brontës during this period, both biographers and fictional biographers tended to regard them from the patronizing perspective of their own modernity. More interested in turning the Parsonage into a set for a soap opera, few really got to grips with questions of the Brontës' creative imagination. None seem to have alluded to their literary apprenticeships in Angria and Gondal, and Rachel Ferguson is unusual in her use of the Brontës as a way in to exploring the theme of fantasy.

After 1941, however, when the American academic Fannie Ratchford published the first in-depth study of the juvenilia, *The Brontës' Web of Childhood,* the idea of using the Brontës as fantasy characters in fiction became more and more popular. Ever since Gaskell, the existence of the early writings had been on record, but they had not yet become a focal part of the Brontë story. Ratchford's pioneering work—since superceded but authoritative in its day—revealed the richness of the young Brontës' imaginary worlds and had the unintended (and sometimes unfortunate) effect of somehow legitimizing enthusiasts' urge to fantasize. As a child, Charlotte had peopled her imagination with real-life heroes, such as the

Duke of Wellington. Her adult admirers took this as a cue to do likewise with the Brontës.

Kathleen Wallace's *Immortal Wheat* (1951) describes itself as "a personal interpretation mainly in fictional form of the life and works of the Brontës"[24] and celebrates them as "for all time, the outstanding example of possession-by-day-dream."[25] It is hard not to find something suspect in the way she elides the mature creativity of the Brontës as adult novelists with her own self-indulgent fantasizing. In the final chapter, "Ballet for Puppets: A Fantasia," lifesize marionettes of Charlotte, Emily, Anne, Jane Eyre, Cathy, and Heathcliff dance about on an imaginary stage with no distinction between the real and the literary characters. Nothing could better illustrate the way in which Brontë worshippers had taken possession of their idols and were pulling the strings.

Yet on a more positive note, the popularization of the juvenilia also led to a new focus on the Brontës' childhood, now seen as a time of excitement and imagination in contrast to Gaskell's grim vision. As an authentic exploration of the child's-eye view, the early chapters of *Jane Eyre* have never perhaps been bettered in literature, and have always appealed to the young—from Emma Cullum Huidekoper, a ten-year-old American girl who in the 1870s surreptitiously obtained a copy of the novel only to have it confiscated as unsuitable at the most exciting moment,[26] to the poet Adrienne Rich, who describes how carried away she was by the whirlwind of Jane's story in her youth.[27] The Brontës themselves began to take on a similar appeal, and if many of the adult fictionalizations of the Brontës' lives are often disappointing as literature, there is something far more heartening about the children's stories in which they now began to appear.

Once the young Brontës were established in the popular imagination as characters in their own right, they appealed particularly to shy, lonely, bookish children, as Margaret Drabble testifies in an account of her own childhood fascination with them.[28] Their creation of fantasy kingdoms, their freedom to walk the moors, the sense of their self-sufficiency in their own world invited identification. A book such as Phyllis Bentley's *The Young Brontës* (1960) told the story straightforwardly. But writers of children's fiction also began to use less conventional strategies in an attempt to get inside the intensity of children's identification with the Brontës, with varying success.

One of the most thoughtful is *Peter's Room* by Antonia Forest (1961), in which a group of youngsters living in a country house are introduced to the Brontë story by fourteen-year-old enthusiast Ginty. Snowed in, and

with the telephone cut off, they decide to entertain themselves by inventing their own version of a Brontë fantasy world. To begin with, they are
inhibited and embarrassed about the role-playing involved, but eventually
the imaginary characters take over: "It was really awfully queer to be able
to feel as frightened as this by a bit of Gondal of her own making."[29] When
one of them lets off a real gun, shattering a window, the dangers of over-
identification in fantasy are spelled out. "I think those Brontës . . . must
have been absolutely mental," ponders one of the characters.[30]

Another book, written for younger children, *The Twelve and the Genii*
by Pauline Clarke (1962), is equally full of allusions to the Brontës' fantasy
world. Eight-year-old Max is staying in an old Yorkshire farmhouse when
he befriends a group of animate wooden soldiers he has seen drilling in the
attic. These toys once belonged to the young Brontës, and the villain of the
piece is an American relic-hunter, Professor Seneca D. Brewer, who wants
them for himself. The soldiers eventually escape on a roller skate, making
their way back to Haworth Parsonage and a happy ending.

Yet the young Brontës could also inspire other sorts of fiction. Unlike
Peter's Room, in which the characters take a ghoulish interest in the Brontës' early deaths, Elisabeth Kyle's *Girl with a Pen* (1963) reduced the level
of drama in favor of a clean-cut all-girls-together tone. Charlotte and
Ellen become the archetypal "best friends," and, oddly, it is the unliterary
Ellen who comes up with the title for *Wuthering Heights*. Charlotte's time
in Brussels becomes as commonplace as an Enid Blyton school story, with
no mention of her obsession for Heger. Beginning after the deaths of Mrs.
Brontë and the two elder sisters, Maria and Elizabeth, the novel ends
before the deaths of Branwell, Emily, and Anne. The disturbing elements
thus removed, it forms a tale as bland as the average term at Mallory
Towers.

Yet titles such as Jane Amster's *Dream Keepers: The Young Brontës—a
Psychobiographical Novella* (1973) or Noel Robinson's *Glasstown: A Play*
(1974) show that the richness of the Brontës' imaginative world continued
to appeal to creative writers into the 1970s. This was also the decade which
saw the Brontës reach television screens for the first time, in Christopher
Fry's six-part drama for Yorkshire TV, *The Brontës of Haworth*, whose
sympathetic portrait has stood the test of time (despite the '70s wigs). The
biographer Mark Bostridge remembers being bowled over by it at the age
of fourteen, finding it so inspiring that it contributed to his own ambition
to become a writer.

Similarly, the novelist Lynn Reid Banks's fictional biography, *Dark*

Quartet (1976), which (like Fry's adaptation) incorporates some of the Brontës' own words, provides an excellent introduction to the Brontë story for young readers. Though initially anxious about approaching such overtrodden territory, Reid Banks was more successful than many of her predecessors in balancing speculation with authenticity and in creating complex characterization. Mainly seen through Charlotte's eyes, the book acknowledges both her rebellious and conformist aspects.

Both Lynn Reid Banks and Christopher Fry had been able to take advantage of Winifred Gérin's path-breaking 1967 biography, *Charlotte Brontë: The Evolution of Genius*. Gérin—already the author of lives of Anne and Branwell—had been drawn to the Brontës by a deep sense of emotional affinity. Together with her second husband, John Lock (who published a full-length life of Patrick), she made her home on the edge of Haworth moor, where she would walk in all weathers, soaking up Brontë atmosphere along with the Yorkshire rain. She "became passionately fond of her subjects, and cherished them as friends or daughters."[31] Yet rather than leading her into sloppy sentimentalism, this devotion prompted her into writing what many regarded as the best biography of Charlotte since Mrs. Gaskell's.

Gérin combined compassion for her subject with erudition. In contrast to the sentimental, semifictional treatments of the interwar years, her life of Charlotte used the apparatus of footnotes and bibliography to document its sources (even a respectable retelling such as Margaret Lane's *The Brontë Story* of 1953 had done without these basic elements of scholarly presentation). That it took so long before Charlotte became the subject of comparatively rigorous research is indicative of the semifictional role she had come to play in the collective imagination. Yet Gérin's chosen subtitle was also significant, suggesting that her main aim was to trace the evolving process by which Charlotte became a novelist, not only taking into account the emotional crises of her life, such as her passion for Heger, but also tracing her development in her juvenilia and her Romantic background. In many of the earlier fictionalized lives, the Brontës' novels were presented as the result of a sudden, out-of-the-blue decision—for example, Branwell returns from a moorland walk having chanced upon a mysterious house, and *Wuthering Heights* is instantly born—but Gérin saw it in terms of a slower, more organic process reaching back into childhood.

André Techiné's flawed filmic treatment of 1979, *Les Soeurs Brontë,* also put the idea of the creative artist at its center. Unlike *Devotion,* which had tried to rework the Brontë story for the commercial mainstream,

Left to right: Isabelle Adjani as Emily, Isabelle Huppert as Anne, Marie-France Pisier as Charlotte in André Techiné's atmospheric but slow-moving *Les Soeurs Brontës* (1979).

Techiné's movie was more of an art film. The three sisters—played by Marie-France Pisier, Isabelle Adjani, and Isabelle Huppert—were far too beautiful, in a languid, pre-Raphaelite, 1970s style, which is perhaps what led the *Sunday Telegraph* to read the film as proof of a "backlash against hard, tough, independent women" taking place in fashionable France.[32] But Techiné's original intention had been to explore definitions of creativity by reading them as different types of the artist: the officially recognized artist (Charlotte), the mythical figure of the genius (Emily), and the craftsman (Anne).[33]

According to Techiné's taxonomy, the "cursed artist" was represented by Branwell, and much of his film focused on the brother's story. For a French audience, not so familiar with the Brontës as an English one, this added an element of suspense, according to a review in *Cahiers du Cinéma*. With his drink, drugs, illicit sex life, and self-destructive urges, it is Branwell who conforms to the cliché of the Romantic genius. Yet it is, unexpectedly, his sisters who turn into the great writers in the end despite the fact that, rather than living their art, they lead an unromantic existence, doing *"rien de spécial."*[34] The trouble with this concept is that the sisters' lives—and thus the film itself—seem slow, empty, and shapeless.

Techiné acknowledged the difficulties of representing a life devoted to literary work on film, but he did not manage to solve what he called "the famous problem of writing"—of representing the act of writing as an element of the drama. Critics found the film disappointing: "sometimes appealing but too often heavy-footed" was the verdict of *Variety,* which complained that the brunt of the action detailed the brother's doomed love affair with Mrs. Robinson rather than the sisters' story.[35]

Despite the difficulties of finding new ways into the subject, novels based on the Brontës remain a recognized English literary genre. Unlike the purpler versions of the interwar period, *Brontë* by Glyn Hughes, published in 1996, seems to have been written under the demythologizing influence of Juliet Barker, whose group biography, *The Brontës,* came out two years previously. In contrast to the traditional melodramatic imagery of tombstones and wuthering winds, Hughes begins his tale from the more downbeat perspective of Arthur Nicholls. The impression is of an attempt to move away from legend-mongering, though whether this actually makes for a better novel is a moot point.

In general, the most interesting recent Brontë fictions are those which approach the topic tangentially. A novel for older children, Garry Kilworth's *The Brontë Girls* (1995), for example, is both unsettling and thought-provoking, casting a sinister light on the phenomenon of obsessive interest in the Haworth family. It tells the story of fifteen-year-old Chris and his forbidden relationship with Emily Craster, a girl his own age whose eccentric, disciplinarian father has tried to bring up his three daughters in imitation of the Brontës, after whom they are named. Together with her sisters, Charlotte and Anne, Emily leads an isolated life on a farm in the Essex marshes, purposefully kept in ignorance of the modern world until Chris appears and shatters this separateness forever.

For James Craster, the father, the Brontës represent a state of social and sexual purity in which he is determined to keep his daughters. In the twentieth century, the Brontës have often been considered appealing because they represent nostalgia for a bygone age. But in Craster this desire to arrest the passage of time is transmuted into a pathological force with disturbingly oedipal undertones: what he really cannot bear is the idea that his virginal daughters will one day grow up. The novel's strength lies in the fact that it alludes to the Brontë story only indirectly rather than offering yet another pedestrian retelling. Even so, the girls' personalities reflect the typology which had, since the 1920s, been associated with the Brontës: Emily is the free-spirited rebel of the family; Charlotte is masochistic and exaggeratedly dutiful, with hinted tendencies to anorexia and self-harm; and Anne is as usual overshadowed by the elder sisters.

The great biographical Brontë novel is, however, yet to be written. Compared to some (though by no means all) of the creative responses which their works have prompted—Henry James's *The Turn of the Screw,* for example, offers a brilliant rewriting of *Jane Eyre*—the Brontës' lives have received disappointing treatment at the hands of dramatists and novelists, which is a pity considering the opportunities they offer for exploring the play between myth and reality, biography and fiction. The imagery commonly associated with them may now seem hackneyed through overuse, but in the hands of a Peter Ackroyd or an A. S. Byatt it could surely be reclaimed. (Byatt's brilliant 1967 novel, *The Game,* goes some way toward this goal, in that its tale of a present-day novelist, Julia, who has to choose between love and art, is shot through with references to nineteenth-century women's writing, including the Brontës, but it is not a biographical novel.)

Instead, the sensational new fictions which keep on coming are likely only to make the serious biographer weep. *The Crimes of Charlotte Brontë* by James Tully (1999) is an extreme case in point. Its preposterous claims include the theory that Emily was made pregnant by Arthur Nicholls and subsequently murdered to hush her up. The book is written in the first-person voice of the Brontës' servant, Martha, and is supposedly a secret witness statement made in 1878. It reads like a historical novel. Yet the publisher's blurb on the hardback confusingly presents the book as fact, offering "a startling vision of the extraordinary truth behind the established Brontë biography" from a "noted criminologist" (the author's previous work concerned Jack the Ripper).

Faced with such a mélange of reality and fantasy, it is hard not to feel with Henry James that "we cease to know, in the presence of such ecstasies, what we have hold of or what we are talking about."[36] Biographical truth may be an ideal that is only ever provisionally achieved, and there may be a close aesthetic kinship between biography and the novel. But this makes it more, not less, important to keep alive some consciousness of the distinction between historical facts and fictional inventions.

II

When the Brontë novels first came out, one of the biggest questions they raised in the public mind was that of gender. What was appropriate for a woman to write? What, indeed, was appropriate for women to read? Critics and pundits were quite explicit in homing in on this issue, around which buzzed a furor of controversy.

In reaction to the subversive image which *Jane Eyre* soon acquired, Elizabeth Gaskell had made determined efforts to detach its author from any imputation that she had been either passionate or a so-called strongminded, emancipated woman. Derivative hagiographies went further and packaged her as the epitome of domestic feminity. Later in the century, campaigners for women's rights, such as Millicent Fawcett, had tried to rewrite Charlotte as a feminist pioneer. Yet it would not be until the women's movement of the 1960s and 1970s that gender would reemerge as the focal issue it had been at the time of *Jane Eyre*'s initial reception.

In fact, the rediscovery of the agenda which had dominated the Brontës' public image in the 1840s and 1850s would eventually be made possible not by modern feminism alone (which could sometimes lead to anachronistic misinterpretation), but by the gradual development of a more scholarly, historicized approach. By the time they appeared, both feminism and scholarship were sorely needed if the Brontës were to be rescued from the deadening grip of sentimentalism.

By the mid-1960s, mutterings against what was derisively called the "purple heather school" of Brontë biography had begun to be heard.[37] The mushy, fictionalized versions of the story which had become so popular were felt by some to have had the effect of belittling the Brontës and travestying the truth. Certainly, the levels of basic factual accuracy in many cases left much to be desired. One popular biography of the 1920s said Emily had written *Wuthering Heights* at the age of twenty-four (in fact she had been twenty-seven) and called the artist who made Charlotte's famous portrait Richardson rather than Richmond;[38] another made the embarrassing mistake of announcing that it was known to all Brontë students that Branwell had been born at Haworth Parsonage, when in fact the family did not move there from the nearby village of Thornton until after Anne's birth.[39] Such niggling errors may not individually signify much, but when combined with gushingly expressed presumed intimacy with the subject, they were symbolic of a lackadaisical attitude toward the idea of re-creating the Brontës on their own terms.

If the fictionalizations of the 1930s, '40s, and '50s were unconcerned with historical precision, they were equally uninterested in what are now called gender issues. Despite the fact that Suffragettes had claimed her as a pioneer before the First World War, Charlotte was not particularly associated with feminism in the middle years of the twentieth century, though she was sometimes melodramatically presented as battling against Victorian patriarchy in the shape of the father who opposed her marriage. Some of the novels and dramas based on the Brontë story had alluded, say, to Charlotte's letter from Southey with its strictures against literature being the business of a woman's life. The actress playing Charlotte in a 1933 production of Alfred Sangster's *The Brontës of Haworth* clearly saw her as a career woman, telling a journalist that she thought her character might have been a barrister had she lived in the twentieth century.[40] But audiences were probably more interested in the theme of the romantic heart pulsating beneath the prim facade. It may have become permissible to discuss love and sexuality, which had been suppressed by Gaskell. But the connection between passion and female self-assertion had been severed.

Back in the 1840s, when *Jane Eyre* was published, some readers felt uncomfortable about the idea of a woman writing a love story from the female point of view in which the heroine uninhibitedly expressed her passion. Those who did not find it distasteful found it exhilarating because it seemed so new and original. Not only do Jane and Rochester hold risqué conversations about his previous sex life, but the hero begs the heroine to elope and live with him as his mistress. Significantly, when Jane confesses to having passions of her own, telling Rochester that women feel just as men feel, this acknowledgment of female desire merges into an acknowledgment of women's need for self-expression, for intellectual or professional fulfillment, both of which, it is implied, are conventionally considered the preserve of men.

By the 1940s, however, the connection between passion and ambition had been severed. Both Jane and Charlotte—who were often confused in the public mind—had lost their subversive edge. This was the period in which *Jane Eyre* and *Wuthering Heights* were transformed by Hollywood into "the greatest love stories ever told," at a cost, as Patsy Stoneman has shown, of making them fit the mold of conventional romance.[41]

In the 1944 film of Charlotte's novel, Joan Fontaine's Jane is a meek creature, lacking the fire of the original in her exchanges with Orson Welles's Rochester. In some ways, her characterization seems in fact to have its roots as much in Charlotte's ladylike post-Gaskell persona as in the novel. The original story is set in the Regency period,[42] but the film brings it forward to the mid-nineteenth century, so that Jane's demure dark dress, white collar, and hairstyle can be modeled on George Richmond's famous portrait of Charlotte, made during one of her trips to

London. On display in literary society, Charlotte had projected a respectable feminine self-image in contradistinction to Jane's reputation for naughtiness. A century on, this personal image was still having the effect of dampening Jane's assertive individualism.

The 1940s and '50s was also the period which saw the rise of mass-market romantic fiction designed for female readers. *Jane Eyre* has often been acknowledged as a forebear of Mills and Boon in terms of its basic plotline: inexperienced girl meets difficult, richer older man—usually with smoldering, dark looks and a secret sorrow—and eventually wins his love after a series of trials and misunderstandings which may include the removal of a rival lover. Yet if the simplified narrative structure of the novel—which also relates at a deeper level to fairy tale—found its way into these fictions, the heroine's dynamism and self-validation fell by the wayside.[43]

A century after Jane's first appearance, there was nothing subversive about the swooning Mills and Boon heroines who were her disempowered descendents. Indeed, it could even be argued that this type of mass-market romantic fiction, typically written by women for women, functioned as a sort of emotional narcotic to dull the boredom of frustrated housewives imprisoned in what Betty Friedan famously called "the feminine mystique."

The effect can be seen in a historical romance of 1951. *In the Steps of the Brontës* takes its inspiration from the sisters' story, but unlike Charlotte, Emily, or Anne, the artistic heroine, Jayne, is passively dependent on masculine help. She wants to sell a picture to pay for a ball gown, but is powerless until the local curate offers to take it to a London dealer for her. He tells her she must follow the example of the Brontës, but precludes her from emulating their independence. "They used men's names to help them; you cannot use a man's name, but you can use a man," he chivalrously concludes.[44] The reappearance of Charlotte in books for girls with Victorian-sounding titles such as *Women of Devotion and Courage* (1956) or *When They Were Girls: Girlhood Stories of Fourteen Famous Women* (1956) again suggests that the 1950s was a retrogressive period for the Brontës.[45]

Seen from a feminist perspective, the Brontë whose posthumous reputation suffered the most was not in fact Charlotte but Anne. Gaskell's presentation of Charlotte's life may have skated over those aspects of her work which had provoked accusations of coarseness, but it also quoted enough of her correspondence to show that the author of *Jane Eyre* had been more than a shrinking violet despite her apparent shyness. In contrast, Charlotte's "Biographical Notice" of her sisters had been so apologetic on behalf of Anne that the youngest Brontë had been almost erased.

When it was first published in 1848, Anne's *Tenant of Wildfell Hall* had offended the shockable sections of society more than the other Brontë novels and had had the effect of intensifying the critical outrage that had gathered around the Bells. In its uncompromising attack on masculine vice and on the laws which bound a wife to an abusive husband, it offered a more explicit piece of social and moral criticism than can be found in the work of Charlotte or Emily. Those who were disgusted (though the disgust was not universal) found it too graphic in its portrayal of Arthur Huntingdon's violence, drunkenness, bad language, adultery, and attempts to corrupt his infant son. The preface Anne wrote for the second edition included the most explicit demand for equality for female writers to come from the Brontës: "I am satisfied that if the book is a good one, it is so whatever the sex of the author may be. . . . I am at a loss to conceive how a man should permit himself to write anything that would be really disgraceful to a woman, or why a woman should be censured for writing anything that would be proper and becoming for a man."[46]

In her attempt to wipe the dust from her sister's reputation, Charlotte had described this, the most shocking of the Bells' books, as a mistake which should never have been written. It is doubtful whether she truly and uncomplicatedly believed what she said: she was writing in a highly defensive mood, and her remarks were primarily designed to soothe the public into sympathy. Yet it was to Emily that Charlotte devoted the most space in her commentary on her sisters, and, as a result, Anne was left on the sidelines.

The effect was to push Anne from the public eye. In the future, she would never gain the iconic status of either of her sisters, and it would take more than a century before she was deemed interesting enough to deserve a proper biography to herself.[47] (*Withering Looks,* a satirical two-woman theater piece created in the 1990s by the company Lip Service, cuts her out completely, leaving Charlotte and Emily to explain her absence as due to government cuts.) May Sinclair, in 1912, asserted that Anne lacked genius, but she nevertheless acknowledged *The Tenant of Wildfell Hall* as a revolutionary work of social criticism.[48] This view, however, did not feed into popular culture. Instead, whenever Anne appeared as a supporting character in the Brontë story, she was usually reduced to the simple stereotype of "gentle Anne" (a novelization of Anne's experiences at Thorp Green, where she observed Branwell's relationship with Mrs. Robinson develop, is called *The Captive Dove*).[49] When George Moore praised *Agnes Grey* in 1924 as "the most perfect prose narrative in English letters," such admiration must have seemed eccentric to some.[50] Received opinion (in the voice of Sir Herbert Toddington in *The Brontës Went to Woolworth's*) was, rather, that "there isn't a quotable line recorded of Anne."[51] Until her work began to be reevaluated in the 1960s—in particular by Inga-Stina Ewbank in *Their Proper Sphere*—she would be presented as weak and ultrafeminine, the complete opposite of her heroine Helen Huntingdon, who fights for herself and her son in the face of an abhorrent social and legal system.[52] Readers and audiences who knew Anne only through the purple-heatherish novels and plays of the mid-twentieth century would have been amazed to discover that she had arguably shocked her contemporaries more than her sisters.

"From her radiates a charm evanescent as a flower. . . . We must love her as we love all delicate frail things" is how one playwright summed up Anne in his list of dramatis personae in 1933.[53] The adjectives routinely applied to her are pretty, little, slight, feminine. Another play, dated 1936, includes an interchange in which Charlotte reads out Southey's comments on female authorship and her sisters respond. Only Emily is allowed a snort of derision for the Poet Laureate. The Anne who wrote *The Tenant of Wildfell Hall* has been transformed into a pliant figure keen to embrace a male-dominated view of womanhood:

> Charlotte: "Literature cannot be the business of a woman's life nor ought it to be."
> Emily (sarcastically): Her whole being must be fully pledged to its fitting duties—blacking grates, kneading dough, mending clothes and comforting her husband.
> Anne: I suppose after all most men's ideal of a woman is a comely housewife. There's something in it too.[54]

Popular fictionalizations may have softened Anne's perspective on the world to a caricatured extent, but the protofeminist aspects of Charlotte's work also continued to be underplayed even by highbrow writers. The psychobiographical approach which remained dominant into the 1970s tended to present her as an uncontrolled neurotic, and often failed to take into sufficient consideration the socially constructed aspects of gender, despite the fact that Charlotte's novels had explicitly explored and chal-

lenged society's definitions of womanhood. Lucile Dooley's psychoanalytical study of 1920 may have suggested that the policy of the Brontë
household—in which the only son was early on defined as the family
hope, pride, and joy—had "fostered a subconscious rebellion that never
found full expression but . . . made her in some ways a forerunner of feminism."[55] But she does not consider the possibility that the author of *Villette*
and *Jane Eyre* had applied her *conscious* intellect to the woman question,
or indeed that it was a question that resonated beyond the nuclear family.
Medicalized articles which used Charlotte as a case study of a masochistic
character or typical depressive tended to ignore the historical and cultural
context to an even greater extent. The patient tended to be placed in a subjective void, her neuroses the product of her unconscious mind alone.

In 1929 Virginia Woolf, in *A Room of One's Own,* had, however, made
the connection between what she saw as Charlotte's "rage" and the fact
that she had been "cramped and thwarted" in a patriarchal world.[56] Yet
this feminist perspective was not generally shared. Rosamund Langbridge's biography, published the same year, laughed at the idea of female
solidarity, "that brilliant and exclusive sisterhood, the Mothers Meeting,"
and seems to have felt that the woman question, like the crinoline, was out
of date.[57] (In fact, Langbridge may have been right in implying that part of
Charlotte would have been tempted to see herself as a female version of
the exceptional man of genius rather than identifying herself with run-of-
the-mill womankind.) It would take another forty years before biographers began to explore Woolf's suggestions in more depth.

Winifred Gérin's *Charlotte Brontë: The Evolution of Genius* of 1967 had
established a new standard, but it had not taken fully into account the
importance of gender as an issue. Elizabeth Rigby's virulent attack on *Jane
Eyre* was interpreted simply as a response to the gossip which had falsely
identified Currer Bell as a cast-off mistress of Thackeray's: it was not put
in the context of any wider social discourse about women's writing. Concentrating on the novel's instant success, Gérin underestimated how much
of a problematic text it was felt to be by contemporaries despite its popularity. Today, on the other hand, it is equally important that modern feminism should not seduce us into underestimating how much Charlotte's
literary talent was appreciated in her own time. In the opening chapter of
this book, I have emphasized the attacks and accusations of coarseness
because it was in particular reaction to this strand of opinion that Charlotte, and later Mrs. Gaskell, began to build up the public image of the
Brontës. This is not to say that all Victorian readers were prudes and

misogynists, or that Charlotte was so divorced from the values of her time that no one was able to share her outlook.

In the 1970s, however, the women's movement meant that female biography took on an ideological coloring it had not had, perhaps, since the First World War. In 1989, exactly a hundred years after Millicent Fawcett championed Charlotte and Emily Brontë as role models for "working women," the American academic Carolyn Heilbrun looked back over the 1970s and '80s as a period of progress, noting that "many new biographies of women have uncovered new facts . . . or sometimes no significant new facts but only new stories." With a somewhat amnesiac view of women's history, which failed to take writers like Fawcett into account, she went on to argue that biography had failed women in the past but that the modern age offered new hope: "Since about 1970, we have had accounts of . . . lives miraculous in their unapplauded achievement. . . . They are all new stories. Only the female life of devotion to male destiny had been told before."[58]

Two American biographies of Charlotte, both published in 1976, show contrasting responses to the influence of feminism. Helene Moglen's *The Self Conceived* is the more academic and is more concerned with how a close reading of Charlotte's novels can give us access into her mind. Yet it also has an ideological edge. The biographer asserts that her work has a present-day political purpose as much as a historical or literary critical one: "In our families, in our society, in our political and sexual lives, we are still the victims of the patriarchal forces which protect our economic structures. We continue to reenact our roles in the romantic mythology which embodies and validates that persuasive power. And as we too strive for autonomous definition we see ourselves reflected in different aspects of the Brontës' struggle."[59]

Moglen's feminist reassessment accepted the premise of the psychobiographers—Charlotte remained a neurotic—but it relocated the cause of her neurosis in patriarchy. Charlotte was doomed because, as a woman, she could not be Zamorna, the Byronic hero of her juvenilia: she was condemned to be "the other." Repressing her rage, she withdrew into the "womblike world of fantasy."[60] Her lack of "self-esteem," and her unconscious internalization of patriarchal pressures, bred masochism. Only after her father succumbed to blindness and her brother declined into alcoholism could her "ego survive at all" in the "patriarchal Victorian family."[61] Sharing the psychobiographers' belief that Charlotte's death was psychosomatically induced, Moglen saw it as a direct result of the literally deadening culture in which her subject lived.

Moglen begins her first chapter with a long quotation from a letter written by Charlotte to William Smith Williams on July 3, 1849 (five weeks after Anne's death, six months after Emily's, and nine months after Branwell's). In it, Charlotte considers her loneliness and loss, but is thankful that Providence has given her the "courage to adopt a career" — without it, she would have been like Noah's "raven, weary of the deluge and without an ark to return to." Rather than stressing Charlotte's courage and career, Moglen picks up the image of the bird and, with Gaskellian fatalism, opens Charlotte's story with a tragic prolepsis: "In six years time, like the wearied raven forced to descend, she too would drown."[62]

More than a hundred years before, Elizabeth Gaskell had created a climate in which Charlotte was hailed as the woman made perfect by sufferings. Ironically, the sort of feminist reading which stressed Charlotte's victimhood unintentionally reproduced the martyrology of the Victorians. Whether or not the women's movement of the 1970s genuinely liberated Charlotte from being trapped in a narrative of "devotion to male destiny" seems a moot point when one reads of her being so oppressed by the men in her life — the father, the brother, the husband, even the teacher (Heger becomes something of a sexual harasser) — that it eventually killed her.

Reading Charlotte's story as a parable of victimhood made it more difficult to acknowledge her strength and determination and the conscious artistry she brought to her writing, which instead became a spontaneous cry of pain. Unlike Millicent Fawcett, who had used Charlotte as a positive role model, Helene Moglen ultimately sees her not as proof of what *was* possible for some ambitious nineteenth-century women, but as a symbol of failure and loss. Though she admires Charlotte's novels for their extraordinary vision of psychosexual relations, not to be matched (she thinks) until the fiction of D. H. Lawrence in the next century, she sees their author as so crippled by lack of self-confidence and masochistic submission that she could not in the end survive.

If Helene Moglen's view of Charlotte was as dependent on seeing her as a symbol of suffering as Gaskell's had been, Margot Peters, whose biography *Unquiet Soul* came out the same year, had a more robust conception of her subject. She began her introduction with a twist on the standard image of the journey up to Haworth. Rather than describing the Brontë family's arrival in 1820, she follows the modern tourist trail and wonders what it is about it that attracts the pilgrims. The Brontës' appeal, she decides, lies in the fact that they are perceived as having "the glamor of fame deified by suffering" and as having been "canonised . . . by the tragedy of their lives."[63] Yet Peters has only distaste for the bogus emotions involved in such adoration. It is just too easy, she argues, in a world of antibiotics and sterile, white hospitals, to get a picturesque frisson from the image of the frail consumptive dying on a sofa. Such sentimentality can only do the Brontës a disservice. One could go even further into the question of why our culture still needs so many of its female icons—from Marilyn Monroe to Princess Diana—to suffer and die, as if we want to see them punished for their fame.

Instead of focusing on the tragedy, Peters wanted to portray Charlotte's life and art as "both an eloquent protest over the cruel and frustrating limitations imposed upon women and a triumph over them."[64] An understanding of the social expectations and everyday lives of Victorian women was essential for understanding Currer Bell. For Peters, the conflicts within Charlotte that gave such electricity to her work were not generated (as they were for the psychobiographers) by mental pathology, but by the tensions commonly experienced by talented and intelligent middle-class women of her time, for whom "life could not be other than a battle between conformity and rebellion."[65]

Rather than reading Charlotte's life as directly relevant to the present-day struggle, as Moglen had done, Peters tried to create more of a sense of historical distance. The desire for foremothers, for martyrs and heroines (expressed in Carolyn Heilbrun's somewhat idealized picture of post-1970 female biography) had brought with it a temptation to re-create Charlotte anachronistically in the light of current ideas of women's liberation. As a result, Peters felt that her version of Charlotte would automatically be judged by readers by the standards of their day, not Currer Bell's: one finds her almost apologizing for the fact that Charlotte "was not officially a feminist" in the modern, political sense and "did not directly engage in the legal struggle for women's rights."[66] Instead, she proffered a more inclusive definition of feminism which could involve "all women who have broken the mold to fulfill their creative, intellectual impetus."[67]

Reluctant to pigeonhole Victorian women as passive victims of social injustice, Peters's own feminism encouraged her to seek out their strength and confidence, resulting, for example, in a highly unusual (and perhaps overrosy) reading of the Brontës' aunt, who had come up from Cornwall after the death of her sister to help Patrick bring up his now motherless children. Usually caricatured as a repressive influence, a Dickensian grotesque clattering about the Parsonage in patterns and absurd false hair, Aunt Branwell now becomes "a woman whom financial independence and a consciousness of good works has rendered self-confident; a woman unawed enough by the world to keep the fashion of her youth."[68] Similarly, Peters presents Charlotte not as a victim, but as a professional whose success as a writer singled her out from the common run of women: if she did not fight for their rights, it was because she personally had achieved the success and power her "less fortunate sisters still cry for."[69]

Whether they stressed her victimhood or her strength, 1970s biographers of Charlotte were newly keen to acknowledge that female authorship in the 1840s involved cultural conflicts which inevitably resonated within the psyche of the writer. At the same time that biographers were rediscovering this social context, literary critics were rescuing *Jane Eyre* as a subversive text. Among academics, *Wuthering Heights* had held the high ground for most of the twentieth century as the single acknowledged Brontë masterpiece. In the midcentury it is commonplace to find Emily described as the sole Brontë genius; to modernists her novel seemed to offer entry into a timeless world of mythic clashing egos, whereas Charlotte's work seemed to remain stuck in what was considered the inferior realm of Victorian social realism. The connection between *Jane Eyre* and mass-market romantic fiction did not do it any favors among highbrow critics, and it suffered in comparison with Emily's novel.[70]

In the 1970s, however, the Victorian view of *Jane Eyre* reasserted itself in a new light: the transgressive aspects of the book were rediscovered, but seen this time as a cause for celebration rather than condemnation. Inspiring the title of one of the seminal works of academic feminist criticism, *The Madwoman in the Attic: The Woman Writer and the Nineteenth-Century Literary Imagination* by Sandra Gilbert and Susan Gubar, Charlotte's novel was redefined as one of the founding texts of feminist fiction. Gilbert and Gubar interpreted Bertha Mason, the insane first Mrs. Rochester, as Jane's sympathetic double—an alter ego expressing the unconscious rage and madness of the heroine at the limitations of the male-dominated world in which she had to live. In this, they followed Jean Rhys's 1966 novel *Wide Sargasso Sea,* a "prequel" which tells the story of Mrs. Rochester's early life in the West Indies from her point of view, and which treats her as a sympathetic figure.[71]

The idea that Bertha is Jane's doppelgänger, able to express what she cannot, has subsequently become something of an orthodoxy in feminist approaches to the novel. For example, it was deployed to brilliant dramatic effect in a stage version of *Jane Eyre* created by the Shared Experience theater company in 1997 and revived in London in 1999. The relationship between Jane's outward quietness and hidden fire has always been difficult for an actress to portray, and has often resulted in rather enervated-seeming Janes (in Zeffirelli's disappointing film of 1996, Charlotte Gainsbourg has fascinating *jolie-laide* features, but they are kept in a state of almost total paralysis, never moving to express her inner turmoil). Expressionist in style, Shared Experience solved the problem by having Jane played by two actresses, the first representing her social face and the second, dressed in ragged red with her hair in wild dreadlocks, her inner rage and passion.

When the child Jane is locked in the Red Room by her aunt as a punishment, it is the figure in red who represents her passionate rage. At school, Jane gradually learns that self-control is a necessary part of self-protection if she is to conform and be accepted in society, and the red figure retreats to the back of the stage. But when she arrives at Thornfield, it becomes clear that her alter ego is occupying the attic and threatening to break out, a symbol for the fact that sexual passion is beginning to be awakened in her by Rochester, whether she wants to acknowledge it or not.

Although it makes for compelling theater, the trouble with this interpretation is that it is not quite true to the book. When the madwoman is discovered and the wedding between Jane and Rochester broken off, the implication of the Shared Experience production is that Jane runs away because she cannot face her own passions. We are left feeling that she should have followed her instinct and united herself with Rochester anyway—that it was only fear and repression which stopped her becoming his lover. However, this suggests a rather anachronistic view of sex outside marriage. In the original text, Jane's escape from Thornfield is presented not just as tragic self-denial but as an act of empowering self-assertion. I may be poor and plain and alone, but *I* care for myself, says Jane, aware that if she became Rochester's mistress she would lose not only her respectability but her self-respect.

As Brontë criticism has become more historically aware, scholars have begun to feel that feminists of the 1970s tended to overstate Charlotte's sympathy for the madwoman and understate the importance of reason as well as passion in the author's moral worldview. Certainly, one gets the sense that they often approached Charlotte's text through the veil of their own ideology. Patsy Stoneman notes that while feminists championed *Jane Eyre* as a bible of female consciousness-raising, critics with an interest in postcolonial studies, who also saw Bertha as the novel's true heroine, began to denounce it for the implicit racism of its Creole subplot.[72] Ironically, this suggests a return to the moralizing criteria which hostile Victorian reviewers brought to bear: the values may be different, but the critics' agenda is equally concerned with judging the novel in terms of its moral goodness or badness, rather than on purely aesthetic or emotional terms.

In contrast, recent critics, keen to understand *Jane Eyre* in terms of its own cultural and literary background, have tended to reject the idea that the text sets up the madwoman as a sympathetic figure.[73] Yet whatever Charlotte's original conception of the character may have been, some men clearly still feel threatened by Bertha. In 1999, the distinguished politician Roy Jenkins described Margaret Thatcher as the "great incubus of John Major's premiership, comparable with Mr Rochester's mad wife in *Jane Eyre*."[74] The first Mrs. Rochester, it seems, has resonance today as an emblem of the fear of female power.

In the 1980s and '90s, a postfeminist consciousness seems to have made it possible, perhaps for the first time since Gaskell, for biographers to stop routinely seeing Charlotte primarily as a victim, whether of the external tragedies in her life, of her own neuroses, or of patriarchal society. Rebecca Fraser's excellent 1988 life felt no need to use Charlotte for present-day ideological purposes. Rather than anachronistically hailing her as a radical forerunner of the modern women's movement, she chose to place her in the context of nineteenth- rather than twentieth-century writings on gender. Like Margot Peters she was less interested in Charlotte the sufferer, more interested in recognizing those aspects of her personality which enabled her to become an ambitious artist. But where Peters had called Charlotte "naive" in her supposed isolation from society—she was too naive, for example, to realize that there was anything "coarse" in her work[75]—Fraser saw Charlotte as in touch with a culture in which the "woman question" was a burning current issue.

The fact that the need to claim Charlotte as an early feminist martyr has receded can be seen in recent biographical treatments of her marriage. The first feminist life, Millicent Fawcett's brief account of 1889, had painted Arthur Nicholls in a negative light: he was blamed for preventing Charlotte from writing and trying to force her into the uncongenial role of conventional clergyman's wife. Helene Moglen's 1976 reading is similarly unsympathetic, characterizing Nicholls as an authority figure, though it internalizes Charlotte's need to be dominated, which is presented as the masochistic product of a lifetime of social conditioning. In the same year, Margot Peters also asserts that the marriage "blighted the great powers of Currer Bell," and goes on to describe her death as a solution to the unsolvable conflict between her art and her marriage.[76]

In 1988, however, Rebecca Fraser paints a warmer portrait of the marriage, and defends Arthur Nicholls from the charge—which he always denied—that he had refused to allow Charlotte to continue writing fiction. This accusation had been leveled against him by both Elizabeth Gaskell and Ellen Nussey, but Fraser shows how biased the views of both these women were of the man who had got in between them and their friend.[77] In fact, Charlotte had found time to think about a new novel—the fragment known as "Emma"—after her marriage, even though, no longer facing lonely, empty days, her time was now much taken up with her husband and his work. She was, we could add, only married for nine months before she died: we cannot know how her life would have developed had she lived, though in Mrs. Gaskell she had as a role model a successful author who was both married and female.

One of the aspects of the marriage which still evokes feminist disapproval is Arthur's attempt to censor Charlotte's letters to Ellen. "Think of Charlotte Brontë, who married after writing three of the greatest novels of the nineteenth century, and was reduced to seeking her husband's approval for writing letters to her best friend," writes Natasha Walter in *The New Feminism,* comparing the power and freedom of modern women to the boxed-up lives of their less fortunate forebears.[78] Having seen the sort of catty comments about mutual friends Charlotte put in her letters to Ellen, Arthur had been afraid of trouble if the wrong people got hold of them. As a result he had indeed intervened in the relationship between the friends and extracted a promise from Ellen that she burn the correspondence. Yet in their exchange over this issue, and in Ellen's written promise (which she had no intention of keeping), the two women seem from their satirical style to be humoring this overcautious specimen of the male sex rather than crushed into silence.

Culturally and emotionally, Arthur Nicholls's reserve and strong need for privacy—expressed in his lack of enthusiasm for the Gaskell biography—must have related, at some level, to his masculinity, particularly to the age-old male fear of female gossip. But whether he can be simply defined as an instrument of patriarchal oppression seems less certain today than it did in the 1970s. Both Arthur and Ellen were possessive of

Charlotte, and his attitude toward the letters may have been informed more by unacknowledged jealousy than by socially conditioned misogyny. Recently, Arthur Nicholls has been given the benefit of the doubt by Lyndall Gordon and Juliet Barker, as well as by Rebecca Fraser, and the marriage has been characterized as a happy one. The personal, these post-feminist biographers seem to be saying, need not always be political.

In recent years, the move toward historicism, which first began in the 1960s in reaction against sentimental fictionalization, has continued as a strong current in Brontë biography. The Brontës are no longer the pre-serve of the purple-heather school, even if they still attract cranks and sentimentalists. Over the past decade or so, scholarly research has been reaping great rewards. The quest to establish definitive texts of Charlotte's writings, particularly her juvenilia and letters, has resulted in landmark editions by Christine Alexander and Margaret Smith, whose dedicated efforts are providing a solid base upon which future biographers will be able to work.

These scholars have had the task of sorting out the legacy of confusion left in the wake of the dispersal of manuscripts originally bought in the 1890s from Ellen Nussey and Arthur Nicholls by the unscrupulous collector and dealer T. J. Wise. Wise—who was later unmasked as a forger of first editions—has become known as something of a villain in the field of Brontë studies. His desire to make maximum profit out of the Brontës meant that rather than keeping the material together, he soon split up the manuscripts he acquired and sold them off to private collectors. Charlotte's letters were thus scattered far and wide, while manuscripts of Branwell's were divided up and confusingly sold as hers.[79]

Ironically, when Wise himself came to co-edit the Shakespeare Head edition of Brontë correspondence in 1932 he was, as Margaret Smith puts it, much "hampered by his own former activities."[80] Many letters were no longer available, and the editors had to rely on expurgated and abridged copies made by Ellen. In other cases, even when the originals were available, they relied on inaccurate second- or thirdhand copies.[81] The completion of Smith's edition—of which two volumes have already appeared—will mean that biographers will no longer have to rely on the inadequate 1932 version and can get that much closer to Charlotte in her own words.

It seems as though we are now living in a golden age for Brontë scholarship. In the 1990s, the quality of books on the sisters to reach the best-seller lists has shown that popularity and serious research are by no means mutually exclusive. Two biographies, which both came out in 1994, Lyndall Gordon's *Charlotte Brontë: A Passionate Life* and Juliet Barker's *The Brontës,* are utterly different in approach. But they each confront the Gaskell myth in new and revealing ways.

Barker's vast biography is presented as a work of demythology: the back of the jacket proclaims it as "the first book to strip away a century of legend and reveal the truth about the Brontës." Having trained as a historian, Barker spent six years as curator and librarian of the Brontë Parsonage Museum, and eleven years immersing herself in Brontë archives worldwide, with the intention of setting the factual record straight. Not only does she explore unpublished Brontë correspondence; her most innovative research involves trawling hitherto unexplored sources such as contemporary local newspapers and parish records. Her book demonstrates the extraordinary tenacity of Gaskell's vision, since the *Life* remains the prime target of Barker's no-nonsense revisionism even after a century and a half.

Yet though Barker is so determined to squash Gaskell's myths, she remains in one respect trapped in Gaskell's agenda, since it is the life history of the family, and not the sisters' works, which interests her most. The amount of care and detail expended on the supporting characters— Patrick, Branwell, Arthur Nicholls—almost makes one forget that these men would never have became biographical subjects in the first place if it had not been for the literary achievements of their female relatives. Barker takes a far less sympathetic view of Charlotte than other recent writers, and in her desire to demystify her some critics felt that she had overnormalized her, almost forgetting the extraordinariness of what she did.[82] It is telling that this biographer seems baffled by Charlotte's letter to Hartley Coleridge, but feels comfortable criticizing her for moaning about having to go out and earn her living as a governess. In terms of factual data, Barker is one of the most trustworthy Brontë biographers: from the documentary viewpoint her work will prove a lasting achievement. But it is far less certain that she gets to the core of Charlotte's genius.

In complete contrast, *Charlotte Brontë: A Passionate Life,* by the Oxford don Lyndall Gordon, is most convincing when exploring the inner workings of the creative life. Compared to Barker's meticulous amassing of detail (to the extent that we learn, for example, that during the sixteen months in which the young Patrick held a curacy in Dewsbury in 1809–10 he performed "nearly 130 marriages"),[83] Gordon's approach to evidence is more like a search for what Virginia Woolf called the "creative fact; the fertile fact; the fact that suggests and engenders."[84]

As a literary critic, whose previous books were on T. S. Eliot and Woolf, Gordon comes to the life through the works rather than the other way around, reversing the pattern initially established by Gaskell. The novels are not used, as so often in the past, as sources of biographical evidence; rather, the facts of Charlotte's life history are put to the service of gaining a deeper understanding of her novels. Life and art go hand in hand, and the character who emerges is subtle and complex. Unlike the psychobiographers who emphasized the internal psyche at the expense of the social self, Gordon is able to bring both to life, exploring the interface between the two.

It is because she puts the writings center stage that Gordon is able to dispense with the need for seeing Charlotte as a victim-heroine (or its venomous reverse, the cold and carping creature found in E. F. Benson and, to an extent, in Barker). Gaskell had used the sorrows of her subject's life as a means of focusing attention away from the works. By putting the works first, Gordon recovers Charlotte's strength: "It is easy to see this life as a series of losses," she writes, "yet loss does not explain the central fact of Charlotte Brontë's existence: her capacity to use her experience as the material of art."[85]

Any history which presents itself in terms of progress rather than process should be treated with a certain amount of suspicion, but it is hard to deny that the recent history of Charlotte's posthumous life has been a success story. During the middle years of the twentieth century the Brontës were frequently travestied in fictional biographies which turned their lives into a soap opera and belittled their literary imaginations. Nowadays, however, it seems that progress really has been made in the journey toward rediscovering the real Charlotte and the world in which she lived.

In a profound sense, however, we will never arrive at the end of that journey. Although textual scholars can aspire to accuracy and historians can establish certain sorts of fact beyond reasonable doubt, the subject's inner life will only ever be reachable by a creative act of imagination. It is all to the good that the raw materials of Charlotte's biography are now more accurately documented than in the past, but her life will still require constant rewriting. Future generations will always need to reconceive the Brontës, to tell their story from a new perspective. Indeed, the emphasis on historicity which characterizes the work of recent critics may itself be relativized by their successors, who may regard it as simply another expression of our current obsession with the past, a cultural phenomenon which extends from interest in "authentic" performance in classical music to the fashion for architectural preservation and restoration.

Literary biography will continue to raise questions which need to be answered and reanswered—about the relationship between fact and truth, and between information and interpretation, as well as about the nature of personality and the relationship between writers and their writings. We should not see biography as a failed empirical science striving to produce definitive, objective results but doomed to failure. Nor should we take the extreme postmodernist line which completely collapses the distinction between biography and fiction, regarding both as undifferentiated "textual constructs." Instead, we should regard it as an amphibious art form, which ideally has *both* to obey the constraints of evidence *and* to respond creatively to the challenge of making shape, form, and meaning.

The future contains an infinite number of Charlotte Brontës in the hands of tomorrow's biographers, each one of whom will forge a different relationship with her. Some will be more valid than others, but we should celebrate, rather than regret, this potential richness as a means of illuminating the extraordinary mind which created *The Professor, Jane Eyre, Shirley,* and *Villette,* and of communicating to each new generation the enduring value of these works.

CHAPTER SEVEN

Interpreting Emily

Our understanding of Charlotte is bound to be flawed and subjective, but it would be wrong to say that we do not know her. In contrast to her elusive sister Emily, we know her very well. Gaskell's *Life of Charlotte Brontë* may have been hagiographic and sometimes misleading, but it put an extraordinary amount of information on record at a very early date. In addition, a biographer working on Charlotte today has a wealth of primary material to go on, including the hundreds of letters one would expect from an eminent Victorian and an enormous volume of juvenilia.

But Emily, who never seems to have made a single significant friend outside her immediate family, had no Elizabeth Gaskell and left little behind her. She was notoriously reserved in life, and seems equally unwilling to share herself in death. Apart from her single novel, *Wuthering Heights,* and her surviving poetry, she has bequeathed her biographers very little. The few anecdotal glimpses we get of her have her literally running away at the sight of strangers. She seems to repel investigation as fiercely as Heathcliff rebuffs those who intrude upon his moorland solitude.

It is no coincidence that Emily has inspired two detective novels.[1] Her remains are so skeletal that the body seems to have gone missing altogether. The personal documents that exist are few and far between: four short "diary papers" spaced out over a period of ten and a half years, three formal, unrevealing notes to her sister's friend Ellen Nussey, a handful of French essays written at school in Brussels, the odd sketch, a fragment of an account book, the occasional other trace.

With so little to go on, Emily's biographers have had more literary sleuthing to do than Charlotte's. But research has yielded little in the way of hard evidence. Ever since Charlotte revealed that the author of *Wuthering Heights* was the retiring daughter of a provincial parson, readers have regarded this fact as some sort of unnatural aberration. Lack of biographical data has made that enigmatic novel seem all the more obscure, and the combination of the two has left Emily riper for mystification than the rest of her family.

From what we can reconstruct, it seems likely that this fiercely private woman would have resented biographers' attempts to pin her down. Above all, she seems to have loved liberty: freedom to think her own heterodox thoughts, freedom from social pressures, freedom from having to submit to the will of others. Although posterity has cast her as a wind-blown waif wafting across the moors in a fug of intuitive trance, the real Emily had both a razor-sharp intellect and a surprisingly down-to-earth imagination capable of taking delight in everyday objects. Her mental resistance to social conventionality meant that she could be infuriatingly difficult in company, reserved to the point of rudeness. It was only at home in Haworth, where she could live unhindered in the world of her own imagination, that Emily was genuinely happy and relaxed.

"Happy" and "relaxed" are not words which one would easily associate with a novel as dark and tense as *Wuthering Heights*. But the impression we get from Emily's secret so-called diary papers is of a person with the capacity to feel at ease with herself. These four fragmentary papers are the only documents which give us anything like access into her personal world. As a result, they are like gold dust for the biographer. But the glimpses they give us are so fleeting, so provisional, so compromised by what they do not tell us, that they are as frustrating as they are fascinating. They invite us into Emily's private space only to warn us about the dangers inherent in biographical interpretation. She may have been at ease when she wrote them, but we cannot wholly relax while reading them because we are always straining to know more than they reveal.

Unlike Emily's carefully honed poetry or novel, her diary papers are spontaneous, unself-conscious scraps of prose in which she speaks in her own voice.[2] They have a disarming realness about them which makes them uniquely attractive. But at the same time they remain slippery and incomplete. Written on small pieces of paper and hidden away, they were intended to be reread in future years, but only by Emily herself and her favorite sister, Anne. Emily was, as Charlotte put it, "not a person of demonstrative character, nor one, on the recesses of whose feelings, even those nearest and dearest to her could, with impunity, intrude unlicensed."[3] Perusing her private diaries feels uncomfortably like trespassing, in the same way that reading Charlotte's Roe Head Journal makes you afraid you are committing a treacherous intrusion.

Yet the tone of these brief notes is much less pent-up than the Roe Head Journal. Emily did not use them for self-analysis or extended reverie, and as a result they are more tantalizing but less explicitly revealing of her innermost thoughts. They record the minute-by-minute occurrences of the day, capturing a moment and preserving it like an insect in amber. Snatches of conversation, accounts of the weather or of what the other members of the family were doing at that very instant, give tiny glimpses into the world of Haworth Parsonage which bring the dead momentarily to life. But it is only for a moment, and the fugitive, evanescent feel of Emily's unruly, dashed-off prose only underscores the transitoriness of time. They give us the illusion of recovering the past, but also show us what we've lost.

The 1837 diary ends with a snippet of recorded dialogue:

Aunt. Come Emily Its past 4 o'clock. Emily Yes Aunt
Anne well do you intend to write in the evening
Emily well what think you

The questions remain open-ended. We will never know whether the sisters did in fact spend the evening of June 26, 1837, writing. The passage concludes with a parenthesis, squashed up to the very edge of the sheet of paper, in which the closing bracket is omitted: "(we agreed to go out 1st to make sure if we get into a humor we may stay."[4] In its incompleteness, the missing bracket symbolizes the absences with which the reader has to deal: the fact that we are not able to ascertain whether the sisters put their plans—either of writing in the evening or of going out—into action stresses the limits of interpretation. We simply cannot know what is the relation of these words to history, whether the future they project is real or purely speculative.

The diary papers are thus shifting, unstable indicators of reality. This seems only too appropriate when one considers what they tell us about Emily's habit of mind. What strikes most is the way in which, for her, the boundary between the real and the imaginary seems to have been unusually porous. The 1834 diary paper juxtaposes reality and fantasy as if there were no difference between them. Two consecutive sentences—"The Gondals are discovering the interior of Gaaldine Sally moseley is washing in the back-kitchin."—suggest that Emily is as comfortable in the invented kingdom of Gondal as she is in the actual world of the washerwoman.[5] She can expand her imagination to fill vast tracts of unexplored land, or she

Emily's diary paper of June 26, 1837, is both revealing and concealing. In the sketch of herself and Anne, we only get to see Emily from behind.

can contract it to the cramped enclosure of the back kitchen. This combination of high-flown fantasy with the solidity of the everyday anticipates the style of *Wuthering Heights,* in which extremes of melodrama coexist with close attention to realist detail, such as the vast oak dresser with its pewter dishes and silver jugs which the narrator, Lockwood, notices as he enters the living room of Heathcliff's home.

Oddly enough, Emily's novel offers us an uncanny if unintended commentary on her diary papers and our own relationship to them as voyeurs and interpreters. Near the beginning of the novel, Lockwood is forced by the weather to spend the night at the Heights. In bed, he discovers Cathy's childhood journal, scribbled, as spontaneously as Emily's own, in the margins of her Bible. Like the diary papers it is both fragmentary and arrestingly immediate. Beginning *in medias res* with the words "An awful Sunday!" it hauls the past right into the present, but remains only partially intelligible because, so far, neither we nor Lockwood have been intro- duced to all the characters involved.

As Lockwood puts it, Cathy's words are "faded hieroglyphics" which need to be "deciphered." They whet his appetite for knowledge—"an immediate interest kindled within me for the unknown Catherine"—but at the same time they fail fully to satisfy it.[6] Like the 1837 diary paper, Cathy's journal ends unresolved, leaving the reader in a state of uncer- tainty. Cathy describes how she and Heathcliff are planning to borrow the dairywoman's cloak and go out for a scamper on the rain-swept moors. But neither Lockwood nor the reader are in a position as readers of the diary to know whether they eventually did so.

In poring over Emily's faded scraps of diary, we are like Lockwood. It is as well to remember that part of his function in the novel is to offer us a cautionary tale about the dangers of interpretation. A bumbling character, he is comically bad at reading signs and embarrasses himself by mistaking a pile of dead rabbits for his hostess's pet cats. His immediate reaction to Cathy's diary is to fall asleep and find himself in a dream about a crazy preacher performing a relentless and surreal exegesis on a scriptural text. This is meaning gone mad, but it shows how protean the written word can be and how dependent it is upon what the reader makes of it.

Wuthering Heights is in fact an intellectually complex work, conscious of its own literariness and aware of the philosophical problems inherent in the business of reading. Full of riddlesome texts which invite explication— such as the inscription over the door of the Heights or Cathy's graffiti on the windowsill—it alerts the reader to the dangers of misreading but also suggests that ambiguity and plurality are inescapable facts. This is a novel whose most famous phrase—Cathy's "I *am* Heathcliff"[7]—undermines the very concept of individual identity. Uncannily, it seems to warn us against trying to make a single, stable, self-consistent entity out of the fragments of Emily Brontë which posterity has left us. We can read what we will into these literary scraps, but we run the risk, like the nightmare preacher Jabes Branderham, of shooting off into our own "private manner of interpret- ing" and missing the point altogether.[8]

Cathy's diary fills Lockwood with such curiosity that he is determined to discover her story. He asks the housekeeper Ellen Dean to fill him in, and it is her account which becomes the central narrative of *Wuthering Heights*. Unlike Charlotte, whose best books are written in the first person, Emily constructed her single novel as a complex tale within a tale: the reader is held at a distance, through multiple narratives, from the main protagonists of the story, and has to rely on the narrators' versions of events.

Much the same is happening when the attempt is made to reconstruct Emily Brontë's own story. The biographer is as desperate to know it as Lockwood is to know Cathy's. But since there is so little direct access to her, it is necessary to rely on the testimonies of others, particularly of Charlotte, who famously remarked that an interpreter should have stood between Emily and the world.

As interpreter, Charlotte does indeed stand *between* posterity and Emily, beckoning us with one hand and waving us away with the other. Since she is almost the only source of biographical information, there is no option but to listen to what she says. But she is a slippery authority whose comments tell us more about her own attitude toward her sister than about the inner workings of Emily's mind. They betray ambivalent feelings: protectiveness tipping over into an urge to dominate, admiration tinged with condescension.

After Emily died, Charlotte took the reins and became the impresario of her posthumous reputation. Her attempts to rewrite her in fiction, criticism, and biography, and as an editor, are often as obfuscating as they are revealing. Quite possibly, Charlotte also destroyed many of the documents which might have given us a clearer picture of Emily's character and artistic development. Her actions—which grew out of her deep, complicated love for her sister, and the unbearable pain of bereavement—were not maliciously intended. Nevertheless, they have had an incalculable—and sometimes damaging—effect on posterity's perceptions, exacerbating the mystery which surrounds Emily to this day.

The story of the Emily myth, therefore, begins with Charlotte. Any account of it must start by unpicking the ways in which the elder sister attempted to remold the younger after her death. Charlotte's controlling attitude may have been unleashed after Emily died, but it had its seeds in the living relationship between the sisters.

Born in 1818, Emily was only two years younger than Charlotte, though it comes as a surprise to realize how close they were in age. Charlotte clearly regarded her as very much the younger sister: she even had a habit of miscalculating how old Emily was, often knocking a year or two off her actual age.[9] The fact that Branwell, born in 1817, came between them may have made the gap seem larger than it was. In childhood and adolescence, Charlotte was closer to her brother, who became her partner and rival in the Angrian adventure, while Emily and Anne formed a separate bond in the imaginary world of Gondal.

As the eldest surviving child in a motherless family, Charlotte was placed in a position of inevitable responsibility toward her younger sisters. While Emily and Anne identified with each other as closely as twins, their elder sister worried about them like an anxious parent. There were times when Charlotte quite literally felt responsible for keeping Emily alive.

At the age of nineteen, when Charlotte went back to teach at Roe Head, seventeen-year-old Emily went with her as a pupil. Her homesickness, amounting to physical illness, caused Charlotte such fear that, as she later remembered, "I felt in my heart she would die if she did not go home, and with this conviction obtained her recall."[10] In Charlotte's version of events, it is she, not Emily herself, who realizes that her sister must go home. Emily is passive, and Charlotte the protector who stirs herself to action just in time to prevent catastrophe. But if Charlotte never believed that Emily was capable of looking after herself, it was equally important to the dynamic of the relationship that Emily was stubborn, independent, and reluctant to submit to her sister's management.

When the two sisters went to study at the Pensionnat Heger, it was the elder who organized the trip and decided that Emily should go too. Thus far, Emily complied. People they met in Brussels, however, perceived the balance of power between them rather differently, noting how Emily seemed to operate on Charlotte with a sort of "unconscious tyranny."[11] Unlike Charlotte, who craved social acceptance, Emily did not care what people thought. Her refusal to behave with conventional ladylike manners—like her perverse but determined choice of unfashionable clothes—caused Charlotte agonies of embarrassment. Both worked hard, but unlike Charlotte, who was looking for a mentor, Emily resented Constantin Heger's teaching methods. She felt her originality would be compromised by his requirement that they imitate the style of other writers. Of the two sisters, she already had more literary self-confidence.

Charlotte's most celebrated attempt to take control of her resistant sister came in the autumn of 1845 when she picked up Emily's private poetry notebook and was inspired by what she found to mastermind the publication of the 1846 *Poems by Currer, Ellis, and Acton Bell*. Unlike Anne, who volunteered to collaborate, Emily was so angry that "it took hours to reconcile her to the discovery I had made, and days to persuade her that such poems merited publication."[12] Charlotte had responded with amazement when she read Emily's poems, as if she was astounded at the talent her little sister had revealed. This may partly explain why Emily was so angry.

Emily's feelings about her own work are, however, characteristically obscure. But we cannot simply assume that she was averse to the idea of publication per se. Her fury may have had more to do with the fact that Charlotte always claimed to know what was best for her. Emily was not so unworldly that she refused any contact at all with the literary world. Although she was happy for Charlotte to negotiate the *Poems* deal with Aylott and Jones, as Ellis Bell she probably conducted her own correspondence with Thomas Newby, *Wuthering Heights*'s publisher.[13]

Intriguingly, Gaskell also mentions in a letter to George Smith that Emily had corresponded with G. H. Lewes.[14] It may be part of Charlotte's posthumous romanticization of her sister to present her as an artist so pure that she shrank from contact with the world of publishers and readers.

Emily was, however, the most determined of the sisters to remain hidden behind her pseudonym. When Charlotte and Anne returned from their revelatory visit to London in the summer of 1848, Emily was upset to discover that Charlotte had let slip the identity of Ellis Bell as well as that of Currer and Acton. Charlotte had to tell William Smith Williams to adopt the charade of pretending he did not know who Ellis was: "Permit me to caution you not to speak of my sisters when you write to me — I mean, do not use the word in the plural. 'Ellis Bell' will not endure to be alluded to under any other appellation than the 'nom de plume.' I committed a grand error in betraying ~~her~~ his identity to you and Mr. Smith[.]"[15] In the context, pronouns become crucial. As Charlotte crosses out "her" and replaces it with "his," we can see her forcing herself to comply with Emily's demands.

Charlotte's experience of Emily as someone who needed placating would become agonizing during the latter's final illness, and it is the context of this dreadful experience that her later attempts to stage-manage Emily's reputation should be viewed. No amount of pleading seemed to have any effect on her increasingly unreachable sister. On October 29, 1848, Charlotte first expressed the extent of her fears to Ellen Nussey:

"Emily's cold and cough are very obstinate . . . she looks very, *very* thin and pale. Her reserved nature occasions one great uneasiness of mind—it is useless to question her—you get no answers—it is still more useless to recommend remedies—they are never adopted."[16] By November 2, the cough and cold had become "something like a slow inflammation of the lungs," but Charlotte still felt impotent in the face of Emily's refusal to accept help, either medical or emotional: "[S]he neither seeks nor will accept sympathy; to put any question, to offer any aid is to annoy . . . you must look on, and see her do what she is unfit to do, and not dare to say a word."[17]

Things had not much changed by the end of the month. Helpless, Charlotte was desperately searching for ways of manipulating Emily into trying a homeopathic remedy: "[I]t is best usually ~~not~~ to leave her to form her own judgment and *especially* not to advocate the side you wish her to favour," she wrote to William Smith Williams on November 22, "if you do, she is sure to lean in the opposite direction, and ten to one will argue herself into non-compliance."[18] Five days later, she was still describing her sister as "too intractable."[19] On the morning of December 19 she wrote to Ellen in desperation: "Moments so dark as these I have never known."[20] Later that day, Emily died.

Future commentators would come up with contradictory readings of Emily's death. Some would argue that she refused medical help because she wanted to die—that, like Heathcliff, she committed passive suicide.[21] Others would say the opposite—that she denied she was ill because she wanted to live, like Hindley Earnshaw's wife in *Wuthering Heights*, who refuses to acknowledge her consumption until within a week of her death.[22] Yet in the letters leading up to Emily's death Charlotte gives us frustratingly little access into her sister's motives or desires. What she calls Emily's "peculiar reserve of character" shuts her out.[23] Later, however, she would remember the death itself as painfully reluctant, telling Ellen in April 1849 that Emily had been "torn conscious, panting, reluctant though resolute out of a happy life."[24]

All of Emily's biographers have had to cope with the absences surrounding her, but Charlotte's public comments on her sister were written under the shadow of a real and agonizing loss. Emily's death was far more of a wrench than Branwell's the previous September or Anne's the following May. "I let Anne go to God and felt He had a right to her," she told William

Smith Williams in June 1849. "I could hardly let Emily go—I wanted to hold her back then—and I want her back hourly now."[25]

The months between September 1848 and May 1849 had been dominated by illness and death. Charlotte's novel *Shirley* had been put on hold. But in June, she returned to the book with energy, determined to make work an antidote to grief. When she picked it up again she decided to focus on the character of Shirley Keeldar, which she later told Mrs. Gaskell was based on what Emily might have been had she been born into health and prosperity.[26] Gaskell herself would eventually write *The Life of Charlotte Brontë* to make up for having failed to save Charlotte's life. In a similar vein, the character of Shirley was Charlotte's way of resurrecting Emily. If she could not root her out of her mind, she would use the novel as a way of defying death.

Shirley was the first of a number of attempts to explain Emily's genius, which would culminate in the "Biographical Notice of Ellis and Acton Bell" and the preface to *Wuthering Heights* of 1850. At first glance, it is hard to see what the novel's heroine has in common with Charlotte's sister. The beautiful, wellborn heiress, attired in gorgeous silks, seems so different from the impression we get of the introverted poet with her frumpish, droopy skirts and abrasive manner. Even its first reviewers, who knew nothing of Shirley's original, found her an unrealistic character compared with the novel's other heroine, Caroline Helstone. Set against the background of the Industrial Revolution, it is an amphibious book, part "condition of England" novel, part idiosyncratic experiment. Caroline belongs to social realism. In her miserable life of enforced idleness she embodies the feminist argument for the expansion of women's lives beyond the home. But Shirley is a poetic creation belonging to idealism. It is in this, rather than as a literal portrait, that she represents Charlotte's attempt to understand Emily.

Ever since she had discovered Emily's poems, Charlotte had been as convinced of her sister's genius as she was of her own. It was a genius she felt in awe of—even afraid of—and which she wanted to make sense of on her own terms. During the twentieth century, the rediscovery of *Wuthering Heights* has meant that Emily has been taken up by academic critics of every persuasion—Marxist, feminist, psychoanalytical, structuralist—who have used her work as a means of bolstering their own intellectual positions. But it was Charlotte who first appropriated Emily for ideological purposes. In *Shirley,* she uses the heroine as the mouthpiece for her most explicit expression of her Christian-Romantic credo. In this act of mythmaking she attempts to make sense of her sister according to her own—though not necessarily Emily's—worldview.

Just as Charlotte and Emily wrote homework essays for Monsieur Heger, Shirley writes a *devoir* for her half-Belgian tutor, Louis Moore. Called "La Première Femme Savante" ("The First Blue-Stocking"), it is, quite literally, a creation myth about the female imagination. In it, Charlotte gives a powerful articulation of her own beliefs. Ironically, however, her manifesto often chafes against what we know of Emily's attitudes. One can also detect in it hints that she felt uncomfortable about the nature of her sister's rebellious imagination.

Indeed, if one turns straight from *Wuthering Heights* to *Shirley,* the very form the *devoir* takes begins to look suspect, as if Charlotte is using it to contradict her sister's skeptical stance on religious reading. In Emily's novel, biblical interpretation is an object of satire, mocked in the crazy figure of Jabes Branderham. Yet Shirley's essay is couched in the form of an extended exegesis of a text from Genesis: like the preacher, Charlotte chooses to base her statement of belief on a reading of Scripture.

Despite her unconventionality in other ways, one has to remember that Charlotte was orthodox in her attitude toward holy writ, in that she regarded it unquestioningly as the revealed word of God. As a child, she declared that the Bible was the best book in the world, and it is the book to which she most often alludes in her adult fiction.[27] The daughter of one clergyman and future wife of another, she was not a free-thinker like the atheist Harriet Martineau or the agnostic George Eliot. Nor, it seems, was she as questioning as her sister, whose attitude toward religion seems to have been far less conservative. It is true that parts of *Shirley* are littered with ironic quotations from the Bible, which are there to remind us how absurdly, say, the curates fail to live up to its example. In the *devoir,* however, it is used nonironically as a marker of the seriousness of Charlotte's myth of female creativity.

The enigmatic text (Genesis 6:1–2) on which Shirley's *devoir* is based describes how, in antediluvian times, the "sons of God" chose wives from among the "daughters of men." Charlotte interprets the text allegorically. The "sons of God" represent the divine spark of genius; the daughters of men are embodied by the human woman, Eva, who is "chosen" by God to receive that Presence into her soul.

Sitting on a lonely crag with only the night sky for company, Eva's sense of God-given self is as strong as Jane Eyre's: "Of all things, herself seemed to herself the centre,—a small, forgotten atom of life, a spark of soul, emitted inadvertent from the great creative source, and now burning unmarked to waste in the heart of a black hollow."[28] Her need to express herself and her belief in her inborn creativity are as potent as the ambition which spurred Charlotte herself to become a writer:

> She asked, was she thus to burn out and perish, her living light doing no good, never seen, never needed . . . ? Could this be, she demanded, when the flame of her intelligence burned so vivid; when her life beat so true, and real, and potent; when something within her stirred disquieted, and restlessly asserted a God-given strength for which it insisted she should find exercise?[29]

Eva's pulsating ego has all the Charlotte hallmarks. The words, are, of course, supposed to have been written by Shirley, who in turn is supposed to be a fictional version of Emily. Yet they are very far from what we can imagine the real Emily writing. If Charlotte's imagination, like Eva's, centered on her powerful sense of self, Emily's seems to have been entirely different, deriving, on the contrary, from her sense of *not*-self. For Emily, the imagination represented freedom from the confines of individual subjectivity as much as it represented liberty from external constraint. In the diary paper of 1845, for example, she records how she and Anne had played at being Gondal characters during a trip to York. "[D]uring our excursion," she writes, "we were Ronald Macelgin, Henry Angora, Juliet Augusteena, Rosobelle? Esualdar, Ella and Julian Egramon[t] Catherine Navarre and Cordelia Fitzaphnold."[30] She does not put "we pretended to be" but "we were." For her, the imagination and the self are altogether more protean and disruptive to the order of things than they are for Charlotte.

In many ways, the story of Eva has less to do with Emily than with Charlotte's strong need to justify herself in the wake of the attacks on the Bells' morality. In this context, her myth of female creativity should be read as an act of self-defense. She shows her critics that there is scriptural authority to prove that the purifying force of divine genius is as likely to be found in women as in men. Unlike Emily, who does not appear to have experienced moral unease about her imagination, the young Charlotte had experienced a religious crisis brought on by guilt about her dependence on her feverish Angrian fantasies. She had wondered whether, in Calvinist terms, she was one of the damned, not the saved. Here, in *Shirley*, she seems to be asserting that the woman artist is instead one of the "chosen," that the imagination which created *Jane Eyre* is divinely derived. Using the sexual metaphor of consummated marriage—this is the "bridal-hour"[31] of Genius and Humanity—her theological myth dramatizes the idea that female passion, whether in love or in ambition, can be pure.

So far, the *devoir* reads like a general rebuff to those critics who had castigated *Jane Eyre* as irreligious. But toward the end, Charlotte seems to be using Eva's story in a more private way, relating specifically to Emily. It concludes, significantly, with the idea of a death made glorious by the protective presence of Genius, as if Charlotte is trying to replace the dreadful memory of Emily torn panting out of a happy life with a more bearable image. At the moment of death, Genius sustains his bride "through the agony of the passage" and restores her to Jehovah, her Maker, crowning her with the crown of Immortality before Angel and Archangel.[32] Here, Charlotte is idealizing Emily's poetic gift—defined not as a mere talent for crafting verses but as the capacity for spiritual transcendence—by trying to imagine how it may have smoothed her passage into the next world.

In contrast, in *Wuthering Heights,* Emily had presented heaven as a far less welcoming prospect. When Cathy dreams that she has been there, it is a place of exile, not rapture: "[H]eaven did not seem to be my home," she tells Nelly, "and I broke my heart with weeping to come back to earth; and the angels were so angry that they flung me out, into the middle of the heath on the top of Wuthering Heights; where I woke sobbing for joy."[33] Anne had died an exemplary Christian death, buoyed up by faith, which Charlotte had found comforting. But Emily's panting end continued to prey upon her mind as if it did not seem to guarantee such a smooth passage to the afterlife. The end of the *devoir* is poignant in its patent wish-fulfillment.

Charlotte's fear that there was something disturbing about Emily's imagination would eventually surface in her preface to *Wuthering Heights,* but there are already hints in "The First Blue-Stocking" of her ambivalence. Genius may have taken female Humanity in his arms, but their after-union, Charlotte tells us, is an equivocal time of "bliss and bale." Genius may be God's emissary in the human woman's soul, but he has to fight the forces of Satan. The imagination has as much potential for evil as for good, and Genius has to put up a fight to keep it pure:

Who shall tell how He, between whom and the Woman God put enmity, forged deadly plots to break the bond or defile its purity? Who shall record the long strife between Serpent and Seraph? How still the Father of Lies insinuated evil into good—pride into wisdom—grossness into glory—pain into bliss—poison into passion? How the "dreadless Angel" defied, resisted, and repelled? How, again and again, he refined the polluted cup, exalted the debased emotion, rectified the perverted impulse, detected the lurking venom, baffled the frontless temptation—purified, justified, watched, and withstood?[34]

In her later comments on Emily's novel, Charlotte would betray anxieties that the novel contained debased emotions and perverted impulses which were not entirely purified. Was it serpent or was it seraph that lay behind the creation of Heathcliff?

In *Shirley,* however, Charlotte mostly suppresses her uncertainty about Emily's genius. She is more concerned with idealizing her sister than with questioning her. She does this by transforming her into an embodiment of Romantic visionary poetics, but in a way which, ambiguously, saps her of adult responsibility for her own creativity. As her later remarks on *Wuthering Heights* show, it was important for Charlotte to believe that Emily was not accountable for her own imagination, because it seemed so threatening.

In one scene, Shirley is rapt in a trance in contemplation of the moonlit landscape outside her window. Through her identification with the natural world—what Wordsworth called "primal sympathy"—she moves, "[b]uoyant, by green steps, by glad hills," into a transcendent state "scarcely lower than that whence angels looked down on the dreamer of Beth-el." The "vision" which comes upon her is, in true Romantic vein, an act of perception which is also an act of creation. Earth is made "an Eden" and life "a poem" for her, as she sits in the parlor in the stillness of the evening.

In terms of Romantic metaphysics, the faculty through which she achieves divine transcendence is the imagination. Such ideas would have reached the Brontës through their magazine reading. *Fraser's,* for example, would have told them about Coleridge's view of the imagination as the faculty which transcends natural experience and discovers objects purely spiritual.[35] Similarly, the account of Shirley's vision reflects the sort of exalted interpretation of Wordsworth's philosophy which a *Blackwood's* article of 1829 finds among his disciples. Charlotte's ideas about poetry and genius changed little throughout her life, and the influence on her thought of magazines from the 1820s and '30s—which are likely to have been kept like books to be reread over the years—can still be felt twenty years on.[36] Significantly, in *Shirley,* her interpretation of these ideas makes the imagination operate independently of the heroine's will, sent direct from heaven, "by no human agency bestowed."

Charlotte goes on to add:

> If Shirley were not an indolent, a reckless, an ignorant being, she would take a pen at such moments; . . . she would fix the apparition, tell the vision revealed. . . . But indolent she is, reckless she is, and most ignorant, for she does not know her dreams are rare — her feelings peculiar: she does not know, has never known, and will die without knowing, the full value of that spring whose bright fresh bubbling in her heart keeps it green.[37]

Emily, of course, was not indolent; she did take up her pen. But there is a vein of Romanticism which "exalt[s] the artist who does not give a material form to his dreams — the poet ecstatic in front of a forever blank page," and to locate the creative act in the inspired experience rather than in the more prosaic activity of writing it down.[38] Here, Charlotte seems to have found a way of interpreting Emily which would explain how the younger sister she thought of as so difficult and immature had been able to produce such exceptional poems. She would go on to use a similar argument to provide an excuse for the disturbing aspects of *Wuthering Heights*. Benign imaginings are sent to Shirley, which are "the pure gift of God to His creature, the free dower of Nature to her child";[39] devilish visions have been the lot of the author of *Wuthering Heights*. But in both cases, their source is beyond the individual's own power.

This loss of power may enhance Shirley's innocence, but it infantilizes her in the process. Shirley is utterly naive, completely without self-consciousness, and totally devoid of the ability to respond analytically to her own imaginative experience. She is, in the words of her teacher-lover, Louis Moore, "a child."[40] Emily's final illness had reinforced Charlotte's belief that her sister needed to be protected from herself. Charlotte had tried, as she had done at Roe Head, to take charge, but this time she had failed to save Emily's life. By rewriting her in *Shirley*, she was at last in a position to mold and manage her as she thought best.

Charlotte's urge to get Emily under control is expressed, unconsciously, in her presentation of the love affair between Shirley and the tutor Louis Moore. At first glance, it may look like an imaginative reworking of Charlotte's own relationship with Heger. But it actually says more about her feelings toward Emily. The novel ends, in traditional style, with a wedding. Yet the marriage between Shirley and Louis could not be more different from the equal partnership with which Jane Eyre and Rochester are rewarded at the close of Charlotte's previous novel.

Louis's job, it seems, is to maintain authority over his rebellious lover, to keep her "little failings" in check. "I delight to find her at fault," he says gleefully.[41] "In managing the wild instincts of the scarce manageable 'bête fauve,' my powers would revel."[42] Repeatedly compared to an animal who needs taming, Shirley at last gives in, saying of Louis, "I am glad I know my keeper and am used to him. Only his voice will I follow; only his hand shall manage me."[43] Once engaged, though, she tries to put off the wedding, but submits at last, "fettered to a fixed day": "Thus vanquished and restricted, she pined, like any other chained denizen of deserts. Her captor alone could cheer her; his society only could make amends for the lost privilege of liberty: in his absence, she sat or wandered alone; spoke little, and ate less."[44] Speaking little and eating less sounds more like Emily in the weeks before her death than like the heroine of a romance preparing to live happily ever after. But Emily, unlike the captive Shirley, had been unmanageable in her illness. After finishing the novel, Charlotte would go back again and again to the idea of taking her in hand.

A year later, when she agreed to edit a posthumous volume of her sisters' works for Smith, Elder, Charlotte returned to the process of interpreting Emily. Buoyed up by the sympathetic response she had received from people such as Gaskell, she had decided to make her sisters' identities known to the world. As she wrote to Williams on September 13, 1850, "If Mr. Smith thinks proper to reprint 'Wuthering Heights & Agnes Grey,' I would prepare a Preface comprising a brief and simple notice of the authors—such as might set at rest all erroneous conjectures respecting their identity—and adding a few poetical remains of each[.]"[45] Charlotte would also provide an additional brief memoir of each sister to introduce her selections from their previously unpublished poems.

Preparing the volume in the autumn of 1850 was a very painful experience. As Charlotte told Ellen, "The reading over of papers, the renewal of remembrances brought back the pang of bereavement and occasioned a depression of spirits well nigh intolerable—for one or two nights I scarcely knew how to get on till morning—and when morning came I was still haunted with a sense of sickening distress[.]"[46] Yet she may have found an ambiguous solace in the fact that her sister was no longer able to rebel. As editor of Emily's poems, she took it upon herself, like Louis in relation to

Shirley, to correct their "little failings." While her approach should not be judged by today's scholarly standards, it is undeniably interventionist. The extent of her editorial changes, bound up inextricably with her emotional response to her sister's death, was not fully recognized until C. W. Hatfield's scholarly edition of *The Complete Poems of Emily Jane Brontë* came out in 1941.[47] They would have the effect of distorting future generations' perceptions of Emily's poetry.

Charlotte's editing of Emily embodies her conflicting feelings. Sometimes she appears as a pernickety teacher figure, making supposed corrections to Emily's idiosyncratic punctuation, or scansion, or use of vocabulary. For example, she might add an extra word or two to regularize the number of beats in a line, or replace an uncommon word—say, "beamy" with the more conventional "sunny."[48] Charlotte believed that the world had not sufficiently appreciated Emily's poetry. Perhaps she thought her improvements would ensure it a better reception, though the changes do little for the poetry beyond stifling Emily's originality.

Yet in combination with this patronizing desire to correct what she called the "rude efforts" of her wayward sister's "unpractised hand," Charlotte was equally determined to heroize her.[49] In her "Biographical Notice of Ellis and Acton Bell," she would rewrite Emily's unwilling death, painting her as a stoic whose "spirit was inexorable to the flesh" and who faced her end with superhuman strength.[50] Similarly, she idealized her sister by misleadingly describing the poem beginning "No coward soul is mine" as the last lines she ever wrote. Readers were invited to believe that this statement of courage and faith in the face of death was written on the very threshold of the grave, though the poem, dated January 2, 1846, was actually written nearly three years before Emily died. On reading it, Matthew Arnold described how Emily's "too-bold dying song / Shook, like a clarion-blast, my soul."[51] Swinburne wrote, "No last words of poet or hero or sage or saint were ever worthy of longer or more reverent remembrance."[52] Would they have been less moved if they had known it was not in fact her swan song?

Elsewhere, Charlotte used the editorial process creatively as a means of expressing her own feelings of bereavement. Emily's original intentions became subordinated to her sister's overwhelming feelings of loss. One particular poem, "The Night-Wind," is a dialogue between the wind and an unidentified speaker. The night-wind tries to persuade the speaker to follow it, arguing in the final stanza that only death can separate them. Thus Emily's original:

"And when thy heart is laid at rest
Beneath the church-yard stone
I shall have time enough to mourn
And thou to be alone" — [53]

In her revised version of this last stanza, Charlotte's changes reinterpret the poem in the light of her own bereavement, replacing the night-wind's voice with her own. The "I" and "thou" become identified with herself and Emily. She replaces "church-yard" with "church-aisle" because Emily was buried in the church rather than in the graveyard outside. She is using Emily's poem as a vehicle for expressing her own sense of loss, regardless of the original context in which it was composed:

"And when thy heart is resting
Beneath the church-aisle stone,
I shall have time for mourning,
And thou for being alone."[54]

Even minor changes have the effect of transforming the sentiments into Charlotte's own. Her italicization of the pronouns "I" and "thou" is characteristic of the sort of overblown emphases she often imposes on Emily's spare and unpunctuated style, but in this case it has the real effect of stressing the contrast, and thus the gulf, between the living and the dead. When Charlotte exchanges infinitives for present participles—"laid at rest" becomes "resting," "to mourn" becomes "mourning," "to be alone" becomes "for being alone"—she does so in the context of her own bereavement. Instead of being a finite event, death becomes a perpetual state, reflecting the mourner's ever-present sense of loss. Emily ended the poem with a dash, which Charlotte changes to a full stop, perhaps seeing herself as putting the finishing touch to a poem which Emily would never finish now that she was dead. But the incomplete poem, the fragment, is a typical Romantic device (the most famous being Coleridge's "Kubla Khan"), and it is possible that Emily left her lyric open-ended by design and had no intention of going back to finish it.[55] It is hard to believe that Emily would have regarded this as anything other than unlicensed intrusion.

There was, however, one aspect of Charlotte's editorial approach which Emily would probably have accepted. This was Charlotte's decision to suppress all references to characters and places associated with Gondal, the fantasy world Emily shared with Anne. From 1844, Emily had transcribed her own poems into two notebooks, one titled "Gondal Poems," the other untitled.

Unlike Charlotte, who eventually abandoned Angria, Emily and Anne continued not just to chronicle the saga but to "play" at it, taking on the roles of its dramatis personae in private games. The women who "were" Ronald Macelgin, Henry Angora, and the rest on their trip to York were adults of twenty five and nearly twenty-seven. In the 1845 diary paper which records that particular fantasy, Emily goes on to say that the "Gondals still flo[u]rish bright as ever" and to note the literary activity in which she and Anne had been involved: "I am at present writing a work on the First Wars—Anne has been writing some articles on this and a book by Henry Sophona—We intend sticking firm by the rascals as long as they delight us which I am glad to say they do at present[.]"[56]

The works to which Emily refers here have not survived. Indeed none of the Gondal prose has ever come to light. As a result, posterity has been able to do no more than guess at the contents of this shadowy world, since Gondal allusions in the poetry are hard to interpret without the prose chronicles, though it seems clear that the kingdom was dominated by a beautiful, imperious queen, a sort of female Zamorna. There have been a number of attempts at imaginative reconstruction. These range from the American scholar Fannie E. Ratchford's account of 1955, *Gondal's Queen,* to *Gondal,* a play by Martin Wade broadcast on BBC Radio 4 in 1993, which supposed that the papers had been found under Emily's bed after her death, and reconstructed the saga with Diana Quick in the role of the heroine Augusta. But they must remain highly speculative.[57] Charlotte's juvenilia provides a picture of the literary influences with which she grew up and allows us to chart the development of her vision and her relationship to her own imagination. The loss of the Gondal prose, which would have stretched back to Emily's childhood, means further mystification of her artistic development, because it makes *Wuthering Heights* appear to have risen out of nowhere, encouraging critics to romanticize it as a miraculous text.

Over a century ago, Clement Shorter was the first to suggest that Charlotte had probably destroyed Emily's and Anne's letters and literary effects.[58] A number of commentators have since concluded that Charlotte destroyed the Gondal legacy. If so, it seems likely that she would have done this in the autumn of 1850 when she was sorting through her sisters' papers. In the brief memoir Charlotte wrote as a preface to those of Emily's previously unpublished poems which she included in the 1850 volume, she remarked that

It would not have been difficult to compile a volume out of the papers left by my sisters, had I, in making the selection, dismissed from my consideration the scruples and the wishes of those whose written thoughts these papers held. But this was impossible: an influence, stronger than could be exercised by any motive of expediency, necessarily regulated the selection. I have, then, culled from the mass only a little poem here and there.[59]

Although the "mass" of material she mentions might refer exclusively to poetry—Charlotte printed only seventeen of Emily's poems in 1850—the "papers" to which she refers could also have included other manuscripts, now lost or destroyed, including the Gondal prose.[60]

Gondal was a private space in which not even Charlotte had a share. When Emily chose a selection of her "Gondal Poems" for the 1846 *Poems by Currer, Ellis, and Acton Bell,* she had herself eliminated all Gondal references. So when Charlotte suppressed the Gondal names in her 1850 selection, she was merely following Emily's lead. If it was at this point that she destroyed the Gondal prose, it may be that she regarded this as a protective act. Where the poems had their own value independent of Gondal, the prose, never perhaps intended for the eyes of anyone but Emily and Anne themselves, could not be read outside the Gondal context, and Charlotte may have felt that her sisters would not have wanted it to survive.

However, if indeed Charlotte destroyed the papers, this may have reflected her own ambivalent attitude. Her feelings about Gondal—which she never, of course, mentioned in public—are not likely to have been wholly accepting. While Emily had no apparent qualms about the lure of fantasy, Charlotte had said farewell to Angria because she had felt guilty about its addictive attractions and idolatrous implications. She felt she had been worshipping the creatures of her own imagination, allowing them to compete with God. It may be that she continued to feel unsure about the compulsive imaginative drive behind Emily's addiction to "the world below,"[61] and wanted to destroy the evidence that her sister had continued to be dependent on it in her maturity.

Charlotte's changes to one of the poems of Emily's she published in 1850 suggest an active attempt on her part to prove that her sister's imagination came from a divine, not an idolatrous, source. In "The First BlueStocking," Charlotte had asserted the God-given nature of genius, while at the same time admitting that it had a rival in the false imagination sent by the Father of Lies. In this poem, which she titled "The Visionary," her editorial additions make it look as though she is trying to dispel any fears concerning the origins of Emily's imagination. Yet her attempt to interpret her sister's genius in this light is particularly ambiguous, as it involves not merely cutting the original poem, but adding two whole stanzas of her own and presenting them as Emily's.

The elder sister's version of this poem would have a substantial distorting effect on posterity's perceptions of Emily. Even though Hatfield made clear in 1941 that the final stanzas were an interpolation, most probably by Charlotte, these particular lines became entrenched in the collective imagination as Emily's. As late as 1982 they were being quoted in the *New Pelican Guide to English Literature* as typical of the younger sister, representing a "glimpse into the fiercely maintained integrity of her inner life" and showing her "true spiritual vision," when in fact all they can tell us is how Charlotte interpreted her.[62] The poem is particularly important because it would be used in the future, time and again, by Emily's biographers to prove that she was a mystic, though in fact as biographical evidence it is extremely shaky.

In its original form, the poem was a long narrative Gondal work entitled "Julian M. and A. G. Rochelle." This version falls into two sections whose narrative relationship to each other remains rather enigmatic. The first twelve lines describe an unidentified figure waiting at night in a silent house for a secret visitor or "Wanderer." The scene then shifts to tell the story of Julian and Rochelle, lovers who were caught on opposite sides in a war. Rochelle was imprisoned in a dungeon but was eventually rescued by Julian. The two unidentified figures of the opening stanzas must also be Julian and Rochelle, though whether he is coming to her or she to him, and whether the secret assignations it describes predate or postdate Rochelle's imprisonment and rescue, are unclear.

With some substantial cuts and a few minor changes, Emily had already published the dungeon section under the title "The Prisoner (A Fragment)" in the 1846 *Poems by Currer, Ellis, and Acton Bell*. In 1850, Charlotte printed the first twelve lines. But instead of leaving it there, she completed the poem by inventing eight completely new lines of her own.[63] By this action she turned what was originally a story about the two Gondal lovers into a poem that asks to be read as a poet's personal testimony to the sources of her inspiration. In this, Charlotte was anticipating many of Emily's subsequent biographers. In the absence of much data, they would use Emily's poetry as source material, often ignoring its original Gondal context and treating it misleadingly as though it were directly autobiographical in content.

Charlotte made no substantial changes to the first three verses, which contrast the warm and cheerful interior of the silent house, where the speaker is waiting for the nightly visitor, with the snowy waste outside.* But the two stanzas she added completely transform their meaning. The speaker in the house and the approaching Wanderer, who were originally the two Gondal lovers, undergo a complete change of identity. Acting as Emily's ventriloquist, Charlotte turns the speaker into the poet herself, as if these are Emily's own words, spoken in her own voice and not in character. She transforms the visitor into a personification of genius, the same Genius who came down to his bride Eva in "The First Blue-Stocking." Here are Charlotte's additional stanzas:

> *What I love shall come like visitant of air,*
> *Safe in secret power from lurking human snare;*
> *What loves me, no word of mine shall e'er betray,*
> *Though for faith unstained my life must forfeit pay.*

> *Burn, then, little lamp; glimmer straight and clear—*
> *Hush! a rustling wing stirs, methinks, the air:*
> *He for whom I wait, thus ever comes to me;*
> *Strange Power! I trust thy might; trust thou my constancy.*[64]

---

*The first three stanzas, given here with Emily's original punctuation as transcribed by Janet Gezari (*The Complete Poems*, p. 177), read as follows:

> *Silent is the House—all are laid asleep;*
> *One, alone, looks out o'er the snow-wreaths deep;*
> *Watching every cloud, dreading every breeze*
> *That whirls the wildering drifts and bends the groaning trees—*

> *Cheerful is the hearth, soft the matted floor*
> *Not one shivering gust creeps through pane or door*
> *The little lamp burns straight; its rays shoot strong and far*
> *I trim it well to be the Wanderer's guiding-star—*

> *Frown, my haughty sire, chide my angry Dame;*
> *Set your slaves to spy, threaten me with shame;*
> *But neither sire nor dame, nor prying serf shall know*
> *What angel nightly tracks that waste of winter snow—*

This may be a private attempt by Charlotte to convince herself that Emily's imagination was God-given. It is similar both to "The First Blue-Stocking" and to the description of Shirley's evening reverie in that the receiver of the vision is portrayed as passive. Chosen by the Strange Power, rather than actively choosing it, the poet becomes a mere vessel. She does not love, she is loved. Where the Power has "might," the poet's greatest virtue is the meek one of "constancy." Charlotte thus pacifies her rebellious sister by presenting her as waiting patiently for the dove to descend unsought.

From the evidence of her poetry, Emily's own imaginative credo seems to have been different from what Charlotte would have liked it to have been. Emily was as steeped in Romantic visionary discourse as Charlotte, but her interpretation of the poet's role was less passive. In Emily's "Plead for Me," the poet addresses a personified imagination as a "radiant angel," but has far more control over this "phantom thing" than Charlotte's Visionary. The poem concludes:

And am I wrong to worship, where
Faith cannot doubt, nor hope despair,
Since my own soul can grant my prayer?
Speak, God of visions, plead for me,
And tell why I have chosen thee! [65]

Here, the poet is active, having consciously "chosen" to follow the imagination, rather than being, like Eva in "The First Blue-Stocking," the "chosen" one. She also claims that the power resides within herself, rather than outside, since her "own soul" can grant her prayer. Significantly, she also acknowledges that some might find this wrong.

In order to feel comfortable with the visionary egoism at the heart of her own aesthetic credo, Charlotte had to attribute it to a divine source. Her strong faith in her own genius was morally justified by her belief that it was a freely given gift from God in which she had no say. Emily, however, seems, in a more pantheistic sense, to be convinced that the divinity is actually immanent within herself. To Charlotte, this may have seemed perilously close to the idolatry of self-worship.

Charlotte's doubts about Emily's vision would resurface in her preface to *Wuthering Heights*. Though apparently couched as an apologia, her comments on the novel are so equivocal that it sometimes seems uncertain whether she is acting for the prosecution or the defense. Like the similarly ambiguous "Biographical Notice of Ellis and Acton Bell," which presented Emily and Anne as simple country girls, the preface is full of tensions and contradictions which reveal conflicting urges on Charlotte's part to blame and to protect, to censure and to admire. Charlotte is a confused mythographer, grappling with contradictory feelings. In interpreting her sister to the world, she would end up mystifying her more than she explained her.

When in protective mode, Charlotte felt any attack on Emily very deeply. In her eyes, Emily was the vulnerable younger sister, and it caused her real pain to see her criticized. This lies behind her distorted interpretation of Ellis Bell's critical reception. Charlotte presents herself as Emily's lone, embattled champion in the face of reviewers' neglect, but this simply does not hold water. On the subject of Emily's contribution to the 1846 *Poems by Currer, Ellis, and Acton Bell,* she writes, "The fixed conviction I held, and hold, of the worth of these poems has not indeed received the confirmation of much favourable criticism[.]"[66]

In reality, although only two copies of the book were actually sold, it received rather enviable review coverage for a first attempt by three unknown writers publishing at their own expense in a climate in which poetry (unlike fiction) was notoriously hard to market. The three papers which reviewed it were encouraging, and Ellis's contribution was unequivocally singled out as the best by the *Athenaeum,*[67] a view which has remained the critical consensus ever since.

Similarly, Charlotte's claim that "[t]he immature but very real powers revealed in *Wuthering Heights* were scarcely recognised" falls somewhat flat on examination.[68] An article in the *American Review* for June 1848 had attested to its popularity among "thousands of young ladies in the country."[69] Although the critics had reservations, both moral and aesthetic, the one thing they did recognize was the novel's "power," a word which recurs again and again in the early reviews. It is true that it attracted some very negative criticism. One of the most poisonous remarks comes from Elizabeth Rigby's sustained attack on the Bells in her *Quarterly Review* article on *Jane Eyre.* Rigby declared that "there can be no interest attached to the writer of *Wuthering Heights*—a novel . . . too odiously and abominably pagan to be palatable even to the most vitiated class of English readers."[70] This particular review, however, did not reach Haworth until after Emily's death, and the press cuttings found in her writing desk include one which positively raved with enthusiasm: "It is not every day that so good a novel makes its appearance. . . . May [the reader] derive from it the delight we ourselves have experienced, and be equally grateful to its author for the genuine pleasure he has afforded him."[71]

It is not really true to say that *Wuthering Heights* was neglected. Any first-time novelist today who received as many notices as Ellis Bell would be extraordinarily lucky.[72] The general impression one has of its reception is one of bafflement among the critics. Frequently called "strange" and "original," it simultaneously aroused admiration and repulsion. "[T]he reader is shocked, disgusted, almost sickened by details of cruelty, inhumanity, and the most diabolical hate and vengeance," said one reviewer, who nevertheless went on to recommend it "strongly," pronouncing it "very puzzling . . . very interesting . . . remarkable."[73]

By exaggerating Emily's lack of critical recognition, Charlotte idealized her as the "neglected genius," an archetype, epitomized in the figure of Chatterton, which had appealed to the Romantics and had long been part of her own poetic landscape. It was also a measure of her grief. In her protectiveness toward the younger sister whose life she had been unable to save, she overemphasized the attacks of others, imagining them to have been crueler and more universal than they actually were. However, in attacking the reviewers for failing to recognize Emily's merits, she was also displacing her own mixed feelings about her sister's work. "I have just read over *Wuthering Heights*," she writes, "and, for the first time, have obtained a clear glimpse of what are termed (and, perhaps, really are) its faults."[74] The parenthesis is telling.

Charlotte's ambivalence toward Emily is underlined by the fact that much of what she says in her defense merely regurgitates the opinions of the reviewers she is so keen to accuse. Her references to Emily's "limited experience"[75] and "immature but very real powers"[76] echo the *Britannia*'s view that the author "displays a considerable power . . . proceeding from a mind of limited experience."[77] Even her famous final image of the novel as a giant half-finished statue, carved with a "rude chisel"[78] out of a granite block, seems to borrow its metaphor from the *Britannia*'s reviewer, who wondered whether Ellis Bell would "remain a rough hewer of marble or become a great and noble sculptor."[79] In her public apologia for her sister Charlotte cannot detach herself from the phraseology of already published opinion.

It is curious that one of Charlotte's arguments for finally revealing the authorship of *Wuthering Heights* rests on the fact that critics had mistakenly identified it as an earlier work by the author of *Jane Eyre,* which Charlotte rather oddly takes to be the cause of the prejudice against it: "That writer who could attempt to palm off an inferior and immature production under cover of one successful effort, must indeed be unduly eager after the secondary and sordid result of authorship, and pitiably indifferent to its true and honourable meed. If reviewers and the public truly believed this, no wonder that they looked darkly on the cheat."[80]

This cannot truly represent Charlotte's real feelings, since only a few months later she went back to her own first novel, *The Professor* (which had been rejected over and over again), and tried unsuccessfully to persuade Smith, Elder, to publish it.[81] What she really could not bear was the idea that people might attribute the disturbing *Wuthering Heights* to her.

Stung as she was by the critics' shock at the novel's raging emotions and amorality, Charlotte could not wholeheartedly defend it, as she shared their doubts. Though Charlotte would have identified with Emily's decision to portray passionate love in *Wuthering Heights,* she found its demonic antihero hard to accept. Our image of the novel today is so influenced by Hollywood's classic 1930s repackaging of it as a conventional love story that it is easy to forget how psychopathic Heathcliff becomes in his pursuit of revenge.

Wuthering Heights has one of the most complex plots in literature, and Heathcliff is one of the most ambiguous heroes. Told through the narratives of Lockwood, a southern visitor to Yorkshire, and of the housekeeper Nelly Dean, the novel follows Heathcliff's story from his mysterious origins to his death. A foundling brought into the Earnshaw household at Wuthering Heights, he develops a symbiotic closeness to his foster sister Catherine, but is bullied by her brother Hindley. Catherine's friendship with the Linton family of Thrushcross Grange alienates Heathcliff, who disappears for three years. On his return he finds Catherine grown up and married to Edgar Linton. In revenge, he marries and sadistically ill-treats Edgar's sister Isabella. His and Catherine's mutual but now forbidden passion precipitates her death in childbirth.

Heathcliff's determination to avenge himself on both the Earnshaw and Linton families reverberates on the next generation. He calculatedly sets out to ruin Hindley, making him drink himself to death, but only after he has manipulated his fortune out of him through gambling; he brutalizes Hindley's son Hareton; and in a bid to get the Linton inheritance for himself, he eventually forces a marriage between his own sickly son and Catherine's daughter, also named Cathy. Heathcliff's own death follows soon after his son's, and the younger Cathy eventually marries Hareton, restoring some sort of equilibrium. The Hollywood version ends with the death of the first Catherine, omitting the second half of the novel, in which Heathcliff pursues his revenge, thus enabling Laurence Olivier to purge the character of much of his evil. But Emily's Heathcliff, as Charlotte puts it, stands unredeemed by any conventional moral standards.

Charlotte was, in a sense, right to acknowledge that *Wuthering Heights* was an unsettling book. Yet it is not just the characterization of Heathcliff which makes it so, or, indeed, its scenes of casual violence, such as the one in which Hareton is found nonchalantly murdering puppies by hanging them from the back of a chair. The very love affair on which the plot centers suggests a disturbing affront to the incest taboo, as Cathy and Heathcliff have been brought up as brother and sister. But it is at an even deeper conceptual level that Emily's novel is truly transgressive.

Indeed, transgression—the dissolving of normative boundaries—could be called the main thematic idea which holds the novel together. As a teenager, Emily had fuzzed the limits between the real and the imaginary, shifting easily between the world of the Gondals and the back kitchen. As a mature writer, she transformed this rebellion against the apparent natural order of things into the basis for a staggeringly sophisticated work of literary fiction.

If Charlotte inherited the egoism of Romanticism, Emily drew on a different, more abstract, strand of the Romantic imagination, concerned with the unstable space between dream and reality, with ambiguity and doubleness. In Charlotte's most famous sentence, "Reader, I married him," the identities of the three individuals—the reader, the "I," and the "him"—are secure and separate. Nothing can truly undermine Jane Eyre's sense of sovereign self. But Emily's most famous sentence, "I *am* Heathcliff," affronts our normal sense of what identity is. Two become one as the line between them is erased.

Recent critics have noted how often images of crossing boundaries crop up in the book.[82] There are frequent references to windows, such as the one through which the ghost-child Cathy grabs Lockwood by the hand, and to doorways, such as the entrance to the Heights itself with its carvings of shameless little boys. It is, significantly, in the margins of her Bible that Cathy writes her childhood diary, disrupting the frame of white space which ought to be holding the text in place, the words spilling out over their natural border. As the shameless cupids suggest, with their naked cavorting on the lintel of the front door, boundaries may be there to create order, but seething within them are the anarchic seeds of their own destruction.

In *Wuthering Heights*, Emily Brontë is constantly setting up oppositions and then threatening to dissolve them. The duality of Cathy and Heathcliff, for example, is undermined as soon as Cathy says "I *am* Heathcliff." On a larger, structural level, the novel's double plot creates a symmetry of mirror opposites. But the fact that the two contrasting heroines—one dark, one fair—are both called Catherine upsets the clear-cut boundary between the two halves. What gives *Wuthering Heights* its electricity is the tension which runs through it between the creation of such boundaries or symmetries and their dissolution. It is a work of the tightest artistic control put continually under pressure by its own self-generating instability.

The very complexity of the novel's plot and structure—events are related as stories within stories within stories, and there don't seem to be enough names to go around—keeps the reader in a state of anxious alertness which is belied by the clarity of Emily's lucid and rational prose style with its short sentences and vernacular vocabulary. It is a teasing novel which seems to present us with riddles which must be solved but whose ultimate meaning is endlessly deferred. As Lockwood wants to "decypher" Cathy's diary, so we want to find a simple answer to the question, What does *Wuthering Heights* mean?

One recent reader ingeniously but spuriously rearranged the letters of the central names in the novel—Catherine, Earnshaw, Heathcliff, Linton—to form an anagram of "How the infernal half-caste can inherit," as if Emily were writing in code.[83] Such irrational interpretative excess— reminiscent of the sort of Scripture-reading you find at the outer reaches of Christian fundamentalism—is an understandable, if crazy, response to a book which seems to be baiting us to behave like Jabes Branderham, the mad exegetical preacher in Lockwood's dream. Perhaps the code-cracker should have listened to the critic J. Hillis Miller, who suggested that the "secret truth about *Wuthering Heights* is that there is no secret truth."[84]

This riddlesome aspect of *Wuthering Heights* relates to the genre of gothic, part of whose function is to titillate the reader with a maze of narrative blind alleys and literary booby traps. Other elements of the novel's transgressive nature also have a gothic feel, such as its use of the supernatural and the sense it gives of scarcely being able to contain its excess of emotion. Yet it cannot simply be classed as a gothic novel. Transgressing even this label, it refuses to be pinned down and, shiftily, incorporates elements from all sorts of genres, from the ghost story to Victorian domestic realism, from religious satire to poetic allegory. Thus, the amorality in *Wuthering Heights* which Charlotte found so hard to take merely reflects the way in which the novel resists certainties at every level.

Charlotte decided that she must do her best to stick up for Emily's book despite her misgivings, but the misgivings won over in the end. In her preface, she tries to defend the novel on moral grounds by holding up Heathcliff's less passionate rival, Edgar Linton, as an exemplar of mercy and forgiveness, "the divinest attributes of the Great Being who made both man and woman." But she knows, despite this, that Emily's "unredeemed" antihero remains at the center of the novel's energy, and she concludes uncomfortably, "Whether it is right or advisable to create things like Heathcliff, I do not know: I scarcely think it is."[85] Her references to Catherine's "perverted passion and passionate perversity"[86] recall the satanic "debased emotion" and "perverted impulse" to which she referred in *Shirley*. For Charlotte, the evil in *Wuthering Heights* remains dangerously unsublimated.

She goes on to paint a mythic picture of the artist as one possessed. Significantly, she does not, as in *Shirley,* attribute the creative gift to a purifyingly divine source, but to the amoral agency of "Fate or Inspiration":

> [T]he writer who possesses the creative gift owns something of which he is not always master—something that at times strangely wills and works for itself. . . . [I]t sets to work on statue-hewing, and you have a Pluto or a Jove, a Tisiphone or a Psyche, a Mermaid or a Madonna, as Fate or Inspiration direct. Be the work grim or glorious, dread or divine, you have little choice left but quiescent adoption. As for you—the nominal artist—your share in it has been to work passively under dictates you neither delivered nor could question—that would not be uttered at your prayer, nor suppressed nor changed at your caprice. If the result be attractive, the World will praise you, who little deserve praise; if it be repulsive, the same World will blame you, who almost as little deserve blame.[87]

In the future, this vision would eventually inspire bastardized versions of Emily as a paranormal phenomenon, the mystic of the moors, swooning into a trance, visited by ghostly presences from the next world, gifted with second sight. In fact, rather than literally describing her sister's methods of composition, Charlotte was harking back to the debates she had had with Constantin Heger in Brussels between classical and Romantic models of the artist. Her comments are indicative of how caught up she was in her own cultural moment and are representative of the sort of Romantic thinking previously expressed, say, in the following by William Hazlitt: "The definition of genius is that it acts unconsciously; and those who have produced immortal works have done so without knowing how or why. . . . The true inspiration of the Muse . . . leaves us little to boast of, for the effort hardly seems to be our own."[88] Mythographers in love with Charlotte's myth of her sister, but unaware of its cultural origins in the Romantic movement, would forget that the real Emily was primarily a writer and treat her instead as a supernatural force.

The fact that Charlotte had doubts of her own about Emily's fiction meant that she was doubly obliged to find excuses for it. She sought sympathy and forgiveness from the public by presenting her sisters as simple rustics, the products of an isolated life. Yet in *Shirley* and her edition of Emily's poems, she had also been drawing on Romanticism to find ways of interpreting her sister. The "Biographical Notice" would combine these two strands in its insistence that Emily had no knowledge of literary tradition. Charlotte's defense of her sisters insists on their unsophistication. "Neither Emily nor Anne," she writes, "was learned; they had no thought of filling their pitchers at the well-spring of other minds; they always wrote from the impulse of nature, the dictates of intuition, and from such stores of observation as their limited experience had enabled them to amass."[89]

If Charlotte underplayed her sisters' reading, this stemmed partly from her desire to prove their innocence, but also from her belief in the supreme importance of originality as the touchstone of artistic value.[90] (Occasionally, one finds Charlotte nervously protective of her own artistic originality, expressing absurd fears of having committed unconscious plagiarism[91] or denying she has read certain books when we know from other sources that she has.[92]) By portraying Emily as an unthinking sibyl, receiving her vision fully formed from the hand of fate, she prevented critics from recognizing, for over seventy years, the careful crafting which had gone into the complex structure of *Wuthering Heights*.[93] As an indirect result of her comments, the novel would, in addition, go on to hold a place of dubious privilege in the English canon as a text uniquely and miraculously disconnected from the rest of literature. In the twentieth century, F. R. Leavis would deny it a place in his "Great Tradition," believing instead that this "astonishing work" came out of nowhere.[94] This belief would gain ground partly because it fitted in with established prejudices about women artists as intuitive rather than reflective.

In fact, Charlotte's suggestion that her sisters were uneducated was disingenuous. Elsewhere in the "Biographical Notice" she described how they were "dependent . . . on books and study, for the enjoyments and occupations of life."[95] The question of cultural influences on Emily is vexed by the lack of direct statements from her, though scholars have offered some convincing, if fragmentary and speculative, accounts of her intellectual background.[96] Evidence as to Charlotte's and Branwell's early reading is present in their juvenilia, but there is little precise documentation about what Emily actually read. However, it makes more sense to assume that she had access to the same books as her brother and sister than to imagine her living in a literary vacuum, separated from the rest of the household as well as culture at large. It seems fair to assume that Emily's literary education must have been similar to her siblings', which was in many ways unconventional but rich nevertheless.

Rather than seeing Emily as an untutored rustic, Constantin Heger had been deeply impressed by her intellect and head for logic. This is borne out by the sophistication of her surviving French essays, which have recently become available in a critical edition.[97] Before Emily's death, Charlotte too had called Emily "somewhat of a theorist," suggesting to William Smith Williams that she would come into her own as an essayist rather than a fiction writer.[98] This suggests that the real Emily was more of a thinker than Charlotte's myth would allow. Indeed, a throwaway comment in Emily's diary paper of 1841 suggests an ambitious writer who regarded literary endeavor as conscious intellectual labor. Emily gives herself a good-humored rap on the knuckles, suggesting she needs a timetable, not "Fate or Inspiration," to help her get on with her writing: "I have a good many books on hands but I am sorry to say that as usual I make small progress with any—however I have just made a new regularity paper! and I ?me[an] ?verb sap—to do great things[.]"[99] It may be, instead, that the books she refers to are ones she is reading rather than writing. If so, that proves that she was not as unlearned as Charlotte made out.

Of course, Emily herself, who chafed against Constantin Heger's requirement that she imitate other authors, may have also believed in her own Romantic myth and held to the idea that her own imagination was independent of influence, derived instead from transcendent sources alone. Yet if so, she was not passive in this belief, like the idle Shirley at her evening reverie. Rather, her poetry constantly questions and reformulates the Romantic model by which the imagination is able to "lift the veil" of the phenomenal world and glimpse the spiritual reality which lies behind it.

She frequently takes as her themes the imagination itself and the relationship between visible nature and the Unseen, constantly reformulating and questioning it. "A Day Dream" describes a visionary moment in which the poet's very breath seems "full of sparks divine" as she lies on a "sunny brae," though the vision is undercut in the final lines, "But Fancy, still, will sometimes deem / Her fond creation true." Similarly, in "To Imagination" she prizes "[t]he world within" for its "voice divine," but ends, again, on a questioning note, wondering whether to trust to its "phantom bliss." In "Stars," poet and nature, perceiver and perceived, become one in another visionary moment, though the epiphany is again impermanent, dissolved as it is by the sunrise.

Whether or not the influence was consciously acknowledged, Emily's visionary poetry shares its emphasis on nature and the imagination with Wordsworth, Coleridge, and the other Romantic writers to whom she had access through *Fraser's* and *Blackwood's*. The latter, for example, carried a lengthy review of *The Poetical Works of S. T. Coleridge*, when it was published in 1834. Some critics have suggested even closer verbal parallels between Emily's work and that of these poets.[100] In addition, many of the Gondal lyrics of love and loss, torment and despair, have been shown to contain verbal echoes of Byron's verse.[101]

Wuthering Heights, too, is not without its literary forebears, even though it offers something completely different from the standard social realism of the period, which is why it baffled its first reviewers. Instead, Emily's novel harks back both to gothic and to the poetry and prose of the Romantic generation. Like Charlotte, she responded particularly to Byron and Walter Scott (chosen as one of the chief men for her island at the age of nine, and the inspiration behind Gondal's mountainous Scottish landscapes). The presence of both can be felt in her novel. The lullaby sung by Nelly Dean in chapter 9 directly quotes a ballad translated from the Danish which appeared in a note to Scott's poem *The Lady of the Lake*, while the names of Heathcliff and the Earnshaw family may derive from Earncliff in Scott's *The Black Dwarf*. Like Lockwood in *Wuthering Heights*, Earncliff finds himself holed up in a solitary moorland dwelling with the eponymous dwarf, a piteous but horrifying character who has, like Heathcliff, turned misanthrope as a result of thwarted passion.[102] More generally, the theme of family feud, particularly sexual and sibling rivalry, can be related to Scott's novels, as can Emily's use of dialect, and her narrative technique of the tale-within-a-tale.[103]

Byron, who was such an influence on the young Charlotte, also made an impact on her sister. Even the diary papers, those apparently spontaneous records of the minute-to-minute occurrences of the day, show evidence of having been consciously composed in imitation of quotations from Byron's journal found in Moore's biography of the poet.[104] Both Byron's life, as told by Moore, and his works can be traced in *Wuthering Heights*. In the biography, the sixteen-year-old Byron falls in love with a girl, Mary Chaworth, but overhears her scornfully telling the servant, "Do you think I could care anything for that lame boy?" Like Heathcliff, who overhears Catherine telling Nelly that it would degrade her to marry him, he then runs off into the night. Moore interprets this ur-rejection as the source of all Byron's subsequent sufferings and errors. He quotes as evidence a poem of 1811, "The Dream," which reads like a summary of Emily's plot, in which a spurned lover returns from abroad to find his beloved married to another and blames on her his future life of "deepening crimes," while she ends in madness.[105]

It can be added that Moore's *Life* also provided a precursor for the literary representation of violent domestic quarrels, complete with pokers, tongs, and vicious dogs. A review in *Blackwood's* of 1830 contains the following, which is reminiscent of the marriage between Heathcliff and Isabella: "Had he not fired off pistols over his wife's head, as it lay on the pillow of their post-nuptial morn—and, as the smoke broke away, had he not, with the face of a fiend, whispered into her ear, delicately veiled in a lace night-cap, that he had married her from revenge and would break her heart?"[106]

But it was in Byron's poetic romances, too, that Emily found the germ of the passion of Cathy and Heathcliff. With its overtones of sibling incest, theirs is a love of identity rather than difference. Her famous "I *am* Heathcliff"[107] is echoed by his despair after her death, "I *cannot* live without my life! I *cannot* live without my soul!"[108] In Byron's *Manfred* (1817), the fatal love between the hero and his spiritual twin and female doppelgänger, Astarte, is a passion which is also mutual torture and ends destructively. She appears to him as a ghost, disappearing as soon as he tries to touch her, just as Heathcliff begs the ghost of Cathy to come back through the open window after she has appeared to Lockwood in a dream.[109] At the time of *Manfred*'s publication it was common speculation in the press that Astarte represented Byron's half sister Augusta, with whom he was (accurately) rumored to have committed incest.[110] In addition, Augusta was one of the names of Gondal's heroine, A. G. A., thought to be an early prototype of Catherine.[111]

Along with these specific borrowings, Emily's art should be seen in the broader context of the Romanticism and sub-Romanticism which permeated the young Brontës' imaginations. The three strands of Romantic influence—Scott-ish, Byronic, and visionary—found in Emily's work can also be seen working together in, for example, a long verse romance by John Wilson which appeared in *Blackwood's* in 1831, *Unimore*.[112] Wilson's setting, a Highland landscape of lochs and glens and gloomy castles, recalls Scott. His antihero, the chieftain Unimore of Morven, is Byronic. Victim of a "wicked love and fatal" for twin girls, his cousins and adoptive sisters, he is a "demon" who destroys them both and spends the rest of the poem "by misery crazed," eventually falling to his death as he chases after their ghosts.[113] "Moody and wild, and with large restless eyes / Coalblack and lamping," he anticipates Heathcliff in looks.[114] His period of disappearance from Morven, during which he visits an Indian isle and becomes a pirate and buccaneer, recalls both Heathcliff's mysterious absence from *Wuthering Heights* and Nelly Dean's orientalist fantasies about his mysterious origins.[115] In addition to its references to Scott and Byron, Wilson's poem, divided into ten "Visions," draws on Coleridgean visionary poetics and pays Wordsworthian attention to nature. As in *Shirley,* the imagination is the active faculty which reveals the divine in the natural landscape.[116]

In addition, another strand of influence on Emily may have come from her interest in German, which she studied while in Brussels. Her use of the uncanny and the supernatural in *Wuthering Heights,* as in Lockwood's dream of the ghostly Catherine, has been related to the stories of Hoffmann, but she is likely to have read more broadly among the German Romantics. As Stevie Davies has suggested in her account of Emily's intellectual context, she probably had contact with the philosophical German Romanticism which had influenced Coleridge and which was popularized in England during the 1820s and '30s by writers such as J. A. Heraud of *Fraser's,* De Quincey, and Thomas Carlyle.[117] We can add for sure that Carlyle's *Sartor Resartus* made it into the Parsonage, as John Elliot Cairns noticed a copy on the shelves when he visited in 1858.[118]

The visionary aspects of her poetry may thus have been informed by the idealist metaphysics (or "Visionary Theories," as they were known) ultimately derived from Kant and explained to the British public by the antimaterialist Carlyle.[119] Yet Emily's interest in philosophy, attested by poems such as "The Old Stoic" and "The Philosopher," may have gone all the way back to her early reading of Thomas Moore's life of Byron, which acknowledged its subject's religious skepticism and quoted his "detached thoughts" on such themes as the immortality of the soul and the nature of the mind. The image of the "chainless soul" in "The Old Stoic" has been recognized as deriving from the ancient philosopher Epictetus, who was popular in the late eighteenth and early nineteenth centuries;[120] what has not been noted is that Moore quotes Byron alluding to it.[121]

Tracing the influences Emily assimilated would not have acquired such significance if Charlotte had not misleadingly presented her as an untutored country girl. The effects of this portrayal are still with us, as can be seen in John Sutherland's essay "Heathcliff's Toothbrush," in his latest collection of wonderfully brainteasing literary conundrums. Sutherland sees literary parallels between *Wuthering Heights* and Bulwer-Lytton's novel, *Eugene Aram,* about a glamorous scholar murderer, originally published in 1832 but reissued in revised form in 1840 with a preface apologizing for the antihero's amorality. Sutherland hedges about, almost apologizing for speculating that the *Eugene Aram* controversy could have been picked up "even in remote Haworth."[122]

In fact, Emily knew the novel. Her diary paper of June 26, 1837, paints the following scene—"A bit past 4 o'Clock Charlotte working in Aunts room Branwell reading Eugene Aram to her"[123]—which proves not only that the book entered the Parsonage, but that it did so in its unexpurgated pre-1840 form. Sutherland has, it seems, been too eager to believe in the myth of Haworth's cultural remoteness which was first established by Charlotte in 1850.

What is in fact remarkable about *Wuthering Heights* is not that it borrows from literary sources (such intertextuality is arguably part of the definition of a literary text) but how it manages to use them as the basis for creating something entirely new. Like Charlotte, Emily transformed her Romantic legacy, and, in doing so, she created a fertile text which has outlived and overshadowed not only the turgid and derivative *Unimore* and the now unread works of Bulwer-Lytton, but the verse romances of Byron himself and even most of the novels of Walter Scott.

If Charlotte had doubts about the amorality of *Wuthering Heights,* she also admired Emily's gift, as her repeated attempts to make sense of it in idealized Romantic terms reveal. These conflicting feelings are at the heart of her mythic re-creation of her sister. Her deep ambivalence also comes through in the greatest of all the mysteries surrounding Emily: the shadowy and as yet unresolved question of her lost second novel. If Charlotte underplayed the bookish influences that went into *Wuthering Heights*, it is also possible that she destroyed the book that came after it, thus further mystifying the enigmatic Emily in an act of destruction she may have perceived as an act of protection.

There are plenty of suggestive hints that Emily had been working on a second novel before her final illness. In the "Biographical Notice," Charlotte acknowledged that, after the publication of their first novels, *both* her sisters were prepared to try again.[124] Anne did indeed follow up *Agnes Grey* with *The Tenant of Wildfell Hall*. However, letters from Charlotte written in November and December 1848 to George Smith and William Smith Williams strongly imply that Ellis Bell had some work in progress at that time. In one of these, Charlotte asserts that, although Ellis is at present too ill "to trouble himself with thoughts either of writing or publishing," he must decide for himself whether or not the unscrupulous publisher Thomas Newby has "forfeited every claim to his second work."[125]

In 1929, further evidence of this second work was discovered in Emily's portable writing desk by the biographer Charles Simpson. After Patrick Brontë's death, Arthur Nicholls had returned to his native Ireland and remarried, taking with him an important cache of Brontë relics, including Emily's desk. The desk was among the items sold by his widow at Sotheby's in 1907 and acquired by the American collector H. H. Bonnell, who in turn bequeathed it to the Brontë Society after he died in 1926. When Charles Simpson examined the desk soon after it arrived in Haworth in 1929, he found inside an envelope addressed to "Ellis Bell, Esq" containing a letter from the publisher Thomas Newby dated February 15, 1848.[126]

In this letter, Newby tells his author not to hurry too fast with "your next novel," for "if it be an improvement on your first you will have established yourself as a first rate novelist, but if it fall short the Critics will be too apt to say that you have expended your talent in your first novel."[127] The snag is that the letter begins with an impersonal "Dear Sir," and, as a result, it has been suggested that it was in fact meant for Anne, whose second novel, *The Tenant of Wildfell Hall*, was published by Newby the following June.[128] However, Newby's comments are undoubtedly more relevant to Emily, as Anne's first novel, *Agnes Grey*, was hardly noticed at all by reviewers, while *Wuthering Heights* had been singled out as a work of real promise, with one critic suggesting that its author "wants but the practised skill to make a great artist."[129]

The lost novel has proved so tantalizing that it has even sparked forgery, by someone keen to prove its existence, of a letter in which Charlotte supposedly discusses her sister's second work.[130] The possibility that it might yet turn up has appealed strongly to detective writers, forming the central plot device of both Austen Lee's *Miss Hogg and the Brontë Murders* and Robert Barnard's *The Missing Brontë*. It may also lie behind attempts by later novelists to provide a sequel to *Wuthering Heights* (whose somewhat unimaginative titles range from *Return to Wuthering Heights* to *Heathcliff* to *Heathcliff: The Return to Wuthering Heights*).[131] Many scholars are convinced that Emily did indeed start this second book, and its most likely fate is to have been destroyed by Charlotte.[132] But, in the absence of direct proof, this remains speculation.

If Emily's second novel was anything like her first, it would not be surprising if Charlotte destroyed it, as she had so many doubts about *Wuthering Heights*. And yet other evidence attests to the fact that Charlotte also admired her sister's fiction enough to imitate it. After she finished *Villette* in 1853, she attempted a couple of beginnings for what would have been her next work, though she never in fact completed another novel. One of these fragments, known as "Emma," is set in a girls' boarding school and has all the Charlotte hallmarks. Yet the fragment known as "The Story of Willie Ellin" is strikingly different from her other work.[133] Focusing on the sadistic treatment of a young boy, its uncompromising violence has far more in common with *Wuthering Heights,* implying that, after molding Emily for posterity, Charlotte was now prepared to be influenced by her.

Whether or not Charlotte destroyed her sister's unfinished second novel, the immediate effect of its disappearance was to bolster the Emily myth. To die young after producing a single masterwork has a particular romantic frisson. The absence of a second novel has made it easier for the myth to take root of Emily as the frail vessel through which *Wuthering Heights* was poured by some inexorable power of fate, its storm and stress destroying her in the process. Matthew Arnold's verse tribute to the Brontës, written in 1855 in the aftermath of Charlotte's death, casts Emily as a Romantic icon consumed by her own genius:

She—
(How shall I sing her?) — whose soul
Knew no fellow for might,
Passion, vehemence, grief,
Daring, since Byron died,
That world-fam'd Son of Fire; She, who sank
Baffled, unknown, self-consum'd[.][134]

At the time, Arnold was unusual in acknowledging Byron's influence on Emily. But his lines tells us more about mid-nineteenth-century stereotypes of the artist—what G. H. Lewes dismissively called "the common cant of genius being a fatal gift—a Nessus-poisoned shirt, that consumes the wearer"[135]—than they do about the real woman who was Emily Brontë. Charlotte's ambivalent actions as her sister's critic, biographer, and literary executor had sparked a myth which would make it all the harder for future generations to resurrect her. As Charles Simpson put it in his 1929 biography—the sanest life of Emily to appear in a period otherwise dominated by lurid legend-mongering—"Those who have thought deeply about Emily Brontë may indulge in one speculation: what they would feel if they could for a moment see Emily in the flesh and compare her with the figure of their imaginations. . . . Seldom has a phantom so vast and so shadowy been raised above a personality so elusive."[136]

CHAPTER EIGHT

A Woman Worthy of Being Avoided

Emily's elusiveness is now an established part of her persona, but it is worth wondering whether she would have become quite such a mystery if she had not been so neglected in the decades after her death. It took until 1883 for the first full-length biography of her to appear, by which time the traces of her life that remained had begun to fade. Until the 1870s, those who did acknowledge her often expressed horror at her nature, which came to be seen as almost bestial. But as the century progressed she began to find her champions. Her posthumous image underwent a metamorphosis, and she became increasingly idealized until she was claimed, by May Sinclair in 1912, as an icon of purity and spirituality.

Charlotte may have intended her 1850 "Biographical Notice" and preface to *Wuthering Heights* as a means of protecting Emily from critical condemnation, but she was overoptimistic if she hoped that her efforts to explain her sister would secure much sympathy. Unlike Gaskell's *Life,* which would be brilliantly effective in dispelling the dubious aura surrounding the author of *Jane Eyre,* Charlotte's words did little to improve Ellis Bell's image, which is not surprising in the light of the mixed feelings with which she wrote them.

When the 1850 volume appeared, the press responded defensively. The *Examiner* was insulted by Charlotte's attack on book reviewers, and the *Leader* riposted that critics had in fact been "excessively indulgent" to *Wuthering Heights.*[1] By conceding that the novel had "faults," Charlotte had made a strategic error. If the author's own sister was ready to find moral flaws in her work, how could reviewers avoid doing the same? The revelation that Ellis Bell was a "home bred country girl"[2] did nothing to soften the attitude of the critic on the *Eclectic Review,* who now described her novel as "one of the most repellant books we ever read."[3]

During the 1850s, the impact of Charlotte's public comments on Emily was equivocal. For the author and journalist Peter Bayne, Charlotte had succeeded in establishing Emily as the greatest Brontë genius, but at a price. Emily's promise, he felt, had been richer than Charlotte's, but her novel remained morally beyond the pale: "It were a strange and distempered criticism which hesitated to pass sentence of condemnation on *Wuthering Heights.* We have no such hesitation ... in pronouncing it unquestionably and irredeemably monstrous."[4] He concluded that the author, though a "wonderful woman," had produced work which was "unhealthy, immature, and worthy of being avoided."[5]

Bayne's pronouncement was prophetic. For the next thirty-odd years the public did indeed find Emily worth avoiding. Unlike Charlotte, whose popularity boomed after the publication of Gaskell's *Life,* Emily remained outside the mainstream. Even those with a personal interest failed to defend her. "I wish my cousin had not written '*Wuthering Heights,*' although it is considered clever by some," wrote one of the Brontës' Penzance relatives in 1860.[6] Ellen Nussey reportedly used to "turn away with something like a shudder" from what she called "that dreadful book."[7] In 1876, Charlotte's biographer Thomas Wemyss Reid noted that "*Wuthering Heights* is now practically unread."[8]

Taking their cue ultimately from Charlotte, those critics who did pay Emily attention felt obliged to adopt an apologetic stance. An essay of 1873 which argued that Emily's novel did not "deserve the wholesale condemnation and unqualified abuse which have been heaped upon it" offered only a qualified defense: "Though a brutal, it is not a sensual book; though coarse, it is not vulgar; though bad, it is not indecent."[9] The fact that some of *Wuthering Heights*'s earliest critics had admired it was forgotten. Paradoxically, the novel's reputation for being ignored outlasted its actual neglect. As late as 1918, by which time Emily had in fact been widely praised and had even become the focus of hero worship in some circles, her novel was still being inaccurately described as "nearly forgotten."[10] In the short term, Charlotte's defense of 1850 contributed to *Wuthering Heights*'s failure to find an appreciative audience. In the longer term, it helped create its deceptive but romantic image as an unacknowledged masterpiece.

Gaskell's *Life* did not do much to endear Emily to the Victorian public when it came out in 1857. The sociable Mrs. Gaskell had never met the reclusive Emily, and she did not much like what she had heard from Charlotte, confessing that "all that I, a stranger, have been able to learn about her has not tended to give either me, or my readers, a pleasant impression of her."[11]

As a character in the *Life,* Emily plays only a supporting role, and is presented very differently from its central protagonist. We see Charlotte in three dimensions. We are encouraged to sympathize with her and are given access into her inner feelings (as Mrs. Gaskell saw them). In Emily's case, however, Gaskell sacrifices subtlety and complexity of characterization for the dramatic potential of a monolithic image seen exclusively from the outside. Making her larger than life, she literally transforms her into a mythological creature, calling her "a remnant of the Titans,— great-grand-daughter of the giants who used to inhabit earth."[12]

Charlotte's portrait of Emily as the genius possessed by demonic powers was too abstract to appeal to Mrs. Gaskell, who was not interested in forging a metaphysical explanation for Emily's literary talent. Like her Unitarian religion, which concentrated on good works in the world rather than contemplative spirituality, her aesthetic was essentially practical. *Wuthering Heights* was even further from her philanthropic approach than Charlotte's novels and did not appeal to her sensibility. She did not want to enter into a debate about the spiritual sources of inspiration. What she wanted for her biography were stories. The anecdotes she chose to include concerning Emily were dramatic, eye-catching, and so memorable that they have found their way into almost every subsequent Brontë biography.

We see Emily beating her disobedient bulldog into a pulp, while Charlotte stands by not daring to interfere; "no one dared," writes Gaskell, "when Emily's eyes glowed in that manner out of the paleness of her face, and when her lips were so compressed into stone." Keeper had been found by the servant, Tabby, asleep upstairs on the forbidden best bed. Gaskell continues:

> [Emily] went up-stairs, and Tabby and Charlotte stood in the gloomy passage below, full of the dark shadows of coming night. Down-stairs came Emily, dragging after her the unwilling Keeper, his hind legs set in a heavy attitude of resistance, held by the "scuft of his neck," but growling low and savagely all the time. The watchers would fain have spoken, but durst not, for fear of taking off Emily's attention, and causing her to avert her head for a moment from the enraged brute. She let him go, planted in a dark corner at the bottom of the stairs; no time was there to fetch stick or rod, for fear of the strangling clutch at her throat—her bare clenched fist struck against his red fierce eyes, before he had time to make his spring, and, in

the language of the turf, she "punished him" till his eyes were swelled up, and the half-blind, stupified beast was led to his accustomed lair, to have his swelled head fomented and cared for by the very Emily herself.[13]

The origins of this anecdote are obscure. There is even some reason to doubt that the incident took place at all. When the economist John Elliot Cairns visited Haworth in 1858, inspired by the *Life,* he questioned the Brontës' servant Martha, who could remember nothing of it, though she did recall Emily courageously extracting Keeper from fights with other dogs. Cairns's conclusion—"I suspect Mrs Gaskell does not scrutinise over-carefully the authority of her stories, if they be only picturesque"— seems reasonable enough.[14]

Yet even if there is a factual basis for the episode, Gaskell gives it a heightened sense of drama, presenting it as vividly as though she were actually there herself. We too are made to identify with the "watchers," rooted to the spot, our eyes fixed on the terrifying scene before us. Colorful adjectives proliferate. There is a melodramatic contrast between the deathlike "paleness" of Emily's face and the sinister "dark shadows of coming night." Her glowing eyes are identified with Keeper's "red fierce eyes," as though the two were members of the same animal species. He does not merely "growl," he growls "savagely." In fact, he is no longer a dog but a "brute," whose home is not a kennel but a "lair." Nor is Emily any longer a woman: she is a pugilist, whom only the "language of the turf" will suit. Having punished the animal, Emily reverts to a conventionally feminine nurturing role to bathe his wounds, but this only heightens the Jekyll-and-Hyde effect.

Gaskell's treatment of this incident derives less from life than from the fight scene in *Wuthering Heights* in which Heathcliff kicks Hindley almost to death and afterward binds his bleeding wrist.[15] Charlotte had declared that beneath Emily's "unpretending outside, lay a secret power and fire that might have informed the brain and kindled the veins of a hero."[16] Influenced by her perception of *Wuthering Heights* as a brutal book, Gaskell seems to suggest that its author is a beast in a woman's body.

In another scene, she describes Emily's response to being bitten by a strange dog she feared was rabid: she had cauterized her own arm with a red-hot iron from the kitchen, without telling anyone "for fear of the terrors that might beset their weaker minds."[17] In the *Life,* this story is used as evidence of Emily's stern nature and superhuman courage, of her lack of normal human sensitivity to pain. We have no reason to doubt the factual truth of the anecdote. Charlotte told Gaskell that the scene in *Shirley* in which the heroine is bitten by a dog and self-cauterizes the wound was taken from a real incident involving her sister.

Charlotte's fictional interpretation, which is strikingly different from Gaskell's, shows how the same story told twice can take on a completely different meaning. Charlotte invites us to perceive Shirley's response to the dog bite as a symptom of her "childish" insecurity rather than proof of her strength.[18] After cauterizing the wound, she is still tortured by a secret fear that she has contracted rabies. When she finally summons up the courage to tell her lover Louis Moore, his sympathy is tempered by amusement. In his protective but patronizing eyes, she is hysterical and hypochondriac. He does not believe that her fears are rationally grounded; he calls her "very nervous and womanish."[19]

When Shirley confesses, "I am neither so strong, nor have I such pride in my strength, as people think, Mr Moore; nor am I so regardless of sympathy,"[20] it seems like wish fulfillment on Charlotte's part, considering Emily's refusal of sympathy in her last illness. Indeed, the whole scene, which presents Shirley as vulnerable and Louis as in control, casts a strange light over Charlotte's attitude. Written after Emily died, it becomes particularly disturbing when the couple begins to discuss death. Shirley begs for euthanasia in the event of being infected with rabies, and Louis humors her by agreeing to perform the act, as though even death could be made bearable under the controlling hand of a loved one.

Charlotte may have wanted to soften Emily in *Shirley,* making her more pliable than she had been in reality, but Mrs. Gaskell's portrait of her in *The Life of Charlotte Brontë* had the opposite effect. Charlotte presumably remembered the beating of Keeper (if indeed she was the source of that story) and the cauterized arm because they were memorable, singular incidents outside the normal run of things. All biography emphasizes the extraordinary at the expense of the ordinary, simply because the everyday is less likely to be recorded. Ellen Nussey once remarked with justice that "[s]o very little is known about Emily Brontë, that every little detail awakens an interest."[21] Gaskell had very little data, but she deployed it so effectively, and with such a nose for dramatic interest, that these two violent incidents appeared to offer a total summation of Emily's personality.

Readers would come away from Gaskell's demonized portrait with the impression that Emily devoted her life to beating up dogs and was scarcely more human than her victims. As one critic put it in a review of the *Life,* "If the respectable bull-dog Keeper could have been endowed with the ambition and the power to describe graphically the passions of his race . . . he would write precisely such a book as *Wuthering Heights;* and as 'Life in the Kennel,' it would be a very striking and clever performance."[22] The implication is that the willfully canine Emily is not so "respectable" as the dog, who cannot help his nature.

Not surprisingly, the Victorian public took Gaskell's saintlike Charlotte more readily to its bosom than her titanic Emily. Although Emily had in fact taken on the greater part of the housekeeping responsibilities at the Parsonage, it was Charlotte who in afterlife became the icon of domestic virtue. Emily was overshadowed by her more famous sister, appearing only on the sidelines. During the 1860s, she effectively disappeared from view, undocumented and underappreciated. Those who paid her any attention at all regarded her as a freak, powerful but somehow perverted. For the most part, she dwindled to a mere cypher.

Emily's marginalization during the 1860s and '70s had one particularly curious and damaging consequence. It set the scene for what might be called the great Brontë conspiracy theory. Of all the weird claims which have been made about the Brontës over the past century and a half, the idea that Branwell was the true author of *Wuthering Heights* has had the most staying power. Though serious scholars have always dismissed it as absurd, it has managed to find champions among successive generations of Brontë obsessives. Yet it seems unlikely that anyone would have had the nerve to deny Emily the authorship of her own masterpiece had she not been so forgotten in the immediate decades after her death. If she had been as fêted as her sister at the time the claim emerged it is unlikely it would have gained such currency, and it might never have been made in the first place.

Once in circulation, the theory that there had been some sort of cover-up over the authorship of *Wuthering Heights* was ready to take on a life of its own. But where did it spring from in the first place? If we look at the context in which it originally surfaced, we can see that the reasoning behind it was anything but disinterested. Instead, it reveals how Victorian prejudices about writing and gender could be powerful enough to inspire men to try to erase the literary reputation of a woman. It is a story of male loyalty and posthumous sibling rivalry fueled by the desire of the unremarkable to bask in the reflected celebrity of the famous dead.

The authorship controversy began on June 15, 1867, when a man named

William Dearden published an article in the *Halifax Guardian* under the headline "Who Wrote *Wuthering Heights?*" A teacher and amateur poet, Dearden's main claim to fame was that he had, in years gone by, been personally acquainted with both male members of the legendary Brontë family. Perhaps he felt that, compared to their womenfolk, posterity had given these men a raw deal. A decade previously, he had loyally written to the papers to defend his old friend Patrick against Gaskell's lurid allegations of hearth-rug burning and other domestic violence.[23] His attempt to propose Branwell as the author of *Wuthering Heights* was probably intended as a similar act of restitution.

It is significant that Dearden, and the other early champions of Branwell's claim to authorship, were not objective researchers but his own friends. They had seen his name blackened in Gaskell's *Life,* which presented him as a talentless moral weakling at the mercy of a seasoned adulteress, groveling in the filth of his own pathetic vices. Attributing the novel to him might, they felt, do something to redress the balance and make him seem more of an achiever.

Branwell had, indeed, achieved more in his life than Gaskell had suggested. He may never have fulfilled his precocious promise. But though his adult writings are nothing like so accomplished as those of his sisters, he was the first Brontë sibling to make it into print, publishing poetry in Yorkshire papers and making a name for himself in local literary circles while his sisters were still unknown. It was as fellow poets that Branwell and Dearden were thrown together in the early 1840s, though Dearden, who was older, had first known Patrick back in 1829.

In his article on *Wuthering Heights,* Dearden described a meeting which had taken place in the summer of 1842 between himself, Branwell, and their sculptor friend Joseph Leyland at the Cross Roads Inn between Haworth and Keighley. A month earlier, the two poets had each agreed to produce a verse composition set in the mythical time before the Deluge. But when Branwell arrived at the appointed pub to show off his handiwork, he found that he had accidentally picked up the wrong manuscript. What he read out was not the antediluvian poem *Azrael, or, Destruction's Eve*[24] he had written in answer to Dearden's challenge, but a fragment whose scene and characters "so far as then developed" were, according to Dearden, "the same as those in *Wuthering Heights,* which Charlotte Brontë [*sic*] confidently asserts was the production of her sister Emily."[25]

On the basis of this, future writers would find much food for speculation. Did Emily steal Branwell's novel and deceitfully take the credit? Was

Wuthering Heights a joint production, the first half written by the brother, the second by the sister? Or had Branwell picked up one of Emily's manuscripts and passed it off to Dearden as his own? Under examination, Dearden's remarks are actually far from conclusive. Despite the confident assertions made at the beginning of his article, he ends on a more timid note, stopping short of positively proclaiming Branwell's authorship. All he in fact concludes is that, whether the novel itself was the work of brother or sister, Branwell's 1842 manuscript contained a prototype of the character of Heathcliff.

If Dearden thought he could detect echoes of Branwell when he eventually read *Wuthering Heights,* no conspiracy theory is needed to explain the coincidence. All the Brontës were subject to the same literary influences, and all their fiction had its ultimate roots in the shared literary experience of their childhood and adolescence. The satanic, self-destructive antihero appealed particularly to both Branwell and Emily. As William Smith Williams noted, different aspects of the same Byronic template can also be detected in *Jane Eyre*'s Rochester and in *The Tenant of Wildfell Hall*'s Arthur Huntingdon.[26] The modern editor of two recently published prose narratives by Branwell finds a number of Heathcliffian parallels in his Angrian characters, and if Branwell read out any of his own prose fiction derived from the Angrian saga, it would not be surprising if Dearden noticed similarities.[27]

Yet whatever Dearden remembered of Branwell's manuscript from that day at the Cross Roads Inn, it must have been hazily impressionistic by the time he connected it with *Wuthering Heights.* In his 1867 article, written a quarter of a century after the event, he admits that it was only in the previous week that the possibility of Branwell's authorship had occurred to him, after reading an article in a newspaper which expressed astonishment that Heathcliff had been conceived by a "timid and retiring female."[28] Yes, says Dearden, suddenly inspired, Heathcliff is simply too "revolting" to have been invented by "an inexperienced girl."[29]

What really undermines Dearden's position is the fact that it is the perceived nonfemininity of the novel, rather than his own memories of Branwell, which really clinches the authorship question for him. Perhaps he felt irked by the fact that one of his own male circle had found no place in the annals of literature while the sisters walked off with the glittering prizes. Dearden certainly used his article on *Wuthering Heights* to promote his own poetic standing. Having presented his evidence in prose, he goes on to elaborate his account of the meeting at the pub in verse. In doing so, he implicitly asserts his own status as a poet, and attempts to glamorize his own literary milieu, while dismissing Emily.

One has to wonder whether he felt some unspoken rivalry with the Brontë women, who had succeeded in putting Yorkshire on the literary map to a far greater extent than any of his coterie. Restating his views on the limitations of the female imagination, he tellingly confesses his "hope" that Emily did not have the brains to write *Wuthering Heights:*

> *Let us hope*
> *In charity, it never entered brain*
> *Of woman to conceive and to produce*
> *A character without a single trait*
> *Of nature to redeem it, and without*
> *A prototype in man or demon—such*
> *Such [sic] as the foul Caliban of "Wuthering Heights."*[30]

This wooden verse, marked by heavy-sounding pedantry ("to conceive and to produce") and contradiction (he denies Heathcliff a prototype only to give him one in Caliban), reveals a talent bathetically inferior to that of the Brontë sisters. If such smugly macho opinion was typical among the local literati back in the 1840s, no wonder Charlotte, Emily, and Anne believed the world was prejudiced against women writers.

Dearden's comments also show how powerfully the Gaskell legend could affect perceptions. In 1857, he had sanely tried to put the record straight regarding her portrait of Patrick. But ten years on, it seems that his memories of the real person who was Branwell have been assimilated into her dramatically simplified character. Though he puts a more glamorous, dangerous spin on her portrait of the doomed addict, Dearden nevertheless follows her in reducing Branwell's complex personality to cliché, explaining the romantic weirdness of *Wuthering Heights* as the result of a brain "kept ever in a state / Of feverous [sic] excitement by the fumes / Of alcohol or opium."[31] In fact, by 1842 Branwell had not yet developed the all-encompassing drug and drink problem which eventually destroyed him. And it seems most unlikely that an authority figure like Dearden—a friend of his father's and a headmaster to boot—would in real life have had such a liberal attitude toward the inspirational effects of substance abuse.

Despite the lack of evidence, Dearden's claim found its supporters. He started a fashion among Branwell's other friends for championing the Brontës' brother in print. These included the engineer Francis Grundy, who as an impressionable teenager had met Branwell while the latter was briefly employed as a railway clerk. He devoted a chapter of his memoirs to him in 1879. Grundy—whose inconsistencies and wildly inaccurate dating of Branwell's letters have made modern biographers[32] highly skeptical of his account—praised Branwell as "a genius of the highest order."[33] He also complained that his old acquaintance had had "a most unnecessary scandal heaped upon" him by his sister's biographer, though in fact his portrayal of Branwell as a madman was as lurid as anything in Gaskell.[34] Following Dearden, Grundy argued that it would be "incredible" for a book "so marvellous in its strength" as *Wuthering Heights* to have been written by "a young girl like Emily Brontë" and went on to assert— without offering corroborative evidence—that Branwell had told him he had written a great portion of it.[35]

Both Dearden and Grundy unwittingly reveal their claims to be based on the shaky foundations of their prejudices about women's writing and their desire for their old friend—and by implication themselves too—to be recognized. Yet their acquaintance with Branwell gave them enough appearance of credibility to ensnare the imaginations of future Brontëphiles. Unsurprisingly, it would find a particular niche in the fictional biographies of the 1920s and '30s, which by their very nature did not need to provide proof.

By 1936, it had become such an irritating distraction that the critic Irene Cooper Willis wrote a coruscating rebuttal, published by Leonard and Virginia Woolf's Hogarth Press. Her book used painstaking linguistic analysis in its efforts to quash the Branwell faction. By identifying characteristic traits of style, and charting them throughout the text, she argued for its unity of construction, denying that it could have been written by more than one hand. She then went on to demolish Branwell's supposed authorship by offering a detailed comparison between *Wuthering Heights* and a known prose fragment of his, *And the Weary Are at Rest*. Probably written in 1845, at around the time his sisters were also turning their minds to publication, this unfinished fiction is so rambling and confused that it is hard for the reader to work out what is going on. Irene Cooper Willis mercilessly juxtaposed its meandering, marathon sentences against the linguistic precision of *Wuthering Heights,* and pronounced it, in her robust idiom, to be boring, badly written "bilge."[36]

With her keen, if bitchy, critical intelligence, Irene Cooper Willis did seem to have offered a devastating blow to those who still clung to the idea that Branwell was responsible for *Wuthering Heights.* Yet even she failed to lay the matter to rest. In 1960, we find Daphne du Maurier still toying with the theory in her *Infernal World of Branwell Brontë*, and it recently resurfaced in the 1990s in James Tully's dubious *Crimes of Charlotte Brontë*. The idea of denying the authorship of *Wuthering Heights* to Emily had originally emerged in the context of her neglect. But although it was never widely accepted, it continued to exert an imaginative pull long after her rediscovery.

The authorship controversy over *Wuthering Heights* may have eventually taken on a life of its own. But to begin with, it was no more than a minor skirmish on the very fringes of Brontë studies and had little impact on Emily's mainstream image. For two decades after the publication of her *Life*, Gaskell's dog-beating caricature remained in the public mind, with Emily cast as the brutal author of a brutal book. Yet by the mid-1870s, some began to suspect that Gaskell's version of life in the Parsonage had been overgrim. The Brontë story was ready for revisionism, and Emily herself was in line for rehabilitation.

In his biography of Charlotte of 1876–77, Thomas Wemyss Reid was determined to soften Gaskell's account, and this included the portrayal of Emily.[37] His portrait was markedly more sentimental than anything previously written about her, yet the downside of his sympathy was that it deprived her of all her power. The only way he felt he could make readers well disposed toward the author of the shocking *Wuthering Heights* was by enfeebling her. He defended her by patronizing her, taking Charlotte's defense of her as an unconscious artist who did not know what she was doing to its logical, infantile conclusion.

"When a woman has lived such a life as that of 'Ellis Bell,' " he writes, "her first literary effort must be regarded as the attempt of an innocent and ignorant child." Emily, it seems, is to be pitied for her arrested mental development: her novel should be regarded as "the work of one who, in everything but years, was a mere child, and its great and glaring faults are to be forgiven as one forgives the mistakes of childhood."[38]

In one rhapsodic scene, based loosely on a reminiscence of Ellen Nussey's, Reid's imagination gets the better of him as he describes the Brontë siblings on a drive through the countryside:

> Emily Brontë does not talk so much as the rest of the party, but her wonderful eyes, brilliant and unfathomable as the pool at the foot of a water-

fall, but radiant also with a wealth of tenderness and warmth, show how her soul is expanding under the influences of the scene; . . . she utters at times a strange, deep guttural sound which those who know her best interpret as the language of a joy too deep for articulate expression.[39]

Unable to communicate except in animal grunts, it is hard to see how this Emily could have written anything at all.

Despite its limitations, Thomas Wemyss Reid's book, with its snapshot of Emily as a weirdly wide-eyed mute, kindled the interest of the poet Algernon Charles Swinburne, who was stimulated into writing an essay on the Brontës in 1877. He would later be credited with having "blown the dust"[40] from Emily's reputation, and his approving portrait of her marked a new departure.

The fact that Emily found a champion in Swinburne goes to show how far beyond the bounds of respectability *Wuthering Heights* remained. A self-conscious rebel from an aristocratic background, everything about him, from his atheism to his overexcited interest in flagellation, was designed to affront bourgeois values. If Emily had inspired some negative press, Swinburne had positively courted notoriety with his *Poems and Ballads* of 1866, whose provocative aesthetic had been read—as it was intended—as a full-frontal assault on Christian morality. Disgusted critics had bridled at his blasphemy and indecency, the *Pall Mall Gazette* had described him as "a mere madman, one who has got maudlin drunk on lewd ideas and lascivious thoughts," and Carlyle had consigned him to the cesspool.[41]

Swinburne's urge to shock, like the glee with which he reports giggling over de Sade, can seem irritatingly puerile, but he was brilliant nonetheless. Steeped in the classics, he had a fine-tuned literary intelligence and great technical facility as a poet. His rejection of God was not a mere pose, but reflected the religious turmoil which, in the age of Darwin, had become endemic among intellectuals.[42] It also harked back to Byron and Shelley, upper-class exhibitionists like himself. Though Swinburne did not know it, Branwell Brontë had also been inspired to flirt with atheism by these Romantic rebels. Whether Emily had too is a matter for debate. But *Wuthering Heights* was certainly alluring in its lack of conventional Christian piety.

A novel which satirized religion in the form of a mad sermon and whose heroine rejected heaven in favor of earth was bound to appeal to Swinburne. In 1848, the reviewer Elizabeth Rigby had thought "pagan" one of the worst insults she could fling at *Wuthering Heights*. Thirty years later, Swinburne was using it as a term of the highest praise. As a poet, he had written in the assumed voice of an ancient Roman, repudiating the pale Galilean God of the Christians at whose breath the world had grown gray. Now, as a critic, he lauded Emily as "a lineal daughter of the earth-born giants, more ancient in their godlike lineage than all modern reigning gods."[43] Admiring her "dark unconscious instinct as of primitive nature-worship," he paid tribute to her "passionate great genius"[44] and labeled her approvingly as "antichristian."[45]

Charlotte's 1850 "Biographical Notice" had put Emily on the road to becoming an icon of death, and Swinburne's interest may also have been connected with his perverse attraction to female figures associated with death and pain. Charlotte's public comments—so different from her private memories of her reluctant sister being torn panting out of a happy life—had presented Emily as a fearless stoic embracing her end. Certainly, Swinburne was exhilarated by Charlotte's misinformation concerning the poem "No coward soul is mine." His belief that these were Emily's last lines led to fantasies about the "lips already whitened but not yet chilled"[46] which had supposedly uttered them. He seems to have found Emily as exciting as the sadistic goddesses in his own erotic poetry, writing to Thomas Wemyss Reid, "I cannot think that anything in her book is at all excessive or unjustifiable,—And with all its horror, it is so beautiful, but I must not go off into fresh rhapsodies about that 'dreadful book.' "[47]

What Swinburne liked about *Wuthering Heights* were precisely those things that had troubled Charlotte: its emotional primitivism, violence, and lack of conventional moral standpoint. Although he clothed Emily in the unrealistic costume of a pagan deity, he also set her on a level with the established literary greats, comparing her novel to Shakespeare and Greek tragedy. In 1848, the *American Review* had declared of Emily's novel that "[i]n conversation we have heard it spoken of by some as next in merit to Shakespeare," but *Wuthering Heights* had not been viewed in such a light for thirty years.[48] Instead of regarding it as one would regard a child's story, Swinburne acknowledged it as a great work of art and went on to redefine it as "essentially and definitely a poem."[49]

His praise of Emily's "nature worship" also anticipated the sea change which would occur in responses to Emily's novel as it moved into the twentieth century. Its early readers had viewed it as a monstrosity, focusing on its shocking scenes of violence and depravity. Swinburne, instead, saw it as a pantheist allegory by a "love[r] of earth for earth's sake." His interpretation derived as much from Charlotte, who had described *Wuthering Heights* as "moorish, and wild, and knotty as the root of heath,"[50] as from the novel itself. By the mid-twentieth century, this sort of elemental reading had worked its way into popular culture, resulting in the clichéd image of Cathy and Heathcliff embracing on a windy hilltop, though in fact the novel contains no scene in which the adult couple appear together out of doors.[51]

Although Swinburne brought a new way of seeing to *Wuthering Heights,* his attraction to the novel and its author still had something to do with the aura of forbidden fruit which hung around them: his admiration remained bound up, at some level, with the book's "dreadful" image and with the fact that it had not quite been accepted into the canon of respectable literature. The book still occupied a place in the alternative, rather than mainstream, culture of the day. But there were many alternative cultures, and those rare, unorthodox individuals who admired the novel did so in startlingly different ways. While Swinburne was making it answer his own provocative paganism, Olive Schreiner, a young governess from colonial southern Africa, was using its inspiration to turn herself into a path-breaking feminist and writer.

In *The Story of an African Farm,* published under the pseudonym of "Ralph Iron" in 1883 after she came to England, Schreiner loosely adapted the plot of *Wuthering Heights* and matched Emily's feel for the Yorkshire landscape with her own incandescent descriptions of the African veldt. The heroine, Lyndall, grows up on an isolated farm, where her childhood companion, Waldo, falls in love with her. But she leaves the farm in search of liberty and culture, gives herself to another lover, and eventually dies, having borne an illegitimate child, but refusing to give up her freedom and marry.[52]

In her questioning of the cultural and spiritual meaning of womanhood, Schreiner was in fact much closer to Charlotte Brontë than to Emily, whose novel offers none of the social criticism or subjectivism found in her elder sister's work. Yet Emily Brontë, less domesticated than Charlotte, clearly appealed to Schreiner's own sense of isolation and rebellion. In many ways, Schreiner out-Brontë'd the Brontës: Haworth was tame compared to the genuine wildness of the scarcely settled Cape Colony where she grew up without formal education. And unlike Charlotte or Emily, she was prepared to play out her resistance to social convention in life as well as art. With no intention of marriage, an institution she opposed, she embarked on a fully consummated love affair with the sexologist Havelock Ellis.[53]

Another admirer who was drawn to Emily around this time was a young woman named Mary Robinson, who was less remarkable than Olive Schreiner but even more committed to the author of *Wuthering Heights*. A well-educated architect's daughter who had published two volumes of verse and several short stories by her mid-twenties, she was ready to be swayed by Swinburne's enthusiasm but keen to develop a vision of Emily that was fundamentally purer and more exonerating. Indeed, she was so impressed by what she saw as Emily's "integrity and passion" that she wrote to Ellen Nussey in 1882 proposing herself as Emily's biographer and asking for help with material.[54] Robinson had been approached by the editor of W. H. Allen & Co.'s Eminent Women Series, who had invited her to contribute a biography on a subject of her own choice. The result was a sympathetic life which would do almost as much to change Emily's image as Gaskell's book had done for Charlotte's.

Unlike Gaskell, however, who had skated over the Bells' novels, Robinson shared Swinburne's admiration for *Wuthering Heights* and wanted to rescue it from critical oblivion. Taking Charlotte's "Biographical Notice" as gospel, she was unaware that the novel had actually been enjoyed by some of its first readers, and believed that Emily had died before a single word of praise had reached her. She exaggerated the novel's critical neglect, supposing that apart from Swinburne, Matthew Arnold, Sydney Dobell, and Thomas Wemyss Reid, no critic had ever appreciated it. She went on to paint an appealing, if somewhat romanticized, picture of how it had found no readership in the establishment. It was only, she said, among the intellectually dispossessed—Yorkshire mill girls and the odd "eager, unsatisfied, passionate child"—that the book had found an audience.[55]

Robinson's aim was to humanize Emily, while acknowledging her as a free spirit. Determined to dispel forever Gaskell's grim vision, she seized on Ellen Nussey's pleasant memories of girlish jollity at the Parsonage in the early 1840s. More specifically, she wanted to get rid of "the fierce, impassioned Vestal who has seated herself in Emily's place of remembrance," and to replace it with the more attractive picture of an "active, genial, warm-hearted girl, full of humour and feeling to those she knew."

Emily's affinity with the animal world was no longer a symptom of subhuman cruelty but of graceful charm. The beating of Keeper was silently dropped from the record. Instead of bulldog nastiness, Emily now possessed "the lithe beauty of the wild creatures that she loved."[56] Instead of the barren scenery described by Gaskell, the moors were now endowed with a gentler beauty of dappling greens and fragrant purples, twittering birds and humming bees.[57] If Emily was a mythological character, she was no longer a titaness but "Athene, leading the nymphs in their headlong chase down the rocky spurs of Olympus, and stopping in full career to lift in her arms the weanlings, tender as dew."[58]

Some of the Gaskell apocrypha remained. Patrick still kept his children on an inadequate non-meat diet, and the young Brontës were still deemed to "have had no childhood."[59] Yet Ellen's pleasant memories also enabled Robinson to add further liveliness to the picture of how the three sisters used to walk around and around the sitting-room table in the evenings discussing literature.[60] Her stress on the delights of sisterly friendship between writers reflected her own situation. From 1880, she had been close to Violet Paget (the novelist Vernon Lee). Both in their twenties, the pair traveled together, rented cottages in which to write together, and became so inseparable that Mary's mother began to resent Violet's regular presence in the Robinson household. As Peter Gunn's biography (*Vernon Lee: Violet Paget 1856–1935*, London, 1964) suggests, it was not a sexual relationship, but it was a passionate one in which Violet—who had a breakdown when Mary became engaged in 1888—lived out her belief in the superiority and purity of female love to what she saw as the corrupting love of men.

Unlike the young Charlotte Brontë, who had focused her enthusiasm and ambition on male role models, Mary Robinson felt drawn to identify with a female literary tradition and to join the Brontës, metaphorically, in their evening walks. Certainly, she was determined to make Emily a more likeable, welcoming figure than she had been hitherto.

Robinson's insistence on Branwell's polluting presence reflected her friend Violet Paget's feminist disgust for masculinity, which she saw as incorrigibly bestial. In the context of the biography, the brother's viciousness had a dual function. First, Robinson wanted to make her subject more likeable. Earlier writers had shuddered with dismay—or pleasure, in Swinburne's case—at the unnatural image of Emily's "frail form standing up undaunted in the scowl of death."[61] Robinson painted a less frightening, more poignant, more feminine picture. On the morning of her death day, the emaciated young girl attempts to comb her own hair, still beautiful "in its plenteous dark abundance," but in her weakness drops the comb into the grate. Robinson goes on, "I have seen that old, broken comb, with a large piece burnt out of it; and have thought it, I own, more pathetic than the bones of the eleven thousand virgins at Cologne, or the time-blackened Holy Face of Lucca."[62] Eventually, five combs with charred teeth would reportedly battle it out for the honor of a place under glass in the Brontë Parsonage Museum,[63] though it is hard to establish for certain the truth of the anecdote, which Mary Robinson allegedly heard from the Brontës' servant Martha Brown.[64] What is important is that Robinson uses it as an occasion to endow Emily with an aura of religious mystery and pathos. Charlotte had until now held the high ground as the single Brontë saint, but Robinson was keen to subject Emily to a new sort of canonization.

Robinson's Emily is a very different sort of saint from the domestic icon which Charlotte had become in the simplistic self-help guides of the Victorian moralists. Her dying heroine with the pre-Raphaelite hair has a more medieval, poeticized flavor. But though Robinson's biography does not dwell on the Gaskellian theme of the woman made perfect by sufferings, it remains an exercise in moral rehabilitation nonetheless. Back in the 1850s, Harriet Martineau had balked at the Brontës' representation of passion, and Gaskell too had found it morbid. In the 1880s, Mary Robinson was far more prepared than most earlier critics to admire Emily's spiritual independence, reading her poetry as evidence of heterodox religious attitudes. But she still felt the need to sanitize the mind that had produced *Wuthering Heights* with a biographical apologia.

Gaskell, of course, had been the first biographer to suggest that Emily's novel had its sources in its author's real-life experiences. She stated, somewhat vaguely, that the violence and coarseness of the Brontë novels did not stem from "internal conception," but from "hard cruel facts, pressed down, by external life, upon their very senses, for long months and years together." All the sisters had done was to "write out what they saw."[65] The reference to "hard cruel facts" was a clear gesture toward the unfortunate Branwell, who could be used to hide a multitude of sins in his sisters. Inspired by this suggestion, Thomas Wemyss Reid went further in his 1877 biography of Charlotte, making Branwell the literal model for Heathcliff. Though Mary Robinson was less crude in her interpretation of that character, she accepted that Branwell was "a page of the book in which his sister studied."[66]

Robinson's interpretation of Branwell's personality was central to her vision. It was important to her to place great stress on the brother's weakness of character, "the miserable flabbiness of his moral fibre"[67] and his "unclean habits."[68] Thus, she makes him "a weed in bud that could only bear a bitter and poisonous fruit"[69] and has already endowed him with a drinking problem by the end of the chapter titled "Childhood." In some ways, her portrait is even less flattering than Gaskell's: she makes him appear more contemptible and less pitiable.

The reasoning behind this interpretation was twofold. First, Robinson wanted to "deal a death blow, once and for all," to the theory that Branwell had written *Wuthering Heights*. She would do this by presenting the brother as too intellectually and morally enervated to have produced "the sustained power and passion of Emily's book."[70] Second, and more important, she needed to find an explanation for how Emily could have created such a dark and dubious novel. Even if she argued that Branwell had not written any of the text, or sat for the portrait of Heathcliff, Robinson still clutched at the demon brother as a means of exonerating Emily. In doing so she continued in the Gaskell tradition of putting biographical circumstances ahead of literary influence in her quest to understand the Brontë imagination. As she explained to Ellen Nussey, "How can I let people think that the many basenesses of her hero's character are the gratuitous inventions of an inexperienced girl? How can I explain the very existence of *Wuthering Heights*? . . . Only by explaining Branwell."[71]

Robinson clung to her faith in this theory even though it was to cause an uncomfortable rift between her and Ellen Nussey, on whose helpful memories she had relied. Ellen, who seems to have got particularly prudish in her old age, hated the idea of the Brontë name being attached to any sort of scandal. She told Mary Robinson that back in 1857 she had been horrified when she discovered that Gaskell's *Life* had publicized Branwell's fall. She also said she had felt betrayed at the amount of Charlotte's correspondence Gaskell had quoted in full, since the biographer had originally promised only to quote short extracts.

Interestingly, when Ellen read Robinson's first draft, she tried to dissuade her from focusing on Branwell's sins by suggesting that it might bring scandal on the *biographer's* head. Robinson, she said, might compromise her own reputation as a lady by dwelling on such disagreeable matters. Ellen, however, was clearly behind the times in her notions of feminine respectability. The young poet answered these objections by confidently asserting that her reputation was that of an artist, "not of an accomplished young lady with talents d'agréments for her decoration," and her vigorous self-justification echoed the arguments that Charlotte and Anne had put before the public as Currer and Acton Bell: "I should feel it a straining cowardice if it seemed to me that such and such a cause explained such and such a result, to say nothing about it because it was unpleasant."[72]

Nevertheless, it was for moral as much as literary reasons that Robinson remained wedded to her belief in Branwell as the main influence behind *Wuthering Heights*. She was the first to construct the plot whereby Emily was closer to her brother than either of her sisters and was the one member of the family who treated the prodigal with compassion. Without access to the juvenilia, Robinson was not aware that it was in fact Charlotte who had grown up collaborating most closely with Branwell in their fantasies of Angria.

Having visited Haworth and questioned locals, she came away with two gossipy anecdotes that bolstered her view of the sympathy between Emily and her brother. One had her putting out a fire, caused by a candle, that threatened to engulf Branwell's bed; the other had her waiting up for him when he came home drunk from the Black Bull. Yet her main evidence came from a poem of Emily's ("Well, some may hate, and some may scorn, / And some may quite forget thy name")[73] which expressed pity for a wretched and ruined figure, comparing his weakness to that of a timid deer or leveret.

The trouble with this biographical reading is that the poem was in fact written in 1839, long before Branwell's final breakdown, and that in it the pitied character is already dead. Yet on the basis of this evidence Robinson took the unwarranted leap of assuming that from earliest childhood "it was Emily and Branwell who were most to each other."[74] She felt she needed to make a strong connection between the two if she was to convince her readers that it was "no perverse fancy which drove that pure and innocent girl into ceaseless brooding on the conquering force of sin," and that Emily's genius was, rather, largely determined by "the sins of this beloved and erring brother."[75]

Robinson's book would not convince everybody. Once published, it had the uncalled-for effect of stimulating another of Branwell's acquaintance into print to defend his memory and reignite the *Wuthering Heights* authorship controversy. In 1886, Francis Leyland (a former bookseller and brother of the sculptor Joseph) brought out a work in two volumes, *The Brontë Family with Special Reference to Patrick Branwell Brontë*. Leyland's book is interesting to the modern biographer because it shows that there was a thriving literary culture in the Brontës' Yorkshire, but it nevertheless dragged Emily back into the mire of conspiracy theory. Leyland took up the idea that Emily had been particularly close to her brother but turned it into a means of bolstering and elaborating on William Dearden's and Francis Grundy's earlier claims about *Wuthering Heights,* arguing that the novel was a work of joint authorship. Without Charlotte's knowledge, Branwell had, Leyland claimed, handed over the unfinished manuscript for his favorite sister, the sympathetic Emily, to complete.

It seems ironic that Robinson, who had been so keen to scotch the rumor that Branwell had written any of *Wuthering Heights,* ended up indirectly providing fodder for the claim. On the whole, however, she was pleased with the reception of her book, which was an international success, well reviewed in Rome and Paris and America as well as London.[76] In terms of image, the biography did not merely succeed in absolving Emily from negative accusations of perversity. In a positive sense, it set her up as a symbol of unaffected, natural energy and "sexless purity,"[77] transforming her into a figure who remained uncontaminated by base passions while running unimpeded over the moors.

The book reached out to women. In America, Emily Dickinson was moved and excited by the story of a female poet as reclusive as herself, and found the book "more electric by far than anything since *Jane Eyre.*"[78] But it was not merely in rarified literary circles that Emily found admirers. The breadth of her newfound appeal was testimony not just to Robinson's persuasiveness as a biographer but to changing social attitudes toward women. In the 1850s, even feminists had wanted to define Charlotte as a suffering martyr. But by the 1890s, forward-thinking New Women no longer wanted heroines of renunciation but role models who symbolized female freedom from the social conventions which had stifled their mothers.

Within a few years of the biography's appearance, young women were confessing their "pious enthusiasm" for Emily in hushed tones, even if her novel retained enough of a pleasurable whiff of the forbidden to make them blush. One young lady revealed her love of the novel to Théodore de Wyzewa, its first French translator, "with a gracious smile, rather embarrassed, head lowered, blushing, as if it were rather too bold a confidence." But she soon took courage when she moved on to discussing her admiration of Emily's character, revealing how she and her friends "had promised each other always to keep a special devotion to this noble memory."[79]

By the 1890s, ambitious girls were becoming jaded with Charlotte. The young Sybylla in Miles Franklin's *My Career Goes Bung* has hopes of one day standing for Parliament, but when she studies the "lives of the great" she finds no relevant role models: "Grace Darling, Charlotte Brontë, Joan of Arc and Mrs Fry passed in review, evidently by dull old professors. These were a long time dead."[80] Robinson's Emily, however, provided a new and more exciting interpretation of the Brontë sisters, who could now be championed by the *Young Woman* magazine as "children of the moor, full of wild untameable energy" who were among "the first to strike that resonant note of revolt against the artificial limitations of a woman's world which is heard everywhere in our literature of today."[81] The nature worship which had once symbolized Swinburne's rejection of Christian values had taken on a healthier aspect: suggesting fresh air and exercise rather than paganism, it had now become suitable for young girls.

By the end of the century Emily had become an object of fascination even among more conservative readers. Forty years previously, it would have been impossible to imagine a magazine with a title like *The Woman at Home* running an admiring article on the monstrous author of *Wuthering Heights*. Yet in 1897, this is where Clement Shorter chose to publish a reverent piece on recently discovered "Relics of Emily Brontë," including reproductions of a number of animal drawings by her and a facsimile of the manuscript of the poem "No coward soul is mine."[82] The sphinx of English literature sat oddly alongside the columns on fashion and beauty.

Mary Robinson had not only succeeded in transforming Emily's image but had gone some of the way to setting the agenda which would dominate biographies right up until the present day. In titling one of her chapters "*Wuthering Heights:* Its Origin," she gave expression to the question which would prompt more speculation and mythmaking than almost any other: What was the source of Emily's creative inspiration? There is some poetic justice in this, as *Wuthering Heights* is itself about unknown origins. Nobody ever knows where the orphan Heathcliff comes from, though Nelly Dean builds castles in the air, suggesting he might be the son of some mysterious eastern potentate.

Swinburne was unconvinced by the theory that Emily had used her brother as the model for her hero. He could not accept that the author of *Wuthering Heights* had such a shallow imagination that she was limited to literal portraiture:

> Those who believe that Heathcliff was called into existence by the accident that his creator had witnessed the agonies of a violent weakling in

love and in disgrace might believe that Shakespeare wrote *King Lear* because he had witnessed the bad effects of parental indulgence, and that Aeschylus wrote the *Eumenides* because he had witnessed the uncomfortable results of matricide.[83]

But by the 1890s the fashion for finding the "originals" of every character and place in the Brontës' novels had become such a mania that fact and fiction often became confused. Bored with searching Emily's personal life for the sources of her novel, some enthusiasts inverted the process and began, even more spuriously, to use *Wuthering Heights* itself as a source for new biographical information concerning its author and her family.

The identification of Branwell with Heathcliff may offer little insight into the world of *Wuthering Heights*. But it retains at least some residual plausibility, compared with some of the other suggestions that had begun to circulate. These reminded one commentator of "nothing so much as of that prophetical literature which once undertook to prove that Napoleon III. [*sic*] was Antichrist, and which still is prepared to fix the date of the end of the world."[84] The desire to prove that the Brontës' fiction was actually fact was so strong in the case of a certain Dr. Wright that in *The Brontës in Ireland: Facts Stranger Than Fiction* (1893) he tried to convince the world—and succeeded to a surprising extent—that the main events of *Wuthering Heights* were a scarcely disguised history of the Brontës' Irish ancestors.[85]

With some exceptions, few looked in what might have seemed one obvious place for the sources of this highly literary novel—to what Emily might have read, rather than what she or her family might have done. In this, they made the same mistake as Lockwood in *Wuthering Heights*, who patronizingly attempts to praise Nelly Dean by suggesting she has an insight into human nature unexpected in an unsophisticated rustic. "I have read more than you would fancy," she replies, denying that she has developed her mind merely by observing the people among whom she lives.[86] In her 1883 biography, Mary Robinson had mentioned Coleridge, Southey, and Scott as possible influences on Emily's poetry but had—oddly—dismissed the possibility that Emily could have known Byron. In her view, Emily would have had "little experience" of such an author in her "remote parsonage."[87]

The belief that Emily could not have had access to such a standard Romantic author—and to many others, less well known—derived from Charlotte's disingenuous presentation of her sisters as unlearned, and from Gaskell's exaggerated portrait of Haworth as a culturally deprived outpost on the farthest fringes of civilization. Ironically, Gaskell's *Life* had in fact offered a surprisingly full record of the books the Brontës had access to. From Charlotte's letters and juvenilia, as quoted by Gaskell, any post-1857 critic could have discovered that the Brontës had access, among many others, to Byron, Wordsworth, Southey, Scott, and Burns as well as to *Blackwood's* and *Fraser's*.[88] But in this case as in so many others, the image of isolation she created was more powerful than the facts she documented.

In the Brontë studies of the 1890s, two voices stand out from the conspiracy theorists as being prepared to contextualize Emily's work, giving it a place in literary history and exploring its roots in Romanticism. The critic Angus Mackay, who took the excitable Dr. Wright to task in *The Brontës: Fact and Fiction,* was one of the first to identify the imagination as a key theme in Emily's poetry, suggesting affinities with Wordsworth and Coleridge. The leading novelist Mrs. Humphry Ward, who was commissioned to write the critical introductions to the Haworth edition of the Brontës' works, refused to be drawn into literal biographical interpretation. Instead, she explicitly acknowledged the influence of English and European literature both on Charlotte (a ravenous reader of French fiction) and on Emily, whose novel she regarded as a brilliant work by a sophisticated literary artist.

Using the evidence available in Gaskell's *Life,* Ward made note of the Brontës' probable reading, mentioning Wordsworth, Coleridge, De Quincey, Southey, James Hogg, and Walter Scott among the British Romantics. She argued that, far from being autobiographical, *Wuthering Heights* had "more than a mere local or personal significance," and she suggested that Emily's novel should be read in the context of German Romanticism, which had been popularized in England in the 1830s in *Fraser's,* among other publications. She took note of the fact—reported in Charlotte's letters of the period and by Mrs. Gaskell—that Emily had learned German while at school in Brussels, and pointed out that a "wild robber-and-magician story" by Tieck had appeared in translation in *Blackwood's* in 1839. One of *Wuthering Heights*'s first reviewers had found the novel reminiscent of Hoffmann's tales. Although she had no direct evidence to prove that Emily had read Hoffmann, Ward thought it probable that she had done so, and concluded:

> *Wuthering Heights* is a book of the later Romantic movement, betraying the influences of German Romantic imagination. . . . The Romantic ten-

dency to invent and delight in monsters, the *exaltation du moi,* which has been said to be the secret of the whole Romantic revolt against classical models and restraints; the love of violence in speech and action, the preference for the hideous in character and the abnormal in situation—of all these there are abundant examples in *Wuthering Heights.* . . . And the violent, clashing egotisms of Heathcliff and Catherine in the last scene of passion before Catherine's death, are as it were an epitome of a whole *genre* in literature, and a whole phase of European feeling.[89]

She went on to sum up *Wuthering Heights* as "the product of romantic imagination, working probably under influences from German literature, and marvellously fused with local knowledge and a realistic power which, within its own range has seldom been surpassed."[90]

Compared to other treatments of the Brontës, Ward's approach was unusual. Suggesting possible sources and analogues for *Wuthering Heights,* she was one of the first critics to treat it as a purely literary text rather than regarding it as the freakish consequence of biographical circumstances. Instead of presenting Emily as a weird aberration she treated her as a conscious artist working within a literary tradition. In doing so, she did not intend to undermine Emily's originality, but to put her on a level with the male authors with whom she compared her. She may have exaggerated the specific importance of the German horror tradition to Emily, but methodologically her approach was striking.

It was, however, to have little influence on the biographical writers who came afterward, who would be extremely reluctant to class Emily as part of an intellectual or aesthetic movement or to give up the Romantic myth, first propagated by Charlotte, of the isolated sibyl receiving her visions direct from the hand of Fate. For much of the twentieth century *Wuthering Heights* would be conceived as a "novel which, without ancestors or progeny, by one superb explosion of genius defies criticism and classification."[91] Twentieth-century scholarship of the Romantics has been criticized for being "dominated by an uncritical absorption into Romanticism's own self-representation," and this is probably more true of Emily Brontë than it is of any other Romantic poet.[92] The reluctance to contextualize her work, combined with a shift of emphasis in the popular mind away from the grimness of Haworth to the beauties of the moors, encouraged readers to define Emily as a natural rather than a cultural phenomenon. As Ernest Dimnet put it in *Les Soeurs Brontë,* "*Wuthering Heights* . . . est . . . un pur produit des *moors* et d'une imagination exclusivement nourrie d'elle-même."[93]

Mrs. Humphry Ward's attempt to explain *Wuthering Heights* by looking at its cultural antecedents did not appeal to May Sinclair, whose influential study of 1912, *The Three Brontës,* would have an enormous influence on perceptions of Emily. The second Brontë sister had always intrigued Sinclair. As a child reading Gaskell's *Life,* she found the forbidding specter of Emily more alluring than Charlotte with her boring literary letters.[94] In adulthood, she continued to be drawn to her mystery, and she transformed her into an etherealized being whose inspiration came not from books but from a higher spiritual plane.

Sinclair hated the idea that the Brontës, or any great women writers, should have been dependent on outside influence for their inspiration. She vehemently denied that Charlotte's work had been affected by what she regarded as her unfortunate relationship with Constantin Heger. In a similar way, she rejected Mary Robinson's view that *Wuthering Heights* had its origins in the sinful spectacle of Branwell. Significantly, she also ignored the possibility that reading could have had any impact on Emily's writings.

This lack of interest in the cultural context of Emily's work derived from Sinclair's resolutely antiempirical stance on creativity. Rather than talking about literature in terms of style or form or influence, her critical vocabulary shows her to have been more concerned with abstract ideas such as soul, divine unconsciousness, transcendence, and the Absolute. Emily was praised above all for her spirituality and her supposed renunciation of the world. Sinclair's interpretation of *Wuthering Heights* reworked Swinburne's view of it as an elemental allegory, but in a purer, more unearthly form. She saw the novel as a "choric hymn" to nature.[95] But her idea of nature did not include the human body, and it certainly excluded sex. "Never," she wrote triumphantly, "was a book written with a more sublime ignorance of the physical."[96] She regarded Emily as more exalted than Charlotte, who had grubbied herself by becoming infatuated with a man.

This vision of Emily would feed into Sinclair's 1914 novel, *The Three Sisters,* whose Yorkshire vicarage setting reflected the situation of the Brontës. Here, Gwenda, the middle sister, is disappointed in love, but finds something better: sublimation through a combination of metaphysics and nature mysticism. Emily, who provided some of the inspiration for Gwenda, was regarded by Sinclair as a holy creature blessed with an intuitive understanding of transcendental philosophy.

In *The Three Brontës,* this supposed spiritual superiority was traced in an analysis of Emily's poetry, which had, by 1910, nearly all been published in one form or another, though not always accurately.[97] Sinclair was the first to popularize the connection between Emily and mysticism, comparing her to St. John of the Cross. Ironically, however, she based her interpretation on those stanzas of "The Visionary" which are now known to have been interpolated by Charlotte, in which the poet receives divine inspiration.[98] In fact, Sinclair was more drawn to Charlotte's idealized version of her sister than to the real Emily. Having read Charlotte's depiction of Shirley's evening reverie, in which the heroine finds divinity in nature, she built up an image of Emily as having privileged access to "a vision of the transcendent reality."[99] Emily was one of those "for whom the Real is the incredible, unapparent harmony that flows above, beneath, and within the gross flux of appearances."[100]

Such hyperspiritual interpretation of Emily did not, however, spring from nowhere. It reflected Sinclair's own ideals and the preoccupation with philosophical idealism and mysticism which had been woven into the fabric of her mind since her teens. The Oxford philosopher T. H. Green, a major early influence, had asserted the primacy of man's spiritual nature and defined the universe as a divinely ordered manifestation of God's consciousness. His primary ethical category was "self-realization," by which he meant the state in which the individual was in touch with his best and highest spiritual nature. Influenced by Kant and German idealism, his rhetoric was often mystical and pantheistic, as was Sinclair's in *The Three Brontës*.[101]

Indeed, her critical response is so bound up with her philosophical beliefs that she uses Emily's poetry subjectively as proof of her own faith. Emily is presented as an ideal figure rising above the phenomenal world and achieving realization of the divine within herself. She is not so much a great writer as a great soul, whose greatness is independent of literary achievement: "[H]er genius was great, not only through her stupendous imagination, but because it fed on the still more withdrawn and secret sources of her soul. If she had had no genius she would yet be great because of what took place within her, the fusion of her soul with the transcendent and enduring life."[102]

Thus, it is important for Sinclair that Emily's spiritual knowledge is "not derived" from reading but self-generated if it is to be true.[103] *Wuthering Heights* must be "absolutely self-begotten and self-born."[104] And Emily must have "had no method," achieving what she did "without knowing it."[105] As Sinclair puts it, "Without a hint, so far as we know, from any philosophy, by a sheer flash of genius she pierced to the secret of the world."[106] Looking at the poetry, Sinclair found evidence of pantheistic and idealist ideas and came to the conclusion that Emily must have derived them from mystical experience and introspection alone.

She used "The Philosopher," a dialogue poem in which a visionary and a doubter debate the existence of God, as proof that Emily had searched after "the Absolute" despite being "destitute of all metaphysical knowledge or training."[107] In reality, though Sinclair did not consider it, Emily would not have had to look further than Byron's "Detached Thoughts," as quoted in Moore's *Life,* to find religious doubt discussed as a branch of philosophy. Yet Sinclair saw a match between her own philosophical preoccupations and what she felt to be similar concepts in Emily's poetry, and concluded that these ideas represented a naked truth independent of culture. She was not able to step far enough back to consider that Emily's rhetoric, and her own, could have come, if indirectly, from the same source.

In fact, the German idealism which had influenced Sinclair may have also, in a different, earlier form, have influenced Emily. As we have seen, not only did Emily study German in Brussels, but she might have had access in English to versions of these ideas through the works of Coleridge or Carlyle or through *Fraser's* magazine. Had Sinclair looked at *Fraser's* she would have discovered that Emily would have had the opportunity for metaphysical reading of a highly intellectual kind in articles such as one on "German Philosophy" which came out in June 1837.[108]

Yet Sinclair would never have considered searching for the cultural origins of Emily's work. Her portrait of her was resolutely supraliterary. For her, Emily was not a talented craftswoman but a being of rare spiritual gifts. The author of *Wuthering Heights* who, half a century before, had been dismissed as doglike and repellent had become instead a symbol of the divine within the human. The mystic of the moors was born.

The effect of Sinclair's idealization of Emily would be widespread but double-edged. On the one hand, she identified the importance of visionary images in Emily's poetry and acknowledged Emily's own interest in ideas of transcendence through nature (though whether Emily takes as optimistic a view of these ideas as Sinclair is a moot point). Yet instead of considering the possibility that these images were metaphors derived from the rhetoric of Romanticism, she interpreted them as literal records of private mystical experiences which had been granted to an innocent girl unawares. Sinclair may have been right in supposing that Emily herself had faith in the reality of these epiphanies, though in fact Emily's visionary poetry is shot through with doubt. But her interpretation—like Charlotte's in *Shirley* and the preface to *Wuthering Heights*—had the uncomfortable effect of implying an absence of conscious artistry which made the poet seem like a mere vessel. It was as if only a divine miracle could explain how a reclusive young woman brought up in provincial obscurity could have achieved so much in literature.

CHAPTER NINE

The Mystic of the Moors

By 1912, when May Sinclair published *The Three Brontës*, the fact that a young woman had produced *Wuthering Heights* was still regarded as a problem in need of a solution, but three main ways of seeing had emerged in the quest to solve Emily's mystery. Essentially following Gaskell, Mary Robinson had looked for a biographical answer in the facts of family life at the Parsonage, using Branwell's chaotic behavior to explain the novel; Mrs. Humphry Ward, in contrast, had preferred to make sense of Emily's work in the context of literary history; while Sinclair herself sought a transcendental explanation.

In the years that followed, all three strands of interpretation would remain in play, though for a long time biographers and pseudobiographers would be less attracted by Ward's impersonal literary approach than by the idea that something must have *happened* to Emily to account for her creativity. While a small amount of new material came to light after the appearance of Mary Robinson's biography—most significantly, the diary papers—the real Emily would remain reconstructable only by speculation. Each new biographer would come to the field in the hope of being the one who would finally crack her code. But like the ghost-child Cathy, who calls through the window to be let in but vanishes as Heathcliff arrives to claim her, she would remain forever just out of reach.

Emily's very shadowiness would contribute to the fashion first popularized by Sinclair for calling her a mystic, a term whose echoes of "mystery" and "mystique" would add to its appeal. Recent biographers have tended to dismiss or underplay the idea that her writings were the result of personally experienced trance states or moments of ecstatic oneness with the divine.[1] Yet this view, presented in a resolutely unhistorical framework, remained a common assumption into the 1970s, the decade which also saw the release of Kate Bush's unearthly single "Wuthering Heights," sung in a freakishly high soprano in a floaty nightdress amid swirls of dry ice.[2]

It is worth revisiting the question and asking whether or not, and if so in

252 · THE BRONTË MYTH

what sense, Emily could have applied the label "mystic" to herself. The two passages from her poetry used time and again as proof that she underwent mystical experiences cannot be said to offer much in the way of evidence. The first was not even written by Emily, since it comprises the two stanzas, already discussed in chapter 7, which Charlotte added to the poem she called "The Visionary," in which the poet waits passively for the Strange Power to descend on her from above.

The second, more relevant, passage is taken from a later narrative section of what had originally been part of the same poem,[3] published in 1846 under the title "The Prisoner (A Fragment)":

> *But, first, a hush of peace—a soundless calm descends;*
> *The struggle of distress, and fierce impatience ends.*
> *Mute music soothes my breast, unuttered harmony,*
> *That I could never dream, till Earth was lost to me.*
>
> *Then dawns the Invisible; the Unseen its truth reveals;*
> *My outward sense is gone, my inward essence feels:*
> *Its wings are almost free—its home, its harbour found,*
> *Measuring the gulf, it stoops, and dares the final bound.*
>
> *Oh, dreadful is the check—intense the agony—*
> *When the ear begins to hear, and the eye begins to see;*
> *When the pulse begins to throb, the brain to think again,*
> *The soul to feel the flesh, and the flesh to feel the chain.*[4]

Later writers would read this passage not just as an account of a personal out-of-body experience, but as an ominous foreshadowing of Emily's own death. Such lines would be regarded as proof that she must have willed herself to "dare the final bound" out of this life. Virginia Moore's sensationalist 1936 biography, for example, would claim that Emily's desire to relive her mystical union with the Absolute had led her to commit suicide by self-neglect "as much as if she had drunk of a deadly poison."[5]

However, biographical interpretation of the stanzas is compromised by the fact that the narrative context in which they appear is Gondal, not personal. The passage refers to the near-death moments of a tortured prisoner, chained in a dungeon, who loses and then regains consciousness, regarding this as a longed-for liberty from pain.[6] On one level at least, Emily must have meant the lines to be taken literally in this sense. Since childhood, she would have known about the physical sufferings of prisoners during the French Revolution, which may have fed into her view of Gondal, a place riven by civil war between Royalists and Republicans. A previously unnoted article on the Terror in *Blackwood's* has sick prisoners praying for death in the dark and the narrator falling into a "deadly stupor" and then coming back to life.[7] A more significant possible literary source is Byron's poem "The Prisoner of Chillon," in which, right at the center of the poem, the narrator experiences a loss of consciousness in a dungeon:

First came the loss of light, and air,
And then of darkness too . . .
There were no stars—no earth—no time
No check—no change—no good—no crime—
But silence, and a stirless breath
Which neither was of life nor death.

Byron's prisoner has a less metaphysically complex experience than Emily's, but the basic theme is present in his text, ready for her to take up, as is some of her imagery. In his related "Sonnet on Chillon," Byron uses Epictetus's idea of the chainless soul, implicit in Emily's "the flesh to feel the chain":

Eternal spirit of the chainless Mind!
Brightest in dungeons, Liberty! thou art.[8]

The fact that Byron could have provided Emily with even the smallest inspirational trigger suggests that her poem should be read as a literary rather than simply autobiographical document.

Though there is nothing in the dungeon passage to indicate that we should read it as a personal testimony, it is hard to deny that, whatever its literal sense, it does have a penumbra of metaphorical meaning. Whether Emily herself would have defined her account of the escape of the soul from the body as "mystical" is unsure, but it is not impossible. It has to be said that during the period in which the Brontës were growing up, the term was often used in a negative sense. In a *Blackwood's* article of 1829, "mystical" is used sarcastically in an attack on Wordsworth's admirers.[9] Similarly, in his essay on the German Romantic writer Novalis written in the same year, and republished in his *Critical and Miscellaneous Essays* of

1839, Thomas Carlyle had to distinguish between the positive use of the term (as a noun) in Germany and "what we English, in common speech, call a Mystic; which means only a man whom we do not understand, and, in self-defence, reckon or would fain reckon a Dunce."[10]

Yet if, as Stevie Davies has suggested, Emily had had contact with the ideas of extreme idealists such as Novalis, either directly through her German studies or through English popularizations such as Carlyle's,[11] she could have thought of "mystic" in its positive sense. In 1849, Charlotte used the adjective in *Shirley* to refer to the heroine's soul as a treasure chest whose secret heart contains jewels of a "mystic glitter," suggesting an occult spirituality associated with the character based on her sister.[12] And while the language of "The Prisoner" does not suggest Emily was literally describing a personal experience, it does indeed echo "mysticism" in the philosophical sense in which Carlyle used it.

Explaining how Novalis interpreted the idealism of Kant, Carlyle summarizes the former's worldview in terms which suggest an uncanny linguistic parallel with Emily's use of the phrases "mute music," "the Invisible," and "the Unseen": "The Invisible World is near us: or rather it is here, in us and about us; were the fleshly coil removed from our Soul, the glories of the Unseen were even now around us; as the Ancients fabled of the Spheral Music."[13] The striking similarity of expression has not before been noticed. It may, of course, be coincidental, but it suggests that Emily's language, rather than being merely private and personal, was part of a public discourse.

As Carlyle uses it, the word "mystic" has a far more abstract, philosophical meaning than it would have a hundred years later when applied to Emily by populist twentieth-century mythographers keen to prove that her poetry derived from paranormal out-of-body experiences she had had up on the moors. It may be that Emily's visionary poems were instead consciously intended as metaphorical explorations of metaphysical ideas. Yet though some biographical writers in the twentieth century would keep alive Mrs. Humphry Ward's idea that Emily's writings should be understood within a cultural context, many would prefer to read her as a symbol of timeless spirituality. In doing so, they would be restating Charlotte's idealization of Emily in *Shirley,* and, implicitly, sentimentalizing her as childlike and naive.

For example, Winifred Gérin's biography of 1971 would remain caught in the supernaturalist rhetoric of Charlotte's preface to *Wuthering Heights.* Here, she interprets the poem "A Day Dream" as describing "a mystical experience of which every detail is sharply defined in terms of sight, sensation, hearing, giving to the incident a factual authentic quality."[14] Whether Gérin regards this as hallucination or genuine visitation is not quite clear. The lines are as follows:

> On a sunny brae, alone I lay
> One summer afternoon; . . .
> Methought, the very breath I breathed
> Was full of sparks divine,
> And all my heather-couch was wreathed
> By that celestial shine!
>
> And, while the wide Earth echoing rang
> To their strange minstrelsy,
> The little glittering spirits sung,
> Or seemed to sing, to me.[15]

It is, however, difficult to see how phrases such as "sparks divine," "celestial shine," and "glittering spirits" could be taken as particular evidence of "factual authenticity." Emily even warns us not to take her metaphors literally with the words "seemed" and "methought." And as so often in her poetry, the visionary moment is soon undercut by hints of doubt. The poem certainly shows her exploring her interest in the imagination, in the sources of poetic inspiration, and in the creative nature of perception. But it may be that she was doing so in a more conscious, less unsophisticated, way than Gérin's interpretation suggests.

Significantly, lines Gérin omits from her quotation contain parallels with Coleridge's "The Rime of the Ancient Mariner," the strongest verbal echo being the visionary "thousand thousand gleaming fires" which contrast with Coleridge's sickening "thousand thousand slimy things."[16] Gérin thus silences the literary context of the poem, making it appear as natural as the visions sent to the innocent Shirley.[17] An alternative reading by Margaret Homans in 1980 instead sees Emily's poem as engaging in a dialogue with Coleridge's,[18] and casts Emily as a conscious artist who created (as did Coleridge) "a myth of imaginative possession."[19] It had taken the best part of a century for scholars to pick up where Mrs. Humphry Ward left off and put Emily back into the context of literary history.

If Emily's "mystic" image had been hard to dislodge, it was because it had become so entrenched as part of her popular persona. In the immediate aftermath of May Sinclair's *Three Brontës,* the idea of Emily as a spiritual being proved highly appealing and contributed to the rehabilitation process begun by Mary Robinson in the 1880s. Over the next few years, Sinclair's views had reemerged in simplified form in the works of lesser writers who accepted them at face value, unaware of their philosophical background.

In 1919, for example, Esther Alice Chadwick—best known as a collector of oral history from Haworth folk who remembered the Brontës— summed Emily up in terms which reveal the direct influence of Sinclair's approach. Defending her from being "unjustly judged . . . a pagan," she employed a somewhat unfocused vocabulary of mysticism, spirituality, and union with the divine in which to praise her, announcing that her poems were "written from . . . spiritual experience."[20] Rather than suggesting that Emily's beliefs were the conscious products of her cultural environment, Chadwick characterized her as the innocent recipient of mystical experiences which came direct from God. Her Emily is less like a poet than a nondenominational, literary version of St. Bernadette, the simple country girl who received visions at Lourdes.

In her youthful rejection of her mother's Christianity for a less dogmatic form of spirituality, May Sinclair had been at the forefront of advanced Victorian thinking. By the 1920s, however, such changes in attitudes toward religion had penetrated society at large, which explains the appeal of Emily's new mystical persona. Charlotte, the dutiful clergyman's wife, had come to represent all that was constrained and doctrinaire about Victorian Anglicanism. Emily in contrast could be canonized in a vaguer, nondenominational faith, and by the 1930s she had become a saint to be spoken of in hushed tones and biblical metaphors. As E. F. Benson put it in his unsympathetic biography of Charlotte, the spiritually superior Emily possessed the "all-sufficient rapture of a mystic who waited the coming of the spirit . . . even as the prophet waited for the temple to be filled by night with the glory of the Lord."[21]

On the other hand, she was also claimed as a religious rebel, as she had been by Swinburne, and to an extent by Mary Robinson, who had read her visionary poems as spiritually heterodox. In Sylvia Townsend Warner's Brontë-inspired short story, "The Salutation" (1932), Emily stares out of the Parsonage window through the rain at her symbolic antagonist, the blackened tower of the church: "[W]as she, perhaps, imagining in herself some power superior to the godliness and deathliness of the object of her satirical scrutiny, a power that could call down the lightning-stroke upon the tower or summon from underground goblin likenesses of the dead to sit perched upon the crowding headstones?"[22] The phallic tower, associated with the Brontës' clergyman father, becomes a symbol of patriarchy in this feminist reading, in which Emily fantasizes about having her own self-created supernatural powers, but remains essentially trapped: Sylvia Townsend Warner suggests that, having internalized the judgments of her repressive father and his God, Emily is terrorized by a fear of her own rebellious imagination. On a similar, though less sophisticated note, a drama of 1933 has Emily standing up to her father, played as the embodiment of the harsh Victorian patriarch. "My God is not your God," she cries, as he accuses her of meeting a lover on the moors at night.[23]

As the word "mystic" became the standard epithet applied to Emily, its meaning became less and less clear. May Sinclair's intellectual notions of spirituality soon gave way to cruder variations on the theme. Isabel C. Clarke, for example, had a knee-jerk reaction to the religious associations of the word "mystic," leaping to the conclusion in her 1927 book, *Haworth Parsonage: A Picture of the Brontë Family,* that Emily must have been a Roman Catholic, which is bizarre if one considers the anti-Papist bigotry which existed in the Brontë household and embarrasses present-day readers of *Villette.* Charlotte had even described how in Brussels Emily's "upright, heretic and English spirit" had recoiled from "the gentle Jesuitry of the foreign and Romish system."[24] But such evidence did not dent Clarke's faith in her version of Emily. Spuriously comparing her to Catholic mystics, she believed that it was "impossible to doubt that Emily experienced certain rare spiritual joys," and concluded, "Of her it can confidently be said that she was 'not far from the Kingdom.' "[25] It would be interesting to know whether or not Clarke had Catholic sympathies of her own. Certainly, the objectivity of the biographer who found specifically Franciscan mysticism in Emily's poems begins to look shaky when one discovers that his previous book had been on St. Francis of Assisi.[26]

"Mysticism" became more and more distorted as it worked its way down through culture. Emily's role as an icon of death, ultimately derived from Charlotte's "Biographical Notice," merged with her reputation for mystical experiences to create a debased vocabulary of ghostly presences, weird out-of-body experiences, and, in the film *Devotion,* misty images of a man on a large black horse who eventually sweeps the dying Emily off to the next world. Supernatural motifs became common, whether in depictions of Haworth as a place "so remote from civilisation that only some ghostly rider . . . or dun, spectral hound with lolling tongue, were fitting company,"[27] or in interpolated scenes such as one in which a mysterious gypsy out on the moors announces that Emily holds the keys to life and death.[28]

In *Wuthering Heights,* Emily had, of course, incorporated the supernatural into her own brand of gothic, creating the most memorable ghost scene in literature, with the phantom Cathy's hand grabbing Lockwood's through the broken window.[29] The success of the scene depends in part on its ambiguity: we are left in a radically unsettled state of not knowing whether the ghost is real—as Heathcliff wants to believe—or a dream. Similarly, at the end of the novel, we hear of sightings by locals of the spectral Cathy and Heathcliff. Do we believe in these, or should we share the more skeptical view of Lockwood, who wonders, at their graveside, "how any one could ever imagine unquiet slumbers, for the sleepers in that quiet earth"?[30] Ultimately, the novel will not allow us to pin down what has happened to the lovers. Have they, like Wordsworth's Lucy, become one with the rocks and stones and trees of the natural world, or do their spirits walk abroad? It is this lack of closure that makes *Wuthering Heights* such a haunting book.

Ambiguity like this is an essentially literary quality, and attempts to reproduce it in the cinema or onstage have been fraught with difficulty. William Wyler's classic 1939 film version literalized the idea of haunting in its camp and faintly comical final image of Cathy and Heathcliff's transparent forms superimposed on a background of the snowy moors. On the other hand, Peter Kosminsky's film of 1991, starring Ralph Fiennes and Juliette Binoche, sought to "resolve" the problem of the ghost-child by transforming her hand into a real branch which has been misinterpreted by the dreaming Lockwood. Neither fully captured the tensions of the original text.

However, attempts by the fictionalizers of the 1930s and '40s to relocate the idea of the supernatural in the persona of Emily herself were even less successful, often plunging to unintended bathos. Rachel Ferguson's 1933 play about the Brontës offered an absurdly literal reading of Charlotte's claim that her sister was the passive vessel through which Fate or Inspiration poured, when Emily tells her sister, "I was on the Withens, this afternoon. . . . There are voices out there . . . that tell one what to do. . . . It's to be called *Wuthering Heights.*"[31] This Emily has a habit of seeing ghostly presences and of breaking off in midconversation to go into a trance:

Anne: . . . Emmy!

Charlotte: Don't speak to her—or touch her.

Anne: What do you mean? Charlotte, you frighten me. Why doesn't she answer? Why does she sit so still with that empty look in her eyes?

Charlotte: Ssh. I don't quite know. I never have known. I am jealous of It. While It possesses her she is no longer mine.[32]

In this context, it is not surprising that the Emily persona came to appeal to spiritualists. In 1940, a psychic clergyman, Charles L. Tweedale, decided to contact her in a séance at Haworth Parsonage with his daughter Dorothy. A somewhat petulant spirit sent back the following message:

[Y]ou must walk round my music stool and play on my piano and say "Emily Brontë I love you." . . .

Then upstairs you must go

To see my dress, and ask that you

May always be dressed in blue.[33]

Clearly, death had done little for the poetic gifts of the famous sphinx of English literature, but Tweedale was not unimpressed. "To be present on these occasions when that splendid soul proved the realisation of her trumpet blast to mankind, and manifested from 'the kingdom of the heavens,' " was, he believed, "a privilege for which to thank God."[34]

Bizarre religious interpretation of Emily probably reached its apogee in 1960 with Millicent Collard's *Wuthering Heights—the Revelation: A Psychical Study of Emily Brontë,* which asked, "[W]hat was it that Emily Brontë was hiding from the world?"[35] and answered that she had a strong psychic nature, contact with the dead, and second sight, basing its arguments on such observations as the fact that there are thirty-four chapters in *Wuthering Heights* and that Jesus died in his thirty-fourth year. As the author's excitement mounts—"the three 'crucified,' Catherine, Isabella and Cathy, the three in one, ONE on the cross. Who is the ONE?"—the prose completely breaks down into mad charts and columns.[36] Half a century down the line, May Sinclair's influential attempt to spiritualize the author of *Wuthering Heights* had mutated into a form of interpretative psychosis.

Millicent Collard's paranoid critique may seem like the work of a lone eccentric, but it reflects the process of mystification, established during the interwar period, in which the figure of Emily had become enmeshed. More

Emily Brontë by Branwell. This haunting profile is all that survives of a portrait which originally included all four Brontë siblings. Its oblique, fragmentary nature seems to echo Emily's elusiveness.

than any other biography, Romer Wilson's 1928 *All Alone: The Life and Private History of Emily Jane Brontë* exemplifies the extent to which Emily had become a magnet for fantasy. Though cast in the form of a factual life, the book tells us more about the extraordinary level of spiritual identification its subject had come to invite. As one reviewer caustically remarked of the biographer, "[O]ne hardly knows whether it is of herself or of her heroine that she is writing."[37]

Romer—christened Roma—Wilson had a number of reasons for identifying with the Brontës. A Yorkshirewoman, she had made something of a sensation with her first novel, *Martin Schüler* (1918), which she published as a young unknown under a male-sounding pseudonym. She also suffered from tuberculosis, from which she would die in her late thirties. The Emily Brontë biography was the last book she completed.

Wilson's approach can be loosely identified with aspects of a certain sort of modernism, though the quality of her work was so suspect that it was known to produce mirth in reviewers. Her best-known novel, *The Death of Society* (1921), was described by the *Times Literary Supplement* as "an ecstasy in five convulsions . . . so rapturous . . . that a prosaic reader may easily be left boggling."[38] Its title, which became a fashionable catch-phrase, reflects the attempts of post–First World War novelists to break away from the social realism of their Victorian and Edwardian predecessors and, in the words of one critic, to turn instead toward the "exploration of the individual personality."[39] As *All Alone,* the title of Wilson's biography, suggests, she would read Emily as a mythic creature existing in a space beyond and above social reality.

Brontëan influences can be traced in the last novel Wilson wrote before turning her attentions to Emily. *Greenlow* (1927) is set in the Derbyshire dales and features Jillian, a girl torn between two lovers: Jim, a local ne'er-do-well she has known since childhood, and John, an intellectual up from Bloomsbury, who is suffering the aftereffects of wartime shell shock. Jillian describes her passion for Jim, a "loose, drinking, strong young man, lazy as the devil,"[40] in language which echoes Cathy's famous "I *am* Heathcliff!": "I love Jim. He is me and I am him."[41] But she ends up with the enervated, Linton-like John, convinced she can repair his damaged soul.

Wilson combines the motif of the love triangle with the nature mysticism that had become associated with *Wuthering Heights.* "I am wild," says the repetitive Jillian. "In our valley there is a wild heart and it is mine. I am the wild heart of the valley, its only heart. . . . The valley and I live as one."[42] In this, Wilson makes use of common themes shared by many writers of the period, including D. H. Lawrence, whom she claimed as an influence in *All Alone,* and who had himself been drawn to the Brontës.

At twenty, still under his puritanical mother's thumb, Lawrence had forbidden his girlfriend Jessie Chambers to read *Wuthering Heights,* as it was still regarded as an "advanced" taste.[43] Clearly, the novel had an appealing dangerousness about it which he wanted to keep to himself. Later, he would draw on it for the plot of his first novel, *The White Peacock* (1911). After the heroine Lettie has given up on her first lover and married another for wealth and security, she has Cathy-like feelings of exclusion from the natural world: "[H]earing the winds of life outside, she clamoured to be out in the black keen storm."[44]

For the young Lawrence, the Brontës' treatment of human passion as a mythic force may have seemed revolutionary. But by the time Romer Wilson was writing, Emily's novel had begun to be sentimentalized in the popular mind, a process which would reach its apogee in the 1939 Hollywood film. In her own fiction, Wilson takes the edge off both the Brontëan and the Lawrentian influences, diluting them out of existence. Where Lawrence's novels were infamous for sexual frankness, Wilson limits physical contact to kisses, though these are usually so earth-shattering they make the heroine faint dead away. And where Emily had represented violent fits of rage with a clear-sighted lack of affectation that her contemporaries found shocking, there is nothing subversive about the insults Jillian flings at her lover, "you mucky toad" being as earthy as they get.[45]

Aspects of the artistic, nature-loving Jillian would feed into Wilson's portrayal of Emily. Charlotte had called her sister "[s]tronger than a man";[46] Jillian wears breeches and cannot think her own thoughts in female dress (though she also indulges in hyperfeminine masochistic fantasies of being beaten by her lord and master). She imagines being Byron, or, more dubiously, "Mussolini's arch-buccaneer."[47] The androgyny theme would be influential on later readings of Emily, and indeed reflected the importance of gender definition to the Brontës' self-perception as writers. Yet the way in which Wilson interpreted it had less to do with the Brontës than with her own overblown imagination.

Modernist writers such as Lytton Strachey and Virginia Woolf may have questioned the idea that facts alone could get to the heart of a life. Wilson, however, took this a stage further and expressed a scorn for accuracy and evidence that Woolf would never have countenanced. "I do not care how erroneous my statements of fact are," she announces boldly in her introduction.[48]

Faced with the paucity of the historical record concerning Emily, Wilson's dubious solution is to take refuge in the certainty of myth and in her own subjectivity. Her life of Emily begins in the standard mode for Brontë biography, with a journey to Haworth, though this time it is a trek on foot across the "bleak and black and brooding" moors rather than up Main Street.[49] She writes in the first person, in a voice that has something of the literary tourist about it: we see her sampling the Yorkshire inns en route and looking out for real-life versions of the servant Joseph from *Wuthering Heights*. Yet her lushly purple prose style soon distinguishes her from the average holiday-maker. This is not just a day trip into Yorkshire, but a journey into the heart of eternal nature, punctuated by incantatory repetitions, in which a white flower "stares like a blind white star out of the sombre afternoon"[50] and the air echoes with the ominous cry of the grouse urging the intruder to "Go back!"[51]

Confusingly, the identity of the "I" who is making the journey soon becomes muddied. In an orgy of narcissism and gender confusion, Wilson identifies herself with the timeless figure of a male hero:

> Foreigners rarely wander here, but I, who belong to these parts, like to be alone on the moors, for I know myself then and walk with myself, hand in hand. I am a hero, my own hero, the man whom no one knows. Nor do I care now that no one knows him. Alone on the moor I care for neither God nor man, but only for myself, who have always been I from the time when other folk called me a child, and before that, always, back to the beginning, if eternity ever began.[52]

The identity of this "hero" is as yet uncertain. Perhaps he is an incarnation of the "Dark Hero," a mythic archetype soon introduced as the key to understanding Emily.

According to Wilson, the Dark Hero—elsewhere called the Dark Thing or simply It—is a force as primeval as the moors themselves, which "descends upon some men and women out of a mysterious region beyond what we know as rational."[53] Taking up its abode in privileged, though tormented, individuals, it is an outcast, brooding, passionate, and ultimately destructive spirit, descended from the fallen angel Satan or perhaps from Prometheus. More recently, we are told, this Prince of Darkness has taken the shape of rebel poets such as Byron and Rimbaud. Its presence in the corporeal frame of Emily Brontë explains how she came to write *Wuthering Heights:* the demonic Heathcliff is the Dark Hero within herself and the novel tells the story of her secret soul.

Though Wilson's rhetoric has a mystical tinge, she also borrows from contemporary psychology in her quest to explain how Emily's soul was prepared for the advent of the Dark Hero. Mysticism and psychoanalysis were sometimes coupled together in the popular mind at this date, and Wilson, accordingly, looks for an emblematic childhood trauma as the key to Emily's life. She decides (on what basis it is hard to tell) that the scene in which the young Jane Eyre is shut in the Red Room as a punishment by her aunt must refer to a real-life incident in which Emily was locked up by

Aunt Branwell in the room in which her mother died.[54] (If this turns Miss Branwell into something of a wicked stepmother, Wilson's portrayal of Emily as the household drudge forced to cook and clean for the family has more than a touch of Cinderella about it.)

Such logic is typical of Wilson's method, which eschews historical reconstruction in favor of a string of symbolic, imaginatively realized moments, sometimes degenerating into slushy passages of autobiography. Hints that she identifies her own talent with Emily's genius—she condescends to explain to her less gifted readers how "[W]e who write, who create, seek and seek for the pure experience,"[55] and she seems to believe that she too has been possessed by the Dark Hero—are difficult to take in the context of her gushing and unruly prose, which could not be more different from the tight verbal economy of *Wuthering Heights*.

Some of Wilson's symbolic interpretations are not without appeal, such as the idea that the characters in *Wuthering Heights* represent aspects of Emily's own mind. Heathcliff, for example, is the rebellious, socially alienated inner self who produced the poetry and novel. Yet the core of her mythic message differs little from those Victorian critics who believed that no woman could have written *Wuthering Heights*. Emily, she argues, must have had "a man's soul in her female body." Only possession by the "Dark Hero" could explain how she had been able to do it.[56]

Romer Wilson's life of Emily came out in 1928 at a time when the Brontës were enjoying a boom, and it is possible that her books—both fiction and biography—were among the many texts which must have been at the back of Stella Gibbons's mind when she wrote her classic novel, *Cold Comfort Farm*, in 1931–32. This sophisticated and very funny book has been called "a comic encyclopedia of the fads and fancies of the period." Among these is included contemporary fascination with the Brontës.[57]

The novel is written through the detached, ironic eyes of Flora Poste, a metropolitan young woman who descends on her country cousins, the Starkadders, at Cold Comfort Farm. Through them, Stella Gibbons takes a swipe at the "loam and lovechild" school of literary ruralism, epitomized in the novels of Mary Webb (author of *Precious Bane*). In her satire on sexual passion as a mystical life force identified with the burgeoning natural world, she also fingers D. H. Lawrence, and indeed sub-Lawrentian texts like Romer Wilson's *Greenlow*. Yet other themes—the family feuds, the use of dialect, the satirical presentation of low church religious mania—reach all the way back to *Wuthering Heights*. The character of Elfine, who feels an affinity with the animal kingdom, writes poetry, and flits about the hills seeking mystic communion with Brother Wind and Sister Sun, even has something in common with current sentimentalized ideas of Emily Brontë herself.

Yet the most explicit reference to fashionable obsession with the Brontë story comes in the shape of Mr. Meyerburg, or, in his strangulated accent, "Mybug," a Bloomsburyish pseud who is working on a life of Branwell. During the 1920s, Branwell was enjoying something of a renaissance. The debate over the authorship of *Wuthering Heights* had been reignited by a minor Yorkshire nature poet named Alice Law in two books designed to bolster his claim.[58] Law's account is sympathetic to the brother at the sisters' expense, idealizing him as a blameless emblem of doomed youth. Perhaps, in the wake of the First World War, a young man's tragedy seemed to have more poignancy than the struggles of young women. Law repeated the old argument that *Wuthering Heights* could not possibly have been the work of a female, pointing to the presence of swear words and even Latinisms as supposed evidence (in fact, as we shall see, Emily must have been something of a classical scholar, since fragmentary translations of Virgil and Horace in her hand have survived).[59]

Fictionalizers of the Brontë story, such as Clemence Dane in her 1932 play *Wild Decembers* or Kathryn MacFarlane in her 1936 novel *Divide the Desolation,* soon picked up on the idea that Branwell was ultimately responsible for the novel. Mr. Mybug, who champions this view in *Cold Comfort Farm,* is thus not a wild eccentric, as readers usually suppose, but has simply jumped on the latest bandwagon. Through him, the antifeminist assumptions behind the theory are mercilessly satirized by Stella Gibbons, who herself suffered something of Emily Brontë's fate at the hands of the press. One reviewer thought her novel too sophisticated to be by a mere girl and suggested it was a pseudonymous work by Evelyn Waugh.[60] According to Mr. Mybug, no "intelligent person in Europe today" doubts Branwell's claim, for *Wuthering Heights* is so clearly "male stuff."[61]

As the narrator Flora is aware, Mybug's views on the Brontës are a reflection of his rampantly masculine viewpoint, summed up in his belief that "a woman's success could only be estimated by her sexual life."[62] His deliciously absurd inversion of the traditional Brontë story reflects his denigration of the female mind. According to his theory, not only did the talentless sisters hate their brother for his genius. They were dipsomaniacs who stole their brother's manuscripts and sold them as their own to pay for drink: Branwell, who had an overdeveloped sense of sacrifice, took the blame for their drunkenness and allowed them to claim the credit for his books.

As a satire on the interpretative methods of biography, Mr. Mybug's pronouncements are horribly apt. With subjects such as the Brontës, who had been "done" so many times before, the biographer was by the 1920s under pressure both to uncover new evidence and to stun the world with a new theory which would, in one tremendous epiphany, provide the definitive explanation for the life. Mr. Mybug does both. An amateur Freudian who sees a phallic symbol in every plant, he is keen to use fashionable psychology as the key to understanding the Brontës, but he also claims to have discovered three new letters, written by Branwell to an elderly aunt in Ireland, which conclusively prove Branwell's authorship of *Wuthering Heights*.

The texts of these letters, Mybug tells Flora, are "masterpieces of repressed passion" and full of clues that betray Branwell's incestuous desire for the old lady. Madly overinterpreting, Mybug reads his subject's enquiries after the health of his aunt's cat as proof of this "perversion." But it is the fact that Branwell does *not* mention *Wuthering Heights* that proves once and for all that he must have written it:

> Look at the question as a psychologist would. Here is a man working fifteen hours a day on a stupendous masterpiece which absorbs almost all his energy. He will scarcely spare the time to eat or sleep. He's like a dynamo driving itself on its own dynamic vitality. Every scrap of his being is concentrated on finishing *Wuthering Heights*. With that little energy he has left he writes to an old aunt in Ireland. Now I ask you, would you expect him to mention that he was working on *Wuthering Heights*?[63]

Such logic is painfully close to the mind-set of conspiracy theorist John Malham-Dembleby, who argued that Charlotte wrote *Wuthering Heights* and believed that any apparent evidence to the contrary must have been planted by her "for obfuscation's sake." But it is also prophetic of the psychoanalytic critic who used the fact that Charlotte rarely mentions her mother as his sole proof for arguing that she had an overwhelming, lifelong fixation with that parent.[64]

In turning Brontë biography into a target for mockery, Stella Gibbons disclosed what a source of mystification it had become by the 1930s. Supernaturalist readings of Emily had enhanced her mystique. But perhaps they had also inadvertently contributed to a climate in which she could be denied the authorship of *Wuthering Heights*, since it seemed hard to believe that such an attenuated, unearthly figure, dependent on visitations from the world beyond, could have written such a passionate novel. Yet while some solved the problem by promoting Branwell's claim—he, at least, was on record as having had an illicit romance with Mrs. Robinson—others had begun to wonder whether the secret of *Wuthering Heights* might lie in a love affair of Emily's own.

In having sex on the brain, *Cold Comfort Farm*'s Mr. Mybug represents a caricature of the twentieth-century biographer. The urge to get into the subject's bedroom, or, failing that, into his or her erotic fantasies, remains part of literary biography to this day. Back in 1912, May Sinclair had had an inkling of how future writers might, as she saw it, contaminate her spiritual heroine. She feared that one day "some awful worshipper of Emily Brontë, impatient of her silence and unsatisfied with her strange, her virgin and inaccessible beauty" might "make up some story of some love-affair, some passion kindred to Catherine Earnshaw's passion for Heathcliff, of which her moors have kept the secret."[65] That fear, in fact, had all too soon been realized. In keeping with late Victorian feminism's emphasis on woman's sexual purity, the Emily of Mary Robinson's 1883 biography had been utterly virginal, her sole contact with passion being through her brother's sinful tragedy, which was presented as the only possible explanation for *Wuthering Heights*. May Sinclair had followed Robinson in her insistence that there was nothing sensual in Emily's makeup.

Yet the publication of the Heger letters in 1913, which so upset Sinclair, put romantic love firmly on the Brontë agenda, and on the basis of a false analogy between the sisters, Emily's admirers did indeed begin to wonder whether Heathcliff, like Paul Emanuel in *Villette*, had been based on a real-life love. Rather than letting Emily's hero remain a literary construct, they could not resist the temptation to turn him into flesh and blood and, in the process, to bring the ethereal Emily down to earth by eroticizing her.

As a result, two parallel but conflicting strands of speculation came to dominate Emily's biographical image. One, based on mystical readings of her visionary poetry, had her as a creature not of this world, while the other, based on *Wuthering Heights,* instead insisted that she had known love. Often both views of Emily came to be found operating rather oddly in tandem, with little attempt on the part of biographers to explain or even acknowledge the apparent paradox.

For example, Esther Alice Chadwick, the collector of oral Brontë history who believed Emily's poems were inspired by a mystical union with God, also held that Emily could not have created Heathcliff without the inspiration of real-life romance. The symbolist poet Maurice Maeterlinck (whose *Pelléas et Mélisande* has distant echoes of Emily's novel) had written a critique of *Wuthering Heights* in which he declared that "[w]e feel that one must have lived for thirty years beneath burning chains of burning kisses to learn what she has learned."[66] Chadwick took this figure of speech with unwonted literalism, and cast around for a possible candidate. She came up with Constantin Heger. "Who but M. Heger could have stood as the original of Heathcliffe [*sic*]?"[67] she asked. This schoolmaster was obviously a "strong, powerful tyrant, with the pure and fierce love of a very god."[68] As for evidence of his passionate nature, almost anything would do: "Witness . . . his beautifully expressed letter of condolence to Mr. Brontë when Miss Branwell died."[69]

A similar flailing around in search of a likely lover can be seen in Isabel C. Clarke's 1927 *Haworth Parsonage.* Like Chadwick, Clarke rather unconvincingly combined a faith in Emily as virgin mystic with the belief that she must have experienced erotic love. "And in searching for the name of that man who first awoke passion within her," she went on rather desperately, "our choice is bound to fall upon the only one . . . she was ever known to tolerate."[70] This man turns out to be William Weightman, the kindhearted, flirtatious curate who was such a favorite in the Brontë household, but whose species of charm could hardly have been more different from that of the demonic antihero of *Wuthering Heights.*

The novelist Elizabeth Goudge took up this random suggestion in her play *The Brontës of Haworth,* which made for some strange dialogue. Here, Weightman gushes in purple prose, which could have come straight out of *Cold Comfort Farm,* and Emily responds with prim understatement:

> Weightman: The moors have made you and so you are made of the moors. Soul and body you are made of heather and bracken, and the west

wind talking in the grasses, and that pulsing wonderful life that runs
through springtime like a flame.

Emily: How nice![71]

Most of the candidates suggested for Emily's lover were certifiably real,
historical people, even when the theories made a mockery of the facts (an
extreme example is *Meeting Point,* a play by Isobel English, in which
Emily gives birth to a child by her own father).[72] But this could not be said
of some other attempts, which flew in the face of all evidence. The 1932 fictionalization *White Windows* featured Harry Deville, a dastardly Don
Juan who announces he will take Emily across his saddle whether she
would or no.[73] One French biographer wondered how on earth a young
girl without experience of love could have created Heathcliff, and immediately set off on a train of thought which ended in a detailed description
of a (completely invented) young farmhand—"fine, tall, with very black
eyes, brown curly hair, pale skin"—with whom Emily *must* have had a
relationship.[74]

Interestingly, the assumption that the love in *Wuthering Heights* must
have been based on personal experience seems to have coincided with the
gradual growth of the novel's popularity and its subsequent taming at the
hands of adaptors for stage and screen. As Patsy Stoneman has shown, at
the turn of the century *Wuthering Heights* was still a somewhat avant
garde or specialist interest, but during the 1930s it began to reach a wider
audience through play versions and eventually through the Hollywood
film of 1939 which would establish it as a love story with genuinely mass
appeal. By 1949, 220 million people had seen the movie.[75]

Just as biographers were trying to literalize Emily's novel by grounding
it in a real love affair, the adaptors of *Wuthering Heights* were "normaliz-
ing" its central relationship, with Cathy transformed into a capricious
Scarlett O'Hara, and the plot re-created as a clichéd narrative of the stable
boy and the lady. Luis Buñuel's 1953 film version, *Abismos de Pasión,* set
in Mexico, may have been more artistically ambitious, but it similarly con-
ventionalized the driving forces at the heart of the novel by assimilating
them into standard patterns of sexual jealousy and adultery. Emily's name,
it seems, has nowadays become a byword for clichéd passion. She was
recently voted twentieth most erotic person of the millennium, just ahead
of Errol Flynn and Josephine Baker, in a poll among the readers of the
Erotic Review.[76]

In fact, the representation of love in Emily's novel is very far from the norm of adult heterosexuality as usually represented in twentieth-century popular culture. Not only is it never consummated, but it is, in a sense, incapable of consummation, since it reaches back to the childhood time before the fall into self and other, when Cathy and Heathcliff were surrogate brother and sister, at one with each other as they scampered over the moors under the dairywoman's cloak. With its analogues in the idealized brother-sister pairings found in Byron, De Quincey, and Shelley, their relationship bears little relation to conventional courtship, unlike Jane Eyre and Rochester's.[77]

Mary Robinson and May Sinclair may have had a point when they stressed the sexless nature of the passion in *Wuthering Heights,* since the erotic and the spiritual seem to have been intriguingly coalescent in Emily's imagination. In her poem "No coward soul is mine," for example, Emily addresses the "Almighty ever-present Deity" in terms which echo Cathy's words about her love for Heathcliff. Just as, in the poem, existence centers on the divinity—

Though Earth and moon were gone
And suns and universes ceased to be
And thou wert left alone
Every Existence would exist in thee[78]

—Cathy's existence centers on Heathcliff: "If all else perished, and *he* remained, I should still continue to be; and, if all else remained, and he were annihilated, the Universe would turn to a mighty stranger. I should not seem a part of it."[79] For Emily herself, the love in *Wuthering Heights* seems to have been far closer to the spirituality of her visionary poetry than many biographers and adaptors of the novel would assume.

Among the various attempts to unearth Emily's supposed lost lover, the most notorious has to be that of Virginia Moore, who committed perhaps the greatest biographical gaffe in the history of Brontë studies in *The Life and Eager Death of Emily Brontë,* first published in 1936.

Unlike Romer Wilson, whose 1928 biography had willfully engaged in the stuff of myth, Moore announced that her aim was to strip aside legend and re-create "the irreducible Emily Brontë, unexaggerated, unaltered, unobscured."[80] She boasted that she had paid "especial and respectful" attention to primary sources.[81] However, she had such difficulty reading old handwriting that, in the course of her manuscript research, she misread the title of a poem, "Love's Farewell," as "Louis Parensell," and went on to invent a spurious lover of that name.

Hatfield, the editor of Emily's poetry, wrote to the *Times Literary Supplement* to point out the mistake.[82] But the mythic Louis went on to spend a colorful speculative existence on the letters page of the *Poetry Review,* where a correspondent suggested that Emily might have met her lover in her brother's studio at Bradford, during Branwell's brief attempt to set himself up as a portrait painter. A mysterious comment in one of the diary papers—that Emily and Anne had enjoyed a trip away from home together "except during a few hours at Bradford"—must, the correspondent concluded, have referred to sorrowful memories of the lost lover Louis.[83]

Once she hit on the idea of using Emily's poetry as biographical evidence, Moore had been overwhelmed. "Collating the poems with her life," she wrote, "was as exciting as working a new-staked gold mine."[84] Often, however, she was not so much "collating" the poetry with the life as using it as direct source material. She was indeed participating in a sort of biographical gold rush, the collective delirium which has sucked in so many of those who have attempted to dig up Emily's secret. Not content with discovering a male lover in "Louis Parensell," Moore made the equally sensational additional claim that Emily had been "a member of that beset band of women who can find their pleasure only in women."[85]

This was not the first time that lesbianism had been associated with the Brontës. E. F. Benson, in his 1932 biography, had called Charlotte's youthful relationship with Ellen Nussey "one of those violent homosexual attachments . . . so common . . . among adolescents."[86] But where Benson had been patronizing, Moore was sympathetic. Writing in the wake of Radclyffe Hall's lesbian novel *The Well of Loneliness,* which had been the subject of a notorious obscenity trial in 1928, she was keen to pose as an enlightened voice, standing up against retrogressive repression and hypocrisy, and firmly telling her readers, "We are not prudes any more."[87]

The subject had become quite a cliché in the minds of fashionable biographers. This is clear from the scene in *Cold Comfort Farm* in which Flora realizes, with a sinking heart, that "sooner or later" Mr. Mybug's conversation will turn to one of his favorite subjects, "the problem of homosexuality." She will be forced to listen to his views on "Lesbians and old maids."[88] Stella Gibbons herself had little time for such speculations. "And I suppose . . . Anne Brontë wrote *The Tenant of Radclyffe Hall*" was her tart response to speculation on the Brontës' sexuality.[89] But Virginia Moore had no such reservations. Fueled by the desire to say something new and up-to-date, she set out to establish herself on the leading edge of revelatory biography.

Moore was keen to show that Emily had been in love with an unidentified girl or woman while at Miss Patchett's school at Law Hill in Halifax, where she taught for some months in 1838–39.[90] But Moore's arguments were based on a reading of a Gondal poem beginning "Light up thy halls!," which is in fact written in the voice of a male lover, Fernando De Samara, despairing at his rejection by a female deceiver, the beautiful, dark A. G. A.[91]

Although Moore does not understand the full implications of Gondal—she mistranscribes "Gondal Poems" as "Glendale Poems"—she is still aware of the possibility that the poem is fiction. But she wants so badly for it to be autobiography that she allows her "instinct" to get the better of her. Because the beloved in the poem is female, Emily, she concludes, must have been in love with a woman. "When Emily says 'she' . . . one feels she means 'she.' Why? Because of the intensity, the immediacy, the fearful urgency of the whole poem. In that mood could she have played and dissembled, even with pronouns? One instinctively answers No."[92] Moving on to *Wuthering Heights,* she decides that Cathy must be the girl Emily fell in love with at Law Hill and that Heathcliff is a self-portrait. Like Romer Wilson, she concludes that his creator had a male soul in a female body.[93]

Despite her loud rejection of Victorian prudery, Moore thus continued to reproduce the prejudices of those nineteenth-century critics who could not believe that *Wuthering Heights* was the work of a woman. By interpreting the "unconceding masculinity" of Emily's prose style as proof of lesbianism, she judged her according to the limited definitions of so-called feminine writing current in the 1840s.[94]

Since the 1920s, biography had become more intimate, more concerned with Freudian psychology, and as a result Moore implicitly tended to marginalize external, cultural issues in favor of the inner psyche. That Emily had a preference for male roles and pseudonyms, that her nickname was "the Major," that Monsieur Heger praised her intellect and said she should have been a great navigator, that villagers remembered her whistling to her dogs, and that she was described rhetorically by Charlotte as stronger than a man are interpreted as comments on Emily's sexual desires rather than on prevailing cultural assumptions regarding "masculine" and "feminine" modes of thought, writing, and social behavior. Interestingly, in the 1880s, Mary Robinson had made Emily's tomboyish characteristics a means of emphasizing her sexlessness, rather than her sexuality. Clearly, the meaning of such social indicators is historically unstable.

How the social and the sexual interacted in individuals' experience of their own gender during the mid-nineteenth century is a far more complex question than Moore allows. It is not self-evident that the "masculine" habits to which she alludes automatically signified lesbianism in the 1830s and '40s, any more than adopting a male pseudonym—something Emily shared with Charlotte and Anne and George Eliot and many others— might have done. Even the bisexual George Sand, who wore men's clothes, did so more in a bid for freedom of movement than to signal her sexual orientation.[95] No biographer has actually suggested that Emily Brontë followed Sand in adopting male dress, though André Techiné's film *Les Soeurs Brontë* has her tramping the moors in trousers. But if her behavior appeared masculine to some of her contemporaries, it was in the context of a culture in which power, privilege, and artistic creativity—as well as whistling and having a head for logic—were routinely gendered male, and in which a woman's uninvited sexual desire, even for a man, could be designated unfeminine.

Where women take on male characteristics in Charlotte's fiction, she does not intend it as a shorthand for same-sex desire. Shirley is called a young squire or "the Captain." But this reflects the social freedom, uncommon for a woman, she has as an unmarried, orphaned heiress. When Lucy Snowe takes the part of a fop in the school play, but refuses to wear trousers, she is afraid of letting herself go. Ginevra Fanshawe, in the role of the heroine, may flirt with Lucy's character onstage. But this is designed as a complicated ruse to capture the attention of Dr. John, the man in the audience both women want. The resulting sexual electricity derives from rivalry between the two women for the same man, not from their mutual attraction.

In fact, Lucy's repressed feelings are more than sexual. They encompass the passion for life, for self-expression, and for power—as well as for Dr. John—which her marginal position as a plain, unsupported single woman prevents her from fulfilling. With little else to recommend her than her respectability, she is aware that public display might, of itself, compromise her amour propre. The trousers she won't put on do not symbolize what they would to Radcliffe Hall's generation. Instead, they indicate a fallen woman. Madame Bovary, one remembers, dons breeches for a masquerade at the moment of her lowest degradation.

Despite the doubtfulness of Virginia Moore's conclusions about Emily's

sexuality, her theory still has its champions. Camille Paglia, the provocative American critic, used Moore as the basis for her lesbian interpretation of Emily in her 1990 book, *Sexual Personae*. Though put off by
Moore's mushy sentimentalism, Paglia was prepared to swallow whole the
unsubstantiated idea of the "teen siren" who had supposedly rejected
Emily's advances at Law Hill, and went on to read the character of Heathcliff, "product of a stunning sex change," as proof of Emily's masculine
nature.[96]

Stevie Davies, too, in her recent *Emily Brontë: Heretic* (1994), revisits
the question of sexuality, but she is far more circumspect. She feels that
Emily may have had a lesbian consciousness, but freely admits she cannot
prove it. She offers a penetrating analysis of the love between Cathy and
Heathcliff as a love of sameness rather than difference. But when she gets
to the point of connecting it with Emily's own sexuality she finds herself
full of doubt as to whether or not the idea can truly be assimilated to the
homoerotic. While it makes sense to talk about the sexuality in *Wuthering
Heights*, it seems far less possible to draw conclusions about Emily's private self, which dissolves just at the moment when it seems to come within
reach.

It seems that biographers are finally ready to abandon the search for
Emily's supposed lover. Generated by a compulsive urge to pin her down
and, in a sense, to "normalize" her, it was a quest which in the end produced some absurd apocrypha. During the first half of the twentieth century, many of Emily's admirers, it seems, had difficulty allowing her to
remain shadowy: they wanted to anchor her in a world of real-life relationships because it would somehow stop her from slipping from their
grasp. Perhaps what was needed, instead, was a form of biography which
could acknowledge her elusive and ambivalent nature, and which was able
to incorporate what Keats called "negative capability": the ability to be "in
uncertainties, mysteries, doubts, without any irritable reaching after fact
and reason."[97]

No one who approaches Emily Brontë can avoid speculation—it is a necessary part of the enterprise—but the débacle of "Louis Parensell" does
seem to have acted on some subsequent biographers as a cautionary tale.
Moore had unwittingly revealed the hubris of her boast that she had discovered the "irreducable Emily." With certain exceptions, her successors
would be less reckless in their claims and would begin to refocus on

Emily's literary imagination. Eventually, Mrs. Humphry Ward's cultural—rather than biographical—interpretation of her works would start to regain currency.

In 1953, the novelist Muriel Spark published a biographical essay whose approach could not have been more different from Virginia Moore's. Instead of looking for a concrete solution to Emily's mystery in the shape of a lover, she simply accepted that her subject's outward existence at the Parsonage had been singularly quiet and uneventful. According to Spark, it was Emily's poems and novel, not anything that happened in her external life, which formed the "principal facts" of her biography.[98]

Spark's Emily has no need for the outside influence of mystical visitations or inspirational love affairs. Instead, she is a self-created being centered in the universe of her own imagination. Focusing on Emily's legendary death, Spark suggests that her posthumous reputation as a dramatic and mythic figure derived from her intense involvement in the literary worlds she created.

In Spark's view, Gondal and *Wuthering Heights* became so central to Emily's life that she ceased to distinguish between the real and the imaginary. Regarding herself as "the hero and cult of her own writings," she came under the illusion that she could "dramatize in her own person the aspirations expressed in her work."[99] Gondal's protagonists had been above the laws of everyday life. In her final illness, Emily too began to believe that she was at liberty to will or not to will death from a fatal disease, though in medical reality she had no such power. Rather than accepting, like Virginia Moore, that Emily chose death, Spark argues more skeptically that she suffered from delusions about the power of her own genius, dramatizing her own dying and believing in her "self-styled superwomanism" until the end.[100] In doing so she communicated a larger-than-life image of herself to Charlotte, who went on to transmit it to the public.

Spark's speculative reading, with its neuroticized, infantilized Emily, has the disadvantage of failing to take into account that Charlotte might have been in the conscious business of mythmaking when she described her sister to the world. One wonders, too, whether her idea that Emily could not tell reality from fantasy unconsciously derived from the semifictional role she had come to play in the popular imagination. But unlike some of its predecessors, which were flabby in construction, this short life does create the sort of coherent characterization one would expect from a good novelist, offering great aesthetic satisfaction to the reader. In doing so, it raises the Stracheyan question of to what extent the biographer should be striving to transform the raw data of biography into a unified story.

Others who approached Emily would have less faith than Spark in their ability to create unity out of the surviving fragments of their subject's life. Skepticism, rather than bold claims at mystery-solving, was beginning to make itself felt. In his 1969 study, John Hewish positively foregrounded the gaps and lacunae in the record. Even those "facts" which most would accept as givens came under scrutiny. Gaskell, for example, had described how Emily might often be found baking with a German book propped up on the kitchen table. Charlotte's letters had reported that Emily did the baking, while *Jane Eyre* had portrayed the Rivers sisters studying German. But, Hewish argued, there was no firsthand eye-witness statement to corroborate the claim that Emily was in the habit of combining the two activities. Perhaps it was Gaskell's imagination which had put them together.[101]

Hewish's skepticism may have a point, especially when one considers quite how Gaskellian the image is. Not only was Gaskell desperate to prove that a woman could pursue the life of the mind without neglecting home duties; she also found the image attractive in novelistic terms, later reusing it in a scene in "Cousin Phillis" in which the heroine studies Dante while peeling apples.[102] Ironically, however, Hewish's attempt at demystification merely creates more mystery.

Occasionally, Hewish's posture of doubt begins to feel somewhat exhausting. The amount of ink spilled over a question made mysterious by inadequate data—exactly how many months, for example, did Emily spend teaching at Law Hill?—can threaten to get out of proportion, when the truth, if it were known, might be utterly banal. It is only the fact that we cannot know the precise answer that makes the subject such a source of fascination. And anyway, what about all those months and days and hours and minutes of the life for which we do not have any record at all and which might have contained far more significant experiences or events? As Julian Barnes puts it in *Flaubert's Parrot*, "But think of everything that got away, that fled with the last deathbed exhalation of the biographee. What chance would the craftiest biographer stand against the subject who saw him coming and decided to amuse himself?"[103]

Despite his interest in the minutiae of the "Law Hill problem," Hewish was in many ways one of the clearest and most rational commentators on Emily to appear so far, primarily because of the central place he gave to the work in the life. He returned to the tradition of Mrs. Humphry Ward, placing Emily's writings in a literary, rather than mystical or purely biographical, context, looking to Byron—particularly Moore's *Life*—as well as Scott, Wordsworth, and Shakespeare in his attempt to build a picture of Emily's reading. He also took into account the periodical literature to which she undoubtedly had access.[104] In conclusion, he stated that "literary relatives of her characters are certainly easier to find than human originals."[105]

Emily's literary background was by now becoming established as something biography needed to take into account. Winifred Gérin's 1971 life may have continued to support the mystical theory of Emily as the recipient of "visitations" which eventually deserted her, leading to her death, but it nevertheless acknowledged that *Wuthering Heights* had been influenced by her reading too. Less successful than her life of Charlotte—perhaps because the biographer felt such trepidation about approaching the more difficult sister—her *Emily Brontë* was also one of the last accounts to incorporate the tradition that Emily had been particularly close to Branwell.

During the 1980s and '90s, the emphasis on Emily's literary context has become more central to her biographical persona. An exception, perhaps, is Katherine Frank's 1990 *Emily Brontë: A Chainless Soul,* which looks back to earlier psychobiographies of Charlotte in its central argument that its subject suffered from anorexia and died as a result of self-starvation. Edward Chitham's life of 1987 and Stevie Davies's of 1994, in contrast, both project images of Emily as a highly literary writer, though this often remains a question of tracing intertextual parallels which may, of course, be coincidental.

Chitham, in particular, sticks his neck out to speculate that Emily may have had a romantic obsession with the figure of Shelley. He centers his argument on a passage from Shelley's *Epipsychidion,* in fact an autobiographical poem about free love, expressed in metaphysical language, and based on the poet's relationships with his various wives, mistresses, and female friends. Shelley addresses "Emily"—actually Emilia Viviani, a beautiful teenage heiress—and asserts the Platonic union of their twin souls in terms which indeed seem to pre-echo *Wuthering Heights.* Shelley's "I am not thine: I am a part of thee" suggests Cathy's "he's more myself than I am" and "I *am* Heathcliff!," while his wish that "we two had been twins of the same mother" parallels Cathy and Heathcliff's childhood sibling relation.[106]

Despite its appeal, the idea that Emily Brontë might have read Shelley's "Emily . . ." as a personal message from the dead poet remains pure speculation. It is true that Emily could have had access to Shelley and his work: he appeared in Moore's life of Byron, he was the subject of an article in *Fraser's* in 1838, and his collected poetry, including *Epipsychidion,* was finally brought out by his widow, Mary, in 1839. Charlotte also alludes to Shelley in her novels.[107] Yet whether, as Chitham contends, certain unidentified figures in Emily's poetry can really be identified with Shelley is far from certain, especially since his name appears nowhere in her writings. In a sense, what Chitham is offering is an intellectualized version of earlier biographers' fruitless searches for a real-life lover.

Stevie Davies is less specific, and thus more convincing, in her claims. Rather than pinning her interpretation on a single text, she offers a more general investigation of the zeitgeist out of which Emily's thought might have developed, giving a suggestive analysis of the German philosophy to which she may have had access. She also reminds us that limiting our view of Emily's reading to the precise books to which we know for certain she had access may be more misleading than any refusal to overestimate her learning. Davies thus sees Emily's poetry and novel not as isolated products of divine inspiration but as embedded in a whole web of other literary sources and analogues. Future biographers, one hopes, will continue to add depth and texture to our understanding of Emily's work in its cultural context, as there is still much to be done in this area.

The appeal of this sort of approach to recent critics derives partly from a positivist urge to demystify the sphinx of English literature, partly from the feminist desire to read Emily as a conscious artist on a level with male writers. The move away from emphasizing Branwell's influence on *Wuthering Heights* can be read as another indirect consequence of feminism, though Emily's writing is less easily assimilated to the preoccupations of women's studies than Charlotte's. Yet the current emphasis on intertextuality may also reflect the poststructuralist ideology which has been such an influence on literary criticism over the past few decades. The postmodern idea of the death of the author seems to have been all but designed for the elusive Emily, who only truly exists for us as an incomplete, fragmentary body of texts.

Stevie Davies's biography is intriguing because it foregrounds the problems inherent in its own enterprise. She acknowledges the combination of exhilaration and frustration Emily excites in her, and gives a vivid picture of the relationship between biographer and fugitive biographee. At one point she describes squinting at a line of dots on a manuscript, wondering if they might not in fact be tiny letters spelling something which she cannot read and whose meaning seems to recede further and further the more she tries to focus. Perhaps any biography's attempt to bring a dead person back to life is an oddly shamanistic enterprise, doomed to failure even when the records are comparatively rich. In the end, we may have to accept that the woman who was Emily Brontë will never be fully recovered.

Yet Emily's very elusiveness has made her a site of often rich invention, a blank screen onto which imaginations can project. After writing her biography, Stevie Davies turned to fiction, perhaps feeling it was a more appropriate medium in which to dramatize this phenomenon. Her light-hearted novel *Four Dreamers and Emily* (1996) centers on a conference in Haworth. Those attending range from narcissistic autodidacts to members of the academic establishment, and Emily plays very different roles in their mental lives. Is the response of a grief-stricken widower who finds solace in seeking Emily's ghost up on the moors any less valid than that of a feminist theoretician with strong views on the Brontës and masturbation? However objective a biographer might try to be, is it right to ignore the emotional force field which surrounds Emily, or should it, as Davies suggests, be part of the investigation?

As we have seen, Emily Brontë has been a focus for speculation, but the sense in which she has become "mythic" is far deeper and more visceral than that suggests. Her myth consists not just in biographical apocrypha but in the symbolic meanings her image has taken on. In her imaginative rewritings of Emily, Charlotte transformed the flesh-and-blood woman who was her sister into something larger, and more abstract, than life: an embodiment of Romantic visionary poetics. Some later writers, too, have remodeled Emily along archetypal lines, untying her from the moorings of history to fit their own psychic universes. While it is appropriate to criticize biographers for misreading the evidence, poetic revisionings of this nature are not subject to the same documentary standards. But they often tell us less about Emily herself than they do about those responding to her magnetism.

One such example is the late British Poet Laureate Ted Hughes, in whose personal mythology Emily was a potent symbol. As Hughes was both Yorkshireman and poet, the Brontës were part of his local, as well as his literary, heritage. He even had a personal connection to the cult of Brontë relics, recording the fact that a distant cousin of his had inherited some of the Parsonage soup dishes.[108] *Wuthering Heights*—famous for its images of violence and the natural landscape—appealed directly to Hughes's sensibility; some of his acquaintance even described him as looking like Heathcliff. But Emily's meaning in his mind was bound up not only with his Yorkshire identity but with his first wife, the American poet Sylvia Plath, who commited suicide in 1963 during the breakup of their relationship.

In 1956, the newly married Hugheses had visited Haworth together and walked over the moors to Top Withens, the ruined farmhouse supposed by some to be the site of Wuthering Heights. This visit would remain as a vivid memory, and his dead wife would become a silent presence in his poems about Brontë country. In the earlier ones, the references are veiled and enigmatic. Later, in *Birthday Letters,* the autobiographical verse narrative he published shortly before he died, he was much more explicit. Emily Brontë's image became a lens through which Hughes viewed Plath's fate as he transformed them both into simplified archetypes of the female poet doomed to self-annihilation.

What is striking—and worrying—about Hughes's version of the Brontës is the way he presents their creativity as a form of destruction. They appear in the 1979 collection *Remains of Elmet,* where the poem "Haworth Parsonage" shows Hughes breathing new, if ambiguous, life into some clichéd Brontë imagery. It takes its cue from the old Gaskellian emphasis on fatalism and death, focusing, like her, on the gravestones and the bleakness of the house and moors. Like many of the popular Brontë fictions of the mid-twentieth century, it also adds a supernatural twist. But where those had often been second rate, unintentionally comical in their references to ghouls and ghosts, Hughes is deadly serious, impressive even. Unlike Gaskell's Brontë sisters, who are innocent martyrs, Hughes's are the "three weird sisters," frightening and destructive hags linked to black magic. It is the male figures in the poem who are the victims. The "stone god" of the gravestones is reduced to "imbecile silence." Branwell, poisoned by the witches' brew, is "The brother / Who tasted the cauldron of thunder." Hughes seems to hold the sisters themselves responsible for having "emptied and scarred black" the landscape.[109] Drawn to the occult and its symbolism, Hughes is quite consciously a mythmaker in the most literal sense, and his Brontë sisters are primitive, monolithic projections of male fear. Creative women, he seems to be saying, are terrifying and vindictive creatures.

"Emily Brontë," in the poem of that name, is as attracted to destruction as the hags in "Haworth Parsonage," but it is a masochistic rather than sadistic love affair. Ever since Charlotte portrayed her in the "Biographical Notice" as embracing death with grim stoicism—a view which contrasts with Charlotte's private account of her sister's end—Emily had been associated in some minds with suicidal impulses.

Hughes turns her into a nature goddess kissed to death by her "darling," the "wind on Crow Hill." By making her both fertile ("The curlew trod in her womb") and drawn to the fatal kiss of the wind (a play on the etymology of "inspiration," with its implications of breath), he transforms her creativity into a death wish. This woman, it seems, can only create in self-destruction.[110]

This echoes what is now known of Hughes's perception of Sylvia Plath. As Erica Wagner puts it, he believed that Plath's artistic endeavor as a poet had "set her on a trajectory towards her death."[111] Hughes originally made no explicit connection with Plath in "Remains of Elmet,"[112] but when he republished it in 1993, he added another poem, "Two Photographs of Top Withens," in which the association with his dead wife suddenly becomes clear. During the newly married couple's visit to the site of Wuthering Heights, Hughes had taken a picture of Plath sitting in a sycamore tree. Here, he alludes to the occasion, remembering how he had "aimed" his camera at her, its gunlike quality suggesting that he saw himself as the agent of her fate. At the time, he remembers, she may have been smiling and cheerful. But Wuthering Heights was a "fouled nest," an emblem of what would happen to their marriage.[113]

It was not until *Birthday Letters,* published in 1998, that Hughes tackled the subject of his first marriage explicitly. He described these poems as "a gathering of the occasions on which I tried to open a direct, private, inner contact with my first wife."[114] For Hughes, Plath had literally become a Cathy-like ghost, and he was the Heathcliff who strained to recapture her presence.

The section of the poem entitled "Wuthering Heights" elaborates the visit to Top Withens. On that day in 1956, Hughes suggests, his breezy, all-American wife may have seemed superficially different from the sternly tragic Emily Brontë. But in fact they were marked out as soul mates. "The moor / Lifted and opened its dark flower / For you too," he tells Plath. "You breathed it all in / With jealous, emulous sniffings. Weren't you / Twice as ambitious as Emily?"[115] Plath eventually died breathing in the poisonous fumes from a gas oven: did she, Hughes asks, always want to outdo her predecessor not only in her art but in her death? A final image has the spectral Emily looking out from death's prison through the broken, mullioned windows of Wuthering Heights, her envy of Plath's life and liberty gradually quenched by the realization of the fate in store for her.

Ted Hughes's appropriation of the figure of Emily Brontë can be seen as part of his attempt to interpret the tragedy of his own marriage in the light of mythic certainties. Plath, he suggests, was doomed from the start, and there was nothing he or she could have done to avert her fate. For Hughes—a believer in astrology—the visit to Brontë country was an omen of a future already written in the stars. Hughes's universe may not be benign, but it offers a form of certainty which may have assuaged his own survivor guilt, something to be clutched at in the quest for closure. Other commentators on Plath's suicide reject the idea that it was an inevitability, suggesting a more messy version of events in which she did not really want to die and expected to be saved. His fatalistic vision may have soothed him, just as Charlotte's efforts to heroize Emily in death were an unconscious attempt to make up for the fact that she had failed to save her.

Artistically, Hughes's appropriation of Emily may have produced some stunning poetic images. But, intellectually, his desire for certainty conflicts with what we know of the real Emily's own mind. As we have seen, the author of *Wuthering Heights* seems to have been drawn instead to ideas of uncertainty, ambiguity, and doubleness. As a result, it is only too appropriate that her literary remains are so fragmentary and inconclusive. Hughes's bid to transform her into a mythic monolith reproduces the attempts of many biographers to unify the fragments and exert control over them, but, at a deeper emotional level, it reflects his impulse to clear up the mess left by Plath's suicide by imposing fatalistic order.

Sylvia Plath also used and reused the image of the honeymoon visit to Top Withens in her writing. But unlike her husband, she was far less interested in squeezing Emily into an archetypal box. The imaginative uses she puts her to are fluid and opportunistic rather than teleological. The trip to Top Withens prompts not only poetry but a gushing letter to her mother,[116] and some story ideas.

In her book *The Haunting of Sylvia Plath*, Jacqueline Rose makes the point that Plath's writings are fragmentary, multiple, unsettled, reflecting the "provisional, precarious nature of self-representation." She describes the difficulty of pinning them down to a single, coherent reading: "From the poems to the stories, to the letters, to the journals, to the novel, what is most striking is the differences between these various utterances, each one contradicting as much as completing the others, each one no less true for the disparity which relates them and sets them apart."[117] In Hughes's imagination, Plath is a static figure, pointing in the single direction of her doom. For Rose, on the contrary, she is a creature of fluidity on whom biographers—and Hughes himself—have tried to impose an artificial unity.

Rose's reading makes sense in the context of Plath's responses to the Haworth visit, which are scattered across her writings, offering widely different styles and perspectives. The account she gave her mother at the time was upbeat, gushing with the good-girl enthusiasm typical of her letters home. "How can I tell you how wonderful it is," she wrote. "Imagine yourself on top of the world, with all the purplish hills curving away."[118] Yet this version of the experience is called into question by her poem "Two Views of Withens," written the following year, whose very title is indicative of ambivalence and double vision. The description sent to her mother has literally had the color sucked out of it: disillusion rather than exhilaration is the emotion with which she greets Cathy and Heathcliff's supposed home: "I found bare moor," she states starkly,

> *A colorless weather,*
> *And the House of Eros*
> *Low-lintelled, no palace.*[119]

Other attempts to put the visit to creative purpose—in the form of story ideas explored in her journal—are different again, revealing its unstable meaning in her imagination. At the time of the visit, she thought of using it as the basis for a ghost story.[120] A year later, she went back and transformed it into two further ideas. One is a highbrow literary fiction, told from the viewpoints of four different characters on a walk to Top Withens, exploring "the eternal paradox of identity" and the clash between "realist" and "spiritist" philosophies. The second, headed "Woman's mag," reuses the same scenario for a tale about relationships, jealousy, and female friendship.[121] Plath, who was highly conscious of writing for a market, would often try out the same theme in different styles or genres.

When she returned once more to the topic in her poem "Wuthering Heights," dated September 1961, she transformed it yet again. This time, the poet is utterly alone at the scene. Even the sycamore tree where Hughes photographed her has disappeared, for she is "the one upright / Among all horizontals." There is no human contact, only the ambiguous presence of nature. The opening image puts the poem's "I" at the heart of a vast conflagration, like a sacrificial victim: "The horizons ring me like faggots." The landscape both lures and threatens: "If I pay the roots of the heather / Too close attention, they will invite me / To whiten my bones among them."[122]

It is this sort of poem which many of Plath's readers have taken as symptomatic of her pathology, her death wish, just as *Wuthering Heights* was taken to be Emily's suicide note, and her death the final fulfillment of poetic images like those explored in "The Prisoner." Yet why should we take "Wuthering Heights" as more "true" to Plath than the story ideas or the letter to her mother? In its tight control of language and imagery, it feels more like a literary exercise than a chaotic outpouring of personal emotion. In fact, as a reading of Emily's *Wuthering Heights,* it is part of the tradition which sees the novel as a pantheistic allegory of human assimilation into nature. The Heights is where Cathy imagines she will go after death, having been thrown out of heaven by the angels. Plath is following her in making this lonely moorland hilltop a place not of this world, divorced from the petty "small change" of life in the valleys.

Plath's differing artistic responses affront the attempt to pin down the meaning of the visit to Withens in her life. Far from having a single, fatalistic significance, as she does for Hughes, Emily Brontë is for Plath an elastic imaginative construct capable of many readings.

What would Emily herself have made of later writers' imaginative responses to her? One tends to feel that the freedom and fluidity of Plath's imagination would have appealed to her more than Hughes's attempt to archetypalize her, especially considering the whiff of misogyny that hangs around his concept of the doomed and destructive female artist. The fact that Emily went on to live an afterlife in the minds of future poets would not of itself have bothered her. She had done the same with Byron, remolding him for her own imaginative purposes. Philosophically, her notion of personality was not fixed but fluid, and she might have reveled in the thought that she would post-exist herself in the imaginations of others. The idea of doing so might even have answered her own spiritual notions of the afterlife, since for her the imagination itself was the transcendent realm beyond the "final bound."

Yet one can never know what she really would have felt. Her personality remains fugitive, though its very mystery will appeal to readers and biographers for years to come. However much one accepts that it is simply not possible to be acquainted with her in any full, objective sense, she will continue to exert an imaginative pull. The few fragments of her which remain will go on posing open-ended questions. Perhaps, more of her writings may yet turn up, having been hidden away in private hands or simply overlooked. One of the diary papers is known to have existed because a photographic facsimile was made, but nobody knows where the original document is now. One tends to assume that, since Emily has attracted so many biographers, none of her extant writings would have been able to escape repeated analysis. Yet, surprisingly, it is still possible to find the odd bit of manuscript that has slipped through the net.

Considering how little prose in Emily's handwriting survives, it is hard to believe that any of it should remain unpublished. But in the King's School at Canterbury, there are two such fragments which have received little or no attention. Except for a passing, incomplete reference by Juliet Barker, neither features in any of the biographies. Indeed, even the content of the longer one was a mystery until it was recently identified by Edward Chitham, and even he had been unaware of its existence when he wrote his biography of Emily in the 1980s.

Since the 1930s, the fragments have been in the possession of the school, when the novelist Hugh Walpole, an ex-pupil, presented a huge collection of manuscripts to his alma mater. King's is an ancient institution, nestling in the shadow of Canterbury Cathedral, which has always had literary connections. It educated Christopher Marlowe in the sixteenth century, and seems an appropriately romantic home for the Walpole Collection, though it is still very much a working school, which now takes girls as well as boys. Emily Brontë hated boarding school, but what would she have thought had she been able to attend one which owned a fragment of Byron's handwriting and the complete manuscript of a novel by Scott?

Emily may not have liked schools, but the manuscripts preserved in King's imply that she did like learning. Both turn out to be translations of Latin poetry. The first, signed and dated 1838, is of the opening lines of Virgil's *Aeneid*. The second, which was only identified in 1996,[123] comprises lengthy sections of Horace's *Ars Poetica*. They suggest, at the very least, that by the age of nineteen Emily was a conscientious Latin scholar. Their evidence dispels once and for all Charlotte's image of Emily as swooning sibyl or simple country girl. They show that, whatever her sister said about her, she did have an ambition to be "learned."

Notes on the grammar of individual words show Emily's mind at work.

The struggle for accuracy is clearly important to her, and strings of question marks mark a place where she is unsure. Nevertheless, the translation, particularly of the Horace, is of a high standard—literal but flexible and skillful. Made when she was undergraduate age, it suggests quick-witted diligence and determination.

Horace's text is a treatise, in verse, on the business of writing poetry, which includes a discussion of the relative values of two qualities in the poet: "ingenium," the innate ability the Brontës would have called "genius"; and "ars," skill acquired through study. Horace satirizes the idea of the mad poet composing in a frenzy of inspiration, dependent on native genius alone. The hard work Emily put into her translation goes to show

Emily's translation of Horace reveals the extent of her classical education. The enigmatic sketches burst out of the page with their scenes of violence.

that in practice she must have taken Horace's views on the importance of "ars" seriously. However much Charlotte may have tried to mythologize her sister as a Romantic genius in the "Kubla Khan" mode, Emily was not a mere vessel for uncontrolled surgings of inspiration, but a thinking writer capable of weighing individual words with great care.

Emily's translations now live in a slim but rather portentously bound red leather book. Like so many Brontë manuscripts they are written on tiny scraps of paper, and have had to be set into larger sheets for the purposes of binding. The minute writing, now brown, is not as neat as Charlotte's, and blotches make it all the more illegible. You have to squint through a magnifying glass to make it out. The effort of doing so makes it feel like a struggle not merely to look at a string of words but to see behind the paper into Emily's mind on "March the 13 1838," the day on which she completed the Virgil. Squiggly doodles, as well as the miniature size of the handwriting, suggest that she was writing these translations not for a teacher to read, but for herself alone.

Halfway down the final page of the Horace, a group of spirited sketches breaks the page in half. A man holds a little boy up by the hair and is about to beat him while another watches. A row of books tips over domino-style. Another man is flogged next to a heap of what seem to be corpses, while a further aggressive figure brandishes a club. Are these vibrant images of violence comic or tragic? What do they mean? They don't seem to bear any direct relation to the text. Except that, a few lines above, Emily has just been translating a section on drama in which Horace argues that horrors such as Medea killing her children or Atreus cooking human flesh should not be directly represented on the stage. Are Emily's pictures—which explicitly show acts of sadism—a sort of witty rebellion against his injunction? Or do they say something darker about the imagination which would go on to produce *Wuthering Heights*?

As with most of what Emily wrote, the manuscript raises more questions than it answers. But we should, perhaps, simply accept as poetic justice the fact that she is so hard to pin down. In a paradoxical way, the endless rewriting of Emily Brontë—which will continue as long as her personality eludes us—ensures that she remains unfettered, which is, in the end, what she wanted to be. As long as posterity is unable to bind her to a fixed identity, she retains something of the independence that she sought.

As Charlotte movingly put it, liberty was the breath of Emily's nostrils. Emily herself expressed something similar through the voice of the "Old Stoic" in her poem of that name:

And if I pray, the only prayer
That moves my lips for me
Is, "Leave the heart that now I bear,
And give me liberty!"

Yes, as my swift days near their goal,
'Tis all that I implore;
In life and death, a chainless soul,
With courage to endure.

Despite the best efforts of biographers, Emily's mystery has endured. While it does, the heart of her will remain her own, elusive and unchained.

Notes

A NOTE ON SOURCES

For the Brontë novels, and for Emily's poetry, I have used Penguin editions:

Charlotte Brontë, *Jane Eyre*, ed. Michael Mason (1996)
Charlotte Brontë, *Shirley*, ed. Andrew and Judith Hook (1985)
Charlotte Brontë, *Villette*, ed. Mark Lilly, intro. Tony Tanner (1981)
Emily Jane Brontë, *The Complete Poems of Emily Brontë*, ed. Janet Gezari (1992)
Emily Jane Brontë, *Wuthering Heights*, ed. Pauline Nestor (1995) (this edition has since been revised, affecting pagination)
Anne Brontë, *Agnes Grey*, ed. Angeline Goreau (1988)
Anne Brontë, *The Tenant of Wildfell Hall*, ed. Stevie Davies (1996)

For Charlotte's letters, plus selected letters from her family and friends, I have used Margaret Smith's new Oxford edition, which has so far reached 1851. For letters after this date, I have had to rely on the Shakespeare Head Brontë edited by Thomas J. Wise and Alexander Symington (1933), despite its inadequacies of dating and transcription compared to Smith.

For other miscellaneous personal writings by Charlotte and Emily I have used Margaret Smith's *The Letters of Charlotte Brontë*. For those not included in Smith, I have used Juliet Barker's *The Brontës: A Life in Letters* (London: Viking, 1997), or I have gone back to the original manuscript source.

ABBREVIATIONS USED IN THE NOTES

Allott   Miriam Allott (ed.), *The Brontës: The Critical Heritage* (London: Routledge and Kegan Paul, 1974).
Barker   Juliet Barker, *The Brontës* (London: Weidenfeld and Nicolson, 1994).
Biographical   Charlotte Brontë, "Biographical Notice of Ellis and Acton Bell,"
Notice   for the 1850 edition of *Wuthering Heights*, reprinted in Emily Brontë, *Wuthering Heights*, ed. Pauline Nestor (London: Penguin, 1995).
BPM   Brontë Parsonage Museum
BST   *Brontë Society Transactions*

C & P	J. A. V. Chapple and Arthur Pollard (eds.), *The Letters of Mrs Gaskell* (Manchester: Mandolin, 1997).
Life	Elizabeth Gaskell, *The Life of Charlotte Brontë* (1857; London: Penguin, 1975, ed. Alan Shelston).
Preface	Charlotte Brontë, preface to the 1850 edition of *Wuthering Heights,* reprinted in Emily Brontë, *Wuthering Heights,* ed. Pauline Nestor (London: Penguin, 1995).
SH	Thomas J. Wise and Alexander Symington (eds.), *The Brontës: Their Lives, Friendships and Correspondence in Four Volumes* (Oxford: Blackwell, in the Shakespeare Head Brontë, 1933).
Smith I	Margaret Smith (ed.), *The Letters of Charlotte Brontë: Volume One, 1829–1847* (Oxford: Clarendon Press, 1995).
Smith II	Margaret Smith (ed.), *The Letters of Charlotte Brontë: Volume Two, 1848–1851* (Oxford: Clarendon Press, 2000).

CHAPTER ONE: *To Be for Ever Known*

1. Biographical Notice, p. xxxii.

2. Charlotte Brontë to Robert Southey, 29 Dec. 1836. Charlotte's letter has not survived, but Southey's reply of 12 March quotes these words of hers. Smith I, p. 166.

3. Ibid. Charlotte describes the Poet Laureate as "stooping from a throne of light & glory."

4. Biographical Notice, p. xxvii.

5. Ibid. "Averse to personal publicity, we veiled our own names . . ."

6. Pam Hirsh, "Charlotte Brontë and George Sand: The Influence of Female Romanticism," *BST* 21 (1996), pp. 209–18.

7. CB to William Smith Williams, 19 Dec. 1849, Smith II, p. 312.

8. See Christine Alexander, *The Early Writings of Charlotte Brontë* (Oxford, 1983).

9. The "Islanders" play was established Dec. 1827. See Charlotte Brontë, "The History of the Year" (1829), Christine Alexander (ed.), *An Edition of the Early Writings of Charlotte Brontë,* vol. I, *The Glass Town Saga, 1826–1832* (Oxford, 1987), p. 5.

10. Charlotte Brontë, "The Origin of the Islanders" (12 March 1829), in ibid., p. 6.

11. Margaret Smith notes that in the period before 1829 during which the Brontës formed their attachment to *Blackwood's,* they borrowed the magazine from a neighbor, Mr. Driver, probably the Reverend Jonas Driver who died aged thirty-five in December 1831. His death would explain why in May 1832 Charlotte writes to Branwell from Roe Head to say she is glad that their aunt has consented to take *Fraser's,* since they would otherwise be without a periodical publication at all. However, it seems that they soon found another source for *Blackwood's.* Sometime in the year ending 8 April 1833, Patrick Brontë joined the Keighley Mechanics' Institute, four miles' walking distance from Haworth, enabling his children to borrow books from its lending library, most probably including *Blackwood's,* to which the library had apparently taken out a subscription. (In 1841 it held eleven volumes of *Blackwood's.*) See Smith I, pp. 112–14, especially notes 7 and 8.

12. Leigh Hunt, "Lord Byron and His Contemporaries," *Blackwood's* 23, March 1828, pp. 362, 364.

13. *Blackwood's* 27, Feb. 1830, p. 389.

14. Alexander, *The Early Writings of Charlotte Brontë* (Oxford, 1983) p. 227.

15. Charlotte Brontë, *The Poetaster* (July 1830), in Alexander, *An Edition of the Early Writings of Charlotte Brontë*, vol. I, *The Glass Town Saga,* pp. 179–96. The manuscript shows Charlotte's ambivalence toward her own role as author: the title page to vol. 1 of the play announces it as being by Lord Charles Wellesley, while the title page to vol. 2 adds the name Charlotte Brontë underneath the pseudonym (pp. 179, 187).

16. Ibid., p. 180.

17. Ibid., p. 181.

18. Sue Lonoff (ed. and trans.), *Charlotte Brontë and Emily Brontë: The Belgian Essays* (New Haven and London, 1996), introduction, p. lii.

19. Signed "Marquis of Douro, Charlotte Brontë," dated 13 Nov. 1830, Tom Winnifrith (ed.), *The Poems of Charlotte Brontë* (Oxford, 1984), p. 128.

20. Ibid., p. 129.

21. See *Blackwood's* 26, Sept. 1829, p. 462. The Wordsworthian poet, with a soul as boundless as nature herself, can transcend what he beholds in nature "by the divine faculty with which he pierces things invisible."

22. Wordsworth's poetry and theory were the subject of a serialized debate in *Blackwood's* 26, Sept.–Dec. 1829, pp. 453–63, 593–609, 774–88, 894–910; Coleridge's philosophy of the imagination was tackled by J. A. Heraud in "Some Account of Coleridge's Philosophy," *Fraser's* 5, June 1832, pp. 585–97.

23. "Unimore. A Dream of the Highlands," by Professor Wilson, *Blackwood's* 30, 1831, p. 141.

24. Alexander, *The Early Writings of Charlotte Brontë* (Oxford, 1983) pp. 21–22.

25. *London and Westminster Review,* 1838, 12 & 55, p. 323. In 1841, the Keighley Mechanics' Institute library had "*Westminster Review,* in parts" among its books. See Clifford Whone, "Where the Brontës Borrowed Books," *BST* 11 (1960), pp. 344–58.

26. Charlotte must have also seen the long review which appeared in *Blackwood's* in February 1830, since she borrowed from it the image of the great poet as a "fixed star" for Rhymer. *Blackwood's* 27, Feb. 1830, p. 389.

27. Macaulay, review of Moore's *Life* of Byron, *Edinburgh Review,* June 1831, reprinted in Andrew Rutherford (ed.), *Byron: The Critical Heritage* (London, 1970), p. 313. This number of the *Edinburgh Review* may have been held by the Keighley Mechanics' Institute library. In 1841, it held "six parts" of the magazine. See Whone, "Where the Brontës."

28. The sub-Byronic heroes of the fashionable novels of the period, such as Edward Bulwer-Lytton's *Pelham* (1828), with their amoral tales of political and sexual intrigue among the aristocracy, may also have influenced her. The 1841 list of books in the Keighley Mechanics' Institute library includes *Pelham.* See Whone, "Where the Brontës."

29. CB to Ellen Nussey, 4 July 1834, Smith I, p. 130.

30. Roe Head Journal, 11 August 1836, Juliet Barker (ed.), *The Brontës: A Life in Letters* (London, 1997), p. 39.

31. Juliet Barker, *The Brontës* (London, 1994), pp. 1–2.

32. The poems she sent to Southey reflected her interest in both types of Romanticism, the Byronic and the visionary: according to Margaret Smith, she probably sent a long Byronic poem in *Don Juan* meter, finished 19 July 1836, and a three-stanza visionary poem of Oct. 1836. Smith I, p. 167.

33. Ibid., pp. 166–67.

34. Ibid., p. 166.

35. As an ardent young man he had been connected with Coleridge's abortive attempt to set up a Utopian community or "Pantisocracy."

36. Smith I, p. 167.

37. CB to Ellen Nussey, 10 May 1836, Smith I, p. 144.

38. CB to Robert Southey, 16 March 1837, Smith I, p. 169.

39. Ibid.

40. Robert Southey to CB, 22 March 1837, Smith I, p. 170.

41. See Smith I, p. 238, note 1.

42. CB to Hartley Coleridge, 10 Dec. 1840, Smith I, p. 241.

43. See Smith I, p. 238, note 4, where she cites Melodie Monahan's suggestion that what Charlotte sent him was a draft of her incomplete early novel, *Ashworth.*

44. Quoted in Hirsh, "The Influence," pp. 209–10.

45. CB to Ellen Nussey, 20 Aug. 1840, Smith I, p. 226.

46. Lonoff, *Charlotte Brontë and Emily Brontë*, p. 362.

47. Particularly interesting is the suggestion that she took some of her Angrian manuscripts with her to Brussels and gave at least one of them to Constantin Heger. See Christine Alexander, *Charlotte Brontë's High Life in Verdopolis: A Story from the Glass Town Saga* (London, 1995), p. ix.

48. CB to Constantin Heger, 24 July 1844, Smith I, p. 358.

49. Charlotte's last surviving letter to Heger is dated 18 Nov. 1845. In it, she begs to be allowed to write to him again the following May. As no subsequent letter survives, Margaret Smith suggests that Heger may have rejected her plea to write again and thus put a final end to the correspondence (Smith I, p. 437, note 10). However, Charlotte may herself have taken the decision not to write, having found distraction from her obsession with Heger in the project of publishing her own and her sisters' poems.

50. CB to Messrs. Aylott and Jones, 28 Jan. 1846, Smith I, p. 445.

51. Biographical Notice, p. xxvii.

52. See CB to W. S. Williams, 15 Dec. 1847, Smith I, p. 576, in which she states that apart from the 1846 *Poems*, " 'Jane Eyre' and a brief translation of some French verses sent anonymously to a Magazine are the sole productions of mine that ever appeared in print." The magazine has not been traced. Gaskell gives an anecdote about Anne (*Life*, p. 291) telling Ellen Nussey that she had had a poem inserted in *Chamber's Journal.*

53. *Dublin University Magazine*, Oct. 1846, Allott, p. 63.

54. *Critic*, 4 July 1846, Allott, p. 59.

55. Biographical Notice, p. xxviii.

56. George Smith, "Charlotte Brontë," *Cornhill Magazine* 9, Dec. 1900, reprinted in Harold Orel (ed.), *The Brontës: Interviews and Recollections* (London, 1997), p. 90.

57. *Atlas,* 23 Oct. 1847, Allott, p. 68.

58. Allott, p. 67.

59. Thackeray to William S. Williams, 23 Oct. 1847, Allott, p. 70.

60. *Fraser's,* Dec. 1847, Allott, p. 86.

61. Allott, p. 84.

62. See Sydney Dobell's comments on *Jane Eyre* in *The Palladium* (Sept. 1850): "This 'I', that seems to have no inheritance in the earth, is an eternity with a heritage in all heavens." Quoted in Kathleen Tillotson, *Novels of the Eighteen-Forties* (Oxford, 1954), p. 299.

63. G. H. Lewes, Allott, p. 84.

64. Ibid., p. 86.

65. *Jane Eyre,* p. 284.

66. W. M. Thackeray to W. S. Williams, 23 Oct. 1847, Allott, p. 70.

67. Compare Charlotte's letter—

My relatives Ellis and Acton Bell and myself, heedless of the repeated warnings of various respectable publishers, have committed the rash act of printing a volume of poems.

The consequences predicted have, of course, overtaken us; our book is found to be a drug; no man needs it or heeds it (CB to Hartley Coleridge, 16 June 1847, Smith I, p. 531).

—and this passage from G. H. Lewes's *Ranthorpe* (Leipzig, 1847, p. 15), in which a young writer tries to sell his poems to a publisher, but discovers that owing to the sluggish market he will have to foot the bill himself if he wants to see them in print (as the Brontës had to in the case of their *Poems*):

"Ah, my dear Sir, you are young yet, or you would know that we *never* purchase such things."

"But if you admire them?"

"The public won't buy them. Poetry, Sir, is a drug; a drug, Sir. I couldn't sell 'Childe Harolde' if it were now first published."

68. *Christian Remembrancer,* April 1848, Allott, p. 88.

69. According to Margaret Smith, J. G. Lockhart reported to Elizabeth Rigby on 13 Nov. 1848 two surmises which had been doing the rounds: that the Bells were three Lancashire weavers and that the author of *Jane Eyre* was Thackeray's lover. The second rumor was probably not in circulation until publication of the second edition of *Jane Eyre,* which Charlotte dedicated to Thackeray, in January 1848. See Smith I, p. 562, note 5.

70. See ibid., p. 587, note 1.

71. See Orel, *The Brontës,* pp. 90–91.

72. CB to Mary Taylor, 4 Sept. 1848, quoted in ibid., p. 118.

73. CB to William Smith Williams, 13 July 1848, Smith II, p. 84.

74. CB to William Smith Williams, 20 April 1848, Smith II, p. 51.

75. CB to Ellen Nussey, 3 May 1848, Smith II, p. 62.

76. CB to William Smith Williams, 4 Jan. 1848, Smith II, pp. 3–4.

77. Ibid.

78. Over a year later, one gossip who was still casting around for ways to be let in on the secret was the novelist and future Brontë biographer Elizabeth Gaskell. Elizabeth Gaskell to Eliza Fox, 26 Nov. 1849, C & P, p. 90.

79. Analyses of the Brontës' critical reception vary. Miriam Allott in her introduction feels that Gaskell exaggerated the abuse heaped on *Jane Eyre* and reminds us that the novel was also admired and appreciated. However, Tom Winnifrith, in *The Brontës and Their Background: Romance and Reality* (Oxford, 1973), chapter 7, concludes that moral objections to the Bells, intensifying particularly after the publication of *The Tenant of Wildfell Hall*, were widespread. Many critics who freely admired the Brontës for their literary power nevertheless still chastised them for coarseness. It seems most true to say that although reactions were often mixed, the novels developed an undoubted *reputation* for scandal, and that it was in reaction against this reputation that the Brontës' public image was first forged by Charlotte and later by Elizabeth Gaskell.

80. *Examiner,* Jan. 1848, Allott, p. 222.

81. *Jane Eyre,* preface to 2nd edition, p. 5.

82. *Christian Remembrancer,* April 1848, Allott, p. 89.

83. *Spectator,* 8 July 1848, Allott, p. 250.

84. CB to Mary Taylor, 4 Sept. 1848, Smith II, p. 113.

85. *Rambler,* Sept. 1848, Allott, p. 267.

86. *Sharpe's London Magazine,* Aug. 1848, Allott, p. 263.

87. *North American Review,* Oct. 1848, Allott p. 97.

88. Elizabeth Rigby, unsigned notice, *Quarterly Review,* Dec. 1848, Allott, p. 106.

89. Ibid., p. 109.

90. Ibid., p. 111.

91. CB to WSW, 25 June 1849, Smith II, p. 224.

92. When William Smith Williams raised objections to the curates, Charlotte asked him if this was "because knowing as you now do the identity of 'Currer Bell'—this scene strikes you as unfeminine—?" She refused to drop the scene. (CB to WSW, ?c. 10 Feb. 1849, Smith II, p. 181.)

93. Smith II, pp. 242–45.

94. CB to WSW, ?31 Aug. 1849, Smith II, p. 246.

95. CB to WSW, ?c. 15 Sept. 1849, Smith II, p. 254.

96. CB to WSW, ?c. 24 Nov. 1849, Smith II, p. 296.

97. CB to George Smith, 19 Nov. 1849, Smith II, p. 290.

98. CB to EN, 22 Nov. 1849, Smith II, pp. 293–94.

99. CB to WSW, 31 July 1848, Smith II, p. 95.

100. *Life,* p. 391.

101. Charles and Frances Brookfield, *Mrs. Brookfield and Her Circle,* SH, vol. III, p. 50.

102. George Smith's account stresses Charlotte's anger, while Elizabeth Gaskell's foregrounds her fear and delicacy. See George Smith, "Charlotte Brontë," *Cornhill Magazine,* Dec. 1900, quoted in Orel, *The Brontës,* p. 99, and *Life,* pp. 446–48.

103. The phrase, from the *North British Review,* is quoted by CB in a letter to WSW, 16 Aug. 1849, Smith II, p. 235.

104. G. H. Lewes, *Edinburgh Review,* Jan. 1850, Allott, p. 163.

105. Reported by George Smith, quoted in Orel, *The Brontës,* p. 100.

106. Plot summarized by Tom Winnifrith in *The Brontës and Their Background,* pp. 101–02.

107. George Smith, quoted in Orel, *The Brontës,* p. 100.

108. Ibid., p. 99.

109. CB to G. H. Lewes, 18 Jan. 1848, Smith II, p. 14.

110. Ibid.

111. See, for example, Elizabeth Gaskell's friend Catherine Winkworth in a letter to Eliza Paterson, 5 Dec. 1849: "In power and in descriptions of scenery, there is nothing in 'Shirley' which seems to me to come up to some parts of 'Jane Eyre,' but then there is nothing also in 'Shirley' like the disagreeable parts of 'Jane Eyre.' " Smith II, p. 303.

112. Biographical Notice, p. xxxii.

113. Ibid., p. xxx.

114. Ibid., p. xxvi.

115. 1850 Preface, *Wuthering Heights,* p. xxxvii.

116. Ibid., p. xxxiii.

117. G. H. Lewes, *Leader,* 28 Dec. 1850, Allott, p. 292.

CHAPTER TWO: *Poor Miss Brontë*

1. Charles Kingsley to Elizabeth Gaskell, 14 May 1857, Allott, p. 343.

2. *Life,* p. 498.

3. Harriet Martineau, *Autobiography,* ed. Maria Weston Chapman (Boston, 1877), vol. II, pp. 21–25, quoted in Harold Orel (ed.), *The Brontës: Interviews and Recollections* (London, 1997), p. 125.

4. *Life,* p. 392.

5. Harriet Martineau to ?Thornton Hunt, 24 Jan. 1851, Smith II, pp. 564–65.

6. Quoted in Elaine Showalter, *A Literature of Their Own* (1977; London, 1982), p. 75.

7. See Deirdre d'Albertis, "Bookmaking out of the Remains of the Dead," in *Victorian Studies,* Autumn 1995, pp. 1–31, for its perspective on the Brontë-Gaskell relationship.

8. Elizabeth Gaskell to Charlotte Froude, c. 25 Aug. 1850, C & P, p. 128.

9. Reginald Blunt, *Memoirs of Gerald Blunt, His Family and Forebears* (London, 1911), p. 66.

10. E. and G. Romieu, *The Brontë Sisters* (London, 1931), p. 253; quoted by Juliet Barker in her introduction to the Brontës' *Selected Poems* (London, 1993), p. xxvii.

11. *Life,* p. 108.

12. EG to ?Anne Shaen, ?24 April 1848, C & P, p. 57.

13. CB to William Smith Williams, ?c. 24 Nov. 1849, Smith II, p. 296.

14. EG to Marianne Gaskell, May–June 1854, C & P, p. 860. Mrs. Gaskell gives her

daughter permission to read the novel: "I am afraid I never told you that I did not mind your reading Jane Eyre."

15. *Life,* p. 495.

16. EG to Charlotte Froude, c. 25 Aug. 1850, C & P, p. 129.

17. EG to Eliza Fox, c. Feb. 1850, C & P, p. 106.

18. Ibid., p. 107.

19. Jenny Uglow, *Elizabeth Gaskell: A Habit of Stories* (London, 1993), p. 3.

20. EG to ?Catherine Winkworth, ?late Nov. 1849, C & P, p. 93.

21. EG to Anne Shaen, 20 Dec. 1849, C & P, p. 96.

22. Ibid., p. 97.

23. CB to EN, 19 Mar. 1850, Smith II, p. 366.

24. EG to Lady Kay-Shuttleworth, 14 May 1850, C & P, p. 116.

25. *Life,* p. 334.

26. *Saturday Review,* 4 April 1857, Angus Easson (ed.), *Elizabeth Gaskell: The Critical Heritage* (London, 1991), p. 378.

27. CB to WSW, 12 May 1848, Smith II, p. 66.

28. EG to Lady Kay-Shuttleworth, 14 May 1850, C & P, p. 117–18.

29. "Woman in Her Psychological Relations," *Journal of Psychological Medicine and Mental Pathology* 4, 1851, p. 35, quoted in Sally Shuttleworth, *Charlotte Brontë and Victorian Psychology* (Cambridge, 1996), p. 200.

30. Shuttleworth, *Charlotte Brontë,* p. 199.

31. "Woman in Her Psychological Relations," p. 35, quoted in ibid., p. 200.

32. EG to Lady K-S, 14 May 1850, C & P, p. 116.

33. E. S. Dallas, *Blackwood's,* July 1857, Easson, *Elizabeth Gaskell,* p. 405.

34. CB to EN, 26 Aug. 1850, Smith II, p. 450.

35. EG to Catherine Winkworth, 25 Aug. 1850, C & P, p. 123.

36. Ibid.

37. Ibid.

38. "Woman in Her Psychological Relations," p. 35, in Shuttleworth, *Charlotte Brontë,* p. 200.

39. EG to Catherine Winkworth, 25 Aug. 1850, C & P, p. 123.

40. Ibid., p. 124.

41. Ibid.

42. *Agnes Grey,* p. 61.

43. EG to Catherine Winkworth, 25 Aug. 1850, C & P, p. 124.

44. For example: Irene Cooper Willis's *The Brontës* (1933); Virginia Moore's *The Life and Eager Death of Emily Brontë* (1936); Ernest Raymond's *In the Steps of the Brontës* (1948); Margot Peters's *Unquiet Soul: A Biography of Charlotte Brontë* (1975); and Katherine Frank's *Emily Brontë: A Chainless Soul* (1990).

45. EG to Catherine Winkworth, 25 Aug. 1850, C & P, pp. 124–25.

46. Barker, pp. 106–09, explodes most of Gaskell's accusations against Patrick Brontë.

47. EG to Catherine Winkworth, 25 Aug. 1850, C & P, p. 125.

48. In a letter of 1835, Patrick Brontë mentions that Charlotte and Emily are soon to leave for Miss Wooler's school at Roe Head and announces his decision to

keep Anne at home "under her Aunt's tuition, and my own." If, as this suggests, he was expecting to teach Anne, it is pretty certain that he might have taught his other daughters too. See Patrick Brontë to Mrs. J. C. Franks, 6 July 1835, Smith I, p. 141.

49. Ibid., p. 126.

50. Lyndall Gordon, *Charlotte Brontë: A Passionate Life* (London, 1994), p. 223.

51. Emily Winkworth to Catherine Winkworth, 30 Aug. 1850, SH, vol. III, p. 151.

52. Ibid.

53. *Life,* p. 56.

54. CB to Margaret Wooler, 27 Sept. 1850, Smith II, p. 477.

55. EG to Eliza Fox, 27 Aug. 1850, C & P, p. 130.

56. CB to WSW, 5 Sept. 1850, Smith II, p. 463.

57. *Life,* p. 495.

58. Ibid.

59. Ibid., p. 532.

60. EG to Catherine Winkworth, 25 Aug. 1850, C & P, p. 125.

61. *Villette,* p. 111.

62. On 31 Aug. 1849, CB had written to WSW of Emily and Anne, "[T]he hour may come when the spirit will move me to speak of them, but it is not come yet" (Smith II, p. 246). On 27 Sept. 1850 she wrote to tell him that she had decided to write a preface to *Wuthering Heights* (Smith II, p. 479).

63. Barker, pp. 92–93.

64. Charles Lemon, *Early Visitors to Haworth* (Haworth, 1996), p. 42.

65. Barker, p. 93.

66. Margaret Connor, "Jane Eyre: The Moravian Connection," *BST* 22 (1997), pp. 37–43.

67. Barker, p. 368.

68. Christine Alexander and Jane Sellars, *The Art of the Brontës* (Cambridge, 1995), pp. 25–26.

69. CB to Ellen Nussey, 11 Feb. 1834, Smith I, p. 126.

70. CB to Branwell Brontë, 17 May 1832, Smith I, p. 112.

71. BB to William Wordsworth, 10 Jan. 1837, Smith I, p. 160.

72. Serialized in *Blackwood's,* 1828–29.

73. Kathleen Wallace, *Immortal Wheat* (London: Heinemann, 1951), p. 38; CB's diary extract, from the so-called Roe Head Journal, was not published until 1941, when it appeared in Fannie E. Ratchford's *The Brontës' Web of Childhood* (New York, 1941).

74. Manuscript in BPM: Bonnell 98 (6v).

75. Dorothy Helen Cornish, *These Were the Brontës* (New York, 1940), p. 1.

76. On one walk in the Lakes, Gaskell used the scenery as an excuse to quiz Charlotte about the moors around Haworth, EG to Unknown, C & P, p. 127.

77. CB to EG, 1 June 1853, SH, vol. IV, p. 70.

78. EG to WSW, 15 Dec. 1855, C & P, p. 375.

79. *Villette,* p. 153.

80. Ibid., p. 421.

81. Ibid., p. 418.

82. CB to G. H. Lewes, 6 Nov. 1847, Smith I, p. 559.

83. EG to Mrs. W. M. James, 29 Oct. 1851, Smith II, p. 707. EG reports the following comment from CB: "If I had to earn my living, I would go out as a governess again, much as I dislike the life; but I think one should only write out of the fulness of one's heart, spontaneously."

84. CB to EG, 27 Aug. 1850, Smith II, p. 456.

85. *Westminster Review* 52, Jan. 1850, pp. 352–78.

86. CB to EG, 27 Aug. 1850, Smith II, p. 457.

87. Despite the metaphors of revolution used in *Jane Eyre*, Charlotte was never really a political feminist. She was more interested in exploring the subjective effects on the female mind of society as it was, than in promoting a program of social reform. Ironically, the Victorian feminism which developed in the 1860s and '70s in reaction against the Contagious Diseases Acts—under which women suspected of prostitution could be locked up and forcibly examined by doctors—would owe less to the Romantic individualism of *Jane Eyre* or *Villette* than to the philanthropic moralism found in Mrs. Gaskell's fiction. *Ruth* was regarded by the campaigner Josephine Butler as one of the founding texts of the social purity movement, which tended to rely on an idealized view of women as the innocent, passionless victims of the corrupt male sexuality, which was held responsible for the evil of prostitution. See Deirdre d'Albertis, *Dissembling Fictions: Elizabeth Gaskell and the Victorian Social Text* (London, 1997), p. 81.

88. EG to Lady K-S, 12 Dec. 1850, C & P, p. 139.

89. CB to George Smith, 22 Sept. 1851, Smith II, p. 699, begins on a cheerful note: "I am sure I am not low-spirited just now, but very happy and in this mood I will write to you."

90. CB to EG, 20 Sept. 1851, Smith II, p. 696, ends in gloomy tones: "You charge me to write about myself. What can I say on that precious topic? My health is pretty good. My spirits are not always alike. Nothing happens to me. I hope and expect little in this world—and am thankful that I do not despond and suffer more."

91. CB to George Smith, 19 April 1851, Smith II, pp. 606–07.

92. For example, *Sharpe's*, quoted in Easson, *Elizabeth Gaskell*, p. 208.

93. *Ruth*, ed. Alan Shelston (1853; Oxford, 1985), p. 44.

94. G. H. Lewes, review of *Villette* and *Ruth* in the *Westminster Review*, April 1853, Allott, pp. 210–11.

95. CB to WSW, 9 March 1853, SH, vol. IV, p. 51.

96. See Sally Shuttleworth's fascinating reading of the novel in *Charlotte Brontë and Victorian Psychology* (Cambridge, 1996), which aligns Charlotte's depiction of mental states with aspects of contemporary psychological theory and discusses the ways in which she both incorporates and challenges these views.

97. Matthew Arnold to Arthur Hugh Clough, 21 March 1853, Cecil Y. Lang (ed.), *The Letters of Matthew Arnold* (London and Charlottesville, 1996), vol. I, p. 258.

98. *Jane Eyre*, p. 498.

99. Matthew Arnold, from a letter to Mrs. Forster, 14 April 1853, Allott, p. 201.

100. *Villette*, pp. 275–78.

101. See Pauline Nestor, *Female Friendships and Communities* (Oxford, 1985), chapter 2, for a rosier view of the Gaskell-Brontë relationship.

102. CB to EG, 9 July 1853, SH, vol. IV, pp. 76–77.

103. *Spectator,* 15 Jan. 1853, Gasson, *Elizabeth Gaskell,* p. 212.

104. CB to EG, 26 April 1852, SH, vol. III, p. 332.

105. EG to Lady Kay-Shuttleworth, 7 April 1853, C & P, p. 228.

106. Ibid., pp. 228–29.

107. CB to GS, 30 Oct. 1852, SH, vol. IV, p. 13.

108. Harriet Martineau, *Daily News,* 3 Feb. 1853, Allott, pp. 172–73.

109. Harriet Martineau to CB, undated, SH, vol. IV, p. 41.

110. CB to Harriet Martineau, undated, SH, vol. IV, p. 42.

111. *Jane Eyre,* p. 125.

112. EG to Anne Robson, before 27 Jan. 1853, C & P, p. 220.

113. Anne Mozley, unsigned review, *Christian Remembrancer,* April 1853, Allott, p. 207.

114. Ibid., p. 203.

115. Ibid., p. 207.

116. CB to the Editor of the *Christian Remembrancer,* 18 July 1853, SH, vol. IV, p. 79.

117. EG to Unknown, end of Sept. 1853, C & P, p. 248.

118. EG to ?John Forster, Sept. 1853, C & P, p. 246.

119. EG to Lady Kay-Shuttleworth, 7 April 1853, C & P, p. 228.

120. Ellen Nussey, *Reminiscences of Charlotte Brontë,* Smith I, p. 592.

121. EG to John Forster, Sept. 1853, C & P, p. 244.

122. EG to Richard Monckton Milnes, 29 October 1853, C & P, p. 253.

123. See Barker, pp. 967–68, note 96; also the appendix to John Maynard's *Charlotte Brontë and Sexuality* (Cambridge, 1984; 1987), pp. 218–24, for another view, which questions the idea that Charlotte was pregnant.

124. EG to John Greenwood, 4 April 1855, C & P, pp. 335–36.

125. EG to John Greenwood, 12 April 1855, C & P, p. 337. That Gaskell used the word "induced" in this technical sense is suggested by Anna Unsworth in "Mrs Gaskell and Charlotte Brontë," *Gaskell Society Newsletter* 8, Aug. 1989, cited in Uglow, *Elizabeth Gaskell,* p. 656, note 4.

126. EG to GS, 4 June 1855, C & P, p. 346.

127. EG to GS, 31 May 1855, C & P, p. 345.

CHAPTER THREE: *Life into Literature*

1. Quoted in Jenny Uglow, *Elizabeth Gaskell: A Habit of Stories* (London: Faber, 1993), p. 397.

2. Henry James, "The Lesson of Balzac," in *Two Lectures* (Boston and New York, 1905), pp. 63–64; cited in Annette Tromly, *The Cover of the Mask: The Autobiographers in Charlotte Brontë's Fiction* (Victoria, 1982), p. 13.

3. Patrick Brontë to Elizabeth Gaskell, 16 June 1855 (misdated 16 July), SH, vol. IV, p. 190.

4. Harriet Martineau, obituary of Charlotte Brontë, *Daily News,* April 1855, Allott, pp. 303–04.

5. Matthew Arnold, "Haworth Churchyard," *Fraser's Magazine,* May 1855, Allott, p. 309.

6. R. W. Franklin (ed.), *The Poems of Emily Dickinson* (Cambridge, Mass., 1998), vol. I, 146, pp. 187–88.

7. Ellen Nussey to Arthur Bell Nicholls, 6 July 1855, SH, vol. IV, p. 189.

8. See Smith I, p. 27, note 1, where it is suggested that the author may have been Frank Smedley, an ex-editor of *Sharpe's* and acquaintance of Catherine Winkworth's.

9. Janet Malcolm, *The Silent Woman* (1993; London, 1994), pp. 10–11.

10. Elizabeth Gaskell to Ellen Nussey, 24 July 1855, C & P, p. 361.

11. Ibid.

12. Ellen Nussey had "more than five hundred" letters from Charlotte, from which she selected a number to be perused by Mrs. Gaskell, who chose to use extracts from 330 for her biography. See Smith I, pp. 28–29.

13. Elizabeth Gaskell to Ellen Nussey, 6 Sept. 1855, C & P, p. 370.

14. *Life,* p. 384.

15. Marion Harland, *Charlotte Brontë at Home* (New York and London, 1899), p. 279.

16. See EG to GS, 15 Nov. 1856, C & P, pp. 420–21; also EG to GS, 22 Nov. 1856, C & P, p. 422.

17. See Alison Kershaw, "The Business of a Woman's Life: Elizabeth Gaskell's *Life of Charlotte Brontë,*" *BST* 20 (1990).

18. *Life,* pp. 444–45.

19. To Unknown, 23 Aug. 1855, C & P, p. 369.

20. James Fitzjames Stephen, unsigned notice, *Edinburgh Review,* July 1857, in Angus Easson (ed.), *Elizabeth Gaskell: The Critical Heritage* (London, 1991), pp. 417–18.

21. Elizabeth Gaskell, *Ruth* (1853; Oxford, 1985), p. 1.

22. *Life,* p. 352.

23. Ibid., p. 182.

24. Rev. W. H. Draper, *Yorkshire Post,* 14 Jan. 1914, press cutting, Brontë Parsonage Museum archive.

25. James, "The Lesson of Balzac," p. 65.

26. *Life,* p. 55.

27. For accounts of the relationship between CB and George Smith, see Lyndall Gordon, *Charlotte Brontë: A Passionate Life* (London, 1994), chapter 7. Also Barker, chapters 22–25.

28. See Barker, p. 784.

29. *Life,* p. 443.

30. Ibid., p. 491.

31. EG to Lady Kay-Shuttleworth, 7 April 1853, C & P, p. 229.

32. EG to George Smith, 1 Aug. 1856, C & P, pp. 400–01.

33. EG to Ellen Nussey, 9 July 1856, C & P, p. 394.

34. Ibid.

35. EG to George Smith, 1 Aug. 1856, C & P, p. 401.

36. EG to George Smith, ?25 July 1856, C & P, p. 398.

37. EG to Emily Shaen, 7 and 8 Sept. 1856, C & P, p. 410.

38. See Charlotte Brontë, *The Professor,* ed. Margaret Smith and Herbert Rosengarten (Oxford, 1987), introduction, p. xxxi.

39. EG to George Smith, 2 Oct. 1856, C & P, p. 417.

40. EG to George Smith, ?25 July 1856, C & P, p. 398.

41. EG to Emily Shaen, 7 and 8 Sept. 1856, C & P, p. 411.

42. *Life,* p. 90.

43. EG to Ellen Nussey, 9 July 1856, C & P, pp. 395–96.

44. Ibid., p. 396.

45. *Life,* p. 98.

46. Ellen Nussey, "Reminiscences of Charlotte Brontë," Smith I, p. 590.

47. Juliet Barker (ed.), *The Brontës: A Life in Letters* (London, 1997), p. 29.

48. *Life,* p. 87.

49. Ibid., p. 210.

50. Ibid., p. 93.

51. Ibid., pp. 116, 115.

52. EG to George Smith, 2 Oct. 1856, C & P, p. 418.

53. Elizabeth Rigby, *Quarterly Review,* Dec. 1848, Allott, p. 111.

54. See Barker, p. 459.

55. *Life,* p. 273.

56. EG to George Smith, 29 Dec. 1856, C & P, p. 432.

57. *Life,* p. 335.

58. Ibid., p. 444.

59. Ibid., p. 281.

60. Ibid., p. 280.

61. Ibid., p. 283.

62. Ibid., p. 281.

63. Ibid., pp. 263–64.

64. Ibid., p. 305.

65. Ibid., p. 511.

66. Elizabeth Rigby, *Quarterly Review,* Dec. 1848, Allott, p. 109.

67. *Life,* p. 295.

68. Ibid., pp. 306–07.

69. Ibid., pp. 316–17.

70. George Smith, "Charlotte Brontë," *Cornhill Magazine,* Dec. 1900, reprinted in Harold Orel (ed.), *The Brontës: Interviews and Recollections* (London, 1997), p. 87.

71. EG to George Smith, 26 Dec. 1856, C & P, pp. 429–30.

72. *Life,* p. 326.

73. Ibid., p. 360.

74. Ibid., p. 334.

75. Ibid., p. 398.

76. Gaskell mistakenly supposes the letter was addressed to Wordsworth. *Life,* pp. 201–02.

77. *Life,* p. 277.

78. Roe Head Journal, c. Oct. 1836, Barker (ed.), *A Life in Letters,* p. 40.

79. May Sinclair, *The Three Brontës* (London, 1912), p. 239.

80. Gaskell's last novel, *Wives and Daughters* (1866), is particularly full of allusions to fairy tale.

81. EG to George Smith, ?early Aug. 1857, C & P, p. 463.

82. EG to Emelyn Story, 8 Feb. 1857, C & P, p. 445.

83. Barker, pp. 795–96. The first edition comprised 2,021 copies.

84. Fifteen hundred extra copies were printed on 22 April, and a further seven hundred on 4 May 1857. Barker, p. 796.

85. *Athenaeum,* SH, vol. IV, p. 224.

86. EG to Ellen Nussey, 16 June 1857, C & P, p. 453.

87. Oscar W. Firkins, *Empurpled Moors* (Minnesota, 1932), p. 144.

88. See Daphne du Maurier, *The Infernal World of Branwell Brontë* (London, 1960), chapter 13.

89. See Barker, p. 897, note 6, and p. 459.

90. See *Life,* p. 41, "A Note on the Text," and appendix A.

91. EG to George Smith, ?early Aug. 1857, C & P, p. 463.

92. See *Life,* pp. 617–18, note 6.

93. Elizabeth Gaskell to Martha Brown, 3 Sept. 1857, C & P, p. 470.

94. K. A. R. Sugden, *A Short History of the Brontës* (Oxford, 1929), p. 108.

95. Pearl Mary Teresa Craigie.

CHAPTER FOUR: *The Angel in the House*

1. Henry William Dulcken, *Worthies of the World: A Series of Historical and Critical Sketches of the Lives, Actions, and Characters of Great and Eminent Men of All Countries and Times* (London, ?1881).

2. Harriet Martineau, *The Westminster Review,* 1 July 1857, Angus Easson (ed.), *Elizabeth Gaskell: The Critical Heritage* (London, 1991), p. 427.

3. *The Spectator,* 4 April 1857, Easson, *Elizabeth Gaskell,* pp. 380, 381.

4. *The Economist,* 18 May 1857, Easson, *Elizabeth Gaskell,* p. 387.

5. *The Manchester Examiner and Times,* 2 May 1857, Easson, *Elizabeth Gaskell,* p. 390.

6. *Fraser's Magazine,* May 1857, Easson, *Elizabeth Gaskell,* p. 397.

7. *The Christian Observer,* July 1857, Easson, *Elizabeth Gaskell,* p. 411.

8. Harriet Martineau, *Westminster Review,* 1 July 1857, Easson, *Elizabeth Gaskell,* p. 427.

9. Samuel Smiles, *Self-Help,* quoted in Ira Bruce Nadel, *Biography: Fiction, Fact, and Form* (London and Basingstoke, 1984), p. 21.

10. Ibid., p. 27.

11. Ibid., p. 20.

12. Anthony Trollope, *The Way We Live Now* (1875; London, 1993), pp. 1–2. Lady Carbury's aim is not to educate her audience but to titillate them with her pictures of "these royal and luxurious sinners."

13. The demand for model lives of women was growing, as is shown by the addition, in 1847, of a supplement of "female examples" to the work which had inspired the young Samuel Smiles, George Craik's successful two-volume *The Pursuit of Knowledge Under Difficulties Illustrated by Anecdotes* (1830–31), see Nadel, *Biography*, p. 23.

14. Charlotte Brontë, Roe Head Journal, 11 Aug. 1836, Barker, *A Life in Letters*, p. 39.

15. Robert Cochrane, *Lives of Good and Great Women* (London and Edinburgh, 1888), preface.

16. Samuel Smiles, *Character* (1871; London, 1897), p. 43. Quoted in Alison Kershaw, "The Business of a Woman's Life: Elizabeth Gaskell's *Life of Charlotte Brontë*," *BST* 20 (1990), p. 16.

17. Quoted in Rebecca Fraser, *Charlotte Brontë* (London, 1988), p. 333.

18. Dorothy Mermin, *Godiva's Ride* (Bloomington and Indianapolis, 1993), p. xiv.

19. William H. Davenport Adams, *Stories of the Lives of Noble Women* (London, 1867; revised ed. 1904), preface.

20. Anon., *Fifty Famous Women: Their Virtues and Failings, and the Lessons of Their Lives* (London, 1864), pp. 1–2.

21. Ibid., p. 3.

22. Anon., *Women of Worth: A Book for Girls* (London, 1859), p. v.

23. *Shirley,* p. 107.

24. Ibid., p. 190.

25. Robert Cochrane, *Lives of Good and Great Women* (London and Edinburgh, 1888), p. 253.

26. Anon., *Women of Worth,* p. 12.

27. J. S. Mill, *On the Subjection of Women,* quoted in Fraser, *Charlotte Brontë,* p. 333.

28. Anon., *Women of Worth,* p. 7.

29. Ibid., pp. 19–20.

30. Davenport Adams, *Stories of the Lives of Noble Women,* p. 287.

31. Charles Bruce, *The Book of Noble Englishwomen: Lives Made Illustrious by Heroism, Goodness and Great Attainments* (London and Edinburgh, 1875), p. 5.

32. Anon., *Women of Worth,* opposite p. 18.

33. Anon., *Worthies of the World,* p. 817.

34. Joseph Johnson, *Heroines of Our Time* (London, 1860), p. 117.

35. Anon., *Women of Worth,* p. 12.

36. Ellen Nussey, "Reminiscences of Charlotte Brontë," *Scribner's Monthly,* May 1871, reprinted in Harold Orel (ed.), *The Brontës: Interviews and Recollections* (London, 1997), p. 14.

37. Thomas Wemyss Reid, *Charlotte Brontë: A Monograph* (London, 1877), p. 229.

38. See Patsy Stoneman, *Brontë Transformations: The Cultural Dissemination of "Jane Eyre" and "Wuthering Heights"* (London, 1996), chapter 1.

39. Margaret Oliphant, *Blackwood's Magazine,* May 1855, Allott, p. 311.

40. Stoneman, *Brontë Transformations,* p. 28.

41. Quoted in Kathleen Tillotson, *Novels of the Eighteen-Forties* (Oxford, 1954), p. 57.

42. Jonathan Gathorne-Hardy, *The Public School Phenomenon* (1977; London: Penguin, 1979), p. 262.

43. Grace Milne Rae, *Thoughts from Charlotte Brontë Gathered from Her Novels* (Edinburgh, 1912).

44. Harold F. B. Wheeler, "On Certain Brontë MSS," *The Bibliophile* 2, no. 12, Feb. 1909, p. 287.

45. Thomas Stanley Wilmot, *Twenty Photographs of the Risen Dead* (London, 1894), p. 54.

46. See Elaine Showalter, *A Literature of Their Own: British Women Novelists from Brontë to Lessing* (1977; revised ed. London, 1982), p. 106.

47. Ibid., p. 103.

48. E. S. Dallas, *Blackwood's,* July 1857, Easson, *Elizabeth Gaskell,* p. 406.

49. Emily Winkworth to Catherine Winkworth, 30 Aug. 1850, SH, vol. III, p. 151.

50. Margaret Oliphant writing in 1897, quoted in Kershaw, "The Business of a Woman's Life," pp. 12–13.

51. May Sinclair, *The Three Brontës* (London, 1912), p. 238.

52. Ibid.

53. Ibid., p. 237.

54. Ibid., p. 238.

55. Ibid.

56. Ibid., p. 239.

57. Suzanne Raitt, *May Sinclair: A Modern Victorian* (Oxford, 2000), p. 23.

58. Theophilus E. M. Boll, *Miss May Sinclair: Novelist* (Cranbury, New Jersey, 1973), p. 27.

59. Ibid., p. 40.

60. Raitt, *May Sinclair,* p. 50.

61. Ibid., p. 109.

62. Paula Bennett, *Emily Dickinson* (Hemel Hempstead, 1990), pp. 14–15.

63. See Judith Farr, *The Passion of Emily Dickinson* (Cambridge, Mass., 1992), chapter 4.

64. R. W. Franklin, ed., *The Poems of Emily Dickinson* (Cambridge, Mass. and London, 1998), 146, vol. I, pp. 187–88.

65. *English-Woman's Journal* 4 (1860), p. 345.

66. *Shirley,* p. 167.

67. Ibid., p. 385.

68. Millicent Garrett Fawcett, *Some Eminent Women of Our Times* (London and New York, 1889), p. v.

69. Ibid., p. 100.

70. Ibid., p. 107.

71. F. L. Clarke, *Golden Friendships: Sketches of the Lives and Characters of True and Sincere Friends* (London, 1884), p. 159.

72. Millicent Garrett Fawcett, *Some Eminent Women,* p. 109.

73. Ibid., p. 110.

74. Clara H. Whitmore, *Women's Works in English Fiction from the Restoration to the Mid-Victorian Period* (New York and London, 1910), preface.

75. *Evening Post,* 28 Oct. 1913, BPM archive.

76. *Lady's Pictorial,* 22 April 1916, p. 571.

77. Maude Goldring, *Charlotte Brontë: The Woman* (London, 1915), pp. 12–13.

78. J. M. Robertson, "Why Charlotte Brontë Still Evokes a Personal Devotion," *Sunday Chronicle,* 9 April 1916.

79. EG to ?John Forster, Sept. 1853, C & P, p. 243.

80. "J. W. E," "A Day at Haworth," *Bradford Observer,* 19 Nov. 1857, p. 8; quoted in Barker, p. 811.

81. W. H. Cooke, "A Winter's Day at Haworth," *St. James's Magazine* 21, Dec. 1867–March 1868, p. 166.

82. Thomas Ackroyd, "A Day at Haworth" (1857), reprinted in Charles Lemon (ed.), *Early Visitors to Haworth* (Haworth, 1996), p. 37.

83. Ibid.

84. Walter White, *A Month in Yorkshire* (1858); quoted in J. Copley, "An Early Visitor to Haworth," *BST* 16 (1973), pp. 219–21; also Lemon, *Early Visitors,* p. 43.

85. John Elliot Cairnes, letter to a friend, 1858, reprinted in Lemon, *Early Visitors,* p. 48.

86. Charles Hale, letter to his mother, 11 Nov. 1861, Lemon, *Early Visitors,* p. 80.

87. Ibid., p. 81.

88. Patrick Brontë to T. Franklin Bacheller, 22 Dec. 1858, MS in Pierpont Morgan Library: Bonnell, MA2696.

89. Margaret Smith, "A Reconstructed Letter," *BST* 20 (1990), pp. 42–47.

90. Charles Mackay, *Extraordinary Popular Delusions and the Madness of Crowds* (1841; Ware, 1995), p. 695.

91. Quoted from a letter to W. W. Yates from an American in the *Reporter,* 17 Feb. 1894, BPM archive.

92. Mary Butterfield, "Face to Face with the Brontës?" *Sunday Times Magazine,* 17 Oct. 1976, p. 65.

93. Helen H. Arnold, "Reminiscences of Emma Huidekoper Cortazzo, 1866–1882," *BST* 13 (1958), p. 222.

94. Emile Langlois, "One Hundred Years Ago," *BST* 16 (1973), p. 223.

95. Charles Lemon, *A Centenary History of the Brontë Society, 1893–1993,* supplement to *BST* 20 (1993), p. 9.

96. Ibid., pp. 6–8.

97. Ibid., pp. 2–3.

98. Ibid. In the event, Reid was ill and his speech was read out by W. S. Cameron, editor of the *Leeds Mercury.*

99. Virginia Woolf, "Haworth, November 1904," in Lemon, *Early Visitors,* p. 126.

100. Ibid., p. 124.

101. For the complex history of the letters, including various abortive earlier attempts at publication, see Smith I, pp. 27–71. See also Barbara Whitehead, *Charlotte Brontë and Her "Dearest Nell"* (Otley, 1993), "The Saga of the Letters," pp. 192–249.

102. See Richard Altick, *The English Common Reader* (Chicago, 1957), chapter 12, for a discussion of book prices in the 1840s.

103. This was Charlotte Brontë's salary from the White family at Rawdon in 1841 after £4 had been deducted for laundry. CB to Ellen Nussey, ?3 March 1841, Smith I, p. 246.

104. See Kathleen Tillotson, "Back to the Beginning of This Century," *BST* 19 (1986), pp. 3–17, for a discussion of the Brontës' mass readership.

105. Chris Baldick, *The Social Mission of English Criticism, 1848–1932* (Oxford, 1987), chapter 3.

106. Joseph Shaylor, *Some Favourite Books and Their Authors* (London, 1901), pp. 35–40.

107. Jeanette Winterson, *Oranges Are Not the Only Fruit* (London, 1985), p. 74.

108. *Leeds Mercury,* 14 May 1913, BPM archive.

109. John Urry, *The Tourist Gaze* (London, 1990), pp. 24–25.

110. Johnnie Gray, *Where to Spend a Half-Holiday: One Hundred and Eighty Pleasant Walks Around Bradford* (Bradford, 1890), p. v.

111. H. Wild, *Holiday Walks in the North-Countree* (London and Manchester, 1912), p. 7.

112. Gray, *Where to Spend,* p. vi.

113. J. S. Fletcher, *Nooks and Corners of Yorkshire* (London, 1911), p. 56.

114. Wild, *Holiday Walks,* p. 149.

115. Rachel Ferguson, *Charlotte Brontë: A Play in Three Acts* (London, 1933), p. 14.

116. Ibid., p. 17.

117. Ibid., p. 13.

118. Ibid., p. 16.

119. *The Times,* 19 Feb. 1994.

120. For the lack of sewers in Haworth, see Barker, p. 95.

121. CB to William Smith Williams, 15 June 1848, Smith II, p. 72.

122. W. H. Cooke, "A Winter's Day at Haworth," *St. James's Magazine* 21, Dec. 1867–March 1868, p. 167.

123. Gray, *Where to Spend,* p. 94.

124. Karen V. Kukil, ed., *The Journals of Sylvia Plath, 1950–62* (London, 2000), pp. 580–82.

125. See Lemon, *A Centenary History,* p. 60.

126. *Telegraph and Argus,* 13 March 1999.

127. Sally Shuttleworth, *Charlotte Brontë and Victorian Psychology* (Cambridge, 1996), p. 22.

128. Lemon, *A Centenary History,* p. 140.

129. Richard Hargreaves, "Why It's Going to Be a Long Hot Summer," *Keighley News,* 28 March 1997.

130. Ibid.

131. J. A. Mackereth, *Storm-Wrack and Other Poems* (London, 1927), p. 3.

132. "Step into the Past" brochure, Past Times, 1999.

133. "How Should Haworth Deal with Tourism?" *Keighley News,* 5 March 1999, p. 7.

134. For example, "Wear Your Wellies to Wuthering Heights," *Independent,* 21

May 1994, Weekend section, p. 42; "Cathy Comes Home to Brontëland," *Sunday Telegraph*, 12 Dec. 1993, Review section, p. 24; "Windswept Heights of Passion," *Daily Telegraph*, 28 Sept. 1996, Arts section, p. 5.

135. Unidentified press cutting.

136. Norman Shrapnel, "The Brontë Shrine: Shivers and Gloom Live," unidentified press cutting.

137. Brontë Natural Spring Water Ltd., P.O. Box 99, Haworth, Yorks.

138. Elizabeth Gaskell to George Smith, 29 Dec. 1856, C & P, p. 434.

139. "Corking Plan to Bottle Brontës," *Independent on Sunday*, 14 March 1993.

CHAPTER FIVE: *Secrets and Psychobiography*

1. A. S. Byatt, *Possession: A Romance* (London, 1990).

2. Clement Shorter's view in the *Times*, 30 July 1913.

3. Madame Heger compared Charlotte's behavior to the hysteria of those *exaltées* schoolgirls she often came across as a headmistress. See M. H. Spielmann, *The Inner History of the Brontë-Heger Letters* (London, 1919), p. 2.

4. Frederika Macdonald's view in *The Secret of Charlotte Brontë* (London, 1914).

5. Many psychobiographies take this line, for example Lucile Dooley in "Psychoanalysis of Charlotte Brontë, as a Type of the Woman of Genius," *American Journal of Psychology* 21, July 1920, pp. 221–72; or Kate Friedlander's 1941 essay, "Charlotte Brontë: A Study of a Masochistic Character," reprinted in Hendrick M. Ruitenbeek, ed., *The Literary Imagination and the Genius of the Writer* (Chicago, 1965).

6. See Fannie E. Ratchford, *The Brontës' Web of Childhood* (New York, 1941), pp. 162–64.

7. See Lyndall Gordon, *Charlotte Brontë: A Passionate Life* (London, 1994), chapter 4.

8. Quoted in Ira Bruce Nadel, *Biography: Fiction, Fact and Form* (London, 1984), p. 144.

9. CB to Ellen Nussey, 6 March 1843, Smith I, p. 311.

10. CB to Ellen Nussey, ?late June 1843, Smith I, p. 325.

11. Spielmann, *The Inner History*, pp. 2–3.

12. CB to Ellen Nussey, May 1842, Smith I, p. 285.

13. Macdonald, *The Secret*, p. 188.

14. CB to Victoire Dubois, 18 May 1844, Smith I, p. 346.

15. To CB from "Mathilde," ?July 1844, Smith I, pp. 353–54 (translation from the French).

16. The Roe Head Journal has Charlotte "toiling for nearly an hour with Miss Lister, Miss Marriott & Ellen Cook striving to teach them the distinction between an article and a substantive." MS in BPM: Bonnell 98(8).

17. CB to Emily Brontë, 2 Sept. 1843, Smith I, p. 330.

18. CB to Ellen Nussey, 13 Oct. 1843, Smith I, p. 334.

19. CB to Constantin Heger, 24 July 1844, Smith I, p. 357 (translation from the French).

20. Ibid., p. 358.

21. CB to Constantin Heger, 8 Jan. 1845, Smith I, p. 379 (translation from the French).

22. Ratchford, *The Brontës' Web*, p. 164.

23. Constantin Heger refers to his cigar in a letter to another former pupil, quoted in Barker, p. 419.

24. See John Maynard, *Charlotte Brontë and Sexuality* (1984; Cambridge, 1987), pp. 69–70, for a discussion of cigars as symbols of virility in the juvenilia.

25. In this last surviving letter, Charlotte asks permission to write to Heger again the following May, but as no more letters survive, this may in fact have been her final letter to him. See Smith I, note 10, p. 437.

26. Gordon, *Charlotte Brontë*, p. 118.

27. It is not known how often Heger wrote to Charlotte. Her letter of 24 July 1844 says it is not her turn to write, implying that there had already been some exchange of correspondence. A lost letter of Charlotte's of 18 May 1845 was perhaps written in answer to one from him: writing on 18 November, she tells him that his letter has sustained her for six months. See Smith I, p. 359, note 1 and p. 437, note 1.

28. Virginia Woolf, *The Waves* (1931; New York, 1959), p. 259, quoted in Nadel, *Biography*, p. 166.

29. CB to Constantin Heger, 24 July 1844, Smith I, p. 359.

30. See Barbara Whitehead, *Charlotte Brontë and Her "Dearest Nell"* (Otley, 1993), pp. 218–19.

31. Thomas Wemyss Reid, *Charlotte Brontë: A Monograph* (London, 1877), p. 2.

32. Ibid., p. 6.

33. Ibid., p. 59.

34. Ibid., p. 63.

35. Ibid., p. 62.

36. Augustine Birrell, *Life of Charlotte Brontë* (London, 1887), p. 78.

37. Ibid., p. 82.

38. Ibid., pp. 77–78.

39. Marion Harland, *Charlotte Brontë at Home* (New York and London, 1899), p. 158.

40. Laura Carter Holloway, *An Hour with Charlotte Brontë, or, Flowers from a Yorkshire Moor* (New York, 1883), p. 9.

41. Ibid., p. 12.

42. Ibid., p. 26.

43. Ibid., p. 10.

44. Ibid., p. 23.

45. John Malham-Dembleby, *The Key to the Brontë Works* (London, 1911), p. 166 and passim.

46. Ibid., p. 104.

47. Ibid., p. 127.

48. The theory derives from Malham-Dembleby recognizing similarities between *Jane Eyre* and "Kitty Bell, the Orphan," a tale within a tale in the serial, which was originally published in English in 1850–51 as a supposed translation of a work by Sue,

in the *London Journal* under the title "Mary Lawson," and was later reissued in French in Paris in abbreviated form as *Miss Mary, ou l'Institutrice*. Instead of concluding the obvious—that "Kitty Bell" was a cheap plagiarism of the recent best-seller *Jane Eyre*—Malham-Dembleby uses the similarities as proof that Sue had access to the secret truth of Charlotte's life, not only as regards the Cowan Bridge–like school in "Kitty Bell," but apropos the love triangle which features in the rest of the fiction, and which he reads as an account of the relationship between Charlotte and the Hegers. Fact and fiction could not be more confused. See also Smith II, p. 499, note 3, for further comment on "Kitty Bell."

49. For example, Herbert E. Wroot, "The Persons and Places of the Brontë Novels," *BST* 3 (1906), pp. 5–237.

50. Reported in the *Sphere*, 16 Aug. 1913, and the *Yorkshire Observer*, 18 Oct 1913, press cuttings, BPM archive.

51. Spielmann, *The Inner History*, p. 1.

52. Paul Heger to M. H. Spielmann, quoted in Macdonald, *The Secret*, p. 33.

53. Ibid., p. 34.

54. *Yorkshire Observer*, 22 Aug. 1913, letter from Stanley Rogers, BPM archive. In fact, Patrick and Mary Burder had been briefly engaged before his first marriage, and he later unsuccessfully courted her again after the death of his wife. See Barker, pp. 19–23, 113–15.

55. Clement Shorter, *Charlotte Brontë and Her Circle* (London, 1896), p. 110.

56. Clement Shorter, interviewed in the *Times*, 30 July 1913, quoted in Macdonald, *The Secret*, p. 40.

57. William Robertson Nicholl, letter to the *Times*, 30 July 1913, BPM archive.

58. *Yorkshire Post*, 22 Aug. 1913, BPM archive.

59. May Sinclair, *The Three Brontës* (London, 1914), p. vi.

60. Ibid., p. v.

61. R. Brimley Johnson, *Some Contemporary Novelists (Women)* (London, 1920), pp. xiv–xv, quoted in Elaine Showalter, *A Literature of Their Own* (1977; revised ed., London, 1982), p. 241.

62. May Sinclair, *The Creators* (1910), quoted in Suzanne Raitt, *May Sinclair: A Modern Victorian* (Oxford, 2000), p. 125.

63. Ibid., p. 122.

64. Sinclair, *The Three Brontës*, p. 26.

65. Ibid., p. 72.

66. Ibid., p. 21.

67. Raitt, *May Sinclair*, p. 64.

68. Ibid., p. 120.

69. Boll, *Miss May Sinclair*, p. 263, note 33.

70. Raitt, *May Sinclair*, p. 120.

71. Quoted in Penny Brown, *The Poison at the Source: The Female Novel of Self-Development in the Early 20th Century* (London, 1992), p. 14.

72. Raitt, *May Sinclair*, pp. 100–02.

73. Quoted in Boll, *Miss May Sinclair*, p. 214.

74. Sinclair, *The Three Brontës*, p. 118.

75. See Sheila Jeffreys, *The Spinster and Her Enemies: Feminism and Sexuality, 1880–1930* (London, 1985).

76. Macdonald, *The Secret*, p. 146.

77. Newspaper cutting, BPM archive. Review of production at the Leeds Art Theatre, 1955.

78. Quoted in Patsy Stoneman, *Brontë Transformations: The Cultural Dissemination of "Jane Eyre" and "Wuthering Heights"* (London, 1996), pp. 176–77.

79. Spielmann, *The Inner History*, p. 11.

80. Angus M. Mackay, *The Brontës: Fact and Fiction* (London, 1897), p. 33.

81. Virginia Woolf, "The Art of Biography," in *Collected Essays* (London, 1966–67), vol. 4, p. 226.

82. *Examiner*, 11 April 1857, Easson, *Elizabeth Gaskell*, pp. 382–83.

83. *Life*, p. 259.

84. *Manchester Examiner and Times*, 2 May 1857, Easson, *Elizabeth Gaskell*, p. 390.

85. *Journal of Psychological Medicine and Mental Pathology*, Forbes Winslow (ed.), no. 10, April 1858, pp. 295–317.

86. Ibid., pp. 313–14.

87. Ibid., p. 317.

88. Sigmund Freud, "Leonardo da Vinci and a Memory of His Childhood" (1910), in Peter Gay (ed.), *The Freud Reader* (London, 1995), p. 448.

89. Lucile Dooley, "Psychoanalysis of Charlotte Brontë, as a Type of the Woman of Genius," *American Journal of Psychology* 21, July 1920, p. 243.

90. Woolf, "The Art of Biography," *Collected Essays*, p. 225.

91. Dooley, "Psychoanalysis of Charlotte Brontë," p. 222.

92. Ibid.

93. Ibid., p. 223.

94. Ibid.

95. Ibid., pp. 252, 223.

96. Ibid., pp. 231, 263.

97. Ibid., pp. 226, 232.

98. Ibid., p. 253.

99. Ibid., p. 258.

100. Ibid.

101. Winifred Gérin in *Charlotte Brontë: The Evolution of Genius* (Oxford, 1967).

102. For the diagnosis of *hyperemesis gravidarum*, see Dr. Phillip Rhodes, "A Medical Appraisal of the Brontës," *BST* 16 (1972), pp. 101–09. For a dissenting view, see the appendix to John Maynard's *Charlotte Brontë and Sexuality*. Rhodes suggests a psychosomatic origin for the illness, which is the main cause of Maynard's objection. However, modern medical opinion has redefined the etiology of the condition as organic rather than neurotic. See also Barker, note 96, p. 967, for an excellent summary.

103. Addison's disease was suggested by Gerson Weiss of the New Jersey Medical

School, as reported in the *Herald Tribune*, 31 March 1992. Gordon, *Charlotte Brontë*, p. 388.

104. Lyndall Gordon suggests that Charlotte had caught "some killer like typhoid" from the elderly servant Tabby, who died in February 1855, a month before her mistress. *Charlotte Brontë*, pp. 312–13.

105. Dooley herself remarks, "It has often been remarked that the keynote of her character was devotion to duty, and this was always shown as the duty of keeping her father's house and caring for him." "Psychoanalysis of Charlotte Brontë," p. 228.

106. Ibid., p. 250.

107. Ibid., p. 261.

108. Sigmund Freud, "Dostoevsky and Parricide" (1928), quoted in Gay, *The Freud Reader*, p. 444.

109. Robert Keefe, *Charlotte Brontë's World of Death* (Austin and London, 1979), introduction, p. xvi.

110. Ibid., p. 44.

111. Ibid., p. 189.

112. Maynard, *Charlotte Brontë*, p. 38.

113. In a letter to Ellen recommending "some books for your perusal," the teenage Charlotte advises her friend to omit *Don Juan* and the comedies of Shakespeare as too risqué, though Charlotte has clearly read them herself. CB to Ellen Nussey, 4 July 1834, Smith I, p. 130.

114. See Sally Shuttleworth, *Charlotte Brontë and Victorian Psychology* (Cambridge, 1996), p. 5 and passim.

115. Maynard, *Charlotte Brontë*, p. 31.

116. See Ibid., p. 238.

117. C. J. Hamilton, *Women Writers: Their Works and Ways* (London, 1892), preface.

118. For example, Kate Friedlander's 1941 essay, "Charlotte Brontë: A Study of a Masochistic Character," reprinted in Hendrick M. Ruitenbeek, ed., *The Literary Imagination and the Genius of the Writer* (Chicago, 1965).

119. Lytton Strachey, *Eminent Victorians* (1918; London, 1948), preface, p. 9.

120. Ibid., p. 10.

121. Rosamond Langbridge, *Charlotte Brontë: A Psychological Study* (London, 1929), p. 235.

122. Ibid., pp. 3–4.

123. Ibid., p. 66.

124. Ibid., p. 245.

125. Ibid., p. 243.

126. Ibid., p. 17.

127. Ibid., p. 5.

128. Ibid., p. 252.

129. Ibid., p. 259.

130. Ibid., pp. 238–39.

131. Ibid., p. 30.

132. Ibid., p. 255.

133. Ibid., p. 258.

134. *Radio Times*, 25 July 1930, p. 171.

135. Kathryn Macfarlane, *Divide the Desolation* (1936), jacket blurb, quoted in Stoneman, *Brontë Transformations*, p. 77.

136. E. F. Benson, *Charlotte Brontë* (London, 1932), p. xi.

137. For a brief period in 1839, CB acted as governess to the children of the Sidgwick family, cousins of the Bensons, as is reported by E.F.'s brother A. C. Benson in his biography of their father, *The Life of Edward White Benson, Sometime Archbishop of Canterbury* (London, 1899).

138. Ibid., p. viii.

139. Ibid., p. ix.

140. Ibid., p. xi.

141. Ibid., pp. ix.

142. Ibid., p. 191.

143. Ibid., pp. 87, 144.

144. Ibid., p. 192.

145. Ibid., p. 214.

146. *Life*, p. 356.

147. Benson, *The Life*, p. 218.

148. *Independent Magazine*, 29 May 1993, p. 59.

149. W. M. Thackeray to Lucy Baxter, 11 March 1853: "The poor little woman of genius! . . . rather than have fame, rather than any other earthly good or mayhap heavenly one she wants some Tomkins or another to love her and be in love with. But you see she is a little bit of a creature without a penny worth of good looks, thirty years old I should think, buried in the country, and eating up her own heart there, and no Tomkins will come" (Allott, pp. 197–98).

150. Lucasta Miller, "Postcard from Haworth," *Independent*, Books section, 11 June 1994.

CHAPTER SIX: *Fiction and Feminism*

1. Kathleen Tillotson, "Back to the Beginning of this Century," *BST* 19 (1986), p. 10.

2. Quoted in Hermione Lee, *Virginia Woolf* (London, 1996), p. 10.

3. J. A. Mackereth, *Storm-Wrack and Other Poems* (London, 1927), pp. 1–3.

4. Ibid., p. 8.

5. Ibid., p. 10.

6. Ibid., p. 14.

7. Ibid., p. 25.

8. See review by Ismene Brown, *Daily Telegraph*, 8 March 1995.

9. Mrs. Oliphant, "The Sisters Brontë," in *Women Novelists of Queen Victoria's Reign* (London, 1897), pp. 55–56.

10. Rachel Ferguson, *The Brontës Went to Woolworth's* (1931; London, 1988), p. 128.

11. Information from BPM.

12. Dan Totheroh, *Moor Born* (New York, 1934), p. 84.

13. Ella Moorhouse, *Stone Walls* (London, 1936), p. 68.

14. Clemence Dane, *Wild Decembers* (London, 1932), pp. 1–2.

15. Moorhouse, *Stone Walls*, p. 23.

16. Dorothy Helen Cornish, *These Were the Brontës* (New York, 1940).

17. Quoted in John Walker, ed., *Halliwell's Film and Video Guide 1999*.

18. *Devotion*, opening titles.

19. Twentieth Century–Fox Studio Archive, Produced Scripts Collection #10, FX-PRS-186, UCLA Arts Library, Special Collections.

20. Clement Shorter, "Relics of Emily Brontë," *Woman at Home* 5, Aug. 1897, p. 912.

21. Quoted in Walker, *Halliwell's*.

22. Ferguson, *The Brontës*, p. 54.

23. Ibid., p. 211.

24. Kathleen Wallace, *Immortal Wheat* (London, 1951), title page.

25. Ibid., p. 6.

26. Helen H. Arnold, "The Reminiscences of Emma Huidekoper Cortazzo," *BST* 13 (1958), p. 221.

27. Quoted in Ruth Parkin-Gounelas, *Fictions of the Female Self* (Macmillan, 1991), p. 34.

28. Margaret Drabble, "The Writer as Recluse: The Theme of Solitude in the Works of the Brontës," *BST* 16 (1974), p. 259.

29. Antonia Forest, *Peter's Room* (London, 1961), pp. 85–86.

30. Ibid., p. 223.

31. *Dictionary of National Biography*.

32. *Sunday Telegraph Magazine*, 22 April 1979.

33. Interview with André Techiné, Cannes Film Festival literature, 1979.

34. *Cahiers du Cinéma* 302, July–Aug. 1979, p. 62.

35. *Variety*, 16 May 1979.

36. Henry James, "The Lesson of Balzac," in *Two Lectures* (Boston and New York, 1905), pp. 63–64.

37. For example, Robert Martin, *The Accents of Persuasion* (London, 1966), p. 18. Tom Winnifrith's *The Brontës and Their Background: Romance and Reality* (London, 1973) also contains a sustained attack on purple heatherism.

38. Ernest Dimnet, *The Brontë Sisters* (London, 1927), pp. 28, 41.

39. Alice Law, *Patrick Branwell Brontë* (London, 1924), p. 18.

40. *Daily Sketch*, 20 July 1933, BPM archive.

41. See Patsy Stoneman, *Brontë Transformations: The Cultural Dissemination of "Jane Eyre" and "Wuthering Heights"* (Hemel Hempstead, 1996), p. 110.

42. As Kathleen Tillotson pointed out in *Novels of the Eighteen-Forties*, in *Jane Eyre* Walter Scott's poem *Marmion* (1808) is referred to as a recent publication.

43. See Stoneman, *Brontë Transformations*, pp. 135–36.

44. Annette Harrison, *In the Steps of the Brontës* (Ilfracombe, 1951), p. 39.

45. Evelyne Elizabeth McIntosh White, *Women of Devotion and Courage* (Lon-

don, 1956); Patrick Pringle, *When They Were Girls: Girlhood Stories of Fourteen Famous Women* (London, 1956).

46. Anne Brontë, *The Tenant of Wildfell Hall*, preface to the 2nd edition (1848; London, 1996), p. 5.

47. Winifred Gérin, *Anne Brontë: A Biography* (London, 1959).

48. May Sinclair, *The Three Brontës* (London, 1912), p. 44.

49. Philippa Stone, *The Captive Dove* (London, 1968).

50. George Moore in Edmund Gosse, *Conversations in Ebury Street* (London, 1924).

51. Ferguson, *The Brontës*, p. 128.

52. Inga-Stina Ewbank, *Their Proper Sphere: A Study of the Brontë Sisters as Early Victorian Novelists* (Cambridge, Mass., 1966).

53. Alfred Sangster, *The Brontës* (London, 1933), p. 4.

54. Moorhouse, *Stone Walls*, p. 44.

55. Lucile Dooley, "Psychoanalysis of Charlotte Brontë, as a Type of the Woman of Genius," *American Journal of Psychology* 21, July 1920, p. 237.

56. Virginia Woolf, *A Room of One's Own* (1929; London, 1977), p. 67.

57. Rosamond Langbridge, *Charlotte Brontë: A Psychological Study* (London, 1929), p. 253.

58. Carolyn G. Heilbrun, *Writing a Woman's Life* (London, 1989), pp. 25–26.

59. Helene Moglen, *Charlotte Brontë: The Self Conceived* (New York, 1976), p. 14.

60. Ibid., p. 42.

61. Ibid., p. 78.

62. Ibid., p. 19.

63. Margot Peters, *Unquiet Soul: A Biography of Charlotte Brontë* (New York, 1975; Doubleday paperback, 1976), p. xvi.

64. Ibid., p. xviii.

65. Ibid., p. 478.

66. Ibid., p. xvii.

67. Ibid., p. xviii.

68. Ibid., p. 21.

69. Ibid., p. xvii.

70. See U. C. Knoepflmacher, *Emily Brontë: Wuthering Heights* (Cambridge, 1989), chapter 4.

71. See Stoneman, *Brontë Transformations*, chapter 6.

72. Ibid., p. 185.

73. For example, Helen Small in *Love's Madness: Medicine, the Novel and Female Insanity, 1800–1865* (Oxford, 1996), p. 178.

74. *Evening Standard*, 18 Oct. 1999, p. 2.

75. Peters, *Unquiet Soul*, p. 478.

76. Ibid., p. 461.

77. Rebecca Fraser, *Charlotte Brontë* (London, 1988), pp. 478–79.

78. Natasha Walter, *The New Feminism* (London, 1998), p. 189.

79. See Smith I, introduction, pp. 52–63, for T. J. Wise and his activities.

80. Ibid., p. 55.

81. Ibid., pp. 66–71, for Smith's commentary on the Shakespeare Head edition.

82. See, for example, Susan Eilenberg, "What Charlotte Did," *London Review of Books*, 6 April 1995, pp. 12–13.

83. Barker, p. 33.

84. Virginia Woolf, "The Art of Biography," *Collected Essays* (London, 1967), vol. 4, p. 228.

85. Lyndall Gordon, *Charlotte Brontë: A Passionate Life* (London, 1994), p. 333.

CHAPTER SEVEN: *Interpreting Emily*

1. Austin Lee, *Miss Hogg and the Brontë Murders* (London, 1956); Robert Barnard, *The Missing Brontë* (London, 1983).

2. The best critical analysis of Emily's diary papers is by Stevie Davies in *Emily Brontë: Heretic* (London, 1994).

3. Biographical Notice, *Wuthering Heights*, p. xxvii.

4. Emily Brontë, Diary Paper, 26 June 1837, MS in BPM, ref. BS105.

5. Emily Brontë, Diary Paper, 24 Nov. 1834, MS in BPM, ref. Bonnell 131.

6. *Wuthering Heights*, p. 20.

7. Ibid., p. 82.

8. Ibid., p. 23.

9. For example, in the statement CB sent to Dr. Epps via William Smith Williams in a last-ditch attempt to get a medical opinion on her dying sister in Dec. 1848, she describes Emily as being in her twenty-ninth year, when she was in fact in her thirty-first (Smith II, p. 150). Similarly, in her prefatory note to her selections from Emily's poems published in 1850, CB describes her sister as having gone to Brussels "[a]fter the age of twenty," when Emily was in fact twenty-three and a half when they left (Smith II, p. 753).

10. Smith II, p. 753.

11. *Life*, p. 231.

12. Biographical Notice, *Wuthering Heights*, p. xxvii.

13. See T. C. Newby to ?Emily Brontë [Ellis Bell], 15 Feb. 1848, Smith II, p. 26.

14. EG to GS, 10 Sept. 1856, C & P, p. 412.

15. CB to WSW, 31 July 1848, Smith II, p. 94.

16. CB to EN, 29 Oct. 1848, Smith II, p. 130.

17. CB to WSW, 2 Nov. 1848, Smith II, p. 132.

18. CB to WSW, 22 Nov. 1848, Smith II, p. 142.

19. CB to EN, 27 Nov. 1848, Smith II, p. 146.

20. CB to EN, 19 Dec. 1848, Smith II, p. 154.

21. Many writers of the mid-twentieth century who believed Emily was a mystic in communion with God saw her as longing for death as the ultimate ecstasy. Later writers with different perspectives also found ways of reading her death as something welcomed, for example, Muriel Spark, who argues that while Emily could not physiologically have willed her own death, she may have wanted to believe she was playing out the tragic destiny of the mythical Romantic hero, just as Heathcliff had (Muriel Spark and Derek Stanford, *Emily Brontë: Her Life and Work* [London,

1953]). Also, see Katherine Frank, who in *Emily Brontë: A Chainless Soul* (London, 1990) reads Emily's death as a denial of the body which was the culmination of years of anorexia nervosa.

22. *Wuthering Heights,* p. 64.

23. The phrase is taken from the description of her sister's case Charlotte sent to Dr. Epps in Dec. 1848, Smith II, p. 150.

24. CB to Ellen Nussey, 12 April 1849, Smith II, p. 200.

25. CB to WSW, 4 June 1849, Smith II, p. 216.

26. *Life,* p. 379.

27. See Charlotte Brontë, *The Professor,* Margaret Smith and Herbert Rosengarten, eds., (Oxford, 1987), appendix VII, "Index of Quotations and Literary Allusions in the Novels of Charlotte Brontë."

28. *Shirley,* p. 457.

29. Ibid., pp. 457–58.

30. Emily Brontë, Diary Paper, 31 July 1845, Smith I, p. 408.

31. *Shirley,* p. 459.

32. Ibid., p. 460.

33. *Wuthering Heights,* p. 80.

34. *Shirley,* pp. 459–60.

35. "Some Account of Coleridge's Philosophy," *Fraser's* 5, June 1832, pp. 585–96. This number of the magazine certainly entered the Brontës' home, as they had begun to take it some time before 17 May 1832 (CB to Branwell Brontë, 17 May 1832, Smith I, p. 112). If the Brontës did not read the article then, they could have done so later, as such periodicals are unlikely to have been thrown away.

36. "An Essay on the Theory and Writings of Wordsworth," part 3, *Blackwood's* 26, Nov. 1829, p. 774. The critic shows a hostility toward Wordsworth's "acolytes" but his account of their beliefs fits Charlotte's depiction of Shirley's vision, suggesting that the Brontës would have counted themselves among the faithful and allied themselves against the cynical critic. The article argues that the famous manifesto in Wordsworth's preface to the *Lyrical Ballads* offers little more than a banal statement that "natural thoughts, clothed in simple language . . . speak at once to the heart," but that the master's disciples had aggrandized his philosophy, deducing from his works "a far more sublime and mystical creed—the 'Revelation.' " This consists in

> a divine discovery by the poet, of the following arcana—namely, a certain accordance, which imaginative minds perceive when, shutting out the clamour of the world, they listen to Nature's still small voice, between the external universe, and the internal microcosm of man;—a purifying influence exerted through the medium of visible objects upon the invisible mental powers;—a sort of *anima mundi* pervading all that is;—a sublime harmony between the natural and the moral creation. It is, in short, the quakerism of philosophy, the transcendentalism of poetry.

37. *Shirley,* p. 374.

38. Mario Praz, *The Romantic Agony* (1933; Oxford, 1970), pp. 14–15.

39. *Shirley,* p. 374.
40. Ibid., p. 488.
41. Ibid., p. 489.
42. Ibid., p. 490.
43. Ibid., p. 579.
44. Ibid., p. 592.
45. CB to WSW, 13 Sept. 1850, Smith II, p. 466.
46. CB to EN, 23 Oct. 1850, Smith II, p. 487.
47. C. W. Hatfield, ed., *The Complete Poems of Emily Jane Brontë* (New York, 1941).
48. See Janet Gezari, ed., Emily Jane Brontë, *The Complete Poems* (London, 1992), pp. 175 and 217 to compare Emily's manuscript version of the poem ("A. E. and R. C.") with Charlotte's 1850 version (retitled "The Two Children").
49. Prefatory note to CB's 1850 "Selections from Poems by Ellis Bell," Smith II, p. 752.
50. Biographical Notice, p. xxxi.
51. Matthew Arnold, "Haworth Churchyard," *Fraser's,* May 1855, Allott, p. 310.
52. A. C. Swinburne, *A Note on Charlotte Brontë* (London, 1877), p. 79.
53. Gezari, *The Complete Poems,* p. 127.
54. Ibid., p. 210.
55. See Thomas McFarland, *Romanticism and the Forms of Ruin: Wordsworth, Coleridge, and the Modalities of Fragmentation* (Princeton, 1981), and Zachary Leader, *Writer's Block* (Baltimore, 1991), pp. 126–33.
56. Emily Brontë, Diary Paper, 31 July 1845, Smith, I, p. 408.
57. See Derek Roper, ed., *The Poems of Emily Brontë* (Oxford, 1995), appendix VII, for summaries of the three main attempts at reconstruction (including Ratchford's) made by scholars.
58. See *Charlotte Brontë and Her Circle* (London, 1896), p. 144.
59. Smith II, p. 752.
60. For accounts of why Charlotte might have destroyed the papers, see Winifred Gérin, *Emily Brontë* (Oxford, 1971), pp. 262–63, 245, and Stevie Davies, *Emily Brontë: Heretic* (London, 1994), p. 238. In *A Life of Emily Brontë* (Oxford, 1987), Edward Chitham, however, suggests that Emily and Anne destroyed Gondal themselves, speculating, somewhat colorfully, that they either tipped the manuscripts onto a bonfire or threw them down the well (p. 218).
61. Charlotte's phrase for her own fantasy world of Angria, CB to Branwell Brontë, 1 May 1843, Smith I, p. 317.
62. Boris Ford, ed., *The New Pelican Guide to English Literature* (London, 1958; revised ed., 1982), vol. 6, "From Dickens to Hardy," pp. 251–52.
63. Hatfield's conclusion (*The Complete Poems,* p. 242) that the added stanzas were Charlotte's invention is supported by Gezari (*The Complete Poems,* p. 278), and more recently by Roper, though he cautiously adds a "probably" in brackets (*The Poems,* p. 269).
64. Gezari, *The Complete Poems.*
65. Ibid., p. 23.

66. Biographical Notice, p. xxviii.

67. Three reviews of *Poems* dating from 1846 are known: from the *Critic,* the *Athenaeum,* and the *Dublin University Magazine.* In November 1848 the volume was reissued under Smith, Elder's imprint, and was reviewed, less enthusiastically than before, in *The Spectator.* See Allott, pp. 59–66.

68. Biographical Notice, p. xxix.

69. *American Review,* June 1848, Allott, p. 236.

70. Elizabeth Rigby, *Quarterly Review,* Dec. 1848, Allott, p. 111.

71. Unidentified review, Allott, p. 244.

72. Allott reprints extracts from twelve reviews; see also *BST* 16 (1975), pp. 383–99; and *BST* 18 (1982).

73. *Douglas Jerrold's Weekly Newspaper,* 15 Jan. 1848, Allott, p. 228.

74. Preface, *Wuthering Heights* (London, 1995), p. xxxiii.

75. Biographical Notice, p. xxxii.

76. Ibid., p. xxix.

77. *Britannia,* 15 Jan. 1848, Allott, p. 224.

78. Preface, p. xxxvii.

79. *Britannia,* 15 Jan. 1848, Allott, p. 226.

80. Biographical Notice, p. xxix.

81. CB to George Smith, 5 Feb. 1851, Smith II, p. 572.

82. See John T. Matthews, "Framing in *Wuthering Heights,*" in Patsy Stoneman, ed., *New Casebook on "Wuthering Heights"* (London, 1993), pp. 54–73.

83. Humphrey Gawthorpe, letter to author, 4 Feb. 2001.

84. Patsy Stoneman, *New Casebook,* p. 101.

85. Preface, pp. xxxv–xxxvi.

86. Ibid., p. xxxvi.

87. Ibid., pp. xxxvi–xxxvii.

88. William Hazlitt, "The Plain Speaker," *Works* 12, pp. 118–19, quoted in M. H. Abrams, *The Mirror and the Lamp* (1953; London, 1960), p. 215.

89. Biographical Notice, p. xxxii.

90. See, for example, CB to WSW, ?early Sept. 1848, Smith II, p. 118: "Were I obliged to copy any former novelist, even the greatest, even Scott, in anything, I would not write—"

91. CB to WSW, 28 Oct. 1847, Smith I, pp. 553–54: "The plot of '*Jane Eyre*['] may be a hackneyed one; Mr. Thackeray remarks that it is familiar to him; but having read comparatively few novels, I never chanced to meet with it, and I thought it original. . . . I hope I shall not find I have been an unconscious imitator" (i.e., of the novelist Mrs. Marsh).

92. In a letter to George Smith of 7 Feb. 1853 (SH, vol. IV, p. 44), Charlotte angrily rebuffs Harriet Martineau's suggestion that there is a likeness between *Villette* and Balzac, "whose works I have not read." In fact, she knew the work of the French author, having been lent two of his novels by G. H. Lewes less than three years previously. (See CB to GHL, 17 Oct. 1850, Smith II, pp. 484–85.)

93. C. P. Sanger's *The Structure of Wuthering Heights* (London, 1926) was a critical watershed. The author, a lawyer, not only showed Emily's sophisticated understand-

ing of the legal issues involved in her novel but her extraordinary control of its internal time scheme.

94. Quoted by U. C. Knoepflmacher in *Emily Brontë: Wuthering Heights* (Cambridge, 1989), p. 26.

95. Biographical Notice, p. xxvi.

96. For a recent exploration of Emily's intellectual background in German as well as English literature, see Stevie Davies, *Emily Brontë: Heretic* (London, 1994).

97. Sue Lonoff, ed. and trans., *Charlotte Brontë and Emily Brontë: The Belgian Essays* (New Haven and London, 1996).

98. CB to WSW, 15 Feb. 1848, Smith II, p. 28.

99. Emily Brontë, Diary Paper, 30 July 1841, Smith I, p. 263.

100. For example, the description of an all-pervading spirit which "animates eternal years" and "changes, sustains, dissolves, creates and rears" in "No coward soul is mine" has been cited as suggesting familiarity with Coleridge's description of the imagination in *Biographia Literaria* (1817): "It dissolves, diffuses, dissipates, in order to recreate. . . . It is essentially *vital*, even as all objects (*as* objects) are essentially fixed and dead." See Gezari, *The Complete Poems*, p. 279. To this can be added another possible echo, from Byron's "Detached Thoughts": "Matter is eternal, always changing, but reproduced, and, as far as we can comprehend eternity, eternal; and why not *mind?*" Quoted in Thomas Moore, *Letters and Journals of Lord Byron with Notices of His Life* (London, 1830), vol. 2, p. 802.

101. See Margaret Homans, *Women Writers and Poetic Identity* (Princeton, 1980), chapter 3; also Helen Brown, "The Influence of Byron on Emily Brontë," *Modern Language Review* 34 (1939), pp. 374–81.

102. F. B. Pinion, "Scott and *Wuthering Heights,*" *BST* 21 (1996), pp. 313–22.

103. See also Rose Lovell-Smith, "Walter Scott and Emily Brontë: The Rhetoric of Love," *BST* 21 (1994), pp. 117–24.

104. John Hewish, *Emily Brontë: A Critical and Biographical Study* (London, 1969), p. 37. Hewish quotes the opening sentence of the diary paper for 24 Nov. 1834—"I fed Rainbow, Diamond, Snowflake, Jasper phaesent (alias) this morning . . ."—and compares its "throwaway style and list of pets" to the following extract from Byron's journal for 6 Jan. 1821, as quoted in Moore's *Life:* "Fed the two cats, the hawk, and the tame (but not tamed) crow."

105. Pinion, "Byron and *Wuthering Heights,*" pp. 195–201. Winifred Gérin previously cited this parallel in *Emily Brontë* (Oxford, 1971).

106. *Blackwood's* 27 (1830), p. 453.

107. *Wuthering Heights,* p. 82.

108. Ibid., p. 167.

109. Pinion quotes direct verbal echoes between Heathcliff's words to the ghost Cathy and Manfred's to Astarte, "Byron and *Wuthering Heights,*" p. 200.

110. Phyllis Grosskurth, *Byron: The Flawed Angel* (London, 1997), p. 314.

111. Edward Chitham, *A Life of Emily Brontë* (Oxford, 1987), p. 93.

112. "Unimore: A Dream of the Highlands," by Professor Wilson, *Blackwood's* 30 (1831), pp. 137ff.

113. Ibid., pp. 190, 168, 191.

114. Ibid., p. 146.

115. Ibid., p. 147.

116. For example, ibid., p. 139: "Morven! this magic lies upon thee now. / Imagination, she it is who bathes / With blue celestial as an angel's eyes / The cloud-sustaining depth which she calls Heaven!"

117. Davies, *Emily Brontë: Heretic*, pp. 49–51.

118. John Elliot Cairns, quoted in Charles Lemon, *Early Visitors to Haworth* (Haworth, 1996), p. 49.

119. See, for example, the summary of this philosophical position in Carlyle's essay on Novalis, *Critical and Miscellaneous Essays* (London, 1839), vol. 2, pp. 82–142 (originally in *Foreign Review* 7, 1829).

120. Gezari, *The Complete Poems*, p. 238, note xxi.

121. Thomas Moore, *Letters and Journals of Lord Byron with Notices of His Life* (London, 1830), vol. 2, p. 801.

122. John Sutherland, *Who Betrays Elizabeth Bennet? Further Puzzles in Classic Fiction* (Oxford, 1999), pp. 70–71.

123. Emily Brontë, Diary Paper, 26 June 1837, in Juliet Barker, ed., *The Brontës: A Life in Letters* (London, 1997), p. 53.

124. Biographical Notice, p. xxx.

125. CB to WSW, 7 Dec. 1848, Smith II, p. 148. See also Edgar Jean Bracco on Emily's second novel, *BST* 16 (1966), pp. 29–33.

126. See Charles Simpson, *Emily Brontë* (London, 1929), pp. 167–186.

127. T. C. Newby to ?Emily Brontë [Ellis Bell], Smith II, p. 26.

128. John Hewish, "Emily Brontë's Missing Novel," letter to the editor, *TLS*, 10 March 1966.

129. *Douglas Jerrold's Weekly Newspaper*, 15 Jan. 1848, Allott, p. 228.

130. A letter to the editor from a certain Arthur Hedley printed in the *TLS*, 6 Sept. 1947, quotes from a supposed letter of Charlotte's of summer 1848 in which she refers to Emily's second novel as a "bold and vigorous piece of work." A number of inconsistencies prove the letter a forgery. I am grateful to Margaret Smith for discussing this with me.

131. *Return to Wuthering Heights* by Anna L'Estrange (New York, 1977); *Heathcliff* by Jeffrey Caine (New York, 1977); Lin Haire-Sargeant's *Heathcliff: The Return to Wuthering Heights* (London, 1992).

132. Winifred Gérin (1971), Stevie Davies (1994), and Juliet Barker (1994).

133. Printed in Tom Winnifrith, ed., *Charlotte Brontë, Unfinished Novels* (Stroud, 1993).

134. Matthew Arnold, "Haworth Churchyard," *Fraser's*, May 1855, Allott, pp. 309–10.

135. G. H. Lewes, *Ranthorpe* (1845; London, 1847), p. 230.

136. Simpson, *Emily Brontë*, p. 1.

CHAPTER EIGHT: *A Woman Worthy of Being Avoided*

1. G. H. Lewes, unsigned review, *Leader*, 28 Dec. 1850, Allott, p. 291.

2. Preface, *Wuthering Heights*, p. xxxiv.

3. *Eclectic Review,* Feb. 1851, Allott, p. 297.

4. Peter Bayne, *Essays in Biographical Criticism,* 1857, Allott, p. 322.

5. Ibid., p. 325.

6. Eliza Jane Kingston, quoted in Fannie E. Ratchford, *Gondal's Queen: A Novel in Verse by Emily Jane Brontë* (Austin and Edinburgh, 1955), p. 36.

7. Thomas Wemyss Reid, *Charlotte Brontë: A Monograph* (London, 1877), pp. 201–02.

8. Ibid., p. 200.

9. "The Life and Writings of Emily Brontë," *Galaxy,* Feb. 1873, Allott, pp. 392–93.

10. Roy T. House, "Emily Brontë," *Nation* 107, 17 Aug. 1918, Allott, pp. 169–70.

11. *Life,* p. 379.

12. Ibid., p. 507.

13. Ibid., p. 269.

14. Charles Lemon, *Early Visitors to Haworth* (Haworth, 1996), p. 50.

15. *Wuthering Heights,* p. 177.

16. Biographical Notice, p. xxxii.

17. *Life,* p. 268.

18. *Shirley,* p. 480.

19. Ibid., p. 479.

20. Ibid., p. 480.

21. Quoted in Clement Shorter, *Charlotte Brontë and Her Circle* (London, 1896), p. 178.

22. *Christian Remembrancer,* July 1857, Allott, p. 367.

23. See Barker, pp. 108–09.

24. The first forty-eight lines of this poem were published in the *Bradford Herald* on 25 Aug. 1842. See Barker, p. 400.

25. William Oakendale (pseud. William Dearden), "Who Wrote *Wuthering Heights?*" *Halifax Guardian,* 15 June 1867, facsimile in *BST* 7 (1927), p. 99.

26. CB to William Smith Williams, 14 Aug. 1848, Smith II, p. 99. Too close to be able to stand back and see the similarities between these male characters, Charlotte disagrees with Williams.

27. Robert G. Collins, ed., *The Hand of the Arch-Sinner: Two Angrian Chronicles of Branwell Brontë* (Oxford, 1993). See introduction.

28. Dearden, "Who Wrote *Wuthering Heights?*" p. 98.

29. Ibid., p. 99.

30. Ibid., p. 100.

31. Ibid., p. 101.

32. See Barker, p. 368.

33. Francis Grundy, *Pictures of the Past* (London, 1879), p. 73.

34. Ibid., p. 74.

35. Ibid., p. 80.

36. Irene Cooper Willis, *The Authorship of Wuthering Heights* (London, 1936), p. 67.

37. Reid's biography came out in book form in 1877, but first appeared in installments in *Macmillan's Magazine* in Sept., Oct., and Nov. 1876.

38. Reid, *Charlotte Brontë*, p. 204.

39. Ibid., pp. 31–32.

40. Mary Robinson, *Emily Brontë* (London, 1883), p. 2.

41. Clyde K. Hyder, ed., *Algernon Swinburne: The Critical Heritage* (London, 1970), pp. xx, xxxiv.

42. See A. N. Wilson, *God's Funeral* (London, 1999), chapter 10.

43. A. C. Swinburne, *A Note on Charlotte Brontë* (London, 1877), p. 86.

44. Ibid., p. 73.

45. Ibid., p. 74.

46. Ibid., p. 79.

47. A. C. Swinburne to Thomas Wemyss Reid, 24 Sept. 1877, Allott, p. 438.

48. *American Review*, June 1848, Allott, p. 241.

49. *Athenaeum*, 16 June 1883, Allott, p. 439.

50. Preface, *Wuthering Heights*, p. xxxiv.

51. Patsy Stoneman offers a lengthy account of the developing popularity of this image in *Brontë Transformations: The Cultural Dissemination of "Jane Eyre" and "Wuthering Heights"* (Hemel Hempstead, 1996).

52. The similarities between *The Story of an African Farm* and *Wuthering Heights* have been noticed by many readers and are discussed by Elaine Showalter in *A Literature of Their Own* (1977, revised ed., 1982; London, 1984), p. 199, and by Stoneman, *Brontë Transformation*, pp. 58–62. *The Story of an African Farm* may not, as Stoneman assumes, be the first time the plot of *Wuthering Heights* was reworked by another writer. See U. C. Knoepflmacher, *Emily Brontë: Wuthering Heights* (Cambridge, 1989), p. 116, where it is suggested that George Eliot's 1858 story "Mr. Gilfil's Love-Story" was influenced by Emily's novel. The heroine is torn between two lovers—one aristocratic, the other lowborn and adopted—and eventually dies in childbirth, mourned by a husband who turns her room into a shrine, though in this resolutely ungothic, realist rewriting no ghost comes back to haunt him.

53. For an account of Schreiner's life, see Ruth Brandon, *The New Women and the Old Men: Love, Sex and the Woman Question* (London, 1990).

54. Mary Robinson to Ellen Nussey, 23 March 1882, SH, vol. IV, p. 268.

55. Mary Robinson, *Emily Brontë* (London, 1883), p. 2.

56. Ibid., p. 48.

57. Ibid., p. 15.

58. Ibid., p. 214.

59. Ibid., p. 26.

60. Ibid., p. 59.

61. Bayne, *Essays*, Allott, p. 322.

62. Ibid., p. 229.

63. "Brontë Legends," in G. F. Bradby, *The Brontës and Other Essays* (Oxford, 1932), p. 37.

64. According to an article in *Cornhill Magazine* 29 (1878), "Old Haworth Folk Who Knew the Brontës," Martha Brown's sister Tabitha also recalled Emily dropping her comb into the fire on her death day. Smith II, pp. 154–55, note 1.

65. *Life*, p. 335.

66. Robinson, *Emily Brontë*, p. 162.

67. Ibid., p. 105.

68. Ibid., p. 94.

69. Ibid., p. 58.

70. Mary Robinson to Ellen Nussey, 15 Aug. 1882, SH, vol. IV, p. 296.

71. Mary Robinson to Ellen Nussey, 17 Aug. 1882, SH, vol. IV, pp. 277–78.

72. Ibid., p. 277.

73. Janet Gezari, ed., *Emily Jane Brontë: The Complete Poems* (London, 1992), p. 26.

74. Robinson, *Emily Brontë*, p. 45.

75. Ibid., p. 6.

76. Mary Robinson to Ellen Nussey, 17 July 1883, SH, vol. IV, p. 283.

77. Robinson, *Emily Brontë*, p. 164.

78. Emily Dickinson to Mrs. J. G. Holland, May 1883, Thomas H. Johnson, ed., *The Letters of Emily Dickinson* (Cambridge, Mass., 1986), p. 775.

79. Théodore de Wyzewa, trans. Effie Brown, *BST* 17 (1976), p. 34.

80. Miles Franklin, *My Career Goes Bung* (Sydney, 1990), pp. 278–79.

81. *Young Woman* 1 (1892–93), p. 173.

82. *The Woman at Home* 5, August 1897, pp. 906–12.

83. A. C. Swinburne, *Athenaeum*, 16 June 1883, Allott, pp. 440–41.

84. Angus M. Mackay, *The Brontës: Fact and Fiction* (London, 1897), p. 88.

85. It seems strange, for example, that Edward Chitham accepts Wright's extravagant claims in *The Brontës' Irish Background* (London, 1986).

86. *Wuthering Heights*, p. 62.

87. Robinson, *Emily Brontë*, pp. 165–66.

88. See *Life*, pp. 151–52, 117, 132.

89. Mrs. Humphry Ward, introduction, Haworth edition of *Wuthering Heights*, Allott, pp. 456–57.

90. Ibid., p. 458.

91. B. G. MacCarthy, *The Female Pen: Women Writers and Novelists* (1944; Cork, 1994), p. 30.

92. Jerome J. McGann, *The Romantic Ideology: A Critical Investigation* (Chicago, 1983), p. 1.

93. Quoted in Esther Alice Chadwick, "Emily Brontë," *Nineteenth Century* 86 (October 1919), p. 680.

94. May Sinclair, *The Three Brontës* (London, 1912), p. 239.

95. Ibid., p. 216.

96. Ibid., p. 214.

97. Derek Roper, ed., *The Poems of Emily Brontë* (Oxford, 1995), p. 292.

98. Sinclair, *The Three Brontës*, p. 178.

99. Ibid., p. 175.

100. Ibid., p. 166.

101. See Penny Brown, *The Poison at the Source: The Female Novel of Self-*

Development in the Early 20th Century (London, 1992), for a discussion of May Sinclair's intellectual background. Also see *May Sinclair* by Hrisey D. Zegger (Boston, 1976).

   102. Sinclair, *The Three Brontës*, p. 171.

   103. Ibid., p. 169.

   104. Ibid., p. 223.

   105. Ibid., p. 125.

   106. Ibid., p. 173.

   107. Ibid., p. 175.

   108. *Fraser's* 15 (June 1837), pp. 716–35.

CHAPTER NINE: *The Mystic of the Moors*

   1. For example, Barker, p. 482.

   2. See Kerry Juby, *Kate Bush: The Whole Story* (London, 1988), pp. 31–32. On British television Bush wore a leotard, but the video released in the U.S.A. had her in a flimsy white dress.

   3. "Julian M. and A. G. Rochelle," Janet Gezari, ed., *Emily Jane Brontë: The Complete Poems* (London, 1992), pp. 177–81. In Emily's manuscript, this poem is dated 9 Oct. 1845.

   4. Ibid., p. 15.

   5. Virginia Moore, *The Life and Eager Death of Emily Brontë* (London, 1936), pp. 355, 360. Winifred Gérin's 1971 biography also follows this line, suggesting that Emily lost the will to live because her visions had deserted her.

   6. See also Barbara Hardy's "The Lyricism of Emily Brontë" in Anne Smith, ed., *The Art of Emily Brontë* (London, 1976), chapter 3.

   7. See "Narrative of an Imprisonment in France During the Reign of Terror," by Samuel Warren, *Blackwood's* 30 (Dec. 1831), pp. 920–53. The description of sick prisoners praying for death in the dark, and the narrator's experience of sinking into a "deadly stupor" and then coming back to life, are striking (p. 935).

   8. Byron, *Complete Poetical Works*, vol. 4 (Oxford, 1986), pp. 11–12, 3.

   9. Wordsworth's followers are said to "deduce from his works . . . a . . . sublime and mystical creed" which is ridiculed in mock-religiose language as "the Revelation," *Blackwood's* 26, (Nov. 1829), p. 774.

   10. Thomas Carlyle, *Critical and Miscellaneous Essays* (London, 1839), vol. 2, p. 104 (originally in *Foreign Review* 7, 1829).

   11. See Stevie Davies, *Emily Brontë: Heretic* (London, 1994); also chapter 7 above.

   12. *Shirley*, p. 428.

   13. Carlyle, *Critical and Miscellaneous Essays*, p. 111.

   14. Winifred Gérin, *Emily Brontë* (Oxford, 1971), p. 152.

   15. Ibid. Gezari transcribes the poem with minor differences of spelling (*The Complete Poems*, p. 17).

   16. Margaret Homans (see note 19 below) is right to assume that Emily had access to Coleridge's poem. *Blackwood's* 6 (Oct. 1834), pp. 542–70, contained a long review of Samuel Taylor Coleridge's recently published *Poetical Works* with a lengthy dis-

cussion, with sustained quotation, of "The Rime of the Ancient Mariner" on pp. 567–70. Charlotte also alludes to the poem in *Jane Eyre, Shirley,* and *Villette.* See appendix VII to the Clarendon edition of Charlotte's *The Professor,* Margaret Smith and Herbert Rosengarten, eds. (Oxford, 1987), p. 331.

17. It is significant that Gérin goes on to compare Emily to Shelley only to contrast her work, described as "purely intuitive and personal," with his, the product of "long study of the Greek philosophers." Ibid., p. 153.

18. Margaret Homans, *Women Writers and Poetic Identity* (Princeton, 1980), p. 144.

19. Ibid., p. 107.

20. Esther Alice Chadwick, "Emily Brontë," *Nineteenth Century* 86 (Oct. 1919), p. 684.

21. E. F. Benson, *Charlotte Brontë* (London, 1932), p. 158.

22. Sylvia Townsend Warner, *The Salutation* (London, 1932), pp. 295–96.

23. Alfred Sangster, *The Brontës* (London, 1933), p. 25.

24. Charlotte Brontë, prefatory note to "Selections from Poems by Ellis Bell" (1850), Smith II, p. 753.

25. Isabel C. Clarke, *Haworth Parsonage: A Picture of the Brontë Family* (London, 1927), pp. 89, 92.

26. Ernest Raymond, *In the Steps of the Brontës* (London, 1948), p. 15.

27. Emily Heaton, *White Windows* (London, 1932), p. xi.

28. Dorothy Helen Cornish, *These Were the Brontës* (1940), p. 199.

29. Emily's interest in the supernatural has been speculatively traced to German Romantic prose fiction. It should also be noted that James Hogg, "the Ettrick Shepherd" and author of the spine-chilling doppelgänger tale *The Private Memoirs and Confessions of a Justified Sinner* (1824), contributed an article on ghosts and apparitions to *Fraser's* in Jan. 1835 (vol. 11, pp. 103–12).

30. *Wuthering Heights,* p. 334.

31. Rachel Ferguson, *Charlotte Brontë: A Play in Three Acts* (London, 1933), p. 49.

32. Ibid., p. 42.

33. Charles L. Tweedale, *News from the Next World* (London, 1940), p. 288.

34. Ibid., p. 292.

35. Millicent Collard, *Wuthering Heights—the Revelation: A Psychical Study of Emily Brontë* (London, 1960), p. 10.

36. Ibid., p. 29.

37. *TLS,* 14 June 1928, p. 446.

38. Ibid., 5 May 1921, p. 290.

39. B. Ifor Evans, *English Literature Between the Wars* (London, 1948), p. 3.

40. Romer Wilson, *Greenlow* (London, 1927), p. 8.

41. Ibid., p. 145.

42. Ibid., p. 3.

43. Jeffrey Meyers, ed., *D. H. Lawrence and Tradition* (London, 1985), p. 11.

44. Quoted in Keith Sagar, *D. H. Lawrence: Life into Art* (London, 1985), p. 17.

45. Wilson, *Greenlow,* p. 173.

46. Biographical Notice, p. xxxi.

47. Wilson, *Greenlow,* p. 4.

48. Romer Wilson, *All Alone: The Life and Private History of Emily Jane Brontë* (London, 1928), pp. xi–xii.

49. Ibid., p. 1.

50. Ibid.

51. Ibid., p. 4.

52. Ibid., pp. 4–5.

53. Ibid., p. 51.

54. Ibid., pp. 27–31.

55. Ibid., p. 26.

56. Ibid., p. 115.

57. Reggie Oliver, *Out of the Woodshed: A Portrait of Stella Gibbons* (London, 1998), p. 121.

58. Alice Law, *Patrick Branwell Brontë* (London, 1924) and *Emily Jane Brontë and the Authorship of "Wuthering Heights"* (Accrington, 1928).

59. Barker, p. 289.

60. Oliver, *Out of the Woodshed,* p. 111.

61. Stella Gibbons, *Cold Comfort Farm* (1932; London, 1994), p. 102.

62. Ibid., p. 122.

63. Ibid., p. 103.

64. Robert Keefe in *Charlotte Brontë's World of Death* (Austin and London, 1979), as already discussed in chapter 5.

65. May Sinclair, *The Three Brontës* (London, 1912), p. 167.

66. Quoted by Esther Alice Chadwick, "Emily Brontë," p. 680.

67. Esther Alice Chadwick, *In the Footsteps of the Brontës* (London, 1914), p. 332.

68. Ibid.

69. Ibid., p. 333.

70. Isabel C. Clarke, *Haworth Parsonage: A Picture of the Brontë Family* (London, 1927), p. 66.

71. Elizabeth Goudge, *The Brontës of Haworth* (London, 1939), p. 141.

72. Obituary of Isobel English, *Times,* 7 June 1994, p. 21.

73. Emily Heaton, *White Windows,* p. 44.

74. Jacques Débû-Bridel, *Le Secret d'Emily Brontë* (Paris, 1950), p. 90.

75. See Stoneman, *Brontë Transformations,* pp. 114–34, 155.

76. Reported in the *Daily Telegraph,* 4 Dec. 1999.

77. Many modern critiques have recognized this, for example, U. C. Knoepflmacher, *Emily Brontë: Wuthering Heights* (Cambridge, 1989), pp. 34–36.

78. Gezari, *The Complete Poems,* p. 182.

79. *Wuthering Heights,* p. 81.

80. Virginia Moore, *The Life and Eager Death of Emily Brontë* (London, 1936), p. xii.

81. Ibid., p. ix.

82. *TLS,* 22 Aug. 1936.

83. *Poetry Review* 1, (January 1943), letter from Marjorie Stuart Barrow.

84. Moore, *The Life*, p. xi.

85. Ibid., p. 189.

86. E. F. Benson, *Charlotte Brontë* (London, 1932), p. 38.

87. Moore, *The Life*, p. 190.

88. Gibbons, *Cold Comfort Farm*, p. 122.

89. Oliver, *Out of the Woodshed*, p. 119.

90. Quite how long Emily stayed at Law Hill is a matter of dispute.

91. Gezari, *The Complete Poems*, p. 82.

92. Moore, *The Life*, p. 193.

93. Ibid., p. 328.

94. Ibid., p. 190.

95. Belinda Jack, *George Sand: A Woman's Life Writ Large* (London, 1999), p. 2.

96. Camille Paglia, *Sexual Personae* (1990; London, 1991), pp. 439–59.

97. John Keats, letter to G. and T. Keats, 21 Dec. 1817. Robert Gittings, ed., *Letters of John Keats: A Selection* (Oxford, 1970), p. 43.

98. Muriel Spark, *Emily Brontë: Her Life and Work* (London, 1953), p. 11.

99. Ibid., p. 81.

100. Ibid., p. 90.

101. John Hewish, *Emily Brontë: A Critical and Biographical Study* (London, 1969), p. 16.

102. Elizabeth Gaskell, "Cousin Phillis" (1864; London, 1976), p. 242.

103. Julian Barnes, *Flaubert's Parrot* (1984; London, 1992), pp. 47–48.

104. In particular, an Irish tale which appeared in *Blackwood's* in 1840 ("The Bridegroom of Barna," by Bartholomew Simmonds), whose themes of separated lovers, the outcast hero, and the maddened dying heroine had pre-echoes of *Wuthering Heights*.

105. Hewish, *Emily Brontë*, p. 169.

106. Edward Chitham, *A Life of Emily Brontë* (Oxford, 1987), p. 1.

107. See Charlotte Brontë, *The Professor*, Margaret Smith and Herbert Rosengarten, eds. (Oxford, 1987), appendix VII, p. 334.

108. Ted Hughes, *Birthday Letters* (London, 1998), p. 59.

109. Ted Hughes, *Remains of Elmet* (London, 1979), p. 37.

110. Ibid., p. 67.

111. Erica Wagner, *Ariel's Gift: Ted Hughes, Sylvia Plath and the Story of "Birthday Letters"* (London, 2000), p. 18.

112. There are, however, implicit connections. For example, the image in "Haworth Parsonage" of electrocution—often used by Plath herself, who underwent electro-convulsive therapy—and the reference to "America" in "Top Withens" allude secretly to Sylvia.

113. Ted Hughes, *Three Books* (London, 1993), p. 15.

114. Quoted in Wagner, *Ariel's Gift*, p. 22.

115. Hughes, *Birthday Letters*, pp. 59–61.

116. Sylvia Plath, *Letters Home (1950–1963)*, ed. Aurelia Plath, (1976; London, 1978), p. 269.

117. Jacqueline Rose, *The Haunting of Sylvia Plath* (London, 1991), pp. 4–5.

118. Sylvia Plath, *Letters Home (1950–1963)*, ed. Aurelia Plath, (1976; London, 1978), p. 269.

119. Sylvia Plath, *Collected Poems* (London, 1981), ed. Ted Hughes, pp. 71–72.

120. Karen V. Kukil, ed., *The Journals of Sylvia Plath, 1950–1962* (London, 2000), Appendix 10, pp. 579–580.

121. Ibid., pp. 302–03.

122. Plath, *Collected Poems*, pp. 167–68.

123. By Edward Chitham. See also Chitham, *The Birth of "Wuthering Heights"* (London, 1998), chapter 2, for his discussion of Emily's Latin translations.

Select Bibliography

Abrams, M. H. *The Mirror and the Lamp*. London, 1960.

Ackroyd, Peter. *Dickens*. London, 1990.

Alexander, Christine. *Charlotte Brontë's "High Life in Verdopolis": A Story from the Glass Town Saga*. London, 1995.

———. *The Early Writings of Charlotte Brontë*. Oxford, 1983.

Alexander, Christine, and Jane Sellars. *The Art of the Brontës*. Cambridge, 1995.

Altick, Richard. *The English Common Reader*. Chicago, 1957.

Amster, Jane. *Dream Keepers: The Young Brontës, a Psychobiographical Novella*. New York, 1973.

Anon. *Fifty Famous Women: Their Virtues and Failings, and the Lessons of Their Lives*. London, 1864.

———. *Women of Worth: A Book for Girls*. London, 1859.

———. *Worthies of the World*. London, 1881.

Arnold, Helen H. "Reminiscences of Emma Huidekoper Cortazzo, 1866–1882." *Brontë Society Transactions* 13, 1958.

Baldick, Chris. *The Social Mission of English Criticism, 1848–1932*. Oxford, 1987.

Barker, Juliet, ed. *The Brontës: A Life in Letters*. London, 1997.

Barnard, Robert. *The Missing Brontë*. London, 1983.

Barnes, Julian. *Flaubert's Parrot*. London, 1992.

Bate, Jonathan. *The Genius of Shakespeare*. London, 1997.

Bennett, Paula. *Emily Dickinson*. Hemel Hempstead, 1990.

Benson, A. C. *The Life of Edward White Benson, Sometime Archbishop of Canterbury*. London, 1899.

Benson, E. F. *Charlotte Brontë*. London, 1932.

Bentley, Phyllis. *The Young Brontës*. London, 1960.

Birrell, Augustine. *Life of Charlotte Brontë*. London, 1887.

Blunt, Reginald. *Memoirs of Gerald Blunt, His Family and Forebears*. London, 1911.

Boll, Theophilus E. M. *Miss May Sinclair: Novelist*. New Jersey, 1973.

Bradby, G. F. *The Brontës and Other Essays*. Oxford, 1932.

Brandon, Ruth. *The New Women and the Old Men: Love, Sex and the Woman Question*. Basingstoke and London, 1990.

Brontë, Branwell. *The Hand of the Arch-Sinner: Two Angrian Chronicles of Branwell Brontë*. Ed. Robert G. Collins. Oxford, 1993.

Brontë, Charlotte. *An Edition of the Early Writings of Charlotte Brontë*. Vol. I. *The Glass Town Saga, 1826–1832*. Ed. Christine Alexander. Oxford, 1987.

——. *The Poems of Charlotte Brontë*. Ed. Tom Winnifrith. Oxford, 1984.

——. *The Professor*. Ed. Margaret Smith and Herbert Rosengarten. Oxford, 1987.

——. Roe Head Journal, manuscripts in Brontë Parsonage Museum, Bonnell 98, and in Pierpont Morgan Library, New York, Bonnell MA2696.

Brontë, Charlotte, and Emily Brontë. *Charlotte Brontë and Emily Brontë: The Belgian Essays*. Ed. and trans. Sue Lonoff. New Haven and London, 1996.

Brontë, Emily Jane. *The Complete Poems of Emily Jane Brontë*. Ed. C. W. Hatfield. New York, 1941.

——. *The Poems of Emily Brontë*. Ed. Derek Roper with Edward Chitham. Oxford, 1995.

Brontë, Patrick. Letter to T. Franklin Bacheller, in Pierpont Morgan Library, Bonnell MA2696.

The Brontës. *Selected Poems*. Ed. Juliet Barker. London, 1993.

Brown, Helen. "The Influence of Byron on Emily Brontë." *Modern Language Review* 34, 1939.

Brown, Penny. *The Poison at the Source: The Female Novel of Self-Development in the Early 20th Century*. London, 1992.

Bruce, Charles. *The Book of Noble Englishwomen: Lives Made Illustrious by Heroism, Goodness and Great Attainments*. London and Edinburgh, 1875.

Bulwer-Lytton, Edward. *Eugene Aram*. London, 1832.

——. *Pelham*. London, 1828.

Butterfield, Mary. "Face to Face with the Brontës?" *Sunday Times Magazine* 17, October 1976.

Byatt, A. S. *Possession: A Romance*. London, 1990.

——. *The Game*. London, 1967.

Caine, Jeffrey. *Heathcliff*. New York, 1977.

Carlyle, Thomas. *Critical and Miscellaneous Essays*. London, 1839.

Carter Holloway, Laura. *An Hour with Charlotte Brontë, or, Flowers from a Yorkshire Moor*. New York, 1883.

Chadwick, Esther Alice. *In the Footsteps of the Brontës*. London, 1914.

Charmley, John, and Eric Homberger. *The Troubled Face of Biography*. London, 1988.

Chitham, Edward. *A Life of Emily Brontë*. Oxford, 1987.

Clarke, F. L. *Golden Friendships: Sketches of the Lives and Characters of True and Sincere Friends*. London, 1884.

Clarke, Isabel C. *Haworth Parsonage: A Picture of the Brontë Family*. London, 1927.

Clarke, Pauline. *The Twelve and the Genii*. London, 1962.

Cochrane, Robert. *Lives of Good and Great Women*. London and Edinburgh, 1888.

Cockshut, A. O. J. *Truth to Life: The Art of Biography in the Nineteenth Century*. London, 1974.

Coleridge, Samuel Taylor. *Biographia Literaria*. 1817.

Collard, Millicent. *Wuthering Heights — the Revelation: A Psychical Study of Emily Brontë*. London, 1960.

Connor, Margaret. "Jane Eyre: The Moravian Connection." *Brontë Society Transactions* 22, 1997.

Cooke, W. H. "A Winter's Day at Haworth." *St. James's Magazine* 21, Dec. 1867–March 1868.

Cooper Willis, Irene. *The Brontës.* London, 1933.

Copley, J. "An Early Visitor to Haworth." *Brontë Society Transactions* 16, 1973.

Cornish, Dorothy Helen. *These Were the Brontës.* New York, 1940.

d'Albertis, Deirdre. *Dissembling Fictions: Elizabeth Gaskell and the Victorian Social Text.* London, 1997.

——. "Bookmaking out of the Remains of the Dead." *Victorian Studies,* autumn 1995.

Dane, Clemence. *Wild Decembers.* London, 1932.

Davenport Adams, William H. *Stories of the Lives of Noble Women.* London, 1904.

Davies, Stevie. *Emily Brontë: Heretic.* London, 1994.

Débû-Bridel, Jacques. *Le Secret d'Emily Brontë.* Paris, 1950.

Dickinson, Emily. *The Letters of Emily Dickinson.* Ed. Thomas H. Johnson. Cambridge, Mass., 1986.

——. *The Poems of Emily Dickinson.* Ed. R. W. Franklin. Cambridge, Mass., and London, 1998.

Dimnet, Ernest. *The Brontë Sisters.* Trans. Louise Morgan Sill. London, 1927. (Originally *Les Soeurs Brontë.* Paris, 1910.)

Dooley, Lucile. "Psychoanalysis of Charlotte Brontë, as a Type of the Woman of Genius." *American Journal of Psychology* 31(3), July 1920.

Drabble, Margaret. "The Writer as Recluse: The Theme of Solitude in the Works of the Brontës." *Brontë Society Transactions* 16, 1974.

Dulcken, Henry William. *Worthies of the World. A Series of Historical and Critical Sketches of the Lives, Actions, and Characters of Great and Eminent Men of All Countries and Times.* London, ?1881.

Du Maurier, Daphne. *The Infernal World of Branwell Brontë.* London, 1960.

Eagleton, Terry. *Myths of Power: A Marxist Study of the Brontës.* Basingstoke and London, 1975; new edition, 1988.

Easson, Angus, ed. *Elizabeth Gaskell: The Critical Heritage.* London, 1991.

Eilenberg, Susan. "What Charlotte Did." *London Review of Books,* 6 April 1995.

Evans, B. Ifor. *English Literature Between the Wars.* London, 1948.

Ewbank, Inga-Stina. *Their Proper Sphere: A Study of the Brontë Sisters as Early Victorian Novelists.* Cambridge, Mass., 1966.

Farr, Judith. *The Passion of Emily Dickinson.* Cambridge, Mass., and London, 1992.

Ferguson, Rachel. *The Brontës Went to Woolworth's.* London, 1988.

——. *Charlotte Brontë: A Play in Three Acts.* London, 1933.

Firkins, Oscar W. *Empurpled Moors.* Minnesota, 1932.

Fletcher, J. S. *Nooks and Corners of Yorkshire.* London, 1911.

Ford, Boris, ed. *The New Pelican Guide to English Literature.* Vol. VI. *From Dickens to Hardy.* London, 1958; revised edition, 1982.

Forest, Antonia. *Peter's Room.* London, 1961.

Frank, Katherine. *Emily Brontë: A Chainless Soul.* London, 1990.

Franklin, Miles. *My Career Goes Bung.* Sydney, 1990.

Fraser, Rebecca. *Charlotte Brontë.* London, 1988.

Freud, Sigmund. "Leonardo da Vinci and a Memory of His Childhood" (1910). In Peter Gay, ed. *The Freud Reader.* London, 1995.

——. "Dostoevsky and Parricide" (1928). In Peter Gay, ed. *The Freud Reader.* London, 1995.

Friedan, Betty. *The Feminine Mystique.* London, 1963.

Friedlander, Kate. "Charlotte Brontë: A Study of a Masochistic Character" (1941). Reprinted in Hendrick M. Ruitenbeek, ed. *The Literary Imagination and the Genius of the Writer.* Chicago, 1965.

Garrett Fawcett, Millicent. *Some Eminent Women of Our Times.* London and New York, 1889.

Gaskell, Elizabeth. *Cousin Phillis.* 1864; London, 1976.

——. *Mary Barton.* London, 1848.

——. *Ruth.* 1853; ed. Alan Shelston, Oxford, 1985.

——. *Wives and Daughters.* London, 1866.

Gathorne-Hardy, Jonathan. *The Public School Phenomenon.* London, 1979.

Gérin, Winifred. *Anne Brontë: A Biography.* London, 1959.

——. *Branwell Brontë.* London, 1961.

——. *Charlotte Brontë: The Evolution of Genius.* Oxford, 1967.

——. *Emily Brontë.* Oxford, 1971.

Gibbons, Stella. *Cold Comfort Farm.* 1932; London, 1994.

Gilbert, Sandra, and Susan Gubar. *The Madwoman in the Attic: The Woman Writer and the Nineteenth-Century Literary Imagination.* New Haven and London, 1979.

Goldring, Maude. *Charlotte Brontë: The Woman.* London, 1915.

Gordon, Lyndall. *Charlotte Brontë: A Passionate Life.* London, 1994.

Goudge, Elizabeth. *The Brontës of Haworth.* London, 1939.

Gray, Johnnie. *Where to Spend a Half-Holiday: One Hundred and Eighty Pleasant Walks Around Bradford.* Bradford, 1890.

Grosskurth, Phyllis. *Byron: The Flawed Angel.* London, 1997.

Grundy, Francis. *Pictures of the Past.* London, 1879.

Gunn, Peter. *Vernon Lee: Violet Paget, 1836–1935.* London, 1964.

Haire-Sargeant, Lin. *Heathcliff: The Return to Wuthering Heights.* London, 1992.

Hamilton, C. J. *Women Writers: Their Works and Ways.* London, 1892.

Harland, Marion. *Charlotte Brontë at Home.* New York and London, 1899.

Harrison, Annette. *In the Steps of the Brontës.* Ilfracombe, 1951.

Heaton, Emily. *White Windows.* London, 1932.

Heilbrun, Carolyn G. *Writing a Woman's Life.* London, 1989.

Heraud, J. A. "Some Account of Coleridge's Philosophy." *Fraser's* 5, June 1832.

Hewish, John. *Emily Brontë: A Critical and Biographical Study.* London, 1969.

Hirsh, Pam. "Charlotte Brontë and George Sand: The Influence of Female Romanticism." *Brontë Society Transactions* 21, 1996.

Homans, Margaret. *Women Writers and Poetic Identity.* Princeton, 1980.

Hughes, Glyn. *Brontë.* London, 1996.

Hughes, Ted. *Birthday Letters.* London, 1998.

——. *Remains of Elmet.* London, 1979.

——. *Three Books.* London, 1993.

Hunt, Leigh. "Lord Byron and His Contemporaries." *Blackwood's* 23, March 1828.

Hyder, Clyde K., ed. *Algernon Swinburne: The Critical Heritage.* London, 1970.

Jack, Belinda. *George Sand: A Woman's Life Writ Large.* London, 1999.

James, Henry. "The Lesson of Balzac." In *Two Lectures.* Boston and New York, 1905.

——. *The Turn of the Screw.* 1898; London, 1993.

Jeffreys, Sheila. *The Spinster and Her Enemies: Feminism and Sexuality, 1880–1930.* London, 1985.

Johnson, Joseph. *Heroines of Our Time.* London, 1860.

Johnson, R. Brimley. *Some Contemporary Novelists (Women).* London, 1920.

Juby, Kerry. *Kate Bush: The Whole Story.* London, 1988.

Keefe, Robert. *Charlotte Brontë's World of Death.* Austin and London, 1979.

Kershaw, Alison. "The Business of a Woman's Life: Elizabeth Gaskell's *Life of Charlotte Brontë.*" *Brontë Society Transactions* 20, 1990.

Kilworth, Garry. *The Bronte Girls.* London, 1995.

Knoepflmacher, U. C. *Emily Brontë: Wuthering Heights.* Cambridge, 1989.

Kukil, Karen V., ed. *The Journals of Sylvia Plath, 1950–1962.* London, 2000.

Kyle, Elisabeth. *Girl with a Pen.* London, 1963.

Lane, Margaret. *The Brontë Story.* London, 1953.

Langbridge, Rosamond. *Charlotte Brontë: A Psychological Study.* London, 1929.

Langlois, Emile. "One Hundred Years Ago." *Brontë Society, Transactions* 16, 1973.

Law, Alice. *Emily Jane Brontë and the Authorship of "Wuthering Heights."* Accrington, 1928.

——. *Patrick Branwell Brontë.* London, 1924.

Lawrence, D. H. *The White Peacock.* 1911.

Leader, Zachary. *Writer's Block.* Baltimore, 1991.

Lee, Austin. *Miss Hogg and the Brontë Murders.* London, 1956.

Lee, Hermione. *Virginia Woolf.* London, 1996.

Lemon, Charles. *A Centenary History of the Brontë Society, 1893–1993.* Supplement to *Brontë Society Transactions* 20, 1993.

——, ed. *Early Visitors to Haworth.* Haworth, 1996.

L'Estrange, Anna. *Return to Wuthering Heights.* New York, 1977.

Lewes, G. H. *Ranthorpe.* London, 1847.

Leyland, Francis. *The Brontë Family with Special Reference to Patrick Branwell Brontë.* London, 1886.

Lovell-Smith, Rose. "Walter Scott and Emily Brontë: The Rhetoric of Love." *Brontë Society Transactions* 21, 1994.

MacCarthy, B. G. *The Female Pen: Women Writers and Novelists.* Cork, 1994.

Macdonald, Frederika. *The Secret of Charlotte Brontë.* London, 1914.

Macfarlane, Kathryn. *Divide the Desolation.* London, 1936.

Mackay, Angus M. *The Brontës: Fact and Fiction.* London, 1897.

Mackay, Charles. *Extraordinary Popular Delusions and the Madness of Crowds.* 1841; Ware, 1995.

Mackereth, J. A. *Storm-Wrack and Other Poems.* London, 1927.

Malcolm, Janet. *The Silent Woman.* London, 1994.

Malham-Dembleby, John. *The Key to the Brontë Works: The Key to Charlotte Brontë's*

"Wuthering Heights," "Jane Eyre," and Her Other Works. Showing the Method of Their Construction and Their Relation to the Facts and People of Her Life. London, 1911.

Martin, Robert. *The Accents of Persuasion.* London, 1966.

Martineau, Harriet. *Autobiography.* Ed. Maria Weston Chapman. Boston, 1877.

Maynard, John. *Charlotte Brontë and Sexuality.* Cambridge, 1984.

McFarland, Thomas. *Romanticism and the Forms of Ruin: Wordsworth, Coleridge, and the Modalities of Fragmentation.* Princeton, 1981.

McGann, Jerome J. *The Romantic Ideology: A Critical Investigation.* Chicago, 1983.

McIntosh White, Evelyne Elizabeth. *Women of Devotion and Courage.* London, 1956.

Mermin, Dorothy. *Godiva's Ride.* Bloomington and Indianapolis, 1993.

Meyers, Jeffrey, ed. *D. H. Lawrence and Tradition.* London, 1985.

Milne Rae, Grace. *Thoughts from Charlotte Brontë Gathered from Her Novels.* Edinburgh, 1912.

Moglen, Helene. *Charlotte Brontë: The Self Conceived.* New York, 1976.

Moore, Thomas. *Letters and Journals of Lord Byron with Notices of His Life.* London, 1830.

Moore, Virginia. *The Life and Eager Death of Emily Brontë.* London, 1936.

Moorhouse, Ella. *Stone Walls.* London, 1936.

Nadel, Ira Bruce. *Biography: Fiction, Fact, and Form.* London and Basingstoke, 1984.

Nestor, Pauline. *Female Friendships and Communities: Charlotte Brontë, George Eliot, and Elizabeth Gaskell.* Oxford, 1985.

Nussey, Ellen. "Reminiscences of Charlotte Brontë." *Scribner's Monthly,* May 1871. Reprinted in Harold Orel, ed. *The Brontës: Interviews and Recollections.* London, 1997.

Oakendale, William (pseud. William Dearden). "Who Wrote *Wuthering Heights*?" *Halifax Guardian,* 15 June 1867. Facsimile in *Brontë Society Transactions* 7, 1927.

Oliphant, Mrs. "The Sisters Brontë." In *Women Novelists of Queen Victoria's Reign.* London, 1897.

Oliver, Reggie. *Out of the Woodshed: A Portrait of Stella Gibbons.* London, 1998.

Orel, Harold, ed. *The Brontës: Interviews and Recollections.* London, 1997.

Paglia, Camille. *Sexual Personae.* London, 1991.

Parkin-Gounelas, Ruth. *Fictions of the Female Self.* London, 1991.

Passel, Anne. *Charlotte and Emily Brontë: An Annotated Bibliography.* New York and London, 1979.

Peters, Margot. *Unquiet Soul: A Biography of Charlotte Brontë.* New York, 1975; Pocket Book paperback, 1976.

Pinion, F. B. "Scott and *Wuthering Heights*." *Brontë Society Transactions* 21, 1996.

Plath, Sylvia. *Collected Poems.* Ed. Ted Hughes. London, 1981.

——. *Journals, 1950–1962.* Ed. Karen V. Kukil. London, 2000.

——. *Letters Home (1950–1963).* Ed. Aurelia Plath. London, 1978.

Praz, Mario. *The Romantic Agony.* 1933; Oxford, 1970.

Pringle, Patrick. *When They Were Girls: Girlhood Stories of Fourteen Famous Women.* London, 1956.

Raitt, Suzanne. *May Sinclair: A Modern Victorian*. Oxford, 2000.

Ratchford, Fannie E. *The Brontës' Web of Childhood*. New York, 1941.

——. *Gondal's Queen: A Novel in Verse by Emily Jane Brontë*. Austin and Edinburgh, 1955.

Raymond, Ernest. *In the Steps of the Brontës*. London, 1948.

Reid, Thomas Wemyss. *Charlotte Brontë: A Monograph*. London, 1877.

Reid Banks, Lynn. *Dark Quartet*. London, 1976; Penguin paperback, 1986.

Rhodes, Dr. Phillip. "A Medical Appraisal of the Brontës." *Brontë Society Transactions* 16, 1972.

Rhys, Jean. *Wide Sargasso Sea*. London, 1966.

Robertson, J. M. "Why Charlotte Brontë Still Evokes a Personal Devotion." *Sunday Chronicle*, 9 April 1916

Robinson, Mary. *Emily Brontë*. London, 1883.

Romieu, E., and G. Romieu. *The Brontë Sisters*. London, 1931.

Rose, Jacqueline. *The Haunting of Sylvia Plath*. London, 1991.

Rutherford, Andrew. *Byron: The Critical Heritage*. London, 1970.

Sagar, Keith. *D. H. Lawrence: Life into Art*. London, 1985.

Salwak, Dale, ed. *The Literary Biography: Problems and Solutions*. Basingstoke and London, 1996.

Sanger, C. P. *The Structure of "Wuthering Heights."* London, 1926.

Sangster, Alfred. *The Brontës of Haworth*. London, 1933.

Schreiner, Olive (pseud. Ralph Iron). *The Story of an African Farm*. 1883; London, 1971.

Shaylor, Joseph. *Some Favourite Books and Their Authors*. London, 1901.

Shorter, Clement. *Charlotte Brontë and Her Circle*. London, 1896.

——. "Relics of Emily Brontë." *The Woman at Home* 5, Aug. 1897.

Showalter, Elaine. *A Literature of Their Own: British Women Novelists from Brontë to Lessing*. 1977; revised edition, London, 1982.

Shuttleworth, Sally. *Charlotte Brontë and Victorian Psychology*. Cambridge, 1996.

Simpson, Charles. *Emily Brontë*. London, 1929.

Sinclair, May. *The Creators*. London, 1910.

——. *The Helpmate*. London, 1907.

——. *The Three Brontës*. London, 1912; also introduction to 2nd edition, 1914.

——. *The Three Sisters*. London, 1914.

Small, Helen. *Love's Madness: Medicine, the Novel and Female Insanity, 1800–1865*. Oxford, 1996.

Smith, Anne. *The Art of Emily Brontë*. London, 1976.

Smith, Margaret. "A Reconstructed Letter." *Brontë Society Transactions* 20, 1990.

Spark, Muriel, and Derek Stanford. *Emily Brontë: Her Life and Work*. London, 1953.

Spielmann, M. H. *The Inner History of the Brontë-Heger Letters*. London, 1919.

Stanley Wilmot, Thomas. *Twenty Photographs of the Risen Dead*. London, 1894.

Stevenson, Anne. *Bitter Fame: A Life of Sylvia Plath*. London, 1990.

Stone, Philippa. *The Captive Dove*. London, 1968.

Stoneman, Patsy. *Brontë Transformations: The Cultural Dissemination of "Jane Eyre" and "Wuthering Heights."* Hemel Hempstead, 1996.

Strachey, Lytton. *Eminent Victorians.* London, 1918; Penguin, 1948.

Sugden, K. A. R. *A Short History of the Brontës.* Oxford, 1929.

Sutherland, John. *Who Betrays Elizabeth Bennet? Further Puzzles in Classic Fiction.* Oxford, 1999.

Swinburne, A. C. *A Note on Charlotte Brontë.* London, 1877.

Taylor, Irene. *Holy Ghosts: The Male Muses of Emily and Charlotte Brontë.* New York, 1990.

Tillotson, Kathleen. "Back to the Beginning of This Century." *Brontë Society Transactions* 19, 1986.

———. *Novels of the Eighteen-Forties.* Oxford, 1954.

Totheroh, Dan. *Moor Born.* New York, 1934.

Townsend Warner, Sylvia. *The Salutation.* London, 1932.

Trollope, Anthony. *The Way We Live Now.* London, 1993.

Tromly, Annette. *The Cover of the Mask: The Autobiographers in Charlotte Brontë's Fiction.* Victoria, 1982.

Tully, James. *The Crimes of Charlotte Brontë.* London, 1999.

Tweedale, Charles L. *News from the Next World.* London, 1940.

Uglow, Jenny. *Elizabeth Gaskell: A Habit of Stories.* London, 1993.

Urry, John. *The Tourist Gaze.* London, 1990.

Wade, Martin. *Gondal.* Play broadcast on Radio 4, 1993.

Wagner, Erica. *Ariel's Gift: Ted Hughes, Sylvia Plath and the Story of "Birthday Letters."* London, 2000.

Walker, John, ed. *Halliwell's Film and Video Guide 1999.*

Wallace, Kathleen. *Immortal Wheat.* London, 1951.

Walter, Natasha. *The New Feminism.* London, 1998.

Warren, Samuel. "Narrative of an Imprisonment in France During the Reign of Terror." *Blackwood's* 30, Dec. 1831.

Webb, Mary. *Precious Bane.* London, 1924.

Wheeler, Harold F. B. "On Certain Brontë MSS." *The Bibliophile* 2(12), Feb. 1909.

Whitehead, Barbara. *Charlotte Brontë and Her "Dearest Nell."* Otley, 1993.

Whitmore, Clara H. *Women's Works in English Fiction from the Restoration to the Mid-Victorian Period.* New York and London, 1910.

Whone, Clifford. "Where the Brontës Borrowed Books." *Brontë Society Transactions* 11, 1950.

Wild, H. *Holiday Walks in the North-Countree.* London and Manchester, 1912.

Wilson, John. "Unimore. A Dream of the Highlands." *Blackwood's* 30, Dec. 1831.

Wilson, Romer. *All Alone: The Life and Private History of Emily Jane Brontë.* London, 1928.

———. *Greenlow.* London, 1927.

Winnifrith, Tom. *The Brontës and Their Background: Romance and Reality.* London, 1973.

———, ed. *Charlotte Brontë, Unfinished Novels.* Stroud, 1993.

———. *The Poems of Charlotte Brontë.* Oxford, 1984.

Winslow, Forbes, ed. *Journal of Psychological Medicine and Mental Pathology* 10, April 1858.

Winterson, Jeanette. *Oranges Are Not the Only Fruit.* London, 1985.

Woolf, Virginia. "The Art of Biography," in *Collected Essays.* Vol. IV. London, 1966–67.

———. *A Room of One's Own.* London, 1928.

Wordsworth, William. *Lyrical Ballads.* London, 1798.

Wright, William. *The Brontës' Irish Background.* London, 1893.

Wroot, Herbert E. "The Persons and Places of the Brontë Novels." *Brontë Society Transactions* 3, 1906.

Yablon, G. Anthony, and John R. Turner. *A Brontë Bibliography.* London and Connecticut, 1978.

Zegger, Hrisey D. *May Sinclair.* Boston, 1976.

Index

Page numbers in *italics* refer to illustrations.

Printed in the United States
by Baker & Taylor Publisher Services